Our Greatest Writers

and their major works

For Ann

howtobooks
Please send for a free copy of the latest catalogue to:
How To Books, 3 Newtec Place, Magdalen Road, Oxford OX4 1RE United Kingdom
email: info@howtobooks.co.uk
http://www.howtobooks.co.uk

The Daily Telegraph

John Carrington

Our Greatest Writers

and their major works

howtobooks

Every effort has been made to identify and acknowledge the sources of the material quoted throughout this book. The author and publishers apologise for any errors or omissions, and would be grateful to be notified of any corrections that should appear in any reprint or new edition.

Published by How To Books Ltd,
3 Newtec Place, Magdalen Road,
Oxford OX4 1RE. United Kingdom.
Tel: (01865) 793806. Fax: (01865) 248780
email: info@howtobooks.co.uk
http://www.howtobooks.co.uk

First published 2003
Second edition 2005

British Library Cataloguing in Publication Data.
A catalogue record for this book is available from the British Library.

Cover design by Oxford designers and illustrators
Cover illustration by David Mostyn
Produced for How To Books by Deer Park Productions, Tavistock
Typeset and design by Baseline Arts Ltd, Oxford
Printed and bound in Great Britain by Bell & Bain Ltd, Glasgow

NOTE: The material contained in this book is set out in good faith for general guidance and no liability can be accepted for loss or expense incurred as a result of relying in particular circumstances on statements made in this book. Laws and regulations are complex and liable to change, and readers should check the current position with the relevant authorities before making personal arrangements.

Contents

How to Use this Book   xi

Beginnings   1

1   'Beowulf'   3
2   William Langland (*c.*1332– *c.*1400)   4
3   'Sir Gawain and the Green Knight'   6
4   Geoffrey Chaucer (*c.*1340–1400)   8
     – his language   8
     – 'Troilus and Criseyde'   11
     – 'The Canterbury Tales'   12
5   Margery Kempe (1373–1438+)   14
6   Early English Theatre   17
     – mystery plays   17
     – morality plays   18
7   Songs and Ballads   20

The Age of Shakespeare   23

8   Four Sixteenth Century Poets   25
     – Thomas Wyatt (1503–1542)   25
     – Henry Howard, Earl of Surrey (1517–1547)   26
     – Philip Sidney (1554–1586)   26
     – Walter Raleigh (1554–1618)   27
9   Edmund Spenser (1552–1599)   28
10   Francis Bacon (1561–1626)   31
11   The Elizabethan and Jacobean Theatre   33
12   Christopher Marlowe (1564–1593)   35
13   William Shakespeare (1564–1616)   37
     – introduction   37
     – the tragedies   40
     – *'Macbeth'*   40
     – *'Hamlet'*   42
     – *'Othello'*   43
     – *'King Lear'*   45
     – the comedies   47
     – "Man, Proud Man"   49

	– politics and power	52
	– the later plays	53
	– the sonnets	55
14	Ben Jonson (1572–1637)	59

The Seventeenth Century   63

15	John Donne (c 1572–1631)	65
	– the love poetry	66
	– Donne's religious writing	68
16	Robert Burton (1577–1640)	69
17	John Webster (c 1580– c 1634)	71
18	Robert Herrick (1591–1674)	73
19	George Herbert (1593–1633)	74
20	John Milton (1608–1674)	76
	– *'Paradise Lost'*	77
	– *'Areopagitica'*	80
	– other poems	80
21	Andrew Marvell (1621–1678)	82
22	Three Devotional Poets	84
	– Richard Crashaw (1612–1649)	84
	– Henry Vaughan (1622–1695)	85
	– Thomas Traherne (1637–1674)	85
23	John Bunyan (1628–1688)	86
24	The Bible in English	87
25	John Dryden (1632–1700)	89
26	Samuel Pepys (1633–1703)	91
27	Restoration Comedy	92

The Augustan Age   97

28	Daniel Defoe (1660–1731)	99
29	Jonathan Swift (1667–1745)	101
30	Coffee House Journalism	104
31	John Gay (1685–1732)	105
32	Alexander Pope (1688–1744)	107
33	Samuel Richardson (1689–1761)	111
34	Henry Fielding (1707–1754)	113
35	Samuel Johnson (1709–1784)	115
36	Laurence Sterne (1713–1768)	118

The Late Eighteenth Century 121

37	Thomas Gray (1716–1771)	123
38	Two Colourful Storytellers	125
	– Horace Walpole (1717–1797)	125
	– Tobias Smollett (1721–1771)	125
39	Christopher Smart (1722–1771)	126
40	Oliver Goldsmith (c 1730–1774)	127
41	William Cowper (1731–1800)	129
42	Richard Brinsley Sheridan (1751–1816)	130
43	Fanny Burney (1752–1840)	132
44	George Crabbe (1755–1832)	133

The Romantic Period 137

45	Romanticism	139
46	William Blake (1757–1827)	140
	– vision	140
	– innocence	141
	– experience	142
	– revolution	143
47	Robert Burns (1759–1796)	144
48	William Cobbett (1763–1835)	146
49	William Wordsworth (1770–1850)	148
	– Wordsworth and memory	148
	– Wordsworth and nature	149
	– Wordsworth and language	150
	– a landmark life	151
50	Walter Scott (1771–1832)	152
	– the poetry	153
	– the novels	154
51	Samuel Taylor Coleridge (1772–1834)	156
	– Coleridge and the supernatural	157
	– the conversational poems	159
	– disappointment and crisis	160
52	Charles Lamb (1775–1834)	161
53	Jane Austen (1775–1817)	162
	– the six great novels	163
	– Charlotte Bronte's 'attack'	165
54	Thomas De Quincey (1785–1859)	166

55	Thomas Love Peacock (1785–1866)	167
56	George Gordon, Lord Byron (1788–1824)	170
57	Percy Bysshe Shelley (1792–1822)	173
58	John Clare (1793–1864)	177
59	John Keats (1795–1821)	179
	– "such miseries to bear"	180
	– the five great odes	181
	– the other poems	182

The Victorians

		185
60	William Barnes (1801–1886)	187
61	Benjamin Disraeli (1804–1881)	188
62	Elizabeth Barrett Browning (1806–1861)	189
63	Edward Fitzgerald (1809–1883)	191
64	Alfred Lord Tennyson (1809–1892)	192
65	Elizabeth Gaskell (1810–1865)	196
66	William Makepeace Thackeray (1811–1863)	198
67	Robert Browning (1812–1889)	200
68	Edward Lear (1812–1888)	202
69	Charles Dickens (1812–1870)	203
	– the intensity of a life	204
	– a poetic inspiration	205
	– character and caricature	207
	– man and society	208
70	Anthony Trollope (1815–1882)	209
71	The Brontes	211
	– Charlotte Bronte (1816–1855)	212
	– Emily Bronte (1818–1848)	214
	– Anne Bronte (1820–1849)	216
72	George Eliot (1819–1880)	217
	– 'Middlemarch'	217
	– 'Adam Bede'	219
	– Mary Ann Evans	221
73	Matthew Arnold (1822–1888)	221

Towards the Turn of the Century   225

74	The Beginnings of Crime Fiction	227
	– Wilkie Collins (1824–1889)	227
	– Arthur Conan Doyle (1859–1930)	227
75	The Pre-Raphaelites and After	228
	– Dante Gabriel Rossetti (1828–1882)	228
	– Christina Rossetti (1830–1894)	229
	– Algernon Charles Swinburne (1837–1909)	229
76	Lewis Carroll (1832–1898)	230
77	Thomas Hardy (1840–1928)	231
	– the novels	232
	– the poems	233
78	Gerard Manley Hopkins (1844–1889)	234
79	Oscar Wilde (1854–1900)	236
80	Drama at the Turn of the Century	238
	– Arthur Wing Pinero (1855–1934)	238
	– George Bernard Shaw (1856–1950)	238
	– John Galsworthy (1867–1933)	239
	– John Millington Synge (1871–1909)	239

The Twentieth Century and After   241

81	Joseph Conrad (1857–1924)	243
82	Contrasts in Englishness	245
	– A.E.Housman (1859–1936)	245
	– Rudyard Kipling (1865–1936)	246
83	William Butler Yeats (1865–1939)	247
84	Science Fiction and Urban Realities	249
	– H.G.Wells (1866–1946)	249
	– Arnold Bennett (1867–1931)	250
85	Classic Literature for Children	251
	– Kenneth Grahame (1859–1932)	251
	– Beatrix Potter (1866–1943)	251
	– A.A.Milne (1882–1956)	252
86	E.M.Forster (1879–1970)	252
87	Sean O'Casey (1880–1964)	255
88	James Joyce (1882–1941)	256
89	Virginia Woolf (1882–1941)	259
90	D.H.Lawrence (1885–1930)	261

91	Poets of the First World War	264
92	T.S.Eliot (1888–1965)	267
93	J.R.R.Tolkien (1892–1973)	270
94	Two Prophetic Novelists	272
	– Aldous Huxley (1894–1963)	272
	– George Orwell (1903–1950)	272
95	L.P.Hartley (1895–1972)	274
96	Social Comedy	275
	– Evelyn Waugh (1902–1966)	275
	– Anthony Powell (1905–2000)	276
97	Graham Greene (1904–1991)	277
98	John Betjeman (1906–1984)	278
99	Samuel Beckett (1906–1989)	280
100	W.H.Auden (1907–1973)	282
101	The Human Condition	284
	– William Golding (1911–1993)	284
	– Charles Causley (1917–2003)	285
102	Distinctive Welsh Voices	286
	– R.S.Thomas (1913–2000)	286
	– Dylan Thomas (1914–1953)	287
103	Patrick O'Brian (1914–2000)	289
104	Experiment in the Modern Novel	292
	– Iris Murdoch (1919–1999)	292
	– John Fowles (1926–)	293
105	Philip Larkin (1922–1985)	294
106	Drama from Rattigan to Osborne	296
107	Harold Pinter (1930–)	298
108	Ted Hughes (1930–1998)	301
109	Sylvia Plath (1932–1963)	303
110	Alan Bennett (1934–)	304
111	Tom Stoppard (1937–)	305
112	Seamus Heaney (1939–)	307
Afterword		310
Appendix on Reading		311
	the reading experience	311
	reading poetry	314
	reading plays	318
	reading novels	323
Bibliography		326
Index		327

How To Use This Book

We have in the British Isles a wonderfully rich store of literature. The purpose of this book is to offer a guide to that inheritance and to invite exploration of the great writers.

All the major figures are here, and in addition many others, not claimed for greatness, whose writing has the quality to give lasting pleasure.

Each section, usually devoted to a single writer, is approached afresh. You will find help towards understanding each writer's work, key biographical detail, extracts from the literature, and suggestions for further reading.

The book is arranged so that writers appear in the chronological order of their birth, from the anonymous Anglo-Saxon author of *Beowulf* through to Seamus Heaney, born in 1939. Read in sequence, the sections build up the unfolding story of our literature. You can use the book, of course, to browse, using the extracts as a small anthology, or with the help of the index checking on one particular author.

Exceptionally, and for obvious reasons, a whole set of sections is devoted to Shakespeare. A few deal with groups of writers, like the poets of the First World War, or the classic writers for children. You will also find units which sketch in important movements of ideas. Throughout the book I have avoided lengthy summaries of the plots of stories and plays, focusing instead on what there is in each writer to stimulate our interest. At the end you will find an appendix on reading, which is designed to provoke thought about reading poetry, novels, and plays, and about the reading experience itself.

A word of caution! When reading literature, simply let the words work. Sometimes we may have to work hard at them (that is part of the joy) but the great thing is that they are always there. You go back to them. They change as we change, and yet they are permanently themselves. As John Bayley reminds us in his comfortable and delightful anthology of favourite pieces, *'Good Companions'*, good reading burrows into the mind. Fragments surface ever after, often for no apparent reason, but to our long-lasting satisfaction.

The body of our literature is not a territory that we need feel obliged to map out in systematic and comprehensive detail. We can enjoy it inconsequentially, dipping into its random pleasures. I hope this book will encourage that, too.

John Carrington

Beginnings

1

'Beowulf'

'Beowulf' is the first great surviving work of English poetry. We nearly lost it. A fire in a library in 1731 threatened to destroy the only manuscript we have. Fortunately it was singed only and not consumed by the flames, and is now kept secure in the British Library. Such are the chances of literary history.

The manuscript dates from about 1000, though debate continues about when the poem itself was written – maybe two or three hundred years earlier. We do not know who wrote it: 'Beowulf' is the name of the hero of the story, not the author. (It is possible, indeed, that more than one writer had a hand in it.)

It is a long narrative poem of some 3,000 lines, written in an early form of English now called Old English, or Anglo-Saxon. Not only the words but the shapes of the lettering are quite different from our modern language, but happily we have translations available, most notably and brilliantly that of Seamus Heaney, published in 1999 by Faber.

The language sings. Heard spoken aloud – which is how it probably found most of its original audience – it has a spell-binding, urgent vitality. In two parts, it tells the story first of how Beowulf comes to the aid of the Danish king Hrothgar whose hall has been terrorised by the attacks of a monster, Grendel. Beowulf kills Grendel and then, the next night, Grendel's mother, who has come for revenge. In the second part, Beowulf, now king of his own people, the Geats, destroys the dragon which has been attacking the Geats, but is himself fatally wounded in the process.

As adventurous epic 'Beowulf' tells an exciting story. It also has depths beyond the narrative, with a recurrent sense of codes of honour and heroism pitted against human mortality, and Christian values in conflict with pagan. Set in Scandinavia, the poem mixes historical elements with the supernatural scale and wonder of the sagas. 'Beowulf' was written in England (though it does not mention Britain). Like the Sutton Hoo treasure it gives us an exhilarating contact with the creativity of a remote past.

Then the wound
dealt by the ground-burner earlier began

to scald and swell; Beowulf discovered
deadly poison suppurating inside him,
surges of nausea, and so, in his wisdom
the prince realised his state and proceeded
towards a seat on the rampart. He steadied his gaze
on those gigantic stones, saw how the earthwork
was braced with arches built over columns.
And now that thane unequalled for goodness
with his own hands washed his lord's wounds,
swabbed the weary prince with water,
bathed him clean, unbuckled his helmet.
Beowulf spoke: in spite of his wounds,
mortal wounds, he still spoke
for he well knew his days in the world
had been lived out to the end: his allotted time
was drawing to a close, death was very near.
Seamus Heaney

2

William Langland (c.1332–c.1400)

The Vision of "Piers the Plowman"

We know little of Langland. He was possibly a religious clerk in minor orders; certainly he was scholarly. He may have been born in Herefordshire; he shows acquaintance with the Malvern Hills and also with London. Above all we know him as the author of the massive and impressive poem, 'Piers Plowman'. In three different versions surviving in forty to fifty manuscripts, it runs to several thousand lines in all and must have been in the crafting for most of Langland's lifetime. Like Dante's 'Divine Comedy', Langland's 'Vision' is a monumental treatment of man's place in God's scheme. It is written with humanity, compassion, and meticulous care.

At its beginning, one sunny May morning on the Malvern Hills, the poet is dressed as a hermit, wandering the world in order to hear "wonders". He rests beside a stream and falls asleep.

Then came I to dream a miraculous dream
That I was in a wilderness quite unknown to me;
As I looked to the east, high up to the sun,
I saw a tower on a hill, wonderfully made.
Below it a deep valley held a dungeon
Of deep and dark ditches, terrible to behold.
Between the two, a fair field, full of folk,
With all manner of men, both rich and poor,
Working and wandering in the way of the world.

We sense here immediately that Langland is creating a symbolic vision. The tower, with its halo of bright light, is "the tower of Truth"; the dark dungeon is untruth, corruption and evil. Wandering between them is the tide of humanity, Langland's *"faire felde ful of folke"*.

As the poem develops, Langland unfolds a rich sequence of humankind – ploughmen, merchants, minstrels, friars – who are variously hard-working or slothful, prayerful or decadent (like the friars, who *"preched the peple for profit of hem-seluen"*). He evokes a particularly strong picture of the lives of the poor.

The poet/dreamer is presented with moral choices by the contrasting symbolic figures of 'Holy Church' and 'Lady Meed' (the temptations of wealth). Piers Plowman makes his first appearance, offering to lead a pilgrimage to Truth. In three large sections which conclude the poem Piers is seen enacting the virtuous life in the style of a parable, becoming identified with the Good Samaritan, and finally as the incarnation of Christ.

'Piers Plowman' is a huge undertaking, intricately achieved, both ambitious and unpretentious. It contains finely-detailed and powerfully-imagined descriptions, for example of the Seven Deadly Sins, of the natural world, and of the crucifixion.

It is written in a Midlands dialect of what we call Middle English – Chaucer's language, from the same period, is London-based, and different – and at first sight looks difficult to read. But it is well worth sampling the original words, which are much closer to us than the Old English of 'Beowulf'. With a little help in vocabulary the poetry becomes surprisingly available and very rewarding. Try the extract below – the original form of the passage at the top of this page.

Thanne gan I to meten a merueilouse sweune,
That I was in a wildernesse wist I neuer where,
As I bihelde in-to the est an heigh to the sonne,

I seigh a toure on a toft trielich ymaked;
A depe dale binethe a dongeon there-inne,
With depe dyches and derke and dredful of sight.
A faire felde ful of folke fonde I there bytwene,
Of alle maner of men the mene and the riche,
Worchyng and wandryng as the worlde asketh.

Notice the skill with which Langland handles the **alliterative verse**, the standard form from Old English until the beginnings of the Sixteenth Century. Each unrhymed line has four main stresses, the first three of which usually are in alliteration with each other.

Translations available include J.F.Goodridge, Terence Tiller and A.V.C.Schmidt. The original edited text can be found in 'The Vision of Piers Plowman: a Complete Edition of the B-Text', by A.V.C.Schmidt.

3
'Sir Gawain and The Green Knight'

It is New Year. In King Arthur's court at Camelot the Knights of the Round Table, the lords and their ladies, are gathered in the great hall for the culmination of fifteen days of Christmas-tide feasting, jousting, dance, and music. The air crackles with merriment.

Suddenly, just as the first course has been served, there is an interruption. A horse clatters in, carrying a huge half-giant of a knight, handsome, superbly dressed, and terrifying. He is not in armour. He carries in one hand a branch of holly; in the other he holds an immense and shining axe. From head to foot he glitters a brilliant green. The revellers are silenced, awe-struck. Their throats run dry.

So begins the poem 'Sir Gawain and the Green Knight', superbly written about 1375 by an unknown author, and one of the masterpieces of England's early literature.

The knight declines Arthur's offer of hospitality, but says he comes in peace. He taunts the company with a challenge. Any man brave enough to take him on in combat may have the axe and strike the first blow with it, on condition that that man seek out the knight at the next new year, and then allow the knight the first stroke. Gawain accepts the challenge, swings the axe, and beheads the green knight.

And then a marvel occurs. The headless trunk reaches down and picks up the head, which speaks. Gawain is honour bound, it says, to keep his word and meet the knight in one year's time at the Green Chapel. The green knight departs, his horse kicking sparks from the stone floor, and the first of the four parts of the story is concluded.

The poetry throughout is exciting and richly-detailed, with an energetic and fertile vocabulary and a fine sense of drama. At a purely narrative level, we have the traditional elements of chivalry, romance, challenge and quest. Supernatural and magical set-pieces interweave with atmospheric natural description, as in Gawain's journey through a winter freeze to find the green chapel. The long poem (2,500 lines) is finely structured, and if we wish we can speculate about the presence in its patterns of ancient myths and rituals, of trials of moral strength, of tensions between Christian and pagan.

The poem is written in a language generally thought to be that of the North West Midlands or Cumbria, and follows the **alliterative verse** tradition we have also seen in '**Piers Plowman**'.

The original text with notes is edited by J.A.Burrow; there are translations by J.R.R.Tolkien and W.R.J.Barron, which also includes the original text.

I have tried to catch something of the poem's flavour in this version of one of the dramatic episodes:

> *The green knight readily sets himself down,*
> *Bending forward his head, baring the flesh,*
> *His long, lovely tresses pulled over the crown,*
> *His naked neck presented ready.*
> *Gawain grips the axe, gathers it high –*
> *His left foot forward, bracing the weight -*
> *Brings it down gently, neatly, on the naked flesh,*
> *As the sharp edge splinters the bones,*
> *Sinks through the fatty white, severs it through,*
> *The shining steel biting the ground.*
> *The fair head cut from the neck falls to the floor*
> *And rolls. They fend it off with their feet.*
> *Blood spurts from the body, and gleams on the green coat.*

But the figure neither falters nor falls.
Raising himself firmly on stiff shanks
He lunges forward, grasping through the throng,
Seizes that fine head, hoists it aloft,
Catches the bridle of his horse,
And steps in the stirrups, swinging high.
His head by the hair he holds in his hand,
Steadying himself in the saddle, headless,
As if these things had never chanced.
His trunk twisted.
His ghastly body bled.
They looked on in fear
As he began to speak.

4

Geoffrey Chaucer (c.1340–1400)

His language

Much admired by poets and readers in succeeding centuries, Chaucer is the first great poet of the English language. A cardinal feature of his importance is the very fact that he decided to write *in English* – at a time when Latin was still the established language of scholarship and the professions, and Norman French dominated many of the official circles in which he moved. Only within Chaucer's lifetime does English begin to replace French as the language of the courts and Parliament; at the ceremonial opening of Parliament, English was first used in 1362. Chaucer pioneered bringing the informal English rhythms of everyday speaking into the more formal world of written literature.

Chaucer's English was the southern English dialect, the vernacular of the London area. It differed, for example, from the Midlands dialect we find in Langland, or the North Western language of the 'Gawain' poet. His so-called Middle English is an early form of the 'standard' English we speak today.

For a modern reader the first sight of Chaucer's language is a touch daunting. It looks unfamiliar. But read it aloud, armed with a few simple principles and some help with vocabulary, and it is surprising how quickly Chaucer becomes for us both fluent and entertaining.

Take for example this verse from 'Troilus and Criseyde', Chaucer's reworking of the famous romance. Troilus, having shut himself away in his room in the palace at Troy, is self-pityingly grieving that his love Cressida has gone to the Greeks:

> *"Wher is myn owene lady, lief and deere?*
> *Wher is hire white brest? Wher is it, where?*
> *Wher ben hire armes and hire eyen cleere,*
> *That yesternyght this tyme with me were?*
> *Now may I wepe allone many a teere,*
> *And graspe aboute I may, but in this place,*
> *Save a pilowe, I fynde naught t'enbrace."*   [Book V lines 218ff]

These are all rhetorical questions, of course. He knows very well where she is. Like many an adolescent, he simply wants to express repeatedly his anger and his distress. Chaucer captures the self-indulgent aspect, as well as the genuine tears, and is there a mildly comic effect in the sorrowful petulance with which Troilus complains that his pillow is a poor substitute for Cressida? Certainly the situation and the character have an easily recognisable reality.

How difficult is it for us to read?

- ◆ We need to know that 'lief' means 'dear' or 'darling'. There may be one or two other details of wording that an editor will help with – eg that 'hire' means 'her', and that 'enbrace' is of course a spelling variation of 'embrace'. (Spelling in the middle ages was very variable, and there are often inconsistencies within the same manuscript.)

- ◆ We also need to know – and this is crucial – that each line has ten syllables to be pronounced for the rhythm to work. That helps us to recognise, for example, that 'owene' ('own') in line 1 has two syllables, rather like the Welsh name Owen. [Chaucer does sometimes use other line lengths, but ten syllables is the norm for his best-known work.]

- ◆ A final principle is that the letter 'e' at the end of a word is usually sounded as a separate syllable, *except* when it is followed by another vowel in the next word. So, for example, 'allone' in line 5 is pronounced with three syllables, but 'graspe' in the next line has only one.

This all comes quickly with a little experimentation – and a sense of humour! The key, again, is to *read it aloud*, with no worry for mistakes. Very quickly Chaucer's fluent and expressive tone becomes clear.

One more example. We can easily 'hear' the lively speech rhythms in this brief extract from 'The Canterbury Tales'. The Friar has just finished telling his tale. The Summoner (a petty court official) can hardly contain his anger; as far as he is concerned, all friars are corrupt. (A nice irony, for Chaucer could count on his audience thinking much the same of summoners.) The Summoner wants the other pilgrims to let him have their ear next.

> *This Somonour in his styropes hye stood;*
>> This Summoner stood high in his stirrups;
> *Upon this Frere his herte was so wood*
>> He was so mad in his heart with this Friar
> *That lyk an aspen leef he quook for ire.*
>> That he shook like an aspen leaf for very anger.
> *""Lordynges," quod he, "but o thyng I desire;*
>> "Gentlemen," he said, "there's only one thing I desire;
> *I yow biseke that, of your curteisye,*
>> I beg you in your kindness,
> *Syn ye han herd this false Frere lye,*
>> Since you have put up with this false Friar's lies,
> *As suffreth me I may my tale telle.*
>> Allow me to tell my tale.
> *This Frere bosteth that he knoweth helle,*
>> This Friar boasts he knows all about hell,
> *And God it woot, that it is litel wonder;*
>> And God knows, that's small wonder.
> *Freres and feendes been but lyte asonder..."*
>> Friars and devils are seldom separated.

Interestingly, the 'translation' above, which I have deliberately kept fairly literal, is dead and colourless beside the original Chaucer, whose animated Summoner mixes his courtesies towards his travelling companions with tart sarcasm at the Friar's expense. Chaucer's words, still fresh for us today, have the vitality and dramatic energy that bring personality to life.

'Troilus and Criseyde'

What we know of Chaucer's life suggests a busy and travelled man of affairs, with both practical and scholarly talents; he was variously a soldier (fighting for Edward III in France, and being ransomed after capture), a diplomat, a customs official, a justice of the peace, and one involved in court services and offices. He was Clerk of the King's Works for Richard II, and John of Gaunt was his patron. He was in receipt of several pensions but also endured a spell of poverty in later life.

He was recognised as a great poet in his lifetime. (A manuscript illustration survives showing him at a lectern reading his poetry to a grandly dressed audience.) On his travels to Italy he probably met Petrarch and possibly Boccaccio. He was well read in Latin, French and Italian, and it is from Boccaccio that he takes the story of Troilus and Cressida. Almost certainly written in Chaucer's maturity as a writer, this retelling of an episode from the Trojan War differs revealingly from Boccaccio's.

The story – which first appears in France, and not in Homer's 'Iliad' – is of the Trojan girl who falls in love with a young Trojan warrior, but who when prisoners are exchanged is forced to leave Troy for the Greek camp, to which her father, Calchas the priest, has already defected. There she betrays Troilus by falling in love with Diomedes.

In Boccaccio, Cressida's cousin, Pandarus, acts as a go-between for the lovers. Chaucer changes Pandarus from cousin to uncle, and so makes it possible to develop a more interesting interplay between young girl and wordly-wise adult. Boccaccio's characterisations are simple; Chaucer develops more complex, psychologically credible figures, and recurrent touches of knowing humour. His poem is huge in scope – over 18,000 lines in five 'books' – and richly achieved: effectively the first successful long narrative poem in early modern English.

Chaucer's entertaining subtleties we may encounter for example in Book II, where Pandarus is with Cressida as Troilus rides past in the street outside. Pandarus asks her to come and watch. She evidently makes an embarrassed move to withdraw from sight (Chaucer leaves that to our imagination) for we next have Pandarus saying:

> *"O fle naught in (he seeth us, I suppose)*
> "Don't disappear – I guess he can see us -
> *Lest he may thynken that ye hym escuwe."*
> In case he thinks that you're rejecting him."
> *"Nay, nay," quod she, and wex as red as rose.*
> "No, no," she said, and blushed a rosy red.

She is touched and impressed as Troilus rides by. Our narrator (Chaucer) says there is little point in his describing what Troilus looked like, for Cressida is clearly smitten.

> *To God hope I, she hath now kaught a thorn,*
> *She shal nat pulle it out this nexte wyke. [week]*
> *God sende mo swich thornes on to pike!*
>   May God send (her) more such thorns to pick at!

The story-teller is sympathetic yet retains an amused detachment. Pandarus strikes while the iron is hot. "Tell me niece, what would you think of a woman who was watching a man die, but felt no pity for him?" She should, says Pandarus, abandon her decorous distance, and "spek with hym in esyng of his herte". But Cressida makes clear she is not for turning yet. Troilus' state of mind is a matter for the gods, not for her. It is too soon for her to grant him "so gret a libertee".

Chaucer wittily observes the cross-currents, and the mix in Cressida's mind of stand-offishness and melting surrender. He is the first writer in our literature to describe such subtle psychological detail. And throughout the poem an extra perspective is provided by Chaucer's excursions into the philosophy of the Roman Boethius, to the effect that we don't have the power to vary our destinies.

'The Canterbury Tales'

The original 'Canterbury Tales' project was for a narrative poem on a massive scale. Chaucer did not finish it, but what we have left is one of the great works: a versatile and entertaining masterpiece, skilfully witty, and abounding in rich characterisations and contrasting kinds of story. There is a loose framework. Thirty pilgrims leave Southwark for Canterbury Cathedral. They agree that to while away the journey each will tell four stories, two on the way there and two on the way back. The teller of the best story will win a free supper.

Writing over the last fifteen years or so of his life, Chaucer got as far as 24 stories. There is additionally a general introduction, or 'Prologue', in which we meet the pilgrims, a divertingly varied group, and the genial Host of the Tabard Inn who will accompany the pilgrims and 'chair' proceedings. Many of the tellers introduce their tales, and there are linking passages in which some of the pilgrims banter and argue.

Chaucer himself is one of the pilgrims and contributes to the storytelling. (In a nice touch of parody, one of his own stories, 'Sir Thopas', is so boring and atrociously told that the Host stops it in its tracks.) But in a wider sense Chaucer as narrator-in-chief is ever-present as the ringmaster of the entire pageant. Sometimes he keeps a low profile, but we can never entirely forget that he is the presiding entertainer, creating the characters who create the characters.

Readers sometimes picture the Chaucer of the 'Canterbury Tales' as a kind of contemporary social historian, collecting the social types of his society. It would be nearer the mark to see him as a showman, sharing his delight in creative versatility, coining stories of many types and levels, and creating characterisations which range in their variety from simple stereotyping to cartoon-like sketching to closely-observed realism.

The styles range from the delicate courtly romance of 'The Knight's Tale' to the earthy knockabout fun of 'The Miller's Tale', in which the lover outside the lady's window one night expects to kiss her lips, but doesn't realise he has been offered her backside instead. He takes revenge on his rival with a red-hot poker in the same department.

Chaucer's characters too are greatly diverse. The canvas includes the humanised animals of the cock-and-fox fable from 'The Nun's Priest's Tale', the courtly love triangle in 'The Knight's Tale', the ribald and buxom Wife of Bath, and the genteel but pretentious Prioress of the 'Prologue'. Each operates within a different fictional convention.

Chaucer has no over-arching moral or philosophical intention. Some of the stories-within-the-story have satirical elements (like the send-up of the Pardoner's hypocrisies); some have allegorical or fable-like elements (as in the folk tale told by the Clerk, or the Pardoner's own tale); some draw heavily on romantic fantasy (like the traditional courtly adventure of 'The Knight's Tale'). Some venture into serious matters of debate (eg, how much free will does a human have?) and some into light diversions (what is it that women most desire? Answer, in 'The Wife of Bath's Tale' – mastery over men!). But the stance and tone of Chaucer himself is one of broad good humour and tolerance. Like Shakespeare, his endlessly fertile creativity is driven by a curiosity and sympathy for life that excludes the judgmental.

There is also an element of teasing and deliberate provocation of his audience, sharing a sense that story-teller and reader are participants in a kind of knowing game. (We find the same good-humoured mastery in Dickens.) In 'The Franklin's Tale', for example, an exquisitely plotted series of situations is developed, each one posing a dilemma for the main character, Aurelius, a squire who has fallen in love with the wife of a knight. The twists and turns of the story keep us constantly on the alert. Each new twist arrives with appealing ingenuity. There are 'cliff-hangers' contrived as skilfully as in the best of modern soap operas. At the end we are asked which of the people in the story was the most "fre", or generous. It's a good talking point, and an entertaining one – but there is no one answer, and none intended.

A key word to guide our response to Chaucer is 'pleye'. Says the Franklin to the Host, about his tale: "I prey to God that it may pleyen yow". The word means entertain, please, tease, amuse.

Dryden called Chaucer "the father of English poetry". Whatever Dryden meant, Chaucer is much more than a significant historical figure and an important influence. With or without the aid of 'translation', his words still lift off the page in their continuing and engaging humanity.

Modern versions of 'The Canterbury Tales' and 'Troilus and Criseyde' are available translated by N.Coghill. The original texts are published in several editions.
A guide to the language and pronunciation of Chaucer is included in 'The Routes of English' by Simon Elmes, and the accompanying two CDs from BBC Radio 4.

5
Margery Kempe (1373–1438+)

She was rumbustious, noisy, hyper-emotional and eccentric. To many she was an irritant and a hysterical nuisance. She was also warm-hearted, loving and ruthlessly self-critical. She could be sad and she could be funny. Margery Kempe was a mystic, in the medieval tradition of those who recorded visionary experiences of divine grace. '**The Book of Margery Kempe**' documents the life and emotional drama of this remarkable woman, who is inseparably both a selfless pilgrim and a demonstrative 'character'.

Margery Kempe was born into a wealthy Norfolk family – her father was five times mayor of Bishop's Lynn (now King's Lynn) – and married a local businessman at the age of 20. They had fourteen children, at what cost to her health we can only guess. In many ways, both in character and background, she was a townswoman-of-the-world. In later life she became, in her loud public tearfulness and visionary distress, a focus of interest wherever she went, attracting both admiration and vilification. In her travels and pilgrimages she was often received with hostility, perceived as at the very least an embarrassing 'pain' and at the worst as an agent of the devil. Some thought her mad.

Her life was transformed by her visions. They began after the birth of the first child, and troubled her with fears of damnation. She nursed memories from her youth of a "secret sin", never more precisely identified. The torment swelled into an impulse towards pilgrimage. One Friday in her early forties – it was "Midsummer Eve, in very hot weather" – she pressed her husband to agree that their sexual relationship would cease permanently. In return, she would forgo her habit of abstaining from eating and drinking with him on Fridays, and would settle his debts before she set off for Jerusalem. Eventually he concedes: "May your body be as freely available to God as it has been to me."

Margery could neither read nor write. In her sixties, she dictated her '**Book**', the story of her life, to a scribe. It was subsequently edited by a priest. Having been long dormant, the manuscript was rediscovered in 1934. So it is that we now possess one of the first autobiographies, one of the first works of spiritual literature in English and one of our first glimpses of a *woman* writing in English. In her feisty rejection of the conventional role mapped out for a woman in her time, and in her rich individuality of temperament, she creates a living picture that is remarkably accessible.

Here she is, on pilgrimage in the Low Countries, in a characteristic confrontation. (The narrative is in the third person, and she refers to herself, here and elsewhere, as "this creature", and never by name):

> And they were most annoyed because she wept so much and spoke all the time about the love and goodness of our Lord, as much at table as in other places. And so they rebuked her shamefully and chided her harshly, and said they would not put up with her as her husband did when she was at home in England.
>
> And she replied meekly to them, 'Our Lord, Almighty God, is as great a lord here as in England, and I have as great cause to love him here as there – blessed may he be.'
>
> At these words her companions were angrier than they were before, and their anger and unkindness were a matter of great unhappiness to this creature, for they were considered very good men, and she greatly desired their love, if she might have had it to the pleasure of God. And then she said to one of them specially, 'You cause me much shame and hurt.'
>
> He replied, 'I pray God that the devil's death may overtake you soon and quickly,' and he said many more cruel words to her than she could repeat...

They cut her gown so short that it only came a little below her knee, and made her put on some white canvas in a kind of sacking apron, so that she would be taken for a fool, and people would not make much of her or hold her in any repute. They made her sit at the end of the table below all the others, so that she scarcely dared speak a word.

And notwithstanding all their malice, she was held in more esteem than they were, wherever they went.

We do not turn to Margery Kempe for theological insights: more for the colour of her personality, the painful record of her stress, and an absorbing impression of the world she moved in.

Also in the tradition of medieval mystical literature, but quite different in the texture of her writing, is **Dame Julian of Norwich** (c.1343–1416+). During a critical illness on 13th May, 1373, she experienced the first of sixteen visions, or 'shewings'. Christ appears to her upon the cross, '*And at once I saw the red blood trickling down from under the garland...*' Fifteen years later she dictated her visions in '**A Revelation of Divine Love**' – like Margery Kempe, she too was unable to write. She became a celebrated anchoress, or hermit, attached to the church of St Julian and St Edward in Norwich, where once amongst her many visitors was a younger Margery Kempe, seeking consolation and spiritual advice.

Dame Julian has a way of conjuring the memorable phrase which for all her other attractions we do not find so much in Margery Kempe. (Margery astonishes us more with the sentiment than the actual words: '*I wept and sobbed so violently that many people were struck with amazement that God had given me so much grace.*') Anticipating William Blake's glimpse of a world in a grain of sand, Dame Julian finds a strikingly homely image to describe the universe as perceived by God: '*a little thing, the quality of a hazelnut*'. And, in words that speak beautifully and hauntingly of spiritual rest and reassurance: '*Sin is behovely* [an encumbrance]. *But all shall be well and all shall be well and all manner of thing shall be well*'.

'The Book of Margery Kempe' is published in an edition by Barry Windeatt, and 'A Revelation of Divine Love' in editions by Marion Glasscoe and Elizabeth Spearing.

6
Early English Theatre

Mystery Plays

From the Fourteenth to the Sixteenth Century there flourished in England and other parts of Europe a popular tradition of outdoor theatre – plays whose origins lie in religious festivals. (The Oberammergau Passion Play is a modern survival of the tradition, and there have been occasional contemporary revivals of some of the English cycles of plays in York, Stratford and London.) Many of the ancient scripts are lost to us, and knowledge of how the plays were presented is insecure, but it seems fairly certain that in the centres for which some texts survive, such as Wakefield, York, and Chester, performers of short plays toured the city, acting at set locations in succession to each other, maybe over a period of several days. (Other cycles in Cornwall appear to have had one performance arena.)

The plays portrayed biblical events, in animated vernacular language and lively verse with touches of comedy. The amateur players were from local guilds or trade associations ('métiers' – hence, probably, 'mysteries'). The performing tradition may have begun with the processions associated with Corpus Christi, first celebrated as a Holy Day in 1311. The mysteries – sometimes also called 'miracle' plays – declined during the Reformation years, and were finally banned in the 1570s.

Something of their down-to-earth flavour is caught in this extract from the First Shepherds' Play in the Wakefield cycle. Note how the broad and simple rhythms are well-suited to an outdoor acoustic:

Second Shepherd	It draws near night, so go we to rest.
	I am well set, I think it the best.
Third Shepherd	In case we be fright, a cross let us kiss.
	Christ's cross, benedicite, east and west,
	In very dread.
	Jesus of Nazareth,
	Crucifixus,
	Marcus, Andreas,
	God be our speed.

The Angel appears

Angel

Hearken shepherds, awake, if loving you are.
He is born for your sake, lord perpetual;
He is come to save and ransom you all,
Your sorrow to slake, king imperial -
  Behold him.
That child is born
At Bethlehem this morn;
You shall find him displayed
Between two beasts.

First Shepherd

In God's dear dominus, what was that song?
It was wondrous strange, with high notes among.
I pray to God save us, now in this throng,
I am afraid, by Jesus, something be wrong.
  Methought
  One screamed aloud,
  I suppose it was a cloud,
  In my ears it sounded, by God.

Second Shepherd

No, that was not it, I say you certain.
For he spoke to us three as if he were a man.
When he lingered on this lee my heart shaked then.
An angel was he I can tell you,
  No doubt.
He spoke of a bairn -
We must seek him, I tell you -
That betokens yon star
  That stands afar off.

[It would not have troubled the medieval imagination for the shepherds to be referring to Christ before Christ had been revealed to them!]

Morality Plays

In a parallel tradition, there were plays probably performed indoors for a more sophisticated audience. The so-called morality plays were allegories in which a figure standing for Man meets moral problems and temptations, represented by characters with names such as Envy and Pride, counterbalanced by others called Good Deeds or Repentance. The anonymous 'Everyman' (c 1510), probably based on a Dutch play, has Everyman facing the prospect of death and realising that Goods, Kindred and others have been only fair weather friends – he has neglected Good Deeds.

A particularly vigorous and entertaining example of the morality tradition is 'Magnyfycence', written by John Skelton about 1500. Described at its beginning as "a plain example of worldly vain-glory", the play presents the corruption, downfall and repentance of Magnyfycence, who has dallied with Courtly Abusion, Cloaked Collusion, Crafty Conveyance and other scoundrels. Skelton, who was tutor to the young Henry VIII, may well have had contemporary figures such as Cardinal Wolsey in mind. The language of 'Magnyfycence' is racy and zestful, and has a pantomime element which works well on stage:

Liberty	I am president of princes, I prick them with pride.
	What is he living that Liberty would lack?
	Wealth without liberty goeth all to wrack.
	But yet, sirs, hardly one thing learn of me: *[firmly]*
	I warn you beware of too much liberty,
	For I am a virtue, if I be well used,
	And I am a vice where I am abused.
Magnyfycence	*lying covered by a blanket*
	Ah, woe worth thee, Liberty, now thou sayest full true!
	That I used thee too much, sore may I rue.
Liberty	What, a very vengeance, I say, who is that?
	What brothel, I say, is yonder bound in a mat?
Magnyfycence	I am Magnyfycence, that sometime thy master was.
Liberty	What, is the world thus come to pass?
	To audience
	Cock's arms, sirs, will ye not see
	How he is undone by the means of me?
	For if Measure had ruled Liberty as he began,
	This lurdain that here lieth had been a nobleman. *[oaf]*

There is an edition of 'Magnyfycence' by Paula Neuss. The Wakefield – also called Towneley – Mystery Plays are edited by A.C.Cawley. Also see 'Everyman and Medieval Miracle Plays', edited A.C.Cawley and 'Everyman and Other Miracle and Mystery Plays', published by Dover.

7

Songs and Ballads

The story is told of Sir Walter Scott angering his elderly mother. She had a vast repertoire of old folk songs. Scott asked her to dictate the words to him slowly, so that he could preserve them. She refused: to write them down would be to kill them.

The ancient medieval songs and ballads that have survived did so because someone collected them, and it is probably true that in the act of preservation some at least of the life went out of them. There is a real dilemma there. The words had lived on as an oral tradition, passed on from one generation to another, and individual singers or reciters doubtless tweaked the words a little or added new verses of their own. The oral literature grew like yeast rising. When we read one of the ballads today, we may not exactly be gazing at a fossil – to vary the metaphor – but perhaps some of the living element has gone.

Nevertheless, the old words still have a power for us – often a dignity, usually a grace, sometimes a relentless tragic tone. That they are all anonymous adds to their elemental timelesssness.

There are songs, light and simple; there are longer narratives, usually dark and sometimes supernatural; there are 'broadsides', or street ballads, printed and sold in towns and fairs. There is no absolute distinction to be made between ballads and folksongs. Printed versions first make their appearance in the early 1500s, but there is no firm evidence that the words of these were freshly minted, and many at least may have been vestiges of the oral tradition in a new form. Interest in the old ballads has been fitful; there were famous published collections in 1765 (**Percy's 'Reliques'**) and in **Child's 'English and Scottish Popular Ballads'** in the 1880s and 1890s. Many of those collected came from Scotland and the Borders.

All have a rhythmic simplicity of a kind that would lend itself to speaking or singing. Some are obviously songs, and maybe dance-songs, like "Summer is icumen in", which works perfectly as a round. (And wittily: the lines "Wel singes thu, cuccu / Ne swik thu never nu" mean "Sing well, cuckoo; you must never stop!")

The narrative ballads are dramatic and stylised, and because there is scant comment and moralising, often stark in their effect.

The wind doth blow today, my love,
And a few small drops of rain;
I never had but one true love;
In cold grave she was lain.   ['**The Unquiet Grave**']

There lived a wife at Usher's Well
And a wealthy wife was she;
She had three stout and stalwart sons
And sent them o'er the sea.

They hadna been a week from her,
A week but barely one,
When word came to the carline wife [country]
That her three sons were gone.
They hadna been a week from her,
A week but barely three,
When word came to the carline wife
That her sons she'd never see.   ['**The Wife of Usher's Well**']

The words contain the satisfactions of symmetries and repetitions, sometimes at the expense of lucidity ('A week but barely three'?). There are murders, betrayals, mysteries, visions. In some ballads the story takes place in a fantasy world, pleasingly fictional, and yet paradoxically its strange details and events evoke a sinister and tragic undertone that disturbs.

The queen o' Fairies she caught me,
In yon green hill to dwell,
And pleasant is the fairy land;
But an eerie tale to tell!

Ay, at the end of seven years
We pay a tiend to hell; [tithe]
I am sae fair and fu' o' flesh
I'm feared it be mysel.   ['**Tam Lin**']

These ballads are frequently anthologised. Try especially 'Lord Randal', 'Edward, Edward', 'Sir Patrick Spens', 'The Lyke-Wake Dirge', 'Clerk Saunders', 'Thomas the Rhymer', and 'Mary Hamilton'.

Ballad metre

Most of the ballads – not all – are written in a familiar, simple form called ballad metre which aids the speaker or singer and makes the words compelling and memorable.

In these ballads each verse has four lines (a **quatrain**). Each line has eight syllables, with the stresses falling on the even syllables (an **iambic** line). The second and fourth lines rhyme.

There are variations, where the first and third lines rhyme, and these lines may be shorter.

There may be extra lines – vestiges, perhaps, of refrains and repetitions from song and dance forms.

The Age of Shakespeare

8

Four Sixteenth Century Poets

Thomas Wyatt (1503–1542)

Henry Howard, Earl of Surrey (1517–1547)

Philip Sidney (1554–1586)

Walter Raleigh (1554–1618)

They were men of affairs in sophisticated courtly circles, Wyatt and Surrey in the reign of Henry VIII, Sidney and Raleigh in the first Elizabethan age. That which survives of their poetry gives us insights into the developing craft and tradition of writing in the English language. Often the poetry presents us with formally-styled and distanced fictions, whose purpose is to entertain and delight with carefully wrought patterns, as in miniatures, madrigals, or tapestries. Sometimes the veil parts, and we glimpse snatches of individual lives.

Sir Thomas Wyatt held a variety of diplomatic and ambassadorial posts. He was imprisoned in The Tower on two occasions: in 1536, following his admission that Anne Boleyn had been his mistress; and in 1542, when he was charged with treason. He was pardoned and died fourteen months later.

His poetry was not published in his lifetime. When some of it first appeared in 1557, in a popular anthology printed by Richard Tottel, it had been doctored: perceived irregularities in line lengths and rhythms were smoothed out. This process continued over the centuries, and only within the last century have attempts been made to recover the 'real' text, with limited success. Interesting issues are raised here, not only about ownership, but about the nature of a poetic line, and whether its rhythms are to be counted syllabically or 'heard' in the intonations of the speaking voice.

Wyatt translated from and imitated Petrarch, and experimented extensively with different forms. Try reading **'Steadfastness'** for a fine example of the strengthening effect of the chosen form upon the sentiment. Probably his most famous and appealing poem is **'Remembrance'**, where explicit description of past sexual encounters and patronage of mistresses is accompanied by a sense of present rejection, and an enigmatic mix of part-rebuke and part-acceptance.

They flee from me, that sometime did me seek
With naked foot, stalking in my chamber.
I have seen them gentle, tame and meek,
That now are wild, and do not remember
That sometime they put themselves in danger
To take bread at my hand; and now they range
Busily seeking with a continual change.

In this first verse the sensuous adventurousness of the women, caught graphically in the image of the stalking naked feet, moves almost imperceptibly from a positive to a negative, from something he possessed to a criticism of their fickleness.

Surrey's name has often been linked with Wyatt's in literary history: the traditional contrast is between Wyatt as rough pioneer and Surrey as smooth perfectionist. Like Wyatt he was a courtier and soldier. His confident progress was arrested by the conflicting rivalry of powerful families and eventually he was charged with treason. The King had him executed at the age of 30, in The Tower. He translated Petrarch and also Virgil, and developed blank verse and what was to become known as the Shakespearean sonnet. His elegant writing is perhaps more impressive than memorable.

Like Wyatt, **Sir Philip Sidney** was unpublished in his relatively brief lifetime. Courtier, soldier, scholar and traveller, he was patron to many poets and much loved and admired. He has become the epitome of Renaissance man, in a legendary ideal which has almost developed a life of its own. He is best known for '**The Arcadia**', a large and much revised mix of pastoral story and poetry which is overall too elaborate for modern tastes; for his essay '**A Defence of Poetry**'; and for the first major sonnet collection in English, '**Astrophel and Stella**'.

Stella is based on Lady Penelope Rich, as Astrophel is on Sidney. They never married, despite her father's dying wish; we don't know why. The sequence of 108 sonnets, punctuated by 11 songs, breaks off without a resolution of the relationship. There is in the sonnets no narrative development. Each offers self-contained reflections and a lucid and pleasant dignity. They can profitably be sampled at will:

Leave me, O Love, which reacheth but to dust;
And thou, my mind, aspire to higher things;
Grow rich in that which never taketh rust;
Whatever fades, but fading pleasure brings.........

And:

> *Come Sleep! O Sleep, the certain knot of peace,*
> *The baiting-place of wit, the balm of woe,*
> *The poor man's wealth, the prisoner's release,*
> *Th'indifferent judge between the high and low.........*

And from 'The Arcadia':

> *My true love hath my heart and I have his,*
> *By just exchange one for the other given;*
> *I hold his dear, and mine he cannot miss,*
> *There never was a better bargain driven.........*

In 'A Defence of Poetry' Sidney argues that poetry is more 'golden' than Nature. In his sonnets thought is in repose; the doubts and tensions of experience are distilled into tranquil resolutions.

Sir Walter Raleigh was called by Spenser "the summer's nightingale". His poetry, much of which has not survived, seems almost incidental to his career as courtier, politician, sailor, soldier, adventurer, explorer and philosopher.

Initially the Queen's favourite, he fell from favour in the 1590s, and in the year of James I's accession was arrested and tried for treason. His death sentence was at the last moment commuted to life imprisonment. He was released in 1616 but beheaded two years later in Whitehall.

There are doubts about whether all of the poems ascribed to Raleigh were indeed written by him. In what we have, there is a firm, brisk voice, proud and unsentimental, as in these two verses from '**The Lie**':

> *Say to the court, it glows*
> *And shines like rotten wood;*
> *Say to the church, it shows*
> *What's good and doth no good.*
> *If church and court reply,*
> *Then give them both the lie.*
>
> *Tell potentates, they live*
> *Acting by others' action,*
> *Not loved unless they give,*

Not strong but by affection.
If potentates reply,
Give potentates the lie.

'**Walsingham**', with a different theme of lost love, has similarly spare, unadorned language:

But true Love is a durable fire
In the mind never burning;
Never sick, never old, never dead,
From itself never turning.

These lines do not move with a liquid metre: what we have is a brusque (but sophisticated) speaking voice. Try reading them *aloud.*

If it is true as sometimes claimed that Raleigh wrote '**The Passionate Man's Pilgrim**' immediately before his execution, we have, in spirit and language, lines which were in the circumstances strikingly calm and leanly self-sufficient:

And this is my eternal plea
To him that made heaven, earth and sea:
Seeing my flesh must die so soon,
And want a head to dine next noon,
Just at the stroke when my veins start and spread,
Set on my soul an everlasting head.
Then am I ready, like a palmer fit,
To tread those blest paths which before I writ.

Further reading: 'A Literary Portrait of Sir Thomas Wyatt', edited by Harold Andrew Mason, and 'Philip Sidney: A Double Life' by Alan Stewart. There is a biography of Raleigh by Raleigh Trevelyan.

9
Edmund Spenser (1552–1599)

Friend to Sir Walter Raleigh and Sir Philip Sidney, Spenser managed to dedicate more of his life to writing than either of his more worldly contemporaries. He served in the households of the Earl of Leicester and later of the Earl of Essex. He spent most of his time in Ireland where he held a variety of official posts – secretary to the Lord Deputy, commissioner for museums, and an "undertaker" for the settlement of Munster, responsible for crushing rebellion. For the latter role he was given the castle of Kilcolman in Cork in 1586, where writing became one of his principal occupations. In 1598 the castle was burned down, but Spenser escaped, eventually returning to London.

Though his poetry is currently rather out of fashion, he has been a remarkable influence on succeeding generations of poets; amongst those who have at some stage imitated or admired him are Milton, Wordsworth, Coleridge, Keats, Byron and Hardy. Wordsworth in his blank verse autobiography 'The Prelude' describes himself at Cambridge reading:

Sweet Spenser, moving through his clouded heaven,
With the moon's beauty and the moon's soft pace.

Yeats referred to the "charmed sleep" of Spenser's verse; T.S.Eliot, describing the bleaknesses of the Twentieth Century in 'The Waste Land', famously incorporates a quotation from Spenser in ironic contrast:

Sweet Thames, run softly, 'till I end my Song.

Spenser was courtly and conservative in his views. His major work, the allegory of **'The Faerie Queene'** (1590–1609) is partly in praise of Queen Elizabeth (from whom, through Raleigh's influence, he received a pension).

An **allegory** – which can be found in prose or verse, and sometimes in pictorial art – is a story which conceals but hints at a philosophical or moral meaning. The intention is to strengthen the morality by giving it an abstract simplicity, as in a fable. Abstract moral qualities may be symbolised in human or animal form.

Sometimes the allegory may parallel or indirectly refer to actual events.

Allegories were a particularly powerful form for the medieval imagination.

Examples of allegorical works would be John Bunyan's 'Pilgrim's Progress' and – much more recently – George Orwell's fable 'Animal Farm', in reality about the rise of totalitarianism in Russia.

Spenser's allegory is huge in scope (the twelve 'book' plan, of which only half were completed, was over fifteen years in the making) and sometimes obscure. It includes the defence of Truth by Anglicanism, the triumph of moderation over self-indulgence, and reference to recent historical events. The overarching idea, never completed, was to show Prince Arthur (representative of all virtue) in quest of and eventually marrying the Faerie Queene (Gloriana, or Elizabeth I).

The poem's appeal for us probably resides less in the grand allegorical pattern than in the extraordinarily vivid and often sensuous visions conveyed by the language. (The words in Spenser are often deliberately archaic, as part of the effect.) Here, the knight reaches the Cave of Despair:

> *The darksome cave they enter, where they find*
> *That cursed man, low sitting on the ground,*
> *Musing full sadly in his sullein mind;*
> *His griesie locks, long growen and unbound,*
> *Disordred hong about his shoulders round,*
> *And hid his face; through which his hollow eyne*
> *Lookt deadly dull, and stared as astound;*
> *His raw-bone cheekes through penurie and pine*
> *Were shronke into his jawes, as he did never dine.*

And here is the witch in the Bower of Bliss:

> *And all that while, right over him she hong,*
> *With her false eyes fast fixed in his sight,*
> *As seeking medicine, whence she was strong,*
> *Or greedily depasturing delight:*
> *And oft inclining downe with kisses light,*
> *For fear of waking him, his lips bedewd,*
> *And through his humid eyes did sucke his spright,*   [his spirit]
> *Quite molten into lust and pleasure lewd;*
> *Wherewith she sighed soft, as if his case she rewd.*

Spenser sustains the texture of his verse with remarkable consistency, expertly in control of the rhythms of the stanzas, which are in a form he himself invented (note the consolidating effect of the longer ninth line in each verse).

Other poems worth discovering are the sonnet 'One day I wrote her name upon the strand' from **'Amoretti'**, and **'Epithalamion'**.

'Epithalamion' is a tour-de-force, celebrating a marriage – very possibly his own to Elizabeth Boyle in 1594. The poem traces the wedding day from dawn to the waking of the bride, the preparations, the wedding itself, and the night in the bridal chamber. It is possible that each stanza relates to a separate hour of the day, and that kind of pleasure in creative patterning on a wide scale would indeed be characteristic of Spenser. The writing brims with energy and brightness, and each last line repeats a theme of the woods echoing to music, praise and song.

Spenser died in poverty and was buried, at the Earl of Essex's expense, in Westminster Abbey.

10
Francis Bacon (1561–1626)

Nothing quite like Bacon's '**Essays**' had appeared before. He kept notebooks all his life – collections of 'sayings', random thoughts and bons mots. His 58 published essays are each brief, pithy discourses on human nature and human affairs. His predecessor Montaigne wrote 'Essais' often explicitly derived from personal experience; Bacon, in contrast, aimed for generality and objectivity.

Bacon described his 'Essays' as "brief notes" and "dispersed meditations", suggesting that he was focused on thoughtfully provocative sentences rather than developed argument. The word 'essay', which Bacon chose with deliberation, means 'an attempt', 'exploration' or 'endeavour', and leads us to recognise that Bacon had broadly two purposes: to try out stimulating ideas, and to add to our knowledge of human nature. (The two are not quite the same as each other, and do not necessarily both lead in the same direction. We can look to Bacon's essays for pleasing ideas attractively expressed, but not so much for a coherent philosophy.)

The 'Essays' have striking beginnings.

- *'What is Truth?' said jesting Pilate; and would not stay for an answer.*
  ['**Of Truth**']

- *A man that is young in years may be old in hours, if he have lost no time.*
  ['**Of Youth and Age**']

Bacon is a master of the arrestingly unexpected, as in '**Of Love**':

> *The stage is more beholding to Love, than the life of man. For as to the stage, love is ever matter of comedies and now and then of tragedies; but in life it doth much mischief; sometimes like a syren, sometimes like a fury.*

The same essay ends less challengingly and on a very different note:

> *'Nuptial love maketh mankind; friendly love perfecteth it; but wanton love corrupteth and embaseth it'.*

Some would see Bacon's 'Essays' as touched by a worldly-wise cynicism, which others would call realism. There are indeed such moments: *'Virtue is like precious odours, most fragrant when they are incensed or crushed'* ['**Of Adversity**']; *'For he that cannot possibly mend his own case will do what he can to impair another's'* ['**Of Envy**']. However, we also find optimistic observations such as the echoes of John Donne in '**Of Goodness and Goodness of Nature**': *'The parts and signs of goodness are many. If a man be gracious and courteous to strangers, it shews he is a citizen of the world, and that his heart is no island cut off from other lands, but a continent that joins to them.'*

The more expansive and delightful essay '**Of Gardens**' is free from moralising comment and gives us interesting insights into Bacon's ideals for the grander gardens of the time. But Bacon's craft lies especially in the fashioning of provocative single sentences, often proverbial, aphoristic or epigrammatic:

> - *Many good matters are undertaken with bad minds* ['**Of Suitors**']
> - *He that hath a satirical vein, as he maketh others afraid of his wit, so he had need be afraid of others' memory* ['**Of Discourse**']
> - *It is generally better to deal by speech than by letter* ['**Of Negotiating**']

Bacon's public career was fractured by his disgrace in 1621. He had enjoyed a distinguished series of offices – Member of Parliament, Solicitor General, Attorney General, Lord Keeper of the Seal and Lord Chancellor. He was knighted in 1603 and created Viscount St Albans in 1621. In the same year he was found guilty of accepting bribes as a judge (which he admitted) and after a spell in the Tower was forced to retire from public life.

As a scholar and polymath – he was well versed not only in the law but in science, natural history and Latin – he had always nursed ambitions to review and improve the state of knowledge in his time. His '**Advancement of Learning**' (1605) began this process. He developed the principles of scientific induction.

Despite his eminence, his reputation was tarnished by the events of 1621, and for some by his successful prosecution in 1601 of the Earl of Essex, his supporter and patron, on the occasion of Essex's plot against Queen Elizabeth's counsellors. Essex was beheaded for high treason. A century later Pope was tartly to describe Bacon as "the wisest, brightest, meanest of mankind".

The first ten of Bacon's 'Essays' had been published in 1597. He added a further 48 in 1625, written mostly in his later and quieter years. He died of a chill caught when he was stuffing a fowl with snow, part of a study of the effect of cold on the preservation of flesh.

Bacon's 'Essays' are published in 'Francis Bacon', edited by Brian Vickers.

11
The Elizabethan and Jacobean Theatre

London in Shakespeare's day had about 200,000 inhabitants. The theatres provided for them one of the most popular forms of entertainment. It is an astonishing reflection that in the period from the 1580s up to the closing of the theatres by the Puritans in 1642 there were upwards of 300 writers providing plays attempting to meet the capital's enormous demand. Had they been operating simultaneously, that would have been one playwright for roughly each 7,000 of the populace! There were 13 public theatres at the height of the output, in addition to private performances and masques at court and elsewhere. Many of the scripts produced were collaborative efforts, necessitated no doubt by the speed at which material was consumed.

It was an unparalleled intensity of output, analogous perhaps to the insatiable scripting requirements of television in our own time. Given the somewhat casual approach to the printing and preservation of drama in that period, it is not surprising that large numbers of plays are totally lost to us. We are aware of many plays by title alone, and doubtless there are countless others which have sunk without trace. Of the plays in which **Thomas Dekker** (*c.*1570–1632) had a hand about 40 are thought to have disappeared. **Thomas Heywood** (1573–1641) claimed part-authorship of over 200 plays, of which only 20 or so survive. A well-known collaborative partnership was that of **Sir Francis Beaumont** (1584–1616) and **John Fletcher** (1579–1625), though each also wrote separately and Fletcher partnered several other dramatists. Debate continues about quite who wrote what and how much has failed to survive.

Fortunately there has been a relatively substantial preservation of the work of the major figures – **Shakespeare** himself, and **Christopher Marlowe** and **Ben Jonson** – though even here there are continuing disputes about texts and authorship. **John Webster** maintains a significant reputation despite the loss of most of his plays.

Aside from the legacy of these four there are many riches to be found. We might briefly select: **Thomas Kyd**'s 'The Spanish Tragedy' (*c.*1589), an intense revenge drama and likely influence on Shakespeare's 'Hamlet', which still works powerfully on stage; Thomas Dekker's song 'Golden slumbers kiss your eyes' from his play 'Patient Grissil', and his energetically characterful comedy of London life 'The Shoemaker's Holiday'; Heywood's domestic tragedy 'A Woman Killed with Kindness'; 'The Revenger's Tragedy' (1607), a concentratedly black and cynically witty drama ascribed variously to **Cyril Tourneur** (*c.*1575–1626) or **Thomas Middleton** (1580–1627); and 'The Knight of the Burning Pestle', a satiric and boisterous comedy with many resemblances to 'Don Quixote', now usually attributed to John Fletcher writing on his own.

Looking at these prolific and extraordinary decades it is not surprising that we can find a huge diversity of styles and tones (though as we move into the 1600s the mood tends to darken).

Compare the tone of Middleton's 'A Mad World, My Masters' with that of 'The Revenger's Tragedy'. In the former, a comedy of ruses and mistaken identities, the light frivolity is caught by the very names of the characters, which include Sir Bounteous Progress, Hairbrain, Follywit, and Penitent Brothel.

In 'The Revenger's Tragedy', in contrast, set in a decadent Italian aristocracy, the deceits and conspiracies are corruptly sinister. The central figure Vendice plots against the duke's son who aims to force himself upon Vendice's unwilling sister. Vendice is appalled to discover that his mother is encouraging this. In this extract Vendice is alone with the audience:

> *O, shall I kill him o' th' wrong side now? No!*
> *Sword, thou wast never a backbiter yet.*
> *I'll pierce him to his face; he shall die looking upon me.*
> *Thy veins are swelled with lust; this shall unfill 'em.*
> *Great men were gods, if beggars could not kill 'em.*
> *Forgive me, Heaven, to call my mother wicked!*

O, lessen not my days upon the earth,
I cannot honour her. By this, I fear me,
Her tongue has turned my sister unto use.
I was a villain not to be forsworn   [perjure myself]
To this our lecherous hope, the duke's son;
For lawyers, merchants, some divines, and all
Count beneficial perjury a sin small.

Notice here that the lines do not move easily upon the page, but we may imagine them becoming sharp and compelling in the hands of a skilled actor. Fascinatingly and disturbingly, Vendice is himself developing the malice and double standards he is ostensibly set against.

12

Christopher Marlowe (1564–1593)

Marlowe's death in a tavern fight at the age of 29 cut short a brilliant writing career which had lasted only five or six years. A prominent and controversial figure as a Cambridge student and then in London, he was a free-thinking intellectual rumoured to be an atheist and a spy (almost certainly he had been recruited as such by Francis Walsingham).

He was born in the same year as Shakespeare; it was Marlowe's "mighty line", in Ben Jonson's phrase, which established dramatic blank verse in London's theatre.

Blank verse became the predominant form for serious and epic writing in English poetry and theatre. It is first used by Surrey (1517–1547) and subsequently by Shakespeare, Milton, Wordsworth, Tennyson, and many others.

There are no rhymes (hence it is 'blank').

Each line is ten syllables long, usually with the stresses on the even words (an iambic pentameter), though variations on this are commonly found.

As a form it lends itself particularly well to the rhythms of a thoughtful speaking voice in English.

Marlowe's dramas are built around powerful central characters who were first established and popularised by the great actor Edward Alleyn (who was reportedly seven feet tall!). His finest play is '**Doctor Faustus**', first performed about 1589.

Faustus, an ambitious scientific scholar, makes a pact with the Devil in which he is guaranteed 24 years of limitless magical power, at the end of which he will be claimed for Hell. The character is based on stories about an early Sixteenth Century German doctor, also called Faust. Marlowe draws too on the medieval fascinations with alchemy and necromancy (calling up the spirits of the dead). The powerful Faustian legend was later to inspire Goethe's poetry, Thomas Mann's novel, and Gounod's opera.

In Marlowe's brilliantly questing and restless language, Faustus craves a totality of power and knowledge.

> *A sound magician is a mighty God.*

After his deal with Mephistophilis, the Devil's agent, he succeeds in conjuring up the Seven Deadly Sins and the spirit of Helen of Troy – "*Was this the face that launched a thousand ships...?*" – but otherwise squanders his supposed powers in a series of fairly pointless magical tricks. In a magnificently written final scene he pleads to escape from his fate, and offers to repent – unsuccessfully, as the net closes, midnight strikes, and devils carry him off to hell. (*"O I'll leap up to my God: who pulls me down?"*)

The final Chorus offers an epitaph – "*Cut is the branch that might have grown full straight*" – which might suggest that simple moral justice has been done. But the play is more complex than this, presenting through Faustus the collision of contrasting views of man's place in the scheme of things: on the one hand, the medieval inheritance where man has a humble place in an ordered universe, and may not *"do more than heavenly power permits"*; on the other hand, the aspiring Renaissance urge to explore new frontiers.

Faustus was free to sell his soul, but that freedom, paradoxically, only brought him a new kind of spiritual imprisonment. He is human, and so possessed with a questing spirit, but equally limited by being human and mortal. *"Yet art thou still but Faustus, and a man."*

In the two parts of '**Tamburlaine the Great**' (1587), his first and popular drama, Marlowe tracks the cruel but ruthlessly efficient conquests of Timur, the Fourteenth Century Turkic warrior. The play does not soar spiritually like "Doctor Faustus", but offers powerful and exciting pageantry nonetheless. The themes of "Faustus" are echoed:

Nature….
Doth teach us all to have aspiring minds.

'The Jew of Malta' (1592) introduces in Barabas a type of scheming villain who, when provoked, will stoop to anything to achieve his ends. (There are similarities in Shakespeare's Shylock and Iago.) The play was originally described as a tragedy, but more recently it has been presented as black comedy in productions which enjoy its macabre, Grand Guignol stage effects.

An interesting recent publication is 'The Reckoning: The Murder of Christopher Marlowe' by Charles Nicholl. Also see David Riggs, 'The World of Christopher Marlowe'.

13
William Shakespeare (1564–1616)

>−⊷−⊙−⊶−⊰

Introduction		37
The tragedies:	**'Macbeth'**	40
	'Hamlet'	42
	'Othello'	43
	'King Lear'	45
The comedies		47
'Man, Proud Man'		49
Politics and power		52
The later plays		53
The sonnets		55

William Shakespeare: an introduction

"He was not of an age, but for all time": Ben Jonson's famous contemporary tribute to his fellow dramatist was farsighted in at least two respects. First, and most obviously, Jonson recognises that Shakespeare's greatness will endure. But also (and I think we can speculate that Jonson meant this) that all succeeding ages will find in Shakespeare what they need, what speaks to them.

For it is an aspect of his genius that his plays explore humanity comprehensively but not definitively. The texts are not holy writ. Indeed, to talk of Shakespeare's "text" can be misleading. Firstly because the words that have come down to us are not always certainly what he wrote (generations of editors have had to grapple with that); but secondly, and much more importantly for our purposes, because when we read a Shakespeare play we are reading a *script*. In the theatre, in performance, we see a script in action. Actors (and directors, in more recent times) have explored, been inspired by, and interpreted the raw words of the script. When we see a Shakespeare play, we experience this creative fusion. No two productions, no two performances, will be identical.

Of course this is true of all drama, of all dramatists. Yet when it comes to Shakespeare, and especially perhaps because of his formidable genius, a strange kind of paralysed reverence sometimes sets in, and we find ourselves consciously or unconsciously assuming that there is one central philosophy, or meaning, or wisdom to be unlocked or revealed. In reality, there is none of this. The plays are not about what Shakespeare thinks, but about what Shakespeare explores. A measure of his greatness is the depth with which he understands and evokes emotions and situations. And in responding to that in the action of the theatre, we can sense a special kind of tolerance, openness, and generosity of spirit.

THE THEATRES

Shakespeare's plays were performed either indoors, perhaps at the inns of court or before royalty, or in the public theatres, especially The Globe. Although the stage furniture and effects were a touch more elaborate at court, we do well to remember that in all the presentations scenery and technical resources would have been very simple in comparison with most of today's practice.

It is the words that do the work. Shakespeare's language has to be the major stimulus to our imagination, as The Chorus reminds us at the opening of 'Henry V':

Think, when we talk of horses, that you see them,
Printing their proud hoofs i'th' receiving earth.

In the very nature of drama there is action. Plays enact patterns of movement. If all is still, there is no drama. At those times when we want to put one of Shakespeare's plays in perspective, to grasp the overall structure of what is happening, it is helpful to remember that we are observing a movement, a sequence.

In all of Shakespeare's plays that movement, at any given point, is either towards harmony, resolution and completeness, or the reverse – towards rupture, collapse and discord. The plays create these movements and counter-movements on many levels. Sometimes it will be the fracturing of an individual psyche, as in King Lear's agonising descent into madness. Sometimes it will be the healing and restitution of a broken relationship, as at the end of '**The Winter's Tale**', when Perdita is restored to her penitent father, Leontes.

The loss or recovery of balance and harmony may be within one personality, or within a family, or between wider social relationships. There may be a political dimension (for example nations in conflict, or a nation at war with itself) and there may be a universal scale to events, the cosmos itself reflecting the disturbances or recoveries. The effects of the harmonies or discords may be travelling outwards from particular individuals, or inwards upon them.

If we look, we will see elements of these movements in both the lighter plays (as, say, in '**The Comedy of Errors**' or '**Twelfth Night**') and in the profounder tragedies (such as '**Hamlet**' and '**King Lear**').

These rhythms and movements Shakespeare represents not simply in the plots of the plays but in their language. There is a danger that we focus exclusively on Shakespeare's characters. The language with which the drama is realised is a major character, and has its powerful intensities and patterns too. The dramatic poetry liberates, moves us, and makes memorable with its images the unfolding patterns of the action. The dance of the language develops and completes in the theatre that satisfying or overwhelming sense that each play has a unity and power of its own, and has stirred us with something greater than the mere sum of the story it has told.

In the discussions of Shakespeare that follow, I shall assume a little acquaintance with the major plays, though not necessarily a detailed knowledge. I have not included summaries of the plots. (These can easily be found if required in most of the standard reference works and companions to English literature.)

Not all of Shakespeare's 37 plays are discussed. (Though we shall look in some detail at each of the four major tragedies.) The intention is to provide a framework and some helpful guidelines from which an interested reader or theatregoer can begin to browse.

The Tragedies

Tragic drama invites an audience to feel and explore the profoundest and most disturbing aspects of human existence.

Let us look at Shakespeare's four indisputably great tragedies – '**Macbeth**', '**Othello**', '**Hamlet**' and '**King Lear**'.

Sometimes other plays are grouped within the heading of Shakespeare's tragedies, for example 'Romeo and Juliet', 'Julius Caesar', or 'Titus Andronicus'. It is pointless to split hairs over what constitutes an acceptable definition of "true" tragedy, and which plays should thereby constitute Shakespeare's tragic canon. However, we can probably accept that 'Romeo and Juliet', for example, poetic and heart-rending though it is, lacks the complexities of passion that make 'Othello' a deeper and mightier play.

'Macbeth'

The first performance of 'Macbeth' occurred about three years after James VI of Scotland became in 1603 James I of England. It is widely assumed that Shakespeare's play was partly intended to flatter and engage the King, who was the patron of Shakespeare's company, and before whom it would have been performed. James Stuart (son of Mary Queen of Scots) claimed descent from the Banquo who figures in Shakespeare's play as as a man of loyal integrity. The Gunpowder Plot of 1605 had recently heightened for many the enormity of threatening a king with murder. In 1597 James had published his '**Daemonologie**', a study of witchcraft. In 1563 the English parliament thought it necessary to pass an act against witchcraft: the death penalty was prescribed for the raising of evil spirits or murder by witchcraft. In the 1570s Raphael Holinshed contributed to '**Chronicles**', a history of Britain with which Shakespeare was well-acquainted, and which includes a reference to *"one Macbeth, a valiant gentleman, and one that if he had not been somewhat cruel of nature might have been thought most worthy the government of a realm"*.

These details provide us with an interesting context. At the same time we recognise that Shakespeare's transforming genius transcends these local matters. There are indeed witches (weird sisters, as they are described) but the play is not an exploration of witchcraft. There are of course savage cruelties in Macbeth's behaviour, but the play focuses on many other aspects of him. And Shakespeare is evidently not concerned simply to replicate the chronicles. Lady Macbeth, fascinatingly, is transposed from Holinshed's account of the murder of another Scottish king.

It is a dark play. Many of the images conjured by the language are of sleeplessness (and sleepwalking), nightmare, frightening visions, unnatural acts, disease. Violence (butchery in battle, murder, infanticide) is explicit and constantly threatens. There are numerous references to blood. A recent professional production began memorably with a shaggy red floorcloth, representing a blood-drenched heath, which heaved like the surface of a cauldron and eventually disgorged the forms of the three witches.

Set against this blackness are two kings: King Duncan of Scotland, portrayed by Shakespeare as gentle and saintly (very different from the figure portrayed in the histories); and Edward the Confessor of England, *"this good King"*, a healer – *"such sanctity hath Heaven given his hand"*. In the invasion of Scotland to purge the sick tyranny of Macbeth, Edward is represented by the honourable integrity of Malcolm and Macduff.

It is tempting then to see the drama as a contest between the huge polarities of Christian virtue, on the one hand, and the pagan bestiality of Macbeth on the other. There is truth in this, but thus to simplify the play would be to overlook the gripping exploration Shakespeare offers of Macbeth's tortured guilt. Nudged by the witches and pressurised by his wife, Macbeth commits himself to Duncan's murder. He does the deed, but perhaps he is not entirely responsible for the act. Afterwards, it comes to haunt him. Wracked by insecurity, qualms of conscience, and *"terrible dreams"*, he wishes to escape the consequences. But *"what's done is done"*. He cannot reverse time, and is a prisoner of his future.

> *Tomorrow, and tomorrow, and tomorrow,*
> *Creeps in this petty pace from day to day,*
> *To the last syllable of recorded time.*

He does not enjoy power. But committed by circumstance to where he is, he can only steep himself further in blood. *"Things bad begun make strong themselves by ill"*. Deserted by his own troops at the end, he can but go down fighting.

> *They have tied me to a stake; I cannot fly.*
> *But bear-like I must fight the course.*

The play does not vindicate his monstrous deeds, but we may feel some sympathy for the figure who is sucked into monstrosity. Interestingly, Lady Macbeth, iron-hard in her ambition and resolution at first, cannot cope with the stresses, loses her sanity, and dies. She too has assumed a role which is destructively inhuman. Explicitly she has asked the dark powers to "unsex" her. She chides Macbeth for his unmanly scruples before Duncan's murder. In their different ways both partners sacrifice the core of their humanity and suffer terrors in consequence, and it is this suffering, necessary but painful, which holds us at the heart of the play.

The play thus evolves a sequence of personal tragedies, both for the guilty and the guiltless victims, and a political tragedy: *"Alas poor country, almost afraid to know itself."* Black arts and ruthless ambitions precipitate for us horrifying images of humanity at its worst. The play ends with a cleansing and a restoration, but perhaps it is *"the affliction of these terrible dreams"* that remains most strongly with us.

'Hamlet'

My tables – meet it is I set it down,
That one may smile, and smile, and be a villain.

Hamlet, confronted by what he suspects is the murderous hypocrisy of his step-father Claudius, expresses a compulsion to make a written record of such duplicity. The actor of Hamlet has significant decisions to make here about Hamlet's state of mind. Consider some of the options: is it that what Hamlet suspects is so shatteringly inconceivable that writing it down will somehow validate the awful truth?; or is there a kind of gloating masochism, luxuriating in the enormity?; is he cynically bitter? Is he naively incredulous? Is this a controlled reaction or a hysterical one? Is what he says to be taken to indicate a literal intention or not?

Such choices – and there are many other possibilities we could consider – highlight for us in just one detail the extraordinary range of interpretative possibilities which has characterised the history of the play. Hamlet has been variously seen as a heroic sufferer in a cruel and alien world, as a romantic icon, as an incompetent ditherer, as a mature intelligence, as a feckless youth. (Brecht contemptuously called the character "an introspective sponger".) T.S.Eliot went so far as to suggest that the play is a flawed masterpiece, whose story is unable to cope with all that Shakespeare intends to evoke from it.

That we can never wholly fathom 'Hamlet' may nevertheless be a reason for the play's compelling fascination – worldwide it is probably the most produced of Shakespeare's plays.

At the heart of the drama huge questions are raised, often explicitly (but not answered): How can evil happen? What can we do about it? Are there limits to a man's actions? What happens after death? Is there a spirit world? The play begins with a question; the first scene abounds in questions. Hamlet questions himself intensively.

The ghost of Hamlet's father is possessed by a pre-Christian ethic as he (it?) chillingly urges blood revenge. Hamlet, with Claudius kneeling in prayer before him, cannot bring himself to take the guilty life. His ostensible reason is that to kill a man at prayer would be to send him to heaven, but is there also a suggestion that to kill would be to tamper sacrilegiously with the unknown? Later, after he returns from England, he seems calmer, more accepting of universal mystery: *"There's a divine providence in the fall of a sparrow..........Let be."* Yet the play ends, ironically, with no sense of justice, divine or otherwise, as the stage is strewn with corpses. *"Casual accidents, accidental slaughters."*

Hamlet's trust in his mother is shattered – that she should have married again so soon after her husband's/his father's funeral. Ophelia, whom he loved distractedly, appears to Hamlet to have been used by her father against him. His old university 'friends', Rosencrantz and Guildenstern, spy on Hamlet, as he senses, at Claudius' request. Hamlet craves love and friendship but feels betrayed and deceived. Horatio is a close companion, but lacks the depth to be a true confidant. Hamlet wholly relaxes only in the company of the players, the travelling actors, whose false seemings are a wholly innocent kind of pretence. Hamlet *enjoys* pretending that he is mad.

So what is "Hamlet" about? Perhaps this isn't the right question, or at least an answerable question. The play certainly explores disturbance – within the mind of the central character, within his family, in his wider relationships, in the state of Denmark, in the hinterland between the mortal world and the hereafter. Yet the play's multiple questions imply multiple unknowns.

Can we agree with Dover Wilson? – "We were never intended to reach the heart of Hamlet's mystery. That it has a heart is an illusion. The secret that lies behind it all is Shakespeare's, not Hamlet's.........The character of Hamlet, like the appearance of his successive impersonators on the stage, is a matter of make-up."

'Othello'

There is a painful climactic moment towards the end of the play which Shakespeare represents simply as "O, O, O!" – an anguished cry as Othello falls on the bed where lies the body of Desdemona, the wife he has just murdered. It is dawning on him, too late, that he may have been grossly deceived, that the wife he passionately loved but then passionately rejected may not after all have been unfaithful to him. It is a devastating moment of truth (and, incidentally, a reminder that Shakespeare's mastery is sometimes inherent in the non-verbal and visual aspect of his theatre).

The whole play has been moving unrelentingly towards this point. Othello has been destroyed. Othello has been led to destroy himself. We have witnessed the seemingly inevitable drive of the action, initiated of course by Iago, who from the outset makes explicit to us his hatred of Othello. The tragic experience, for us, has been to observe the progressive and seemingly irreversible ruin of a good man and his marriage.

We may say "good man". Some discussions of this play look to blame Othello for his fate. He is said to be vain or gullible or self-centred. Or he is insanely jealous. Ironically, however, some of the most convincing descriptions of Othello's positive qualities come from Iago himself:

> *The Moor – howbe't that I endure him not -*
> *Is of a constant, loving, noble nature*

And

> *The Moor is of a free and open nature*
> *That thinks men honest that but seem to be so....*

Certainly Othello is trusting. Some would say too trusting, naïve. But perhaps to focus on Othello's alleged faults is to distort the nature of the play, as if Shakespeare were writing some kind of moral fable inviting us to beware of jealousy or whatever. This would be absurdly narrowing.

At the heart of the tragedy is the breakdown of a personality. It is engineered by Iago's virulent, cold-blooded single-mindedness. It is facilitated by Othello's trusting nature *and his circumstances*. The play's sub-title reminds us that he is a 'Moor of Venice'. In a society of "super-subtle Venetians" he is valued for his military prowess, but he is not at home. He speaks to Desdemona of his romantic, exotic adventures. He has royal origins. His blackness and his history indicate that he belongs to a different culture. Iago trades devastatingly upon the potential insecurity of one who, if pressed, cannot be confident that he *knows* the workings of a Venetian's mind, of Desdemona's mind.

Nevertheless, Othello requires from Iago evidence. And in a further tragic twist finds 'proof' in the discovery of the handkerchief, which is no proof at all.

And what of Iago? Why does he do it? He offers reasons – his lack of preferment, Othello's alleged adultery with his wife, simple dislike of the man – but either singly or collectively these explanations do not seem adequately to explain his sheer malevolence. Perhaps indeed the question is unanswerable. He simply embodies a destructive malignancy. Once its force is spent, his meaning is gone. "From this time forth I never will speak word" is his closing line.

There is a view that this is Iago's play, that he steals the show. He certainly ingratiates himself with the audience, and despite our natures, perhaps, we become fascinated and absorbed by that which repels us. There is also the view that the play presents in Othello and Iago "mighty opposites" (to borrow a phrase from 'Hamlet'), a collision course between two equal, powerful but ultimately incompatible forces.

Notice the striking and subtle ways in which Shakespeare uses language to delineate the differences between Othello and Iago. They speak differently. Compare Othello's speech before the senate ("Most potent, grave, and reverend signors....." in Act I Scene 3) with Iago's closing words in the same scene. Othello's words are measured, courteous, evocative; Iago's busy, quick-witted, practical. There is no poetry in Iago. Conversely, Othello's words resonate and inspire. As the play develops, watch how Othello's language deteriorates. As his mind and his emotions fragment, so his words become disconnected and even at moments incoherent.

When Othello's lieutenant Cassio disgraces himself in drunkenness (contrived by Iago) he remorsefully describes his deterioration from a "sensible man" to a "beast". In miniature, Cassio's career reflects Othello's. Both men blame themselves. But as we contemplate the emotional wreckage at the end of the play we probably tend not towards blame but to a sympathy for those destroyed and an uncomprehending awe before the evil that caused the destruction.

'King Lear'

> *Why should a dog, a horse, a rat have life,*
> *And thou no breath at all? Thou'lt come no more,*
> *Never, never, never, never, never!*

At the end of the play, Lear enters with Cordelia dead in his arms. She has been hanged by their enemies. It is a heart-rending spectacle, the more painful because he has only just been reunited in love and poignant forgiveness with the daughter he had rejected at the beginning of the play. Lear himself now dies in an outpouring of love for her:

Do you see this? Look on her. Look, her lips.
Look there. Look there.   (He dies)

For many years the sheer sadness and perceived injustice of this ending caused the play to be shunned. Nahum Tate in 1681 famously rewrote it, substituting a happy ending in which the reunited pair live on. Samuel Johnson in 1765 wrote: "I was many years ago so shocked by Cordelia's death, that I knew not whether I ever endured to read again the last scenes of the play till I undertook to revise them as an editor".

In Shakespeare's drama, a cruel universe offers no easy consolations. At the same time, this great tragedy affirms the human spirit and values which burn the more strongly as they are contrasted with the glowering barbarism which poisons so many of the relationships in the play. Lear's love at the end shines unchallenged. *"Look there. Look there."*

The story, from Lear's petty and irascible rejection and banishment of Cordelia at the outset, is a sequence of cruelty. Children contemptuously scheme against their fathers. Vanities and sexual jealousies destroy trust. Goneril, Regan, Cornwall and Edmund lustfully pursue an amoral self-interest. The civilities and kindnesses of blood, friendship and service are abandoned. Gloucester, in perhaps the scene of starkest cruelty in English theatre, has his eyes gouged out by Cornwall.

Lear suffers first the hurt and indignity of insubordination and dispossession, but then – more profoundly – the pain of confronting his true self as in madness he reaches a deeper humanity:

I am bound
Upon a wheel of fire, that mine own tears
Do scald like molten lead.

In this odyssey he is befriended and assisted by the loyal Kent, and by his Fool, who does what he can to open Lear's eyes. In a parallel movement, Gloucester's son Edgar acts in disguise to comfort and heal his bewildered and beleaguered father. The blinded Gloucester begins to see more clearly. *"I stumbled when I saw."*

The scale of the play is immense, both in its plot and in the metaphorical reach of its language. What begins as a squalid domestic dispute in Lear's court moves out into the rawness of nature on the heath, where deprivation, nakedness and raging storm are the environment for Lear's self-discovery and regeneration. Such are the intensities of the human suffering and the tempest that the whole universe seems to be in flux. On one metaphorical level the play opens out visions of the end of existence, the apocalypse. When Lear enters with the dead Cordelia in his arms, it is to the death of the universe that Kent alludes in his question *"Is this the promised end?"*, and Edgar too as he echoes Kent: *"Or image of that horror?"*

It is characteristic of the world's great tragic drama that through the presentation of bleakness and unthinkable horror, positive human values are affirmed. Precisely because 'Lear' is an enacted, shared experience in a theatre, a ritual that is not life itself, an uplifting sense of man's nobility survives beyond the sufferings we have seen. The great paradox is that at the close, with the deaths of Cordelia and Lear, we can be both profoundly moved and exhilaratingly stirred.

The play's intense grandeur has encouraged some to feel it is unperformable. How can one production, one stage, encompass all this? Indeed there are technical difficulties to be surmounted, such as how the actor of Lear can compete vocally with the thunder and effects of the famous storm scene; how the scene of the gouging of Gloucester's eyes can avoid gratuitous sensationalism. The answer to the doubts has to be that Shakespeare's language imaginatively transcends the limitations of any stage. The power of the poetry, if well-delivered, will make the performance compelling and memorable.

The Comedies

'The Comedies' is the term usually loosely assigned to ten or so plays which divert from the harrowing world of the tragedies. The emphasis shifts from intense individual and universal experience to lighter social interactions. Characteristic ingredients are courtship, rivalry in love, disguise, mistaken identity, and the mocking of stupidity and pretentiousness. The mood is skittish, playful, occasionally satirical, sometimes wistful and melancholy, but rarely bleak.

The plays commonly draw aside from the pressing realities and burdens of actual living. They enter a temporary escapist world, a holiday carelessness, where many workaday assumptions and conventions cease to operate. **'As You Like It'** takes place in the forest of Arden, **'Twelfth Night'** in a make-believe Illyria, **'A Midsummer Night's Dream'** in a fairy world outside Athens.

Twelfth Night – January 6th, the Feast of the Epiphany – was in pre-Christian times still a midwinter festive day. On this day in Shakespeare's time, and for centuries earlier, there were carnival-like revels in which, frequently, social hierarchies were turned upside down. Servants became masters. Important figures could be gently satirised without fear of recrimination. (Vestiges of these traditions are faintly echoed in our own time by the dying remnants of April Fool's Day, 'trick or treat', or Mischief Night.) Shakespeare's 'Twelfth Night' is not about the day as such, but was almost certainly written for it, and partakes of its spirit. Its subtitle, we may recall, is 'What You Will'.

The comedies have established rich and sparkling characters who have entered our folklore of cherished fictions almost independently of the works in which they appear (as also happens, for example, with figures from Dickens). We are entertained and provoked by the memory of Toby Belch, Andrew Aguecheek, Malvolio, Beatrice and Benedick, Rosalind, Dogberry, and many others. Shakespeare creates lively cameos who dance through absurd plots without greatly risking the deepest of feelings. Even Malvolio, whose pompous pretensions are ridiculed, departs 'Twelfth Night' a chastised but not a broken man.

Yet, in 'As You Like It' and 'Twelfth Night' particularly, there are explicit reminders that the seemingly timeless carnival world of holiday is only timeless for as long as it lasts. The leaves will fall, the seasons will change, the holiday will end, and life and death will take up their accustomed rhythms. A sad melancholy is woven into the texture of the comedies. Winter bites in Arden.

This resigned wistfulness is often caught in song, and in the words of Touchstone, Jaques, and Feste. Like Don John in 'Much Ado About Nothing', Jaques in 'As You Like It' offers a sour and jaundiced view of life which is off-set against the general tenor of the play. We may accept his discordant notes not as an irritant but as a necessary corrective. As he says:

> *Give me leave*
> *To speak my mind, and I will through and through*
> *Cleanse the foul body of th'infected world,*
> *If they will patiently receive my medicine.*

It is of course Jaques who speaks the famous *"All the world's a stage"* lines, and we may ask ourselves whether their tone is playfully affectionate or philosophically resigned.

The songs, like those of Feste in 'Twelfth Night' (*"Come away, come away death"* and *"When that I was and a little tiny boy"*), often have the interesting effect of freezing the action as we contemplate the textures of life in a detached and reflective manner.

The language in the comedies is frequently busy with puns and other forms of wordplay clearly popular with contemporary audiences. The wittiness glitters even where, as frequently, the actual joke skitters away too fast to be fully comprehended. This is especially true of the earlier comedies such as 'Love's Labours Lost' and 'The Comedy of Errors'.

This verbal dexterity is paralleled by the complex ingenuities of the plots. We happily accept that a Duke, who is in love with Love, is loved by a woman whom he thinks to be a man; that the woman he idealises happens to fall in love with the 'man' who as woman is in love with him; and that the arrival on the scene of this woman's identical twin brother allows for a four-way knot to be tied. Whether or not the plots approach any kind of credibility is not of course an issue for us. The sheer theatricality, the weaving and unravelling, is in itself a central feature of the entertainment.

"Man, Proud Man"

Some of Shakespeare's plays, not deeply tragic in tone nor wholly the stuff of comedy either, survey human behaviour in a manner which is serious, sometimes sceptical, and sometimes sombre. Amongst these we may include 'Measure for Measure', 'Antony and Cleopatra', 'The Merchant of Venice', and 'Troilus and Cressida'.

In 'Measure for Measure', rather as the title suggests, people who have adopted stringent moral disciplines are thereby brought into conflict with each other. Angelo, upholding a cold and fiercely self-disciplined outlook, is charged by the absent Duke to enforce Vienna's laws against immorality. Isabella, an intended nun, dedicates herself to her vow of chastity. The Duke, as himself and disguised as a friar, attempts what is virtually a clinically-controlled experiment upon Angelo.

All these high intentions falter. Angelo struggles with his lust for Isabella. Isabella is placed on the spot by Angelo's offer to cancel the death sentence on her brother Claudio in exchange for her virginity. The Duke's principled detachment is compromised by his failure to make it work. Out of the blue at the end of the play he proposes marriage to Isabella, which she receives in (shocked?) silence.

The play ends in unsatisfactorily contrived ways, discrepant with its earlier searching psychological explorations. Otherwise, it convincingly dramatises the tensions between high ideals and the practicalities and compromises of being human. Having been out of fashion for its supposed indecency in the Victorian and Edwardian years, 'Measure for Measure' enjoyed a restored popularity in the second half of the Twentieth Century.

'The Merchant of Venice' also presents some of the complications of justice. The merchant, of course, is Antonio, not Shylock, though it is Shylock's personality which dominates the play. Love and generosity are locked in conflict with possessiveness and Shylock's famously rigorous pursuit of his rights in law. The story of the caskets and Portia's marriage belongs to the world of the comedies, but the ambiguities of Shylock are much more provocative. Is he villain or victim? Is the Jew, in Venetian society, a beleaguered outsider or an unscrupulous manipulator? How far does he win our sympathies?

Antony and Cleopatra have the status of legendary lovers. Shakespeare absorbingly explores the relationship between the public perceptions which each creates (and, in a sense, has to live up to) and their private identities. Fascinating questions are raised: are they shaped by their mythical reputations to the extent that they are not sure of themselves privately?

The language in 'Antony and Cleopatra' is excitingly dense and suggestive, amongst the richest to be found in Shakespeare. Take the description from Act V of the Emperor that Antony was:

> *In his livery*
> *Walked crowns and crownets, realms and islands were*
> *As plates dropped from his pocket.*

We have here an impression of almost casual opulence, power worn with consummate and extravagant ease. Yet at the same time we notice that this is a generalised description, and a deliberately flattering one, more a projected image than an actual individual. And if we take the hint (and we may be prompted to do so by the rest of the play) there is an implication of self-indulgent luxuriousness.

It is Cleopatra who speaks here of her dead lover. Surely, we may wonder, she would not at this moment be critical of her Antony? Maybe not, but one of the subtle brilliances of Shakespeare's language is that it can suggest and resonate for us beyond the immediate characterisation of the speaker. Immediately after these lines, Cleopatra qualifies them:

> *Think you there was, or might be, such a man*
> *As this I dreamt of?*

Maybe after all she recognises that she is merely romancing. But, in a further twist, she goes on to say that even an imagined Antony is a reality that puts other fancies in the shade.

And Cleopatra herself – how does the play portray her? Worldly-wise or tense and insecure? An enigmatic enchantress, a femme fatale, or a girlish flirt? Is the Cleopatra of the play the figure of legend, or more complicatedly a woman whose private self is partly dictated by the public perception of her? There are no simple answers, but part of the play's enduring appeal is that it intrigues us with the questions.

'**Antony and Cleopatra**' is a magnificent love story, in which the transcendent central relationship is crossed but not broken by politics and shifting loyalties. Antony's aide Enobarbus, whose tough unsentimentality is broached by tenderness, is one of the great minor characters in Shakespeare.

'**Troilus and Cressida**' is set at the siege of Troy, and Shakespeare draws partly from the epic tale of Homer's '**Iliad**' and Chaucer's '**Troilus and Criseyde**'. But there is no romance here. The keynote is satiric and cynical. It is an amoral world:

> *Like or find fault, do as your pleasures are,*
> *Now good or bad, 'tis but the chance of war.*

Helen is no idealised beauty, but presented as a slut. The heroic pretensions of the Trojans seem hollow and blind. In the Greek camp runs a strain of anti-heroic practicality which is unprincipled and destructive. Cressida is a cheat and Pandarus her father a dubious love broker. There are some positives to balance against the general negativity: integrity in Aeneas and Nestor, and some shreds of chivalry in the interchanges of the Trojans and the Greeks. Ulysses' affirmation of the importance of order and concord is powerfully spoken, but it is unsupported by the ambience of the play.

Thersites savagely cuts everything down to size:

> *All the argument is a whore and a cuckold....*
> *War and lechery confound all.*

And later:

> *Lechery, lechery; still wars and lechery; nothing else holds fashion.*

Man's pretensions to human values are diminished by a sense of insignificance before time, in this absorbing but cumulatively bleak play which lacks the deeper, redemptive notes of the tragedies:

> *What's past, and what's to come, is strewed with husks*
> *And formless ruins of oblivion.*

Politics and Power

Shakespeare is fascinated by the qualities of leadership, the manipulation of power, and political rivalries. This appears especially strongly in the English history plays, and the two Roman plays 'Julius Caesar' and 'Coriolanus'.

We do not turn to these plays for historical accuracy, not only because Shakespeare's sources were frequently inaccurate in themselves, but because Shakespeare's primary interest is not in chronicling a narrative. There is a case to be made for seeing the sequence of eight English plays from 'Richard II' to 'Richard III' as in some part a celebration of the emergence of the Tudors after the Wars of the Roses, and an anticipation of the "golden age" of Elizabeth I. But we must be cautious. Each play is complete in itself, and searches the issues of power and responsibility, and the pressures upon those ambitious to exercise responsibility. Nor were the plays written in chronological sequence.

What we can safely say is that the plays display a passion for the stuff of history, the cut and thrust of personality and the thrill of events. They were probably written over a ten year span, and we can observe Shakespeare's style and language evolving richly over that period.

An article of faith received from the middle ages was that a king was God's agent upon earth. Usurpation or regicide were consequently sacrilegious. A contrary, pragmatic view has it that if a weak king remains inviolate, worse disorders will follow. The dilemma consequent upon these opposing viewpoints activates much of the debate and agony within the plays following Henry Bolingbroke's deposition of Richard II. The deposition is seen metaphorically as imposing a curse on succeeding generations that is exorcised only with the destruction of Richard III.

"To be a King and wear a crown is more glorious to them that see it, than it is a pleasure to them that bear it" – Elizabeth I's words echo a recurrent theme of the plays. 'Henry V' has regularly been enjoyed as a patriotic epic (which sentiment inspired Olivier's wartime film version) but the play focuses as much upon Henry's misgivings about his capacity to bear the responsibilities, and his awareness that only he can be truly aware of the pressures put on him by others' expectations. Subjects can be fickle in their allegiances. As much at the heart of the play as the battle of Agincourt and Henry's rousing inspiration are the scenes before the battle where Henry privately contemplates his role:

Upon the King.
'Let us our lives, our souls, our debts, our care-full wives,
Our children and our sins lay on the King.'
We must bear all. O hard condition.....
....What infinite heartsease
Must kings neglect that private men enjoy?

When Henry in disguise speaks to the ordinary soldier John Bates, he reflects: *"The King is but a man, as I am".* This picks up on a recurrent Shakespearean theme, found in both the tragedies and the comedies, that to strip away office, ceremony and pretension is to reveal common humanity, a poor forked animal, "the thing itself".

The much celebrated character of Sir John Falstaff – self-indulgent, loveable, a good-hearted rogue – plays a central part in this theme. In the **Henry IV** plays he is the comically boisterous and warmly affectionate friend to Prince Hal, whose company Hal feels he has to reject as he becomes king. It is perhaps an easy simplification to see Falstaff as a personification of Vice which is incompatible with kingship. In reality Hal has, in abandoning Falstaff, painfully to sacrifice some of his own humanity.

In '**Coriolanus**', an austere and little-performed play, the emperor is a hardened and insensitive leader who is finally killed as the indirect result of the manipulative pressures of his mother, Volumnia. There are no fine values in this political wilderness.

Julius Caesar, we need to remember, is assassinated early in his play, which is less about the man himself than the conspiracy to kill him and the aftermath of the political murder. Ultimately his death rebounds on the heads of the conspirators, both Cassius and Brutus (harrowed with self-doubt) commit suicide, and a further dictatorship is established.

The message of these plays, if message there be, is not that power corrupts, but that power, ironically much coveted, is a dubious friend. Uneasy lies the head that wears a crown.

The Later Plays

Of Shakespeare's last plays ('**The Winter's Tale**', '**The Tempest**', '**Cymbeline**' and '**Pericles**') the most commonly performed are 'The Winter's Tale' and 'The Tempest'. The plots take the form of fables, in which emotional discord and injustice are eventually righted, often through the intervention of magic and the supernatural. The closing note is of harmony and resolution, though qualified, especially in '**The Tempest**', by enigmatic doubts.

The magical and ritualistic aspects of the plays have often attracted directors to spectacular and exotic stage effects, especially in the last two centuries. Charles Kean in 1867 boasted of the 140 stagehands required to operate the stage machinery and effects in his production of 'The Tempest'. At another extreme, there is a view that the plays' poetry appeals most to a reader's imagination or sense of fantasy, and that the texts are likely to be less successful on stage.

In fact from their earliest performances the plays clearly depended significantly on visual appeal. There are strong elements of dance, pageant, mime and transformation effects: the simple but powerful spectacle of Hermione's 'statue' coming to life at the end of 'The Winter's Tale' is an excellent example. Good productions work on this. Equally, they will exploit the theatrical power of vivid words allied to an actor's strong stage presence. A strong Prospero or Leontes commands the theatre.

Prospero in 'The Tempest' has magical powers, effecting miracles in controlling the seas and the storm. The spirit Ariel is at his beck and call until released at the end of the play. But Prospero finally breaks his magic staff, and when Miranda expresses delight in *a brave, new world"* Prospero qualifies her innocent optimism with *" 'Tis new to thee"*. He has powers over the natural world, but no power to control human nature itself. Often identified with Shakespeare, he speaks directly to the audience at the end, a solitary figure as he retires to Milan, his powers spent:

> *Now my charms are all o'erthrown,*
> *And what strength I have's my own,*
> *Which is most faint.*

While in 'The Tempest' the restoration of relationships and purging of human vices is not wholly complete, there is a stronger sense of blessing in 'The Winter's Tale', where time itself is seen to have been a great healer. Mid-way through the play the shepherd who finds the abandoned babe, Perdita (Leontes' cast-out daughter), says: *"Thou met'st with things dying.....I with things new born"*. Rebirth and refreshment of spirit become the keynotes of the second part of the play.

Leontes' tortured jealousy with which 'The Winter's Tale' opens has some parallels, perhaps, with Othello. But to make the comparison is to realise that the style and movement of Shakespeare's later plays is different from that of his great tragedies. In the tragic dramas the central figures are plunged into a scalding pain from which, with the exception of Lear, they barely emerge. In 'The Winter's Tale', in theatrical modes which are symbolic and allegorical, the achievement of benediction and restoration is much more significant. It substantially occupies the second movement of the play.

The plays celebrate the potential of the human spirit and the religious power of love. In 'The Tempest' Caliban, a figure who seems the very incarnation of the gross and sub-human, is movingly half-alert at one point to finer things beyond his comprehension (*"sounds and sweet airs that give delight and hurt not"*), but his brute insensitivity acts as a powerful benchmark against which we are able to measure the burgeoning love of Miranda and Ferdinand, and the gathering wisdoms of Prospero.

Ariel tells Prospero that if he were to behold the enemies he has made prisoners, *"your affections would become tender"*. Surprised, Prospero responds: *"Dost thou think so, spirit?"*

Ariel: Mine would, sir, were I human.
Prospero: And mine shall.....
                 The rarer action is
                 In virtue than in vengeance.....
                 My charms I'll break, their senses I'll restore,
                 And they shall be themselves.

In these last plays, for all the shift of style, there is no escapism and there are no simple answers. Prospero, like Marlowe's Dr Faustus before him, resolves to burn his magic books. He learns forgiveness as Leontes learns to *"awake his faith"*. But there is no sense of easy idealism at the play's end, rather a weariness. In Prospero's own words from earlier in the play:

> *We are such stuff*
> *As dreams are made on, and our little life*
> *Is rounded with a sleep.*

The Sonnets

Technically speaking, the traditional sonnet is a poem of fourteen lines; each line has ten syllables (a pentameter) and there is a tight rhyming scheme. The sonnet form was introduced to England by Sir Thomas Wyatt in the early Sixteenth Century, through his translations of the love poems of the Fourteenth Century Italian poet, Petrarch. These sonnets were much imitated by a variety of English poets.

Shakespeare adopted the form but with a changed rhyme scheme. In Petrarch the first eight lines and the final six lines form two sub-sections; Shakespeare (following Surrey before him) uses four units: three quatrains (four-line sections each) and a concluding couplet, with the rhyme scheme *abab, cdcd, efef, gg*.

One might at first think that to write in a set poetic form with this rigour would be constricting, but of course a form that works well becomes especially satisfying and memorable in its polished intricacy. (Consider, at a much simpler level, the excellent effect achieved by a good limerick.) Shakespeare's three quatrains can develop a theme with subtle extensions and counter-movements, and the last two rhyming lines supply a consolidation or twist that gives a pleasing completeness.

There are 154 sonnets. There is no evident logic to the sequence, though some sub-groups have links. Some seem to be based on real occasions; some may be fictions. Some are addressed to a man, others to a 'Dark Lady'. Scholars have speculated endlessly and inconclusively about the identity of these two (it may of course be more than two) and of "Mr W.H." to whom the printer dedicated the first printing.

Such diversions doubtless have their interests. In the meantime, the sonnets stand: absorbing, endlessly provoking, beautifully set. The tone varies. Some are lightly playful; others enigmatic and dark. Some are wittily tongue-in-cheek; some impassioned and soul-searching.

Take, for example, Sonnet 130:

> *My mistress' eyes are nothing like the sun;*
> *Coral is far more red than her lips' red;*
> *If snow be white, why then her breasts are dun;*
> *If hairs be wires, black wires grow on her head.*
> *I have seen roses damasked, red and white,*
> *But no such roses see I in her cheeks;*
> *And in some perfumes is there more delight*
> *Than in the breath that from my mistress reeks.*
> *I love to hear her speak, yet well I know*
> *That music hath a far more pleasing sound;*
> *I grant I never saw a goddess go -*
> *My mistress when she walks treads on the ground.*
> *And yet, by heaven, I think my love as rare*
> *As any she belied with false compare.*

This is good fun. The tactic is a simple one. *His* mistress does not conform at all to the conventional stereotypes of beauty, as found in many poems of the time: to have eyes that radiate like the sun, lips that are coral red, breasts that are snowy white, and so on. We are at first tricked into assuming that this comparison is to her disadvantage: she must be an ugly specimen! Our assumption seems confirmed by the daringly unconventional reference to her "breath" and the comic jolt of the word "reeks". She does not glide like a goddess – her feet are all too mortally and heavily rooted to the ground. (Does "treads" suggest a heavyweight?)

But then the last two lines spring a surprise. Shakespeare affirms that she is in fact as "rare" as anyone who has been misrepresented by false comparisons. We are amused to realise that we have been deceived into misinterpreting the description of her. And is there then a double twist? There's just a hint that her "rarity", her distinctiveness, may on reflection be a grossness rather than a fineness. If so, we have been teased into a second misreading, which flicks us back into reassessing the first.

This sonnet is essentially lightweight, playing entertaining games with our responses. It is a kind of wit that was a popular diversion of the time, and it is quite possible that the mistress is a total fiction – she exists for the purposes of the joke.

Compare Sonnet 130 with Sonnet 129. We sense immediately that we are in very different territory:

> *Th'expense of spirit in a waste of shame*
> *Is lust in action; and till action, lust*
> *Is perjured, murderous, bloody, full of blame,*
> *Savage, extreme, rude, cruel, not to trust;*
> *Enjoyed no sooner but despised straight;*
> *Past reason hunted, and, no sooner had,*
> *Past reason hated, as a swallowed bait,*
> *On purpose laid to make the taker mad -*
> *Mad in pursuit, and in possession so;*
> *Had, having, and in quest to have, extreme;*
> *A bliss in proof, and proved, a very woe;*
> *Before, a joy proposed; behind, a dream.*
> *All this the world well knows; yet none knows well*
> *To shun the heaven that leads men to this hell.*

This is powerfully compressed language, pursuing its subject tightly. "Lust" is described as unworthy but irresistible. At the very moment when lust is fulfilled, it becomes "despised", "hated", a "woe". The words are the more forceful because of the well-knit rhythm of the lines. Look at line 4 ("Savage, extreme....."), and the accumulating implication that no one word is adequate to express the felt disgust. Or line 10 ("Had, having...."), where a wealth of meaning is most economically expressed – that the wildest and least controllable aspects of ourselves are in play in the anticipation, experience and after-effect of lust.

The final couplet states with an almost proverbial memorability that awareness of the pit does not prevent us from falling into it. Notice that throughout this sonnet the language does not let go, the momentum is unrelenting. The writing has an extraordinary mix of urgent energy and sharp analysis. Is it driven by personal guilt and self-disgust, or by the more generalised wisdom of digested experience? Is the "lust" wholly sexual? homosexual? simply greed? Whatever our conclusion, the sonnet's unresting tensions linger uncomfortably.

Browsing in the sonnets can bring many rewards. Make a start, perhaps, with Sonnets 30, 33, 55, 71, 73, 87, 94, 116, and 138.

The sonnets circulated privately amongst Shakespeare's friends until they were published in 1609, still in Shakespeare's lifetime though possibly not under his direct control. Shakespeare seems to have shown little interest in the publication of his work. Only half of the plays were printed while he lived, many in dubious versions, and the first collected edition of texts even approaching reliability was not until the First Folio of 1623, seven years after his death.

From whence came the inspiration that fired Shakespeare's imagination? We know so little of Shakespeare's life that we can but guess at the influences that shaped his art. Certainly he absorbed a vast amount from his reading. But even if we had a full biography available to us, it is likely that the mysteries of his creative brilliance would remain as indecipherable as genius always is.

There are of course numerous books about Shakespeare. There is interesting introductory material in 'Shakespeare for all Time' by Stanley Wells, and 'After Shakespeare: an Anthology', edited by John Gross. An excellent recent academic work is Frank Kermode's 'Shakespeare's Language'. See also 'Shakespeare' by Anthony Burgess and 'In Search of Shakespeare' by Michael Wood.

14
Ben Jonson (1572-1637)

He had a neat wit, and a measured, worldly sense of experience. Across the range of Ben Jonson's poetry we find a note of reflective assurance. He also had a sweeping contempt for lesser talents – "chattering [mag]pies" – and a warm and generous affection for Shakespeare, "the wonder of our stage". His verse tribute to Shakespeare, **'To the Memory of My Beloved Mr William Shakespeare'**, praises with convincing extravagance. At its end he inverts Virgil's famous dictum, *"Poeta nascitur, non fit"* ('A poet is born, not made') and adds a technically shrewd half line:

> *For a good poet's made as well as born.*
> *And such wert thou....*

He writes in amusingly cultivated and relaxed vein in **'Inviting a Friend to Supper'**, but is equally at home with sharp and even acid satire:

> *For what is life, if measured by the space,*
> *Not by the act?*
> *Or masked man, if valued by his face,*
> *Above his fact?*
> *Here's one out-lived his peers,*
> *And told forth fourscore years;*
> *He vexed time, and busied the whole State,*
> *Troubled both foes and friends;*
> *But ever to no ends:*
> *What did this stirrer but die late?*
> *How well at twenty had he fallen or stood!*
> *For three of his fourscore he did no good.*
> (From **'To the Immortal Memory and Friendship of that Noble Pair,**
> **Sir Lucius Cary and Sir Henry Morison'**)

Compare this with the sophisticated and jewelled movement of **'Simplex Munditiis'**, from his play 'Epicene', which also has a lethal last line:

> *Still to be neat, still to be drest,*
> *As you were going to a feast;*
> *Still to be powdered, still perfumed,*

Lady, it is to be presumed,
Though art's hid causes are not found,
All is not sweet, all is not sound.

Give me a look, give me a face,
That makes simplicity a grace;
Robes loosely flowing, hair as free:
Such sweet neglect more taketh me
Than all the adulteries of art;
They strike mine eyes, but not my heart.

Jonson had an extraordinary variety to his life. He worked as a bricklayer, a soldier and an actor. He killed a fellow-actor in a duel, but successfully pleaded benefit of clergy to avoid hanging. He was twice in trouble for alleged seditious writing. He wrote numerous court entertainments and was given a pension by James I in 1616. He received honorary degrees from Oxford and Cambridge and tutored Sir Walter Raleigh's son in France.

He did not suffer fools gladly. In addition to masques he wrote light comedies (Shakespeare acted in his **'Every Man in his Humour'**) and tragedies, but he is best remembered for his vigorous satiric work in **'Volpone'** (1606), **'Epicene'** (1609), **'The Alchemist'** (1610) and **'Bartholemew Fair'** (1614). These plays succeed probably despite rather than because of Jonson's theory that a stage characterisation could be best modelled on a single foible or 'humour'.

'Volpone', his most performed masterpiece, has a wonderfully diverting and intricate plot, full of cunning plans and unexpected hitches. Volpone – the 'Fox' – is a wealthy and greedy merchant who is entangled in plot and counter-plot with Mosca, his devious and equally avaricious servant. Both end hoist on their own petards.

To Jonson we owe, perhaps without realising it, a whole host of sayings and phrases now firmly part of the language, such as "I have it here in black and white"; "no love lost"; and "castles in the air". It was Jonson who wrote the song (to Celia) **"Drink to me only with thine eyes"**.

Ben Jonson's daughter died at six months and his son died aged seven. His poem **'On My Son'** is one of the most touching of epitaphs. It ends:

Rest in soft peace, and, asked, say here doth lie
Ben Jonson, his best piece of poetry.
For whose sake, henceforth, all his vows be such
As what he loves may never like too much.

Jonson's own epitaph, inscribed on his tomb in Westminster Abbey, is justly famous – "O rare Ben Jonson". We are encouraged not only towards admiration of his talents, but to the pleasing confirmation that he was recognised in his time.

The Seventeenth Century

15
John Donne (c.1572–1631)

Donne is often described as a leading **metaphysical** poet.

The term 'metaphysical', first used in a hostile sense by Dryden and then Dr Johnson, refers to poetry which uses elaborate or far-fetched similes and metaphors, and enjoys paradoxes.

Other Seventeenth Century poets sometimes included in the group are George Herbert, Andrew Marvell and Henry Vaughan. The term has stuck, but is not very helpful: in truth the poets are very different from each other.

Donne designed his own tomb. (We see the monument still in St Paul's Cathedral.) He had himself painted in his death shroud, and kept the picture by his bed. There is an element of bold self-dramatisation here, perhaps, but this complex and fascinating man could also be introspective and troubled. Like Webster he is in his later years "much possessed by death". But unlike Webster, in whose plays the fact of mortality confidently belittles the general human depravity, in Donne's later writings we often find angst and insecurity, an inner wrestling with what he felt were his spiritual inadequacies.

Donne's appeal strengthened considerably in the Twentieth Century, and we think of him now as one of the major figures. In his own time he was little published. His poetry was circulated among his friends; he did not think of himself as in any sense a 'professional' poet. The earlier love poetry was a diversion. Later religious poetry often takes the form of private confessional. Only in the famous sermons, after he had in 1621 been appointed Dean of St Paul's, do we hear a public voice.

His life was in many ways a struggle. He studied law, but as a Catholic was not allowed to take his degree. At this time he led a profligate existence of many affairs – he was, Izaak Walton was to write drily, "a great visitor of ladies". He became chief Secretary to Sir Thomas Egerton, Lord Keeper of the Privy Seal, and in 1601 was secretly married in defiance of her father to Egerton's niece, Anne, who was 17. When this was discovered, he lost everything except the marriage itself. ("John Donne – Anne Donne – Undone", he wrote.) He went through a period of depression and was occasionally suicidal. The death of Anne at the age of 33 in 1617 devastated him. She had borne him twelve children, of whom seven survived.

During this time he began to move away from Catholicism – some say for careerist reasons, others as a product of genuine soul-searchings. Essays which were aimed to persuade Catholics to take the oath of allegiance attracted the attention of James I, who tried to persuade Donne to take holy orders. This he eventually did in 1615, as royal chaplain, with two livings two years later, and he was Dean of St Paul's for the last ten years of his life.

The love poetry

The love poems of Donne's 'Songs and Sonnets' were probably written in the wild oats period before his marriage. They are variously playful, flirtatious, tender and lustful: there is great variety of tone. Often they are ingeniously witty. The old conventions of courtly worship of the loved one are cast aside; instead we find a live, fresh speaking voice, determined on intelligent originality.

The gentle 'Song' ("Sweetest love, I do not go / For weariness of thee") affirms that their love will remain strong despite his absence:

> *They who one another keep*
> *Alive, ne'er parted be.*

This theme is developed more complicatedly in "A Valediction: Forbidding Mourning":

> *Our two souls therefore, which are one,*
>   *Though I must go, endure not yet*
> *A breach, but an expansion*
>   *Like gold to aery thinness beat.*
>
> *If they be two, they are two so*
>   *As stiff twin compasses are two;*
> *Thy soul, the fixed foot, makes no show*
>   *To move, but doth, if the other do.*
>
> *And though it in the centre sit,*
>   *Yet when the other far doth roam*
> *It leans, and hearkens after it,*
>   *And grows erect, as it comes home.*

Such wilt thou be to me, who must
Like the other foot, obliquely run;
Thy firmness makes my circle just,
And makes me end where I begun.

The analogy between the lovers and the two feet of a pair of compasses is designed to be intellectually pleasing, and the rhythmic neatness reinforces this; the last two lines have a satisfying symmetry both within themselves and as a conclusion of the argument. It isn't if pressed a wholly convincing argument, of course – his circle does not in fact end at the centre, in union with her. Look at it this way, and separateness and distance is confirmed. But to take the ideas that literally is to miss the point of the poetry. Donne's intention is to create an *illusion* of logic, which he and we (or his friends) are happy to share and be entertained by. The cleverness is in the trick.

This kind of elaborate parallel or simile is what was called a **conceit** – what Izaak Walton (again) had in mind when he described Donne as "a great writer of conceited verses". Examples abound. In **'The Ecstasy'**, *"Our eye-beams twisted, and did thread / Our eyes upon one double string."* (**'The Ecstasy'**, incidentally, is one of the first poems in the language to use the word "sex" to mean sexual activity; even today one experiences a mild shock at finding it there.) For a frivolous instance, try **'The Flea'** – a tongue-in-cheek justification of 'her' accepting 'his' seduction of her. (We do not need to be concerned whether the women and the situations were actual: some probably were, some may have been, others are almost certainly fictions.)

Many of Donne's conceits play on the idea of the unity of lovers being an image of the wholeness of the world, with their relationship as the centre of creation. With this as the core metaphor, all manner of paradoxes follow: 'we' are 'everything'; 'your' transient beauty is 'unchangeable'; when 'we' weep the whole world drowns. Expressed in this mundane way, these ideas have become no more than clichés. But discover them as handled by Donne's quick wit and adventurous imagination and they become, at his best, tours de force.

All of the 'Songs and Sonnets' are worth sampling. Try especially 'The Sunne Rising', 'Lover's Infiniteness', 'A Valediction: Of Weeping', and 'A Nocturnal Upon St. Lucies Day'.

Look also at his 'Elegies' and 'Satires' of the same period, especially Elegy IV -'The Perfume', Elegy XVI – 'On His Mistress', and the erotic Elegy XIX – 'To His Mistress Going to Bed'. Try Satire II and Satire III.

Donne's religious writing

From the early 1600s religious poetry and prose meditation replace man-about-town wit as the mainstream of Donne's writing.

In the '**Holy Sonnets**', in the prose '**Meditations**' (or 'Devotions upon Emergent Occasions'), and in his **Sermons** we have a fine legacy. The moods range from spiritual restlessness and self-doubt to challenging affirmation. The wording is characteristically bold and energetic, and often memorable. His celebrated lines, "No man is an island....", are to be found in **Meditation XVII**:

> *No man is an island, entire of itself; every man is a piece of the continent, a part of the main; if a clod be washed away by the sea, Europe is the less, as well as if a promontory were, as well as if a manor of thy friend's or of thine own were. Any man's death diminishes me, because I am involved in mankind. And therefore never send to know for whom the bell tolls; it tolls for thee.*

Memorability is not simply in the sentiment, but in the manner of the saying. Donne at his best has the authority of a ringing voice.

Even his insecurities find expression in dramatic eloquence, as we see particularly in the nineteen '**Holy Sonnets**'. Their full impact is gained by reading them as a sequence. There is a strong sense of unworthiness, of past sin, and of the imminence of his leaving *"the world, the flesh, the devil"*. His spirit is disturbed – *"this holy discontent"* – and he courts God for a purging and a healing.

Impending death is faced with resigned acceptance in **Sonnet VI** –

> *This is my play's last scene, here heavens appoint*
> *My pilgrimage's last mile.*

– and with a defiant rhetorical transcendence in **Sonnet X**, "Death be not proud":

> *One short sleep past, we wake eternally,*
> *And death shall be no more; death, thou shalt die.*

Sonnet XIV ends with a remarkable conceit, the double paradoxes of God's controlling and possessing him being both liberating and purifying:

Take me to you, imprison me, for I
Except you enthral me, never shall be free,
Nor ever chaste, except you ravish me.

He uses a similar image in **Sermon XXXVI (1625)** – *"This consolation from the Holy Ghost …..makes my death-bed a marriage-bed".* The sermons are powerfully weighted with the theme of atonement. *"The death of the righteous is a sleep; first as it delivers them to a present rest....And then, lastly, it is so also as it promises a future waiting in a glorious resurrection"* (**Sermon XV, 1627**).

In words that almost serve as an epitaph, Donne had written:

Only death adds t'our length; nor are we grown
In stature to be men, till we are none.

He preached his last sermon on February 25th, 1630, before James I in Whitehall. The text was printed in 1632, prefaced by a note to the reader from the otherwise unknown publisher, Richard Redmer. It is movingly eloquent:

It hath been observed of this reverend man, that his faculty in preaching continually increased; and that as he exceeded others at first, so at last he exceeded himself. This is his last sermon. I will not say it is therefore his best, because all his were excellent. Yet this much: a dying man's words, if they concern ourselves, do usually make the deepest impression, as being spoken most feelingly, and with least affectation. …May we make such use of this and other the like preparatives, that neither death, whensoever it shall come, may seem terrible; nor life tedious, how long soever it shall last.

16
Robert Burton (1577–1640)

>─┼◄►─O─◄►┼─<

'**The Anatomy of Melancholy**' (1621), one of the finest works of English prose, and Burton's most significant book, is an extraordinary encyclopaedic tour-de-force, a high mix of science, philosophy and satiric comedy. Huge in its scope (and its size – it is 500,000 words long), it sets out to explore the causes and character of what medical science assumed to be one of the four controlling 'humours' of the human body, but along the way it offers a kaleidoscope of wit and knowledge on topics as diverse as theology and war, education and parenthood, love and alcohol. Burton has had many admirers. This was the only book, according to Boswell, that Samuel Johnson would rise early to read with pleasure. In our own time, Anthony Burgess celebrated 'The Anatomy of Melancholy' as, despite its title, "one of the great *comic* works of the world".

Writing under the pseudonym 'Democritus Junior' – Democritus was the "laughing philosopher" of the ancient world – Burton starts from the proposition that '*all the world is mad*'. And by 'mad' he means absurd: a fit object for ridicule and satire. Like his contemporary **Bacon**, Burton was a polymath, widely read across a vast range of scholarship and literature. But whereas Bacon's forte was to concentrate, to reduce thought to elegant and pithy nuggets, Burton moves in an opposite direction: expansive, digressive, informal and tartly good-humoured.

He was a churchman, and, from 1599, a fellow of Brasenose College, Oxford. "His company," observed a contemporary, "was very merry." Here he is, in full flow, excoriating those entering the church for careerist reasons:

> *Vile and shameless souls (as Luther calls them somewhere) in search of gain, they fly to the tables of the nobility like flies to the milk pail, and in hope of getting a church living or any other post or honour, betake themselves to any hall or town. They will accept any employment, like marionettes pulled by strings, always on the scent, and like parrots babbling anything for the sake of a morsel: complaisant parasites (as Erasmus calls them) who will teach, write, say, recommend, approve anything, even against their consciences, not to edify their flock but to improve their own fortunes.*

Elsewhere, he targets university colleges which boost their income by taking weak students:

> *Hence it comes that such a pack of vile buffoons, ignoramuses wandering in the twilight of learning, ghosts of clergymen, itinerant quacks, dolts, clods, asses, mere cattle, intrude with unwashed feet upon the sacred precincts of theology, bringing with them nothing save brazen impudence, and some hackneyed quillets and scholastic trifles not good enough for a crowd at a street corner.*

This kind of entertaining knockabout is interwoven with sober philosophising and a sprinkling of gems from other authors – Burton quotes from over 1,500 writers. We also owe to him a host of sayings which have embedded themselves in our culture: '*one religion is as true as another*'; '*penny wise, pound foolish*'; '*birds of a feather will gather together'*; *'a dwarf standing on the shoulders of a giant may see farther than the giant himself'*; *'set a beggar on horseback and he will ride a gallop'*; *'no rule was so general, which admits not some exception'*.

'The Anatomy of Melancholy' was a great success in Burton's lifetime – it went through six editions. To be dipped into rather than read dutifully, it is an eccentric off-beat delight.

There is a complete, six-volume modern edition, but also a handy paperback produced by the New York Review of Books.

17
John Webster (c.1580–c.1634)

A play of Webster's is full of the feverish and ghastly turmoil of a nest of maggots.
Rupert Brooke (1916)

Webster was much possessed by death
And saw the skull beneath the skin.
T.S.Eliot (1919)

We know virtually nothing of Webster's life – the dates of birth and death themselves are conjectural – and most of his plays and collaborations are now lost. But two plays in particular, **'The White Devil'** and **'The Duchess of Malfi'** (written about 1612–13), are celebrated survivors, and have been especially popular in the Twentieth Century.

Both plays, set in Renaissance Italy, present a smoking world of intrigue, sexual jealousy and political manipulation. Torture and murder are commonplace. Corruption breeds upon itself. Flashes of conscience or moral defiance are soon extinguished.

Both tell complex stories, the bare bones of which, taken simply as narrative, may well stretch credulity.

The Duchess of Malfi, for instance, is a widow, who is warned against remarriage by her two brothers, one a duke, Ferdinand, and the other a cardinal. The brothers are greedy to preserve their high status and to inherit her possessions, and there is a hint that Ferdinand is incestuously jealous of her. However, she secretly marries her steward, Antonio. The brothers suspect the worst and appoint an escaped slave, Bosola, as their agent to spy on her. He duly reports the marriage and a pregnancy. Aware of her vulnerability, she and Antonio flee, but she is captured, imprisoned, mentally tortured and strangled. Her children are murdered.

Bosola, disturbed by her defiance of her fate, changes his colours and decides to exact revenge upon the brothers. They meanwhile decide they have to eliminate him. Bosola kills a man he thinks is the cardinal, who turns out to be Antonio. Ferdinand goes mad. Bosola kills the real cardinal, and is himself killed by the mad Ferdinand. Ferdinand is killed by Antonio's friends.

A bare summary such as this highlights the thickly twisted plot, and its apparent improbabilities. (In fact Webster based both plays on supposed facts, though doubtless treated them with creative licence.)

However, we have here a good example of how easy it is to misrepresent or misunderstand drama by focusing simply on the story told. Webster is essentially a man *of the theatre*, and good productions of the plays are extraordinarily powerful experiences, sensational in the best sense. Webster has sometimes been criticised for writing "mere" melodrama, a hotchpotch of unconvincingly exaggerated situations and emotions, but it would be fairer to say that he makes of melodramatic material something finer and more alive.

The decadent and degraded world he evokes is excitingly appalling. (One recent production adopted an icy stylisation in which white- and green-faced figures moved slowly about an enormous chess board.) Individual scenes and speeches can be exhilaratingly tense and moving. The Duchess, and Vittoria in '**The White Devil**', develop a memorable grandeur as they defy their persecutors – *"I am Duchess of Malfi still"*.

Webster's is a bleak world in which individuality glints briefly against the darkness. There is no way out:

> - *I have caught an everlasting cold.* (Flamineo in '**The White Devil**")
> - *I am 'i th' way to study a long silence.* (Flamineo again)

In lines which echo Gloucester in Shakespeare's '**King Lear**':

> *We are merely the stars' tennis balls, struck and bandied*
> *Which way please them.* (Bosola)

Perhaps catching something of that strain of brooding melancholy we often find in the Jacobean period, Flamineo reflects in '**The White Devil**':

'Tis just like a summer bird-cage in a garden: the birds that are without despair to get in, and the birds that are within despair and are in a consumption for fear they shall never get out.

Webster relishes words and relishes theatre. Whether he also relishes the unsavoury stew he concocts, or alternatively is offering a tragic moral vision, is a matter for continuing debate.

18

Robert Herrick (1591–1674)

Herrick was a poet of pleasure. Chambers Biographical Dictionary describes him as "the most pagan of English poets".

He came of a wealthy family and lived well. Ben Jonson was a good friend. In 1630 he became parish priest of Dean Prior in Devon. He was a royalist, in the times of Civil War and Cromwell's Protectorate, but his poetry is barely touched by the national tensions. Parliament displaced him from Dean Prior in 1647; he was reinstated after the Restoration and remained in Devon until his death.

His delight in the sensuous possibilities of language drives the well-known six line poem '**Upon Julia's Clothes**', where the word "liquefaction" – an inspired choice – mimes his melting relish:

Whenas in silks my Julia goes,
Then, then, methinks how sweetly flows
That liquefaction of her clothes!

Next, when I cast mine eyes and see
That brave vibration each way free,
- O how that glittering taketh me!

He writes with the precision of a miniaturist (both his father and an uncle were goldsmiths; for six years he was apprenticed to his uncle). His main themes of sex and beauty, loss, and the transience of life, are not agonised over but distilled as if into exquisitely worked jewellery. He can be erotic without being salacious.

In 'To the Virgins, to Make Much of Time' (better known by its first line, *"Gather ye rosebuds while ye may"*) the subject is treated with graceful lightness:

> *That age is best which is the first,*
> *When youth and blood are warmer;*
> *But being spent, the worse, the worst*
> *Times still succeed the former.*
>
> *Then be not coy, but use your time,*
> *And while ye may, go marry:*
> *For having lost but once your prime*
> *You may for ever tarry.*

Similarly, in **'Corinna's Going a Maying'**, we find a pleasing surface perfection quite different in tone from other poets' treatments of the same familiar theme: compare it, say, with the witty knowingness of Andrew Marvell's **'To His Coy Mistress'**, or the wistful brooding of Thomas Hardy.

Herrick is not a challenging poet; he is for leisurely repose –

> *Melting melodious words, to lutes of amber.* (**'Upon Julia's Voice'**)

19
George Herbert (1593–1633)

In his final year, Herbert sent his major collection of poems to a friend with the instruction to publish them if he thought fit, or otherwise burn them. Happily, they were published as '**The Temple**' in 1633, and became immediately popular.

Born into an aristocratic family, and a brilliant scholar, Herbert at one time seemed set on a political and worldly career. But, maybe disillusioned, he turned to the church. He became a canon of Lincoln Cathedral in 1626, took holy orders in 1630, and was the parish priest at Bemerton near Salisbury for the last three years of his life.

Whereas in Donne's poetry the **conceits** are often deliberately provocative and ostentatious, in Herbert, while they are still elaborate, they are quieter, and usually inseparable from the meaning. "How can one tell the dancer from the dance?" Yeats was to ask, and in Herbert's much admired poems it is indeed impossible to subtract the conceits and leave an essence behind. The image *is* the poem.

Take **"Love"**.

> *Love bade me welcome; yet my soul drew back*
> > *Guilty of dust and sin.*
> *But quick-eyed Love, observing me grow slack*
> > *From my first entrance in,*
> *Drew near to me, sweetly questioning,*
> > *If I lacked anything.*
>
> *'A guest', I answered, 'worthy to be here.'*
> > *Love said, 'You shall be he.'*
> *'I, the unkind, ungrateful? Ah, my dear,*
> > *I cannot look on thee.'*
> *Love took my hand, and smiling did reply,*
> > *'Who made the eyes but I?'*
>
> *'Truth, Lord, but I have marred them; let my shame*
> > *Go where it doth deserve.'*
> *'And know you not', says Love, 'who bore the blame?'*
> > *'My dear, then I will serve.'*
> *'You must sit down', says Love, 'and taste my meat.'*
> > *So I did sit and eat.*

The simple symbolism of Christ and the unworthy guest, or sinner, structures the entire poem. Pervading it is an unspoken pun on the word 'host' – Christ as the welcoming host, and the Host which is the bread consecrated in the Eucharist. The sharing of food with Love becomes an image of communion, as well as a picture of acceptance and forgiveness. The identification of the poet with a guest reinforces his status as one who owes the courtesies of deference. There is a hint of unworthy trespassing. There is also a hint of the traveller – "guilty of dust" – reaching a haven.

The suggestiveness of the central image is inexhaustible. Perhaps a source of the pleasure we can take from the poem is that the central metaphor reverberates endlessly for us.

Look at one further example from 'Virtue'.

> *Only a sweet and virtuous soul,*
> *Like seasoned timber never gives;*
> *But though the whole world turn to coal,*
> *Then chiefly lives.*

The parallel between the virtuous soul and seasoned timber is explicitly affirming the soul's supreme strength. Timber lasts. But timber is physical as the soul is abstract, and the subtle suggestion of the last two lines, with the image of the decaying of physical things, is of the spirit transcending mutability.

Similarly provoking and satisfying are poems like 'The Pulley', 'The Collar', 'Church Music', 'The Church Porch' and 'The Elixir', all from the collection called 'The Temple'. ('The Elixir' has become the well-known hymn, 'Teach Me My God and King'.) It is a touching historical footnote that Charles I, awaiting execution, had a copy of 'The Temple' among his favourite reading.

20
John Milton (1608–1674)

Single-handedly, Milton attempted to reinvent the English language when he wrote his massive epic poem '**Paradise Lost**'. The poem's Old Testament theme is the Fall of Man. In twelve 'books' of 10,500 blank verse lines, Milton describes the rebellion against God of Satan and other angels, their ejection from heaven, and Satan's revenge in successfully tempting Adam and Eve to disobey their creator.

Milton announces that his purpose is to:

> *…assert Eternal Providence*
> *And justify the ways of God to men.*

He aimed to give an epic and tragic stature to man's fallen state, to affirm God's power and mystery, and to inspire his readers to an elevated prayerfulness. It was a huge ambition. The writing of it required of him, he felt, "things unattempted yet in prose or rhyme".

The unique style which Milton developed in writing 'Paradise Lost' became a gigantic milestone in English literary history. So-called 'Miltonic' verse has been over the centuries much imitated, much discussed, much admired and much disliked. Whatever our final view may be, 'Paradise Lost' is a prodigious achievement, the product of turbulent times and an extraordinary man's dedication.

Milton was politically a radical and controversial figure in his own day. In pamphlets he campaigned powerfully for liberty, for free speech and a free press, and for new attitudes to divorce. He argued strongly against bishops, church ritual, and any perceived threat to freedom, which included both the monarchy and presbyterians.

He was financially independent and so under no pressure to find a career. His father, born a Catholic, was a puritan convert. Milton's time at Cambridge, which was socially chequered and unsatisfactory, consolidated his scholarly interest in poetry and Latin. After leaving Cambridge he devoted his time in the 1630s first to private study at his father's home and then to travels abroad. From 1639 his political pamphleteering began. He more or less stopped writing poetry during the Civil War. Upon the execution of Charles I he became Latin secretary to the new council of state, and its official propagandist. With the Restoration in 1660 he went into hiding but was arrested and imprisoned. It seems quite likely that he would have been executed had not Marvell intervened in Parliament on his behalf. (Marvell's argument was that Milton was too old and blind to represent a threat.) After 1660 he devoted himself wholly to poetry.

He was three times married. His first wife, Mary Powell, was 17 when he married her, aged 33, in 1642. Within six weeks she had refused to return to him from a visit to her parents (who were royalists). She came back three years later, but it was an unhappy marriage that played its part in precipitating the divorce pamphlets.

'Paradise Lost'

Milton's sensitive skill with words developed early. At 15, while still a schoolboy, he wrote the poem which we now know as the hymn **'Let us with a gladsome mind'**. And his love of music (his father, John, was a scrivener and composer) undoubtedly influenced his ear for poetic effects.

The notion of writing a large-scale epic poem had been with him for some time. Originally the subject was to have been the Arthurian legends, but as religious politics came more and more to dominate his life the theme of the Fall emerged. He began to write in the 1650s – dictating, as he became totally blind from 1651.

Milton chose to abandon rhyme and use the **blank verse** form which hitherto had been used mostly in drama. Here, in Book I, he describes Satan, flung out of heaven by God, and taking in his new environment:

> *Him the almighty power*
> *Hurl'd headlong flaming from th'ethereal sky*
> *With hideous ruin and combustion down*
> *To bottomless perdition, there to dwell*
> *In adamantine chains and penal fire,*
> *Who durst defy th'omnipotent to arms.*
> *Nine times the space that measures day and night*
> *To mortal men, he with his horrid crew*
> *Lay vanquish'd, rolling in the fiery gulf*
> *Confounded though immortal: but his doom*
> *Reserv'd him to more wrath; for now the thought*
> *Both of lost happiness and lasting pain*
> *Torments him; round he throws his baleful eyes*
> *That witness'd huge affliction and dismay*
> *Mix'd with obdurate pride and steadfast hate:*
> *At once as far as angels ken he views*
> *The dismal situation waste and wild,*
> *A dungeon horrible, on all sides round*
> *As one great furnace flam'd, yet from those flames*
> *No light, but rather darkness visible*
> *Serv'd only to discover sights of woe,*
> *Regions of sorrow, doleful shades, where peace*
> *And rest can never dwell, hope never comes*
> *That comes to all; but torture without end*
> *Still urges, and a fiery deluge, fed*
> *With ever-burning sulphur unconsum'd:*
> *Such place eternal justice had prepar'd*
> *For those rebellious, here their prison ordain'd*
> *In utter darkness, and their portion set*
> *As far remov'd from God and light of heaven*
> *As from the centre thrice to th' utmost pole.*

Try reading that again, slowly. The scale of the conception and of the writing is astonishing. In Milton's punctuation, there are two sentences; we might make it four, but even then note how they are structured in elaborate waves. Main verbs and principal statements are held back; qualifying phrases build on each other in rolling cadences. This is *orchestrated* writing, and heavily influenced by Latin in its patterns.

EPIC

The term has developed a variety of meanings, most loosely in modern publishing or cinema where anything attempted on a large scale is advertised as 'epic'.

The Oxford Dictionary dates the original English language usage to 1589, derived from Latin and Greek, where 'epic' referred to narrative poetry which celebrated the achievements of a heroic person in history or tradition. In later developments the heroism might reside in the subject and scale of the narrative and not necessarily in a person.

For Milton, steeped in the classics of the ancient world, Homer and Virgil were inspirational epic poets. His epic ambition was to write an extensive poem in English in the elevated language appropriate to the solemnity and grandeur of his theme.

Earlier epics in the English tradition are **'Beowulf'** and Spenser's **'Faerie Queene'**.

It is Milton's solution to the challenge of finding an English which has the dramatic sweep, dignity, and impressiveness appropriate to his ambitious theme.

The chaos in which Satan finds himself is sharply but not literally imagined. It is a moral wilderness, where Satan's experience is paradoxically both happening in time and also perpetual and timeless. The 'ever-burning' sulphur is 'unconsumed'; there is no light, but the utter darkness is *visible* (a famous oxymoron); Satan's torture is and will be as much mental as physical. Satan is not described but imagined as a phenomenon, an abstraction. The length of Satan's plummeting descent from heaven, the distance of hell from God, is placed metaphorically as a moral vast beyond universal geography. There is vividness without literalism. (Could it be that Milton's imagination is *enhanced* by his blindness? As maybe Beethoven's music is by his deafness?)

Reactions to Milton's achievement have been mixed. Addison declared: "Our language sunk under him"; Dr Johnson praised the sanctity of thought but found 'Paradise Lost' burdensome to read and lacking in human interest; Marvell thought both the theme and the poetry "sublime"; Blake controversially saw Milton as "a true poet" who was instinctively on the Devil's side without realising it. Wordsworth in his sonnet on Milton praises his versification: "Thou hast a voice whose sound was like the sea; / Pure as the naked heavens, majestic, free".

In the Twentieth Century F.R.Leavis attacked Milton's "impoverishment" of the English language; C.S.Lewis argued alternatively that "Many of those who say they dislike Milton's God only mean that they dislike God". Christopher Ricks in 'Milton's Grand Style', 1963, makes the case for subtlety of detail as well as grandeur in the poetry.

When all is said, we do not find in 'Paradise Lost' the religious self-questioning that we see, for example, in Donne or Herbert. Milton's beliefs were assured and unyielding, and his intention was to affirm truth for an audience which in his own words would be "fit…though few". Whatever we make of it, we are bound to acknowledge 'Paradise Lost' as a colossus, towering in its accomplishment.

The particularly rewarding sections of 'Paradise Lost' are Books I, II, IV, IX and X.

'Areopagitica'

This is Milton's celebrated argument against the censorship of printing. In the form of a speech, it is addressed to the 'Lords and Commons of England', who had enacted in 1643 that no book might be printed without having been first approved and licensed. Possibly motivated by attempts to have his own pamphlet on divorce suppressed, Milton writes with cogent reasoning and compelling rhetoric. (The Areopagus is the name of the hills near the Acropolis where the upper council met – the heart of Athenian democracy.)

> *As good almost kill a man as kill a good book: who kills a man kills a reasonable creature, God's image; but he who destroys a good book, kills reason itself, kills the image of God, as it were in the eye……a good book is the precious life-blood of a master spirit, embalmed and treasured up on purpose to a life beyond life.*

Attempts to quell unpalatable ideas through refusing the licence to print, he says, are reminiscent of "the gallant man who thought to pound up the crows by shutting the park gate".

Other poems

Aside from 'Paradise Lost' Milton left a substantial body of poetry in Latin as well as in English. He was a serious poet. He writes for solemn purposes rather than diversion. Varied though the poetic forms are that he used, there is usually in Milton a tone of sculptured thoughtfulness. We may briefly sample this in four poems.

In firm and ringing terms Milton in 1629 celebrated the nativity in poetry which associates the divine order with music. Christ's birth, he writes, inspires harmonies in nature, music never heard since the Creation.

Ring out ye crystal spheres,
Once bless our human ears
(If ye have power to touch our senses so)
And let your silver chime
Move in melodious time;
And let the bass of heaven's deep organ blow
And with your ninefold harmony
Make up full consort to th'angelic symphony.
'On The Morning of Christ's Nativity'

Milton's ear for rhythmic authority creates a note of monumental dignity here. We pick it up again in his 1630 epitaph 'On Shakespeare', where the commonplace that a writer's real monument is his work is transformed into an impressive reverence:

What needs my Shakespeare for his honoured bones
The labour of an age in piled stones......?

In contrast, his sonnet **'On the late Massacre in Piedmont'** thunders an imperious anger:

Avenge O Lord thy slaughtered saints, whose bones
Lie scattered on the alpine mountains cold......

While **Sonnet XX**, on his own blindness ("When I consider how my light is spent..."), works through to an altruistic dedication to the service of God in its famous last line –

They also serve who only stand and wait.

21
Andrew Marvell (1621–1678)

The Civil War, Cromwell's Protectorate, and the Restoration of the monarchy defined Marvell's political lifetime. From 1659 until his death he was MP for Hull. In 1657 he had succeeded the blind Milton as Latin Secretary to Cromwell's Council of State. In the early 1650s he was the tutor first to the daughter of Lord Fairfax (who in 1645, as commander-in-chief of the parliamentarians, defeated Charles I at the battle of Naseby) and then tutor to the ward of Cromwell himself.

In addition to his parliamentary duties, he wrote. His later poetry, often satirical, is slanted against tyranny and political ineptitude. He argued for religious toleration. His '**Horatian Ode on the Return of Cromwell from Ireland**', written in 1650, is one of the finest political poems in the language. He wrote earlier lyrics (though 'Miscellaneous Poems' was not published until after his death in 1681) in which delicate and witty pastoral and philosophical poems are steeped in his Latin scholarship. He enjoyed the subtle wordplay and ingenious punning that we also find in temperaments as different as Donne and Herbert.

His poetry is essentially humane – poised, civilised, amused and wise. He is more cavalier than roundhead, in the broadest sense of those terms. He has appealed especially to the Twentieth Century, which appreciated his wit, his sophistication and his experienced dispassion.

The '**Horatian Ode**' is anything but crudely partisan. There is a clear admiration for the dignity of Charles I at the scene of his execution. (Part of the memorability of these lines comes from the subtle rhythmic variations – notice how the word "down" slows almost to motionlessness our image of the critical moment.)

> *He nothing common did or mean*
> *Upon that memorable scene,*
> *But with his keener eye*
> *The axe's edge did try;*
>
> *Nor called the Gods, with vulgar spite,*
> *To vindicate his helpless right;*
> *But bowed his comely head*
> *Down, as upon a bed.*

In a chilling detail, the soldiery in the background *"did clap their bloody hands"*.

Cromwell is portrayed as like *"three-forked lightning"*, an agent of *"angry Heaven's flame"*, whose *"forced power"* has the inevitability of political circumstance. He is *"fit for highest trust"*, but his future is not assured:

> *The same arts that did gain*
> *A power, must it maintain.*

Marvell is both involved and detached. His balanced perspective we find again in the quite different tone and circumstance of **"The Garden of Appleton House"**, one of the poems most probably written in the tranquil Yorkshire setting of his tutoring days with Mary Fairfax.

Here a description of a garden's delights moves from the gentle conceits of regimental flowers at dawn firing silent volleys of scents into the air to expression of regret that humanity has invented war. The Garden of Eden has been betrayed by the Fall. *"What luckless apple did we taste?"*

In the similarly titled '**The Garden**' there are again parallels with Eden. Marvell moves from rich, sensual imaginings (*"The luscious clusters of the vine / Upon my mouth do crush their wine"*) to the neat speculation that flowers and bees create a sense of time for us just as much as do the gardener's sundial and the sun's travel.

'**To His Coy Mistress**', one of the great poems and much anthologised, puts a witty gloss upon the ancient theme of *Carpe Diem* or 'Seize the Day'. Persuasively and amusingly Marvell argues that death will eventually render absurd the mistress's prolongation of her virginity.

> *The grave's a fine and private place,*
> *But none, I think, do there embrace.*

The comparison with Donne's '**The Flea**' is interesting. In both Donne and Marvell the tone is unserious and sportive, but as in all Marvell we also sense a wryness and a standing back, a balancing feel for the perspective time lends to human histories. Marvell does not write directly about himself, but reading him we are constantly in touch with an urbane and agreeable personality.

'World Enough and Time: The Life of Andrew Marvell' is by Nicholas Murray.

22
Three Devotional Poets

Richard Crashaw (1612–1649)
Henry Vaughan (1622–1695)
Thomas Traherne (1637–1674)

A popular theme in much Seventeenth Century writing is the association between the tiny, even microscopic, existence of the individual and the huge scale of the vastnesses beyond. Developments in the physical sciences, in astrology, in navigation and exploration, in philosophy and in the pseudo-science of Hermetics, derived from alchemy, all helped to fuel this intellectual excitement. Images derived from this fascination are to be found in both secular and religious poetry.

Occasionally described as the relationship between the microcosm and the macrocosm, this theme sometimes marries with the tradition of mysticism deriving from the middle ages, in which divines contemplated the nature of the bond between the body and the soul, the individual and the Creator, life and eternity.

Richard Crashaw was a friend of Nicholas Ferrar, who first published George Herbert's poems, and who founded the Anglican religious community Little Gidding in Huntingdonshire (which was to become a significant religious icon in T.S.Eliot's 'Four Quartets'.) He was converted to Catholicism in 1645 and left England for France and Italy. His **'Steps to the Temple'** of 1646 includes **'A Hymn to the Name and Honour of the Admirable Saint Teresa'**, which begins with the arresting words

> *Love, thou art absolute, sole Lord*
> *Of life and death.*

Crashaw addresses Saint Teresa:

> *Each heavenly word, by whose hid flame*
> *Our hard hearts shall strike fire, the same*
> *Shall flourish on thy brows, and be*
> *Both fire to us, and flame to thee;*
> *Whose light shall live bright in thy face*
> *By glory, in our hearts by grace.*

In 1650 **Henry Vaughan** uses a strikingly similar image in his collection of poems '**Silex Scintillans**', the 'Sparkling Flint', in which he describes the heart responding to the adversities of life with *"divine rays"* like *"sparks of fire"*. Vaughan, a Welsh physician, expressed his debt to Herbert, "whose holy life and verse gained many pious converts, of whom I am the least".

Vaughan was a mystic, perceiving the divine in the natural world. Eternity is apprehended in a vision of flame, light and brightness which cuts through mist, cloud and fog – metaphors he regularly uses. The confident visionary ring of his poetry is exemplified in the opening to '**The World**':

> *I saw Eternity the other night*
> *Like a great Ring of pure and endless light,*
> *   All calm as it were bright;*
> *And round beneath it, Time, in hours, days, years,*
> *   Driven by the spheres,*
> *Like a vast shadow moved, in which the world*
> *   And all her train were hurled.*

Thomas Traherne's poetry, like Vaughan's, creates powerfully a sense of mystical bliss in creation. In a remarkable discovery, his poems – '**Centuries**' – came to light in a notebook on a market bookstall in the 1890s, and were first published in 1903. Traherne was rector of Credenhill near Hereford, where he had been born and brought up. Childhood was one of his important themes: the child was unwittingly touched by holiness. Traherne's words are fresh, unforced, and freely-moving:

> *But little did the infant dream*
> *That all the treasures of the world were by:*
> *   And that himself was so the cream*
> *And crown of all which round about did lie.*
> *   Yet thus it was: the Gem*
> *   The Diadem,*
> *   The ring enclosing all*
> *That stood upon this earthy ball,*
> *   The Heavenly eye,*
> *   Much wider than the sky,*
> *Wherein they all included were,*
> *   The glorious Soul, that was the King*
> *Made to possess them, did appear*
> *   A small and little thing!*

23
John Bunyan (1628–1688)

>─┼─>─·─⊙─·─<─┼─<

Best-known for his masterpiece 'The Pilgrim's Progress', the first part of which he wrote in Bedford gaol, Bunyan was his own man. He was the son of a tinker, and learnt to read and write at the local school in Elstow near Bedford before becoming a tinker himself. At 16 he was drafted into the parliamentary army. Macaulay describes him as "a young man of singular gravity and innocence". When he was discharged he returned to Elstow and tinkering, and married a girl from a poor family. About this time he had some sort of breakdown, with continuing disturbed visions and fears, and reading his wife's religious books he convinced himself that he was a condemned sinner.

At 25 he joined a non-conformist congregation in Bedford and became an unlicensed preacher, frequently in conflict with established clergy. After the restoration in 1660 he was arrested and tried for preaching to unlawful assemblies, refused to undertake to give up preaching, and was gaoled for 12 years. He was released in 1672 but within a year rearrested and gaoled for a further six months. It was then that he finished the first part of 'The Pilgrim's Progress', which was published in 1678, the complete work following in 1684. He preached without interference, though rather grudgingly tolerated by the authorities, for the last fifteen years of his life.

'The Pilgrim's Progress' is a dream allegory, in which the pilgrim Christian travels through a variety of symbolic landscapes, including the Slough of Despond, Vanity Fair and Doubting Castle, until he arrives at the Celestial City. On the way he is assisted by some figures, such as Faithful, and hindered by others, like Mr Worldly Wiseman. In Part II he is followed by his wife Christiana, their children, and their neighbour Mercy.

Bunyan's style has crystal purity, and a beautiful, dignified simplicity. Here is the end to Part II, where the 'gatekeeper to the Celestial City' greets Christiana:

> *Then he took her by the hand and led her in, and said also suffer little children to come with me, and with that he shut up the gate. This done, he called to a trumpeter that was above, over the gate, to entertain Christiana with shouting, and to sound a trumpet for joy. So he obeyed and sounded, and filled the air with his melodious notes.*

There is debate over whether Bunyan's writing is or is not dominated by the style of the 1611 Bible, the so-called Authorised Version. Clearly there are echoes, but some maintain that he is equally if not more in debt to the rhythms of colloquial speech. (The evidence tends to suggest that while Bunyan could read, he was not widely read. He has been described, probably unfairly, as illiterate. He had two books with him in prison: the Bible, unsurprisingly, and Foxe's Book of Martyrs.)

He certainly had an instinct for fluent, well-paced and semi-ritualised structures. Perhaps we can detect the skill of the populist preacher in the patterns and repetitions. Here is the beginning of the work, where Christian is witnessed in spiritual distress after reading that "our city will be burned with fire from heaven":

> As I walked through the wilderness of this world, I lighted on a certain place where was a Den, and I laid me down in that place to sleep, and as I slept, I dreamed a dream. I dreamed, and behold, I saw a man clothed with rags, standing in a certain place, with his face from his own house, a book in his hand, and a great burden upon his back. I looked, and saw him open the book, and read therein; and as he read, he wept, and trembled; and being not able longer to contain, he broke out with a lamentable cry, saying, what shall I do?

'The Pilgrim's Progress' was an immediate success. In Bunyan's lifetime it was published in several languages; today it runs into over a hundred translations. Among his other works are the vivid autobiography, 'Grace Abounding' (1666) and the hymn "He Who Would Valiant Be".

'An Introduction to the Life and Works of John Bunyan' is written by D.N.Marshall.

24
The Bible in English

>⊷◦⊶⊰

The Latin Vulgate preceded the first Anglo-Saxon manuscripts. **John Wycliffe** (c.1320–1384) initiated the first translation into middle English. **William Tyndale** (c.1494–1536), whose Protestantism and professed desire for a Bible in the vernacular language were heretical in the England of his day, left for the continent in 1524, never to return. He translated most of the Old and New Testaments from the Hebrew and Greek, writing with an admirable grace. His work, produced with the assistance of **Miles Coverdale**, became in 1535 the first published version in modern English. Five more translations appeared in the Sixteenth Century.

What came to be called the **Authorised Version** – though in fact it was never officially "authorised" – was printed in 1611. A team of scholars, convened by James I, worked on this text, which owes a great deal to Tyndale and to the 1560 'Geneva' Bible. (Nine tenths of the AV's New Testament is Tyndale's, and much of the first half of the Old Testament – that which he had completed before his death at the stake.) Over one hundred translations have appeared since 1611, but to the Authorised Version is commonly attributed a huge influence on subsequent writings in English literature. Its resonant phrasing has passed into the common stock of the language.

It is interesting to compare the Authorised Version with later Twentieth Century texts, which aim for transparency of meaning, but are not always charged with the same cadences. For example, look at these two renderings of *Ecclesiastes, Chapter XII, verses 1–8*:

Authorised Version, 1611

> *Remember now thy Creator in the days of thy youth, while the evil days come not, nor the years draw nigh, when thou shalt say, I have no pleasure in them;*
> *While the sun, or the light, or the moon, or the stars, be not darkened, nor the clouds return after the rain:*
> *In the day when the keepers of the house shall tremble, and the strong men shall bow themselves, and the grinders cease because they are few, and those that look out of the windows be darkened,*
> *And the doors shall be shut in the streets, when the sound of the grinding is low, and he shall rise up at the voice of the bird, and all the daughters of musick shall be brought low;*
> *Also then they shall be afraid of that which is high, and fears shall be in the way, and the almond tree shall flourish, and the grasshopper shall be a burden, and desire shall fail: because man goeth to his long home, and the mourners go about the streets:*
> *Or ever the silver cord be loosed, or the golden bowl be broken, or the pitcher be broken at the fountain, or the wheel broken at the cistern.*
> *Then shall the dust return to the earth as it was: and the spirit shall return unto God who gave it.*
> *Vanity of vanities, saith the preacher; all is vanity.*

New English Bible, 1970

> *Remember your Creator in the days of your youth, before the time of trouble comes and the years draw near when you will say, "I see no purpose in them."*
> *Remember him before the sun and the light of day give place to darkness, before*

the moon and the stars grow dim, and the clouds return with the rain – when
the guardians of the house tremble, and the strong men stoop, when the women
grinding the meal cease work because they are few, and those who look through the
windows look no longer, when the street-doors are shut, when the noise of the mill
is low, when the chirping of the sparrow grows faint and the song-birds fall silent;
when men are afraid of a steep place and the street is full of terrors, when the
blossom whitens on the almond-tree and the locust's paunch is swollen and caper-
buds have no more zest. For man goes to his everlasting home, and the mourners
go about the streets. Remember him before the silver cord is snapped and the golden
bowl is broken, before the pitcher is shattered at the spring and the wheel broken at
the well, before the dust returns to the earth as it began and the spirit returns to
God who gave it. Emptiness, emptiness, says the Speaker, all is empty.

*A stimulating book on the genesis of the Authorised Version is '**Power and Glory**' by*
Adam Nicholson.

25

John Dryden (1632–1700)

Dryden saw out the Seventeenth Century, but in his smooth urbanity was a man of the Eighteenth Century. In contrast to Donne's delight in convoluted intellectual trickery, and spiritual agonising, or Milton's Latinate gravity, we find in Dryden a tone of relaxed and amused assurance. He was one of the first and best of political satirists. (His many plays now receive little attention, with the exception of '**All for Love**', his reworking of Shakespeare's '**Antony and Cleopatra**'.) He was the first of the 'Augustans' in English literature, named after the emperor of the classic period of ancient Rome. It was to be a new **Augustan Age**, sometimes referred to as the **Age of Enlightenment**, regarding itself as synonymous with Reason, civility, and the polished confidence of common sense.

Dryden was poet laureate from 1668 until 1688, when his Catholicism caused him to be replaced. (He was born of a puritan family, and had converted from Protestantism in 1686.) In 1659 he wrote '**Heroic Stanzas**' in praise of the late Cromwell; in 1660 his '**Astraea Redux**' celebrated the restoration of the monarchy. He has been accused of cynical political opportunism, but his instinct was to side with the stability of the status quo.

In his satires he perfected the use of the **heroic couplet**, which was to become a standard form in the Eighteenth Century. The heroic couplet is a pair of rhyming, iambic ten-syllable lines. (In **iambic** rhythms, the stress falls regularly on all the even-numbered syllables.) When used in satire, the couplet rhyme is especially suited to clinching a put-down comment:

> *Shadwell alone, of all my sons, is he*
> *Who stands confirmed in full stupidity.*
> *The rest to some faint meaning make pretence,*
> *But Shadwell never deviates into sense.*

The lines come from '**MacFlecknoe**' (1682) in which Dryden satirises a rival dramatist and poet, Thomas Shadwell, who ironically succeeded Dryden as poet laureate.

Dryden's finest satire is '**Absalom and Achitophel**', written in 1681, in which he derides the Earl of Shaftesbury (Achitophel) for Shaftesbury's opposition to the future succession of the Catholic, James II, in favour of the Duke of Monmouth (Absalom), the bastard son of Charles II. (Absalom and his adviser Achitopel, opponents of King David, are borrowed by Dryden from the second book of Samuel in the Old Testament.)

Notice in this extract how the heroic couplets – and one triple – effect a series of stylish dismissals of Shaftesbury. And identifying him with Achitophel of course 'places' him neatly as a villain:

> *Of these the false Achitophel was first,*
> *A name to all succeeding ages curst:*
> *For close designs and crooked counsels fit,*
> *Sagacious, bold, and turbulent of wit,*
> *Restless, unfixed in principles and place,*
> *In power unpleased, impatient of disgrace;*
> *A fiery soul, which, working out its way,*
> *Fretted the pigmy body to decay*
> *And o'er-informed the tenement of clay......*
> *Great wits are sure to madness near allied*
> *And thin partitions do their bounds divide;*
> *Else, why should he, with wealth and honour blest,*
> *Refuse his age the needful hours of rest?*

This character assassination – Shaftesbury is a crook, too clever for his own boots – is accomplished not through evidence or argument, we may note, but through a skilled placing of words. The tone is relaxed: the style uncomplicated: the language settled. It is Dryden's trademark. Nearly two hundred years later Gerard Manley Hopkins was to deliver a lasting tribute: "His style and his rhythms lay the strongest stress of all our literature on the naked thew and sinew of the English language".

26

Samuel Pepys (1633–1703)

Pepys may not have intended his **diary** for publication: he wrote it in code. It was among the papers he bequeathed to his old college, Magdalene, Cambridge, and extracts were decrypted and first printed in 1825.

Perhaps because it was a private document, the diary is engagingly candid and unselfconscious. No holds are barred. His sexual adventures are recorded with an explicitness that may explain why a complete and uncensored version did not appear until 1970. In its vivid wealth of detail it is a most entertaining and colourful autobiography, social history and political witness of the decade 1660 – 1669, until fears for his failing eyesight caused Pepys to discontinue writing.

Pepys as a key civil servant was in a perfect position for a diarist, at the hub of London events great and small. He had risen through the ranks of the naval civil service under the patronage of the Earl of Sandwich, becoming Treasurer to the Fleet in 1660. He was to become Chief Secretary to the Navy, its "right hand", and reported to the House of Commons on naval affairs. (The diary records his nervousness before big speeches, and subsequent triumphs in the role.) He was later President of the Royal Society, 1684–1686.

Though originally he rejoiced at the execution of Charles I, he had no difficulty in celebrating the Restoration. His eyewitness accounts of the Great Plague of London, the Fire of London, and the sailing of the Dutch fleet up the Thames are graphic and absorbing, as are his encounters with all levels of society, the ups and downs of his marriage and his restless philandering.

The 11-volume complete edition edited by Robert Latham and William Matthews was completed in 1983. Many anthology selections are available, including 'The Shorter Pepys', also edited by Robert Latham.

We may savour Pepys' engaging style in these brief and characteristic extracts:

May 2, 1660 – *Great yesterday at London; and at night more bonfires than ever and ringing of bells and drinking of the King's health upon their knees in the streets, which methinks a little too much*

May 25, 1660 – *I went [accompanying the King to shore] with a dog that the King loved (which shit in the boat, which made us laugh and me think that a king and all that belongs to him are but just as others are)*

September 25, 1660 – *did send for a cup of tea (a China drink) of which I never had drank before*

October 13, 1660 -*I went to Charing Cross to see Major-General Harrison [who had participated in the execution of Charles I] hanged, drawn and quartered – which was done there, he looking as cheerfully as any man could in that condition.....Thus it was my chance to see the King beheaded at Whitehall and the first blood shed in revenge*

January 23, 1662 – *to my uncle Fenners, where I find his new wife, a pitiful, ugly, ill-bred woman in a hat, a midwife*

January 22, 1668 – *Betty Turner.... what a beast she is to singing, not knowing how to sing one note in tune. I would not for 40 shillings hear her sing a tune...worse than my wife a thousand times, so that it doth a little reconcile me to her. So, late to bed.*

Pepys' diaries make an interesting contrast with those of his contemporary, John Evelyn (1620-1706), which have great documentary value but reveal much less of their author's personality.

*There is a fine new biography of Pepys, '**The Unequalled Self**' by Claire Tomalin.*

27

Restoration Comedy

In 1697 the clergyman **Jeremy Collier** wrote on the 'Immorality and Profaneness of the English Stage'. Some playwrights riposted vigorously, but **William Congreve**, maybe chastened, soon stopped writing. Collier was one of the influences leading to the decline of a robust style of drama, Restoration Comedy, which had flourished on the London stage since 1660.

The puritans closed the theatres in 1642. When they were permitted to reopen in 1660, only two theatrical managements were licensed, one of which set up the first

Theatre Royal, Drury Lane, seating over a thousand. Audiences came almost entirely from the court, high society, and hangers-on who included mistresses and high-class prostitutes. (**Pepys**, a great frequentor of plays, tells the amusing story of the woman in the audience who inadvertently spat on him from the seat in front; he took no offence, he says, once he realised she was a woman of high breeding.) The tone was set by the court. It was racy and rakish, camp and dissolute. One of its representative figures was the minor poet and wit the **Earl of Rochester**, a debauched favourite of Charles II. (Rochester died in 1680 of alcohol and venereal disease.) Attitudes were also influenced by the amoral philosophy of **Thomas Hobbes**, especially in his 'Leviathan', 1651, which advocates the materialistic pursuit of self-interest.

So developed a social climate which cultivated the **comedy of manners** – drama of artifice in behaviour and body language, highly stylised, with cleverly contrived plots of sexual intrigue. Stage characters are driven by a quest for sex and money. The setting is usually the high life of the sophisticated City; figures who stray in from the contrasting Country tend to be naively virtuous. (In response to Collier, some writers were to claim, not entirely convincingly, that their plays were serious social satires.)

The 1660s saw the first actresses (**Nell Gwyn** and other court mistresses among them). Women, both within the plays and in the reality of society, occupied an ambivalent position: they have all the appearance of being sexually liberated and often dominant, but financially they have nowhere to go and are essentially exploited.

Restoration comedy eventually succumbed to changes in fashion, the rise of London's middle classes and their different preoccupations, and the fading of royal patronage, especially as court circles became preoccupied with such crises as the 'Popish plot' and the controversy over the succession to Charles II. In recent years there has been a strong revival of interest in Restoration comedies, and productions have been enjoyed for their extravagant characterisations, colourful presentation and fast-paced, sometimes farcical, bawdy humour.

Britain's first woman playwright, **Aphra Behn** (1640–1689), belongs to this period. Her output catered mainly for the earthy comedy required by the market, in such plays as '**The Forced Marriage**' (1670) and the popular '**The Rover**' (in two parts, 1676 and 1681). She was to be championed by Virginia Woolf as the first *professional* woman writer.

Other prominent playwrights of the period are:

Sir George Etherege (1635–1691): 'The Comical Revenge' (1664); 'She Would If She Could' (1668); 'The Man of Mode' (1676).

William Wycherley (1640–1716): 'The Country Wife' (1675); 'The Plain Dealer' (1676).
Sir John Vanbrugh (1664–1726): 'The Relapse' (1696); 'The Provoked Wife' (1697).
William Congreve (1670–1729): 'The Double Dealer' (1693); 'Love For Love' (1695); 'The Way of the World' (1700).
George Farquahar (1678–1707): 'The Recruiting Officer' (1706); 'The Beaux Strategem' (1707).

In these plays the *names* of the characters are often a good guide to the flavour of the drama. In Vanbrugh's **'Relapse'**, for example, we find Lord Foppington, Sir Tunbelly Clumsey and his daughter Hoyden, and a homosexual matchmaker, Couple.

In this extract from Wycherley's **'Country Wife'** Mrs Pinchwife has attracted the attentions of a womaniser called Horner. Her husband orders her to write a letter to Horner, rejecting his advances.

Pinchwife	*Come, begin.* (Dictates) *'Sir…'*
Mrs Pinchwife	*Shan't I say 'Dear Sir'? You know one says always something more than bare 'Sir'.*
Pinchwife	*Write as I bid you, or I will write 'whore' with this penknife in your face.*
Mrs Pinchwife	*Nay, good bud.* (She writes) *'Sir'.*
Pinchwife	*'Though I suffered last night your nauseous, loathed kisses and embraces…' – Write.*
Mrs Pinchwife	*Nay, why should I say so? You know I told you he had a sweet breath.*
Pinchwife	*Write!*
Mrs Pinchwife	*Let me but put out 'loathed'.*
Pinchwife	*Write, I say.*
Mrs Pinchwife	*Well, then.* (Writes)
Pinchwife	*Let's see what you have writ.* (Takes the paper and reads) *'Though I suffered last night your kisses and embraces' – thou impudent creature! Where is 'nauseous' and 'loathed'?*
Mrs Pinchwife	*I can't abide to write such filthy words.*
Pinchwife	*Once more write as I'd have you, and question it not, or I will spoil thy writing with this.* (Holds up the penknife) *I'll stab out those eyes that cause my mischief.*
Mrs Pinchwife	*O Lord, I will!*

[He completes the dictation of a repentant letter, in which she apologises for her 'frolic' in man's clothes the evening before, and disowns him.]

Mrs Pinchwife	*I vow, husband, he'll ne'er believe I should write such a letter.*
Pinchwife	*What, he'd expect a kinder from you? Come now, your name only.*
Mrs Pinchwife	*What, shan't I say 'Your most faithful, humble servant 'till death'?*
Pinchwife	*No, tormenting fiend!* (Aside) *Her style, I find, would be very soft. – Come, wrap it up now, whilst I go fetch wax and a candle, and write on the back side 'For Mr Horner'.* (Exit)
Mrs Pinchwife	*'For Mr Horner' – So, I am glad he has told me his name.*

And she now proceeds to hastily rewrite the letter before Pinchwife returns....
There is both verbal and visual comedy here – we don't take Pinchwife's threatening penknife *seriously* – and notice how Wycherley develops the fun of Mrs Pinchwife controlling the situation, despite Pinchwife himself thinking *he* is the boss.

The Augustan Age

28
Daniel Defoe (1660–1731)

Defoe's achievements were extraordinary. Single-handedly he founded British journalism with his periodical, 'The Review'. He is arguably the first novelist, with **'Robinson Crusoe'** the first novel. He invented what we might now call 'documentary fiction'. His publications number over 500 – more than any other body of work in the English literary tradition.

He was a professional journalist from the age of 43 and his major fiction was not produced until he was in his 60s: **'Robinson Crusoe'**, 1719–20; **'A Journal of the Plague Year'** and **'Moll Flanders'** both in 1722.

His formal education began when he was 14; from a Presbyterian dissenting background he initially trained for the ministry, but instead married and started a hosiery business. He travelled, learnt four European languages in addition to Latin and Greek, fought for Monmouth in the Rebellion of 1685 and for William III in 1688. He was for a period an under-cover informer (both Tory *and* Whig!). He was twice imprisoned, both times as a result of ironic satirical pamphlets, **'The Shortest Way With The Dissenters'** in 1702 and **'Reasons Against The Succession of the House of Hanover'** in 1712. He ran 'The Review' for nine years from 1704, a journal of comment and opinion on political and social affairs written almost entirely by himself. Remarkably, while originally a weekly, 'The Review' graduated to twice-weekly and in its last years came out three times a week.

He was popular as a radical individualist with the general public, who appreciated his plain, 'brass-tacks' style. He sold well: **'Robinson Crusoe'** immediately went into many translations and imitations.

'Robinson Crusoe' is a pseudo-autobiography, fiction pretending to be truth. It is based on the true writings of Alexander Selkirk, who was at his own request abandoned on an uninhabited Pacific island, from which he was rescued after five years. (Crusoe stays on his island for 28.) On one level this is an adventure story about resourcefulness and survival. But it also shows Crusoe coping with his situation psychologically and spiritually, which marks the book as a precursor of the modern novel. This aspect may not be handled with immense profundity, but it gives rise to the speculation that Defoe is engaged in a kind of allegory, fable or popular myth, following in the footsteps of the drama **'Everyman'** and Bunyan's **'Pilgrim's Progress'**.

Defoe's dissenting background is evident. In Chapter XI Crusoe discovers the print of a man's foot on the sand. He describes how he is frightened, and his fears get out of control; he tries to persuade himself that the print is a delusion, or possibly his own footprint – but when he tries it, it doesn't fit. All this is absorbingly convincing. But, on another level, Crusoe with the benefit of hindsight recognises spiritual truths in his experience:

> *Thus my fear banished all my religious hope, all that former confidence in God, which was founded upon such wonderful experience as I had had of his Goodness…How strange a chequer-work of Providence is the life of man! …for I, whose only affliction was that I seemed banished from human society, that I was alone, circumscribed by the boundless ocean, cut off from mankind, and condemned to what I call silent life; that I was as one whom Heaven thought not worthy to be numbered among the living, or to appear among the rest of His creatures; that to have seen one of my own species would have seemed to me a raising me from death to life, and the greatest blessing that Heaven itself, next to the supreme blessing of salvation, could bestow; I say, that I should now tremble at the very apprehensions of seeing a man, and was ready to sink into the ground at but the shadow or silent appearance of a man having set his foot in the island…Such is the uneven state of human life; and it afforded me a great many curious speculations afterwards…I then reflected, that as God, who was not only righteous but omnipotent, had thought fit thus to punish and afflict me, so He was able to deliver me.*

We may ask ourselves whether Defoe here is a religious advocate, or whether he is skilfully and convincingly fashioning the mindset of such a character – a very different undertaking.

'A Journal of the Plague Year', as its title suggests, purports to record an eye-witness account of the terrible events in London from 1664–5 (which Defoe had lived through as a youngster). Defoe's name does not appear in the original printing; the 'author' of this supposed documentary is one 'H.F.', who is never identified. That in itself is a neat touch of verisimilitude. (Interestingly, Defoe's uncle was Henry Foe.)

This 'Journal' is fiction, but utterly convincing. The account is vivid, detailed, and appalling. Quotation from official documents and pseudo-documents lends an extra feel of authenticity. Charges in his own day and later that there is a kind of dishonesty in Defoe's enterprise are surely wide of the mark. We could well argue – and subsequent writers have – that judicious fiction can create a more powerful apprehension of truths than much merely factual recording. (Laurie Lee made a virtue of the fact that his autobiography, **'Cider With Rosie'**, was full of "lies"; the debate has continued over the merits and demerits of the television hybrid, 'documentary drama.')

A good example of Defoe's technique is in Chapter III, in which he describes how many of the poor wore 'charms' and signs of the zodiac to protect themselves against the plague, as if it came from 'an evil spirit' rather than 'the hand of God'.

> *I might spend a great deal of time in my exclamations against the follies, and indeed the wickedness, of those things, in a time of such danger, in a matter of such consequences as this, of a national infection. But my memorandums of these things relate rather to take notice only of the fact, and mention only that it was so. How the poor people found the insufficiency of those things, and how many of them were afterwards carried away in the dead-carts and thrown into the common graves of every parish with these hellish charms and trumpery hanging about their necks, remains to be spoken of as we go along.*

This is masterly: the supposed 'narrator' cannot help letting his feelings get in the way of his professed duty to record objectively, and the supposed authenticity of the account is cunningly reinforced. 'A Journal of the Plague Year' is one of the most convincing and compelling reconstuctions of history yet written.

'The Life and Strange Adventures of Daniel Defoe' is written by Richard West.

29
Jonathan Swift (1667–1745)

Swift was a robust and devastating satirist, whose jaundiced view of humankind inspired at least two masterpieces in **'Gulliver's Travels'**, published in 1726, and **'A Modest Proposal'**, 1729. His first satiric work was **'The Battle of the Books'** (1697), followed by **'A Tale of a Tub'** (1704), aimed at "corruptions in religion and learning", which he thought one of his best.

He stood for rational and humane common sense. This led him to be intolerant of 'enthusiasts', dissenters and freethinkers, pedants, most politicians, many scientists, and 'modern' learning that he thought misapplied. He fired off political, religious and satirical pamphlets at regular intervals. He had allies in the Scriblerus Club in London, which he founded with kindred spirits like Alexander Pope and John Gay, whose object was to ridicule "all the false tastes in learning". He befriended the essayists Addison and Steele. He was a staunch Anglican and Tory (after some initial Whig sympathies).

Born in Dublin of English parents, Swift claimed to dislike Ireland. However he spent most of his life in Dublin in various clerical roles (as Dean of St Patrick's from 1713), was popular there, championed Irish rights, and spent one third of his income on Irish charities. In his early life he had hoped for preferment in England and settled in Surrey as secretary to Sir William Temple, but Temple's death in 1699 left Swift 'unprovided' and he returned to Ireland. Thereafter he kept in contact with London literary and political circles through correspondence and occasional visits. He was put off by the new Whig administration after 1714 and imposed 'exile' upon himself – his last visit to London was in 1727.

His satires have a smooth and unruffled surface, but they are driven by exasperation and anger, in contrast with Dryden's more comfortable disdain. His aim in 'Gulliver' was "to vex the world rather than divert it". And Swift did not go for individuals so much as groups of mankind, and on occasion the entire species.

Part of Swift's skill is to fool us as readers into agreeing with the very attitudes he is satirising, until at some point the inadequacy or absurdity of our position is exposed. This can be demoralising and salutary. An irony we think we are grasping is suddenly turned against us. "Satire", he wrote in the preface to 'The Battle of the Books', "is a sort of glass, wherein beholders do generally discover everybody's face but their own." His masterpiece in this style is **'A Modest Proposal'**, probably the finest example of sustained satiric argument yet written in English.

The subtitle identifies that the Proposal is *"for preventing the children of poor people from being a burden to their parents or the country [Ireland], and for making them beneficial to the public"*. Swift writes in the form of a scholarly, reasoned and considered proposition, the essence of which is that poverty and over-population in Ireland would be substantially alleviated if babies were bred to be sold as meat.

> *I do therefore humbly offer it to public consideration, that of the hundred and twenty thousand children, already computed, twenty thousand may be reserved for breed, whereof only one fourth part to be males, which is more than we allow to sheep, black cattle, or swine, and my reason is that these children are seldom the fruits of marriage, a circumstance not much regarded by our savages, therefore one male will be sufficient to serve four females. That the remaining hundred thousand may at a year old be offered in sale to the persons of quality and fortune through the kingdom, always advising the mother to let them suck plentifully in the last month so as to*

render them plump, and fat for a good table. A child will make two dishes at an entertainment for friends, and when the family dines alone, the fore or hind quarter will make a reasonable dish, and seasoned with a little pepper or salt will be very good boiled on the fourth day, especially in winter.

Much of the force of this satiric enormity derives from Swift's parody of measured reasonableness. The logic is inescapable. His proposal, he continues, will ensure that good meat is always available, reduce the number of beggars, and improve the lot of mothers, not least because men will look after them better as 'breeders'. It will also "lessen the number of Papists, with whom we are yearly overrun". The last point is a neat example of how Swift sometimes aims to catch some of his readers off guard.

Swift's target is political indifference to Irish poverty, and neglect and exploitation by absentee English landlords. He may also have had in mind one William Petty, who in 1687 published his 'Treatise of Ireland', in which Petty seriously recommends solving the Irish problem by transporting all the Irish to England.

'Gulliver's Travels', not least in abridged versions, is an entertaining children's story. Unabridged and carefully read, it is an amusing commentary on political and religious pettiness (in the Lilliputian political rivalry between 'High Heels' and 'Low Heels', and the debates over the best end to crack an egg, which are Swift's gloss on trivial religious disputations). The Royal Society and the misappliance of science are mocked in Book III, where Gulliver observes various inventors' schemes, for example attempts to extract sunshine from cucumbers.

Gulliver is amazed in Book IV at the bestial Yahoos, with *"their strange disposition to nastiness and dirt"*. Innocently, Gulliver does not make the connection between the Yahoos (and indeed much of what he observes throughout his adventures) and the absurdities and depravities of mankind. Swift's use of a naïve narrator figure enhances for the acute reader the inescapable conclusions which Gulliver is slow to grasp.

Says the King of Brobdingnag to Gulliver, who has talked guilelessly about European ways of life, *"I cannot but conclude the bulk of your natives to be the most pernicious race of little odious vermin that nature ever suffered to crawl upon the surface of the earth."* It seems Swift's sentiment, too. There is real bile there. Debate continues over whether Swift was ultimately driven mad by disillusionment, or by Méniere's disease, or whether indeed he became demented at all. Whatever the truth of that, we may feel that Swift identifies with Gulliver's increasing repulsion from human physicality. When Gulliver's wife kisses him on his return, he swoons at *"the touch of that odious animal"*, and the very smell of his wife and children he finds intolerable. When faith in human nature has collapsed, there are few consolations.

30
Coffee House Journalism

Joseph Addison (1672–1719)
Sir Richard Steele (1672–1729)

➤┤◆❭•Ο•❬◆├◄

It was said of Socrates, that he brought philosophy down from Heaven to inhabit among men; and I shall be ambitious to have it said of me that I have brought philosophy out of closets and libraries, schools and colleges, to dwell in clubs and assemblies, at tea-tables and in coffee houses.

So wrote Addison in 1711, as he joined with Steele in founding 'The Spectator'. The London coffee houses flourished in the early Eighteenth Century as meeting places and talking shops, and talk was often prompted by one of the latest issues of the many periodicals that were springing up. Steele effectively invented the journalistic essay. The new publications carried a little news, but their prime content was light satire, popular literary criticism, sketches of contemporary characters, and comment on science, politics and issues in morality and philosophy.

Steele (having unsucessfully tried his hand at stage comedy) started 'The Tatler', a thrice-weekly, in 1709. (It came out on the days when the post left London.) Addison was a contributor over the two years of its existence before they jointly started 'The Spectator'. Steele founded three other journals – 'The Guardian', 'The Englishman' and 'The Theatre' – and Addison launched a political paper, 'The Freeholder', in 1715.

Undoubtedly these publications helped broaden the culture of the times. **Dr Johnson** was to note in his 1779 **'Life of Addison'**: *"That general knowledge which now circulates in common talk was in his time rarely to be found. Men not professing learning were not ashamed of ignorance; and, in the female world, any acquaintance with books was distinguished only to be censured".*

Addison and Steele both attacked Restoration comedy for its "corruption and degeneracy" – Steele's words. Their own writing pursued civilised elegance without extravagance, what Johnson called a "middle style", with middle class values. Addison admired the simplicity of classic architecture, and we hear in his essays what James Sutherland has called "the unhurried conversation of an Eighteenth Century gentleman". Addison declared his intention to "enliven morality with wit, and to temper wit with morality". The tone of the writing favoured by Addison and Steele is temperate and balanced, pleasant but often inconsequential, as in the gentle character comedy of Steele in his representative essay 'The Spectator Club':

> *We have amongst us the gallant Will Honeycomb, a gentleman who*
> *according to his years should be in the decline of his life, but having been*
> *very careful of his person, and always had a very easy fortune, time has*
> *made but very little impression, either by wrinkles on his forehead, or traces*
> *on his brain…He is very ready at that sort of discourse with which men*
> *usually entertain women. He has all his life dressed very well, and*
> *remembers habits as others do men. He can smile when one speaks to him,*
> *and laughs easily. He knows the history of every mode, and can inform you*
> *from which of the French king's wenches our wives and daughters had this*
> *manner of curling their hair, that way of placing their hoods…In a word,*
> *all his conversation and knowledge has been in the female world…This way*
> *of talking of his very much enlivens the conversation among us of a more*
> *sedate turn; and I find there is not one of the company, but myself, who*
> *rarely speak at all, but speaks of him as that sort of man who is usually*
> *called a well-bred fine gentleman. To conclude his character, where women*
> *are not concerned he is an honest worthy man.*

Leisurely writing for leisurely readers has become a new literary industry.

31
John Gay (1685–1732)

Gay's '**The Beggar's Opera**' played for an unprecedented 62 nights on its first production in 1728. Overnight it became one of the most popular entertainments of the century. It was to inspire the collaboration of Berthold Brecht and Kurt Weill on 'The Threepenny Opera' in 1928; its anti-establishment flavour and boundary-breaking mix of popular music and flexible theatrical idioms is reminiscent of the work of Joan Littlewood and her Theatre Workshop in the 1960s. Congreve will have recognised the radical character of the script when he told Gay it would either be a huge flop or a runaway success. James Boswell was to write of a later production: "There is in it so much of real London life, so much brilliant wit, and such a variety of airs…that no performance which the theatre exhibits delights me more". Conversely, the play's libertine atmosphere was denounced by, among others, the then Archbishop of Canterbury and Daniel Defoe.

Gay combines a send-up of Italian opera, newly arrived in London, a racy love story set in London's underworld and Newgate prison, and satire of corruption in Walpole's government. (A sequel, 'Polly', was banned from the stage by Walpole, which perhaps predictably ensured successful sales of the printed version.)

The music, arranged for Gay by Johann Pepusch, a German composer settled in London, is derived from popular ballads and street songs – there are 69 numbers in all. Some sort of "Newgate pastoral" had been suggested to Gay by Swift; the story – not quite a 'pastoral'! – is of Macheath, a highwayman, who marries Polly, the daughter of Peachum, a receiver of stolen goods. Peachum informs on Macheath who is condemned to death and imprisoned in Newgate, where he falls in love with Lucy, the warden's daughter. (*'How happy could I be with either / Were t'other dear charmer away!'* sings Macheath.) Lucy assists Macheath's escape. He is recaptured, but pardoned through the intervention of one of the cast on behalf of "the taste of the town".

The satirical and popular slant is established at the beginning by 'The Beggar's' remark, "I hope I may be forgiven that I have not made my opera throughout unnatural"; and by Peachum's song:

> *Through all the employments of life,*
> *Each neighbour abuses his brother;*
> *Whore and rogue, they call husband and wife:*
> *All professions be-rogue one another.*
> *The priest calls the lawyer a cheat:*
> *The lawyer be-knaves the divine:*
> *And the statesman, because he's so great,*
> *Thinks his trade as honest as mine.*

The dialogue is colourful and wittily paced; there are anticipations of Oscar Wilde in places:

Peachum	*And how do you propose to live, child?*
Polly	*Like other women, sir; upon the industry of my husband.*
Mrs Peachum	*What! Is the wench turned fool? A highwayman's wife, like a soldier's, hath as little of his pay as of his company.*
Peachum	*And had not you the common views of a gentlewoman in your marriage, Polly?*
Polly	*I don't know what you mean, sir.*
Peachum	*Of a jointure* [property inheritance], *and of being a widow?*

Polly	*But I love him, sir; how then could I have thoughts of parting with him?*
Peachum	*Parting with him! Why that is the whole scheme and intention of all marriages…*

Gay was a gregarious, well-liked figure in his circles (though Samuel Johnson thought him too idle). He pursued a hedonistic lifestyle of gambling and drinking when he eventually came into money, having lost heavily in the South Sea 'Bubble' crash of 1720. He enjoyed the company of Pope, Swift, Congreve and others in the Scriblerus Club. He had some success with poems and pamphlets, and one or two satirical comedies, and wrote the libretto for Handel's 'Acis and Galatea'. But 'The Beggar's Opera' was his triumph.

He wrote his own epitaph, displayed where he is buried in Westminster Abbey:

> *Life is a jest, and all things show it.*
> *I thought so once – and now I know it.*

Pope, who had said that Gay was more liked than respected, nevertheless wrote him a fond epitaph of his own:

> *Of manners gentle, of affections mild;*
> *In wit, a man; simplicity, a child…*
> *A safe companion and an easy friend,*
> *Unblamed through life, lamented in thy end…*

32
Alexander Pope (1688–1744)

The leading poet of his day, Pope from an early age controlled words with the poise and wit of a virtuoso. Following in the steps of Dryden, he perfected the heroic couplet as a vehicle for satire, his especial talent. His principal targets were pomposity, stupidity, and inept writing. Many of his victims are long since forgotten – except insofar as his satire immortalises them – but the abiding pleasure we still take from Pope's writing is in his supremely deft craftsmanship. Like Mozart, he has in his chosen medium an exquisite ear for form, pattern and balance.

Pope amuses and delights through his assured sophistication. There is no subjective exploration of feelings. The absence of emotional spontaneity and colour was to be seen as a fault by the succeeding generations of the Romantic age, but in Pope's own time controlled reason was the benchmark of **Augustan** values. Hazlitt's later stricture, that Pope was "the poet not of nature but of art", would in Pope's lifetime most likely have been taken as a compliment. In the early Eighteenth Century the English language, in its polished, classical urbanity, was thought to have come of age, shedding the 'barbarities' of the past. Artifice – in literature, in painting, in architecture – represented civilised values. Pope's own interest in landscape gardening, in which he became a consulted expert, illustrates the fashion for due proportion and symmetries – the picturesque as opposed to nature in its own disorder. As Bonamy Dobrée puts it, "Pope is the great poet, not of man's communication with God, but of the social sense, of the individual's responsibility for civilisation".

Some of Pope's phrasings have passed memorably into the language – 'a little learning is a dangerous thing'; 'to err is human, to forgive, divine'; 'damn with faint praise'. It is the neat arranging of words and their rhythms that makes for memorability, as in his two-line poem, '**Epigram Engraved on the Collar of a Dog which I gave to His Royal Highness** [the Prince of Wales, father of George III]':

> *I am his Highness' dog at Kew;*
> *Pray tell me, sir, whose dog are you?*

One of Pope's finest achievements is '**The Rape of the Lock**' (1712–14), a comic mock epic which Pope based on an actual event. Lord Petre had cut off a lock of Arabella Fermor's hair, which precipitated a family quarrel. Pope dedicates his poem to Arabella. He tells the tale of the 'rape' of Belinda's 'lock', her anger, and the lock's final resting place as a star adorning the heavens through the whimsical influences of gnomes and sylphs. The poem is a gentle satire upon genteel society. Here is Belinda preoccupied with the divine mysteries of her cosmetics:

> *And now, unveiled, the toilet stands displayed,*
> *Each silver vase in mystic order laid.*
> *First, robed in white, the nymph intent adores,*
> *With head uncovered, the cosmetic powers.*
> *A heavenly image in the glass appears,*
> *To that she bends, to that her eye she rears;*
> *Th'inferior priestess, at her altar's side,*
> *Trembling, begins the sacred rites of pride.*
> *Unnumbered treasures ope at once, and here*

The various offerings of the world appear;
From each she nicely culls with curious toil,   [skilful]
And decks the goddess with the glitt'ring spoil.
This casket India's glowing gems unlocks,
And all Arabia breathes from yonder box.
The tortoise here and elephant unite,
Transformed to combs, the speckled and the white.
Here files of pins extend their shining rows,
Puffs, powders, patches, Bibles, billet-doux.
Now awful beauty puts on all its arms;
The fair each moment rises in her charms,
Repairs her smiles, awakens every grace,
And calls forth all the wonders of her face:
See by degrees a purer blush arise,
And keener lightnings quicken in her eyes.

The elaborate, elevated references to religious ceremonial are juxtaposed entertainingly with Belinda's little vanities and worldly goods. Those 'Bibles' are clearly social accessories, and Belinda's cosmetically-enhanced blush she thinks to be purer than the real thing – Pope considered the words *'bidden'* and *'vacant'* before he settled on the masterstroke of *'purer'*.

Later in the poem the great and the good gather socially at the royal palace, Hampton Court:

Hither the heroes and the nymphs resort,
To taste awhile the pleasures of a court;
In various talk th'instructive hours they passed,
Who gave the ball, or paid the visit last;
One speaks the glory of the British Queen,
And one describes a charming Indian screen;
A third interprets motions, looks, and eyes;
At every word a reputation dies...
Meanwhile, declining from the noon of day,
The sun obliquely shoots his burning ray;
The hungry judges soon the sentence sign,
And wretches hang that jurymen may dine;
The merchant from th'exchange returns in peace,
And the long labours of the toilet cease.

With stiletto precision Pope witheringly nails the gossips, the judges and the juries, and as the sun sets we realise that Belinda's ministrations have been going on for hours. Pope is deliciously acute.

Pope's scathing attacks elsewhere on fools and charlatans in literature and public life are vigorously handled – "Yet let me flap this bug with gilded wings, / This painted child of dirt, that stinks and sings" (Lord Hervey, in **'The Dunciad'**) – but the individual feuds have relatively little interest for us now. 'The Dunciad', a long piece written over the years 1728–42, is directed in general at 'Dullness' in contemporary culture, and in particular at Colly Cibber, Poet Laureate from 1730, and incidentally the actor-manager who had turned down Gays' **'Beggar's Opera'**.

'The Rape of the Lock' gave Pope financial independence, a freedom from patrons which was unusual for the time. He had coped with various disadvantages. A Catholic, he was debarred from university, and while very bright, he had to be largely self-taught. After the Jacobite Rebellion of 1715 he was banned from residence in the city of London, moving out to Twickenham, his home for the rest of his life. When 12 he was permanently disabled by tuberculosis which caused a severe distortion to his spine. He never grew taller than 4ft 6in, and from middle age could not stand without a stiff corset which painfully hunched his posture.

Despite these problems he was outgoing in spirit. In his preface to the satire, **'Epistle to Dr Arbuthnot'**, 1735, he declared himself desirous to please – *"if anything* [is] *offensive, it will be only to those I am least sorry to offend, the vicious or the ungenerous"*. As a member of the Scriblerus Club he was a good friend to Swift and to Gay. (He had moved away from his original Whig friends, who included Addison.)

His philosophy is represented in the **'Essay on Man'**, 1733–4, where he states 'That true self-love and social are the same'. In what has been described as Cosmic Toryism, he saw a benevolent and rational deity directing all:

> *All Nature is but art, unknown to thee*
> *All chance, direction, which thou canst not see;*
> *All discord, harmony not understood;*
> *All partial evil, universal good:*
> *And, spite of pride, in erring reason's spite,*
> *One truth is clear, Whatever is, is right.*

His gift for neat parallelisms – which became an especial feature of his style and are so perfectly facilitated by the couplet form – is well caught in **'An Essay in Criticism'**:

True wit is Nature to advantage dressed;
What oft was thought, but ne'er so well expressed.

Pope's genius showed early. 'An Essay in Criticism' was written, remarkably, when he was in his teens.

Pope's 'Life' has been written by Maynard Mack.

33
Samuel Richardson (1689–1761)

Defoe had created fiction by simulating diaries and journals; Richardson simulated letters. He called himself the 'editor' rather than the author of what came to be called epistolary novels; there is no narrator – the story is put together by the reader, picking up on what the sequence of letters tells him. In his first novel '**Pamela**' (1739-41) there are six correspondents; in '**Clarissa**' (1747–8), Richardson's major work, there are four. (He used the same form in his last novel, '**Sir Charles Grandison**', published in 1753–4.)

The epistolary form allows for detailed revelations of characters' thoughts and feelings, and the unfolding sequence allows us to see how characters viewed each

---

THE NOVEL

The Oxford Dictionary records the first use of 'the novel' meaning a literary form in 1757.

The earliest prose fiction from the Middle Ages took the form of short stories, usually romances, focusing on incidents and narrative rather than characterisation.
In the Seventeenth Century longer narratives portraying characters and events from real life begin to appear in France and England, in the guise of memoirs, journals and diaries (see **Daniel Defoe**).

Samuel Richardson extends and develops the novel in his use of characters' letters. The convention of the omniscient author with unlimited insight into his characters evolves during the Eighteenth Century (**Fielding, Smollett, Sterne**) and is fully established and refined by the great figures of the Nineteenth Century.

other. Richardson tells how from the age of 13 he wrote love letters for young servant girls. 'Pamela' grew out of a project in which he was writing for publication (he was himself a printer) sample letters on common problems.

In '**Pamela**', which is subtitled 'Virtue Rewarded', a teenage maid is pursued by Mr B, the son of Her Ladyship who has just died. She is torn by conflicting feelings about him and his behaviour, and will not surrender her virginity, but eventually marries him. **Clarissa**, a well-bred young woman, loves Richard Lovelace, unaware that he is a rake. Her parents oppose the relationship: she rejects their choice of man for her. Lovelace abducts her and rapes her. Mortified, she dies.

These are bald summaries of lengthy works. They are very long – '**Pamela**' has four volumes and '**Clarissa**' seven. Richardson attempted to downsize them (*"Length is my principle disgust"*) but, as Samuel Johnson testily remarked, *"If you were to read Richardson for the story, your impatience would be so much fretted that you would hang yourself"*. '**Clarissa**', at over one million words, is the longest English novel.

In reactions to Richardson, both in his own time and since, there is a great divide. Richardson's declared concern was for propriety and morality, and he opposed the kind of bad taste which he thought had been shown for example in Aphra Behn's '**Love Letters Between a Nobleman and his Sister**' (1683). He received much acclaim from the public, and struck a chord, particularly with women in his treatment of females helpless before male power. Simultaneously there were complaints about indecency. He made changes accordingly. All the same, the will-she-won't-she aspect of both novels' prolonged situations is inadvertently titillating, and some of the descriptions, especially of Clarissa's rape, are offensive to many. D.H.Lawrence called Richardson a pornographer. He wasn't, but it is hard to deny that there are in some places unconscious elements of prurience.

Those who find Richardson simply boring or unconvincing will enjoy Fielding's 1749 send-up, '**An Apology for the Life of Mrs Shamela Andrews**'. But Richardson's importance remains a fact. Some claim him as the founder of the modern novel. His technique allowed for deeper introspection by characters than earlier writings, and the letters create a strong sense of immediacy and authenticity. His humourless solemnity perhaps blinded him to some of his faults, but Dr Johnson, characteristically taking a balanced view, thought he *"enlarged the knowledge of human nature"*, and '**Clarissa**' in particular significantly enlarges the possibilities of fiction.

34

Henry Fielding (1707–1754)

While Richardson's fictional world looks inwards, sometimes with obsessive detail, Fielding's looks outwards. All human life is there. He has much in common with his friend **Hogarth**, the great satirical painter and engraver: both have a zest for the crowd, an eye for unsentimental detail, and a profound comic vision.

Fielding became at Bow Street one of London's most distinguished magistrates; he knew at first hand and campaigned against the squalor of much Eighteenth Century low life, and this dimension informs parts of his novels. He is a critic of crime, corruption, and hypocrisy. The tone, however, is anything but grim. Fielding builds a convivial relationship with his reader, often through direct address, and his cheerful brio lends itself to a generalised sense of good-hearted sanity.

Though of aristocratic descent Fielding was not a wealthy man and had to make his way in the world. He trained later as a lawyer, but began a writing career as a dramatist, producing 25 plays and two adaptations of Moliere from 1728–1737. His most successful drama was 'Tom Thumb', now little known because like many of the other plays it is packed with contemporary references, jokes, and satirical jibes which no longer mean a great deal. ('Tom Thumb' was one of the plays that provoked the Licensing Act of 1737 and instituted censorship of plays by the Lord Chamberlain – the reaction of a government increasingly riled by political satire on the stage. The Lord Chamberlain's role survived in various forms until its abolition in 1968.)

And so Fielding turned to fiction – he had instant success in 1742 with '**Joseph Andrews**', followed by '**Jonathan Wild The Great**' (1743), which with unremitting irony 'celebrates' the career of a famous criminal who was executed in 1725. Then came the brilliant '**Tom Jones**' (1749), and the best-selling '**Amelia**' in 1751, set amidst the degradation of London's worst environments. Fielding was active in journalism and pamphleteering, making proposals for the welfare of the poor and for the abolition of public hanging.

As a novelist he stands proud for his techniques – many of the major traditions of the English novel are rooted in Fielding. '**Joseph Andrews**' is subtitled *"in imitation of Cervantes, author of Don Quixote"*, and from Spain Fielding introduces to England the form of the **picaresque** novel, in which roguery and humorous incidents are strung out along a journey. Fielding's 'comic epics in prose' – his own description –

anticipate Dickens. He rightly saw himself as an innovator, fusing the picaresque, the satirical and the realistic into a supreme comic art. In his satire, Swift was a strong influence, and Hogarth he described as one of the most "useful satirists that any age has produced". Following Hogarth, he aimed to create characterisations which, while comically exaggerated, reflected convincingly real personalities with psychological truth. He is a moralist, but there is no narrowness in his outlook. He prefers the great-hearted scoundrel to the mean-minded worthy.

Here, from '**Joseph Andrews**', is the episode in which Joseph has been robbed, beaten up, and left stripped naked by the roadside. A coach comes along, but Joseph is modestly reluctant to get in unless he can be decently covered:

> *Though there were several great-coats about the coach, it was not easy to get over this difficulty which Joseph had started. The two gentlemen complained they were cold, and could not spare a rag; the man of wit saying, with a laugh, that charity began at home; and the coachman, who had two great-coats spread under him, refused to lend either, lest they should be made bloody: the lady's footman desired to be excused for the same reason, which the lady herself, notwithstanding her abhorrence of a naked man, approved; and it is more than probable that Joseph, who obstinately adhered to his modest resolution, must have perished, unless the postillion (a lad who since has been transported for robbing a hen-roost) had voluntarily stripped off a great-coat, his only garment; at the same time swearing a great oath, for which he was rebuked by the passengers, that he would rather ride in his shirt all his life, than suffer a fellow passenger to lie in so miserable a condition.*

The ironies in this are typical of Fielding – gentle but authoritative. The novel is wonderfully funny, taking us on a genial wandering through Georgian England with memorable comic creations, such as Parson Adams, Joseph's companion, who is delightfully innocent and accident-prone, or Parson Trulliber, a boorish blunderer who appears in only one chapter but leaves an indelible impression. (In a wittily mischievous touch, Fielding suggests Joseph to be the brother of Richardson's '**Pamela**'.)

'**Tom Jones**', like '**Joseph Andrews**', has a carefully plotted story, in which Tom pursues his love and discovers his true identity, but in many ways the characters are more important than the plot. The fast-moving action is interspersed with prefaces from author to reader at the beginning of each chapter – another of Fielding's innovations; these interludes offer a relaxed moral commentary and a direct contact with the author, which adds an extra dimension to the comedy. The novel is much more than the romp that it became in the film adaptation. Tom is engagingly created: a fallible hero, but his heart in the right place. The book was very popular, though there were some, including Richardson and Dr Johnson, who thought it improper for the novelist to forgive Tom his indiscretions. Several of the characters Fielding declared to have been inspired directly by Hogarth's pictures – Bridget Allworthy, Partridge, and Square. (The lady in the coach in the '**Joseph Andrews**' passage we have just looked at, who looks at the naked man through the sticks of her fan, is to be found in plate 8 of Hogarth's '**A Rake's Progress**', similarly engaged in leering through her fan at a naked man in Bedlam.)

Fielding's declared aim in his Dedication to '**Tom Jones**' is *"to recommend goodness and innocence"*. It is his general theme, which he pursues with gusto.

35
Samuel Johnson (1709–1784)

Samuel Johnson – Doctor Johnson, after his honorary degree from Oxford in 1775 – is inseparable from our image of Augustan literary England. He exerts still a powerful presence as scholar, reviewer, editor, lexicographer and poet. He was celebrated as a conversationalist and a sage. Impassioned, eccentric, generous, formidably witty and often melancholy, he stood for common sense and measured clarity.

To his friend and biographer **James Boswell** we owe the recording of those trenchant and entertaining remarks which help to flesh out our picture of him:

- *Patriotism is the last refuge of a scoundrel.*

- *A man who exposes himself when he is intoxicated has not the art of getting drunk.*

- *What is written without effort is in general read without pleasure.*

- *Depend upon it , sir – when a man knows he is to be hanged in a fortnight, it concentrates his mind wonderfully.*

- *Q: Why, sir, in your dictionary, do you define 'pastern' as the 'knee' of a horse? A: Ignorance, madam, pure ignorance.*

*- Milton, madam, was a genius that could cut a colossus from a rock; but he
could not carve heads upon cherry stones.*

*- When a man is tired of London he is tired of life; for there is in London
all that life can afford.*

*- Were it not for imagination, sir, a man would be as happy in the arms of
a chambermaid as of a duchess.*

*- Q: Sir, what is poetry?
A: Why, sir, it is much easier to say what it is not.*

- A man should keep his friendship in constant repair.

- It matters not how a man dies, but how he lives.

A citizen of Litchfield, Johnson read extensively as a child – his father kept a bookshop. He studied at Oxford, where he was desperately poor and did not complete his degree. (Poverty was to afflict him greatly until in 1760 he was granted a pension by George III. He never forgot the struggle.) After some unsuccessful attempts at schoolteaching, in 1737 he moved to London with his wife Tetty, accompanied by the actor-to-be David Garrick, a former pupil. Tetty's death in 1752 sparked a deep depression. In later years he was looked after by Mrs Hester Thrale, the wife of a friend. Her remarriage after the friend died left Johnson desolated and angry, and he suffered further profound depressions in his last months. All his life he feared insanity.

Journalism kept the wolf from the door. On arrival in London Johnson started to contribute poems, reviews and parliamentary reports for '**The Gentleman's Magazine**'. From 1750–52, virtually single-handed, he founded, edited and wrote '**The Rambler**', a periodical that survived for 208 issues. From 1758–60 he wrote 91 of the 103 issues of '**The Idler**', a weekly of light reading. In 1764 he established the famous 'Club', an artistic and literary group which was to include Garrick, Boswell, Edmund Burke, Joshua Reynolds and Oliver Goldsmith.

His best literary work began in 1744 with his '**Life of Richard Savage**', a fellow poet and friend of two years, whose destitute and harassed existence attracted Johnson's compassion. The 'Life' of Savage is magnificently and touchingly written. In it Johnson paints an unforgettable picture of Grub Street, the struggling world of London's writers and hacks. This is the first of Johnson's magisterial biographies of literary figures, which culminated in his indispensable '**Lives of the Poets**'.

Other landmarks include 'Rasselas', a novel published in 1759, and in 1765 an edition of Shakespeare whose **Preface** is still authoritative. His celebrated **Dictionary of the English Tongue** appeared in 1755, having been nine years in the making. It was not the first dictionary, but it immediately became a dominating and influential reference. Working largely on his own (he had six amanuenses), Johnson had culled the works of literature and science from the Elizabethan period onwards. The **Dictionary** lists 40,000 words. Into a few of the definitions Johnson slips famously droll asides, such as for 'lexicographer' – "a harmless drudge". More acidly, the definition of 'patron' includes "commonly a wretch who supports with insolence, and is paid with flattery" – a swipe at the likes of Lord Chesterfield, who had offered Johnson money only when it was too late to be really of use, and who was robustly snubbed by Johnson in one of the world's great letters. A browse in Johnson's **Dictionary** is still an education and a pleasure.

Three of Johnson's poems are especially memorable. In '**London**' (1738) he attacks London's vices, and Walpole's administration, which he held responsible for them. *"All crimes are safe but hated poverty."*

He wrote '**The Vanity of Human Wishes**' (1749) in imitation of Juvenal, the Roman satirist. As the title suggests, he writes to condemn the weaknesses of human nature. The tone is imperious and balanced. Johnson's couplets move with a slow, sad gravity:

> *'Enlarge my life with multitude of days!'*
> *In health, in sickness, thus the suppliant prays:*
> *Hides from himself its state, and shuns to know,*
> *That life protracted is protracted woe.*
> *Time hovers o'er, impatient to destroy,*
> *And shuts up all the passages of joy.*

A sceptical eye is cast on both worldly and scholarly ambition:

> *Deign on the passing world to turn thine eyes,*
> *And pause awhile from letters to be wise;*
> *There mark what ills the scholar's life assail,*
> *Toil, envy, want, the patron and the jail.*

In the first edition the word "patron" had been "gibbet". Johnson made the alteration feelingly. Years later, reading these lines aloud, he burst into tears.

'**On The Death of Dr Robert Levet**' (1782), a shorter poem, praises the unpretentious careeer of an old friend, a doctor who had lived in Johnson's house for twenty years. Levet's rough-hewn but kindly ordinariness is warmly and movingly affirmed:

> *Well tried through many a varying year,*
> *See Levet to the grave descend;*
> *Officious, innocent, sincere,*   [officious: diligent, charitable]
> *Of every friendless name the friend.*

Johnson's fine dignity of expression gives Levet a permanent memorial. The poem is well worth savouring in its entirety.

Johnson met the younger Boswell (he was thirty-one years his junior) in 1763. Boswell has had his critics as a biographer, but his **Life of Johnson** (1791) continues to offer rich impressions and anecdotes.

Johnson is buried in Westminster Abbey. His London home at 17, Gough Square, off Fleet Street, where he compiled the **Dictionary** and wrote for '**The Rambler**', has been substantially refurbished, and reopened to the public in 2001.

There is a biography of Johnson by John Wain. Also see 'Dr Johnson and Mrs Savage' by Richard Holmes, and 'Boswell's Presumptuous Task' by Adam Sisman.

36
Laurence Sterne (1713-1768)

>⋅⋖>⋅⊙⋅<⋗⋅⋌

At the climax of the act of his conception, **Tristram Shandy**'s mother asks his father if he has remembered to wind the clock. To this solecism Tristram attributes the possibility of various defects in his character. It is a good joke (or two good jokes) in one of the great comic novels.

Sterne's 'Tristram Shandy' is gloriously unconventional and experimental. Writing his book in nine volumes from 1759 to 1767, at a time when the novel is newly establishing itself, Sterne plays teasing games with the new literary form. 'Tristram Shandy' purports to be Tristram's autobiography, and Sterne whimsically exploits the fact that an autobiography can never be completed; in book four, Tristram announces that it has taken him a year of writing to get as far as describing his first day of life. "It must follow, an' please your worships, that the more I write, the more

I shall have to write." (It is the kind of logical conundrum that **Lewis Carroll** was to have such fun with in the 'Alice' books a century later.)

Sterne's narrative has virtually no plot, and his hero's life gets only scanty attention. We begin with Shandy's conception and birth – he isn't born until three books on – and he effectively disappears from view two-thirds of the way through, at the age of five. Sterne hops backwards and forwards into digressions and character sketches, sharing a mock perplexity with us as he does so. "Is it not a shame to make two chapters of what passed in going down one flight of stairs?...I drop it – strike a line here across the paper, Tristram – I strike it – and hey for a new chapter!" The punctuation (as in that last sentence) and the typography are inventively free-wheeling. Blank pages suddenly appear. We come upon rows of asterisks, and diagrams. In a spectacular about-turn, he writes in volume three that as his characters are in one way or another busy, " 'tis the first time I have had a moment to spare – and I'll make use of it, and write my preface". As readers we never know quite where we are.

Sterne is parodying the notion that a novelist is in control of a fixed world that has its own reality in time. His deliberate inconsequentiality imitates the random workings of the mind, and in this he anticipates the 'stream of consciousness' techniques which will feature in the avant-garde novels of **James Joyce** and others. [He is much influenced by **John Locke**'s 'Essay Concerning Human Understanding' (1690), which discusses our limited grasp of the 'reality' beyond ourselves.]

Sterne well describes his novel as "a civil, nonsensical, good-humoured book". The story assembles a splendid range of comic characters: Tristram's father, Walter, given to long-winded and impractical philosophising; his Uncle Toby, forced to retire from the army by a groin injury, and now playing toy soldiers in the garden with Corporal Trim, while trying to evade the designs upon him of Widow Wadman; Doctor Slop, who when delivering him mistakes Tristram's hip for his nose, which he permanently distorts with his forceps.

'Tristram Shandy' was Sterne's most satisfying achievement; each volume was an instant success, and Sterne began to flourish when, a cult author, he moved to London in 1760. As a boy he had led a peripatetic military life; his father was an ensign in an infantry regiment, and left no money to the family when he died. Sterne was a sizar, a scholar selected from the poor, at Jesus College, Cambridge, and subsequently was never really happy in the role of a Yorkshire clergyman – he was ordained in 1738.

Sterne's playful bawdiness and nonsense has not pleased every reader, but it is easy to respond positively to his warmth about human nature and human feelings – his 'sentiment', to use the vogue word of the time. In his **'Sentimental Journey Through France and Italy'** (1768), narrated by the character Parson Yorick from 'Tristram Shandy', Sterne's express purpose is "to teach us to love the world and our fellow creatures better than we do".

The Late
Eighteenth Century

37

Thomas Gray (1716–1771)

Gray is remembered especially for three poems: 'Ode on a Distant Prospect of Eton College' (1747), 'Ode on the Death of a Favourite Cat Drowned in a Tub of Gold Fishes' (1748) and, supremely, 'Elegy Written in a Country Churchyard' (1751).

A wistful melancholy pervades much of the poetry; Gray's sad notes have a sureness of touch that strikes a chord with most readers. He writes quietly. Life's trials are viewed with hurt resignation.

The 'Eton College' Ode begins with the distant view of Eton (from Stoke Poges, where he was brought up, and where lies the 'country churchyard' in which he is buried). But the poem is not centred on the view, or on nostalgic evocation of happy schooldays. Its thrust is that the young schoolboys are fortunately *"regardless of their doom"*, just as he as a schoolboy was *"a stranger yet to pain"*. *"Black Misfortune"* lies ahead; long may their innocence last:

> *And happiness too swiftly flies.*
> *Thought would destroy their paradise.*
> *No more; where ignorance is bliss,*
> *'Tis folly to be wise.*

The 'Elegy', wrote Dr Johnson, abounds "with sentiments to which every bosom returns an echo". Many other poems of the period pursue the themes of mutability and mortality, often in a dead husk of language. Gray's 'Elegy' has the vocabulary of capitalised abstraction and generalisation typical of its time ("Ambition", "Honour", etc) yet his words are genuine. This is not an expressly personal poem, but it seems personally felt. We cannot know what depths he was writing from.

The graves in the churchyard, says Gray, are of the anonymous poor, *"rude forefathers...far from the madding crowd's ignoble strife"*, who may for all we know have found fame, had they had the education or the means. *"Full many a flower is born to blush unseen."* Only ill-written words on the gravestones memorialise them now.

And yet at least they have their *"frail memorial"*. In an unexpected turn, the poem ends with the sentiment that we all yearn (Gray especially?) to be mourned and remembered, and given an epitaph which will say:

Here rests his head upon the lap of earth
A youth to Fortune and to Fame unknown.
Fair Science frowned not on his humble birth,
And Melancholy marked him for her own.

The poem carries a complex and unresolved view on whether earthly recognition is desirable – "the paths of glory lead but to the grave".

In great contrast the brief and light '**Ode**' on the drowned cat (it was Horace Walpole's) is a perfect jeu d'esprit. Selima in her smug greed slips to her demise in the goldfish bowl. Her fate, suggests Gray's delicate mock heroic, is the comeuppance awaiting all presumptuous and unthinking females:

From hence, ye beauties, undeceived,
Know one false step is ne'er retrieved,
    And be with caution bold.
Not all that tempts your wandering eyes
And heedless hearts is lawful prize;
    Nor all that glisters gold.

Gray studied at Eton and Cambridge. He travelled in France and Italy with Horace Walpole, one of his firm Eton friends. His father died in 1741, and there were financial insecurities. The next year he returned for the rest of his life to scholarship at Cambridge, first Peterhouse and then Pembroke. In 1757 he declined the offer of the Poet Laureateship. He became Regius Professor of Modern History in 1768.

One contemporary Cambridge account mocked him for his eccentric walk. You feel drawn to this meticulous, learned and unhappy man. There's a personal history here that the poetry hints at, but doesn't reveal.

38

Two colourful storytellers

Horace Walpole (1717–1797)
Tobias Smollett (1721–1771)

>─┤⟨⟩─O─⟨⟩┤─<

Horace Walpole, friend to Thomas Gray, wrote an early version of what came to be called the **Gothic novel**, a form especially popular in the 1790s. The plots are supernatural, melodramatic and contrived, and enjoyable for large-scale atmospheric effects. Characterisation is minimal, but there are purple patches of fear and horror. Walpole's contribution to the genre is '**The Castle of Otranto: A Gothic Story**' (1764) which has a pseudo-medieval setting.

Walpole also influenced trends in design with his pet project in Twickenham, Strawberry Hill, which he called "a little Gothic castle". A dream involving the halls and staircases of Strawberry Hill gave Walpole his inspiration for 'Otranto'.

*Among later exponents of the Gothic style are **Ann Radcliffe** ('**The Mysteries of Udolpho**', 1794) and **Mary Shelley**, whose very successful '**Frankenstein**' of 1818 has spawned a host of imitations and films. Grotesque fantasies were to be revived in the Twentieth Century by **Mervyn Peake** (1911–1968) in his Gothic trilogy '**Titus Groan**', '**Gormenghast**' and '**Titus Alone**', completed in 1959.*

Tobias Smollett, the son of a Scottish laird, took a medical degree at Glasgow before he became a ship's surgeon in the British Navy, seeing action in the West Indies. He then settled as a surgeon in London. Amidst much hack work, he wrote novels in the **picaresque** tradition. Rumbustious and extrovert in character, they are shapeless but lively stories, set at sea, or travelling in England, Wales, Scotland and France.

His three most attractive novels are '**The Adventures of Roderick Random**' (1748), written in the first person, '**The Adventures of Peregrine Pickle**' (1751) with a conventional omniscient narrator, and '**The Expedition of Humphry Clinker**' (1771) in the letter form introduced by Richardson.

Smollett's stories sometimes depict violence or depravity, and are sometimes earthily humorous. The attraction is particularly in his prose style, which is cantankerous, sometimes carping and sometimes crude, but always intelligent. He creates caricatures rather than fully-rounded characters, and in this aspect of his craft had a strong influence on some of Dickens' work; he was Dickens' favourite reading as a boy.

In 1766 Smollett published his entertainingly pungent '**Travels Through France and Italy**', which occasioned Sterne to give him the nickname Smelfungus, "who set out with the spleen and jaundice, and every object he passed by was discoloured and distorted".

See Jeremy Lewis's biography, 'Tobias Smollet'.

39
Christopher Smart (1722–1771)

Smart was plagued throughout his life by problems of mental health and problems of debt. He was a fine classical and Hebrew scholar. Like Sterne, he was a sizar at Cambridge; he was elected to a fellowship at Pembroke in 1745. Two years later he was arrested for debt. He moved to London in 1749, trying to eke out a living with poetry and reviews. Increasingly erratic, he spent from 1756 to 1763 in mental asylums. In 1770, declining into further poverty and debt, he was again arrested, and died in a debtors' prison.

Upon his misfortunes Dr Johnson, who befriended him, reflected: "I did not think he ought to be shut up. His infirmities were not noxious to society. He insisted on people praying with him; and I'd as lief pray with Kit Smart as anyone else. Another charge was that he did not love clean linen; and I have no passion for it."

Smart's reputation has been strongest in the Twentieth Century. His '**Song to David**', published in 1763 as he came out of the asylum, made little impact in his day. Its firmly simple stanzas give it a durable and uplifting quality. In praise of David, Smart celebrates the natural bounty of Creation, and the Incarnation.

> *For Adoration, in the dome*
> *Of Christ the sparrows find a home;*
> *   And on his olives perch:*
> *The swallow also dwells with thee,*
> *O man of God's humility,*
> *   Within his saviour's Church.*

The poem is knit with surging rhythms and the incantatory repetition of key words such as 'glorious', which introduces each line of the penultimate stanzas, leading to the climax:

Glorious – more glorious is the crown
Of him that brought salvation down
　　By meekness called thy Son;
Thou that stupendous truth believed
And now the matchless deed's achieved,
　　Determined, dared, and done.

'**Jubilate Agno**' was not published until 1939. Its language is remarkable: free verse held together by Smart's rhythmic instinct, and like 'Song to David' hymning the presence of God in all things. It is a long, unfinished and highly original work, composed within the asylum, and includes the now famous lines on Smart's cat Jeoffrey, some of which were set to music by Benjamin Britten:

For I will consider my cat Jeoffrey.
For he is the servant of the Living God, duly and daily serving him.
For at the first glance of the glory of God in the East he worships in his way.
For this is done by wreathing his body seven times round with elegant quickness.
For then he leaps up to catch the musk, which is the blessing of God upon
his prayer......
For when the day's work is done his business more properly begins.
For he keeps the Lord's watch in the night against the adversary.
For he counteracts the powers of darkness by his electrical skin and glaring eyes.
For he counteracts the Devil, who is death, by brisking about the life.

Smart's words are not self-regarding. They serve the vision with which his prayerfulness is sustained. His particular kind of integrity deserves a wider audience.

40
Oliver Goldsmith (c.1730–1774)

Born in Ireland of an Anglo-Irish clerical family, Goldsmith attended Trinity College, Dublin, but gambled away the money intended to help him study law. His application for ordination was turned down. Poor and struggling, he ended up in London, getting by first as a teacher and medical assistant and then as a Grub Street reviewer and essayist of considerable versatility.

His meeting with Samuel Johnson in 1761 was crucial. He became one of the founding members of Johnson's literary 'Club', and Johnson gave him the friendship and support that helped him to make his name. In 1766 with Johnson's help he secured publication of his one novel, '**The Vicar of Wakefield**', which almost certainly averted his arrest for debt.

Affectionately mocked by his contemporaries for eccentricities, clumsiness, and quirks of conversation, Goldsmith nevertheless gained popular success with three works in particular: '**The Vicar of Wakefield**', his poem '**The Deserted Village**' (1770) and his play '**She Stoops To Conquer**' (1773).

'**The Vicar of Wakefield**' has a light and complex plot with stock characters such as the evil squire, the "good" uncle in disguise, and the amusingly unworldly vicar himself. A pleasant rural family falls on hard times which are resolved in happy endings and marriages.

Of stronger interest for us now is '**The Deserted Village**', which records Goldsmith's distress at the passing of the old rural ways of life afflicted by the Industrial Revolution. "Laws grind the poor and rich men rule the law" he had written in his 1764 poem '**The Traveller**'. As populations moved to the industrial centres, enclosure and commerce became for Goldsmith the new forms of exploitation:

> *Ill fares the land, to hastening ills a prey,*
> *Where wealth accumulates, and men decay.*

He describes a fictional and idealised village, Auburn,

> *Where health and plenty cheered the labouring swain,*
> *Where smiling spring its earliest visit paid.*

Auburn in its former glory is a mix of English pastoral and – probably – nostalgic memories of Goldsmith's Irish childhood. Now it is destroyed:

> *Amidst thy bowers the tyrant's hand is seen*
> *And desolation saddens all thy green:*
> *One only master grasps the whole domain,*
> *And half a tillage stints thy smiling plain;*
> *No more thy glassy brook reflects the day,*
> *But choked with sedges, works its weedy way.*

The sentiments are strongly felt. But Goldsmith's descriptions of the 'charm' (his own word) of the vanished Auburn sentimentalise it. What he 'observes' is coloured by literary artifice; his stylised Augustan diction distances and generalises. We will find more immediacy in the natural descriptions of Goldsmith's contemporary **William Cowper**.

'She Stoops To Conquer', a late flourish in Goldsmith's life and the best of his plays, is light situation comedy. Sub-titled 'The Mistakes of a Night', it develops the misunderstandings which arise from the mistaking of a private house for an inn. The play was instantly successful, and modern productions continue to divert audiences.

41
William Cowper (1731–1800)

On a sunny but cold winter's morning, Cowper takes a country walk:

> *The verdure of the plain lies buried deep*
> *Beneath the dazzling deluge; and the bents*
> *And coarser grass, upspearing o'er the rest,*
> *Of late unsightly and unseen, now shine*
> *Conspicuous, and, in bright apparel clad*
> *And fledg'd with icy feathers, nod superb.*
> *The cattle mourn in corners where the fence*
> *Screens them, and seem half petrified to sleep*
> *In unrecumbent sadness. There they wait*
> *Their wonted fodder...*

Earlier, he notices his elongated shadow:

> *Mine, spindling into longitude immense,*
> *In spite of gravity, and sage remark*
> *That I myself am but a fleeting shade*
> *Provokes me to a smile.*

These extracts come from 'The Task' (1785). Cowper's friend Lady Austen had suggested he write a poem about his sofa. Accepting the challenge – the 'task' – he begins with the sofa but broadens into six 'books' of description of the pleasures of country living and a gentle response to its creatures. 'The Task' was written, he said, "to recommend rural ease and leisure as friendly to the case of piety and virtue… God made the country and man made the town."

For Cowper, the victim of depressions, breakdown, and suicide attempts – he described himself as a "stricken deer" – the countryside was restorative and his writing no doubt therapeutic. He had been bullied at school and, though trained as a lawyer, could not bring himself to practise. Good friends took care of him. He was unambitious as a writer and lived defensively: "I am a castaway, deserted and condemned".

His feeling for words is acute. Go back to "spindling", describing that shadow unravelling before him as he walks, and the pleasing weight and humour of the whole phrase, "spindling into longitude immense". His blank verse moves easily and naturally, as we see in 'The Task'. In contrast with much of the poetic description of nature in his time he responds directly rather than through literary artifice. The grasses, "fledg'd with icy feathers", are simply "superb".

A lonely figure, Cowper has not been a mainstream author, in his day or since. Yet in Cowper's writing we see the beginnings of Romanticism and those fresher ways of describing nature which were to become a programme for Wordsworth and Coleridge. His unpretentious poetry has a gentle and enduring appeal.

Cowper also wrote several hymns, of which the best known is "God moves in a mysterious way", and the comic ballad 'John Gilpin'. His attractive short poem 'The Poplar Field' is in many anthologies.

42
Richard Brinsley Sheridan
(1751–1816)

The 1770s was a prime decade for theatrical comedy. In addition to **Goldsmith's** 'She Stoops to Conquer', the period saw the first performances of Sheridan's enduring classics '**The Rivals**' (1775) and '**The School for Scandal**' (1777), together with his burlesque '**The Critic**' and the comic opera '**The Duenna**'. In 1777, the year of his triumph with 'The School for Scandal', Sheridan's stature as a writer was confirmed when he was elected a member of Johnson's 'Club'.

Sheridan's stance as a comic writer was, like Goldsmith's, to ridicule human absurdities, rather than to be indulgent as had been the recent fashion. His satire of pretentious social manners and hypocrisies was entertainingly pungent, and after an 'iffy' first performance of '**The Rivals**' the script had to be toned down to accommodate those who found some of the characterisations offensive. From the second performance, eleven days later, success was assured.

Set in Bath, the comedy begins with Jack Absolute disguising himself as a poor soldier in order to woo Lydia Languish, who intends to forfeit her dowry and marry a pauper to ensure a marriage of idyllic romantic hardship. Meanwhile Jack's father Sir Anthony approaches Lydia's guardian, Mrs Malaprop, intent on arranging a society marriage between his son and Lydia. The complications deriving from Jack rivalling himself for the hand of Lydia, as well as two other suitors, a country squire and a fortune-hunting Irish knight, form the heart of the entertainment.

In this extract, Sir Anthony and Mrs Malaprop discuss Lydia, who has made it clear that she refuses to be part of an arranged marriage:

Mrs Malaprop   *There's a little intricate hussy for you.*

Sir Anthony   *It is not to be wondered at, Ma'am – all this is the natural consequence of teaching girls to read. Had I a thousand daughters, by heaven! I'd as soon have them taught the black art as their alphabet.*

Mrs Malaprop   *Nay, nay, Sir Anthony, you are an absolute misanthropy!*

Sir Anthony   *In my way hither, Mrs Malaprop, I observed your niece's maid coming forth from a circulating library! She had a book in each hand – they were half-bound volumes, with marble covers! From that moment I guessed how full of duty I should see her mistress!*

Mrs Malaprop   *Those are vile places, indeed!*

Sir Anthony   *Madam, a circulating library in a town is as an ever-green tree. Of diabolical knowledge! It blossoms through the year! And depend on it, Mrs Malaprop, that they who are so fond of handling the leaves, will long for the fruit at last.*

These are neat caricatures. Mrs Malaprop's mishandlings of language, which become comically grotesque as the play develops, are now part of literary legend. The two schemers affect a sophistication which in fact they lack – a characteristic theme in Sheridan. As senior figures, they assume they are in control, though in fact it is the manoeuvrings of the young and amorous which make the running. (There are interesting echoes of Sheridan's own life here. His romance with Elizabeth Linley, a professional singer who was engaged to a wealthy and much older man, scandalised society in Bath and London. They eloped to France in defiance of both their fathers.

Sheridan fought two duels on her behalf. They contracted an invalid form of marriage. Eventually in 1773 there was family reconciliation and a legal ceremony.)

Sheridan cultivates a knowing artificiality of theatrical style, as in asides to the audience which make them complicit in the comedy. There is a strong visual element – it is important not to miss this when reading the text – as in the famous "screen scene" in '**The School for Scandal**', where two characters independently conceal themselves behind screens, and are discovered by the other figures on stage in a brilliant coup de theatre when the screens collapse.

In 1776 and 1778 Sheridan bought from Garrick a major share in the Drury Lane Theatre, of which he became manager. The theatre was closed as unsafe in 1792. A replacement building opened two years later, but was burnt down in 1809 – a financial disaster for Sheridan, who spent beyond his means throughout his life and was arrested as a debtor in 1813.

Ironically, despite his theatrical successes, and the fact that his father had been an actor-manager in Dublin and his mother a writer of novels and plays, Sheridan's preferred career had been politics. After his election as an MP in 1780 he impressed contemporaries with his superb Commons oratory for the next twelve years. Apart from one German adaptation in 1799, he wrote no more plays.

'A Traitor's Kiss: the life of Richard Brinsley Sheridan' is by Fintan O'Toole.

43
Fanny Burney (1752–1840)

>─┤◄►∙─O─∙◄►┤─◄

Her writing caught the eye of Jane Austen, whom she influenced, and she was admired by Samuel Johnson, Garrick, Sheridan, Joshua Reynolds and others of Johnson's circle, to which she had been introduced by her father, the musician Charles Burney. Fanny Burney wrote three successful novels, of which '**Evelina**' (1778) was the first and best.

Although her identity leaked out, she shunned publicity. 'Evelina' was published anonymously, prompted by Fanny's sense of propriety and modesty – an interesting reflection of the continuing awkwardnesses for women in literary life.

Fanny Burney described her "incurable itch to write". From the age of ten she dabbled in stories, poems and plays. The three adult novels ('**Evelina**', '**Cecilia**' and '**Camilla**') each describe a young and innocent upper-middle-class girl gaining experience of the metropolitan social world. She aimed for character study that was psychologically true, and narratives which develop a sense of adventure. The keynote at her best is of witty and sometimes satirical domestic comedy.

A reviewer wrote of '**Evelina**': "readers will weep, will laugh and grow wiser". Subtitled 'A Young Lady's Entrance into The World' [i.e. London], the novel is written in the epistolary form used by Richardson. In one letter, Evelina describes the initiation of herself and a friend into the world of grand balls:

> *The gentlemen, as they passed and repassed, looked as if they thought we were quite at their disposal, and only waiting for the honour of their commands; and they sauntered about in a careless, indolent manner as if with a view to keep us in suspense. I don't speak of this in regard to Miss Mirvan and myself only, but to the ladies in general; and I thought it so provoking, that I determined in my own mind that far from humouring such airs, I would rather not dance at all...*

She is approached by a fop "of ridiculous solemnity", whose address to her beautifully catches his absurdity: *"I humbly beg pardon, Madam, and of you too, my Lord, for breaking in upon such agreeable conversation which must doubtless be more delectable than what I have the honour to offer, but..."*

In 1786 Fanny Burney was appointed Second Keeper of the Robes to Queen Caroline, a role that she found uncomfortably hidebound, but her *journals* and *diaries* have left us with entertainingly humorous glimpses of her life at court.

There is a biography of Fanny Burney by Claire Harman.

44

George Crabbe (1755–1832)

It is the bleak realism of his poetry which gives Crabbe his distinguished voice. A man of Suffolk, his principal subjects were the vast East Anglian landscapes and seascapes, and the hardships of the rural population. Byron approvingly described him as "Nature's sternest painter yet".

In 'The Village' (1783) he describes himself as *"cast by Fortune on a frowning coast"*. It is no happy landscape of groves and picturesque valleys; his mission is to write *"as Truth will paint it, and as Bards will not"*. The dismissive reference to "Bards" is to those Augustan poets whose *"tinsel trappings"* – their smooth, literary pastoral – were to Crabbe not only barren but insensitive, insulting to the *"poor laborious natives of the place"*.

While Crabbe rejects the idealising tendency of some contemporary landscape poetry, he retains for most of his verse that firm Augustan standby, the heroic couplet, and the Augustan preference for calm and rational language. At the same time, he fascinatingly reflects and influences the changes as Augustan values gradually give way to Romanticism. He died aged 77. His roots were in the Eighteenth Century. He was befriended by Burke who introduced him to many of the great Augustan figures. But he died in the full flourish of the new Romanticism of Coleridge and Wordsworth, with whom he was acquainted. He was a close friend of Walter Scott. His later works were published simultaneously with those of Jane Austen – he was her favourite poet, as he was Scott's.

Here is Crabbe in 1810, in 'The Borough', describing his character Peter Grimes, the fisherman who has become a deranged outcast after ill-treating and murdering child apprentices:

> *When tides were neap, and, in the sultry day,*
> *Through the tall bounding mud-banks made their way,*
> *Which on each side rose swelling, and below*
> *The dark warm flood ran silently and slow;*
> *There anchoring, Peter chose from man to hide,*
> *There hang his head, and view the lazy tide*
> *In its hot slimy channel slowly glide;*
> *Where the small eels that left the deeper way*
> *For the warm shore, within the shallows play;*
> *Where gaping mussels, left upon the mud,*
> *Slope their slow passage to the fallen flood:*
> *Here dull and hopeless he'd lie down and trace*
> *How sidelong crabs had scrawled their crooked race;*
> *Or sadly listen to the tuneless cry*
> *Of fishing gull or clanging golden-eye;*
> *What time the sea-birds to the marsh would come,*
> *And the loud bittern, from the bull-rush home,*
> *Gave from the salt-ditch side the bellowing boom:*
> *He nursed the feelings these dull scenes produce,*

And loved to stop beside the opening sluice;
Where the small stream, confined in narrow bound,
Ran with a dull, unvaried, saddening sound;
Where all, presented to the eye or ear,
Oppressed the soul with misery, grief, and fear.

The heat and the slowness evoke an almost timeless sense of stilled refuge. Almost, but not quite: the tides move, the sluice runs, the birds, the eels and the crabs travel. Grimes aches in sympathy with the dull, the sad, and the tuneless, but there is no enduring solace for him here.

This is subtle, and beautifully detailed. The careful, close observation reminds us that Crabbe was an amateur botanist. He aims for realism of impression, eschewing sentiment and idealisation. He understands mental oppression (his wife suffered a manic-depressive illness).

Crabbe was born in Aldeburgh, and practised as a surgeon there before trying his luck as a writer in London. This didn't work; Burke bailed him out, and he avoided imprisonment for debt. (This financial pressure, as we have seen, was a recurring theme in Eighteenth Century London's literary life. It was just about possible then to live on occasional literary earnings, but it was often a close-run thing.)

Encouraged by Burke, Crabbe took holy orders, and was variously chaplain to the Duke of Rutland, and parish priest in Leicestershire and Wiltshire. Suffolk remained his spiritual home. He was never a metropolitan man.

'**The Village**', a poem in two books, focused on distress, especially that of the country poor. After a long gap in which nothing was published came 'The Borough' in 1810, which had been written over an eight year period. Based on Aldeburgh, the poem takes the form of 24 'letters', purportedly from "a burgess in a large sea-port". Seven of these trace the life stories of local figures, and portray institutions such as the church, the school, and the workhouse. Among the subjects is our Peter Grimes, whose story became the opera by Benjamin Britten (who co-founded the Aldeburgh Festival with Peter Pears and Eric Crozier in 1948).

In 1812 Crabbe published '**Tales**', twenty-one short stories in verse, and often regarded as the best work of this compelling and admirable writer.

Biographies of Crabbe include the 'Life' by T.E.Kebbel and P.Kenniket, and 'Restless Ocean: the story of George Crabbe, the Aldeburgh Poet' by Neville Blackburne.

The Romantic Period

45

Romanticism

Literary periods are often only recognisable after they have happened. British Romanticism was not a coherent and self-regarding 'movement'. It occurred diversely and individually. The shift of outlook and styles had no one beginning or focal point, though there were important symptoms and influences in the Industrial Revolution, the 1776 American Declaration of Independence, the French Revolution of 1789, and the Preface to the second edition of Wordsworth and Coleridge's 'Lyrical Ballads' of 1800.

In the late Eighteenth Century there occurred in the movement of ideas a steady shift away from the Augustan stress on the general and the rational, and an increasing valuation of the individual and the emotional. The imagination, which the Augustans called 'fancy', was seen by them as a decorative faculty in writing; for the Romantics it became central. Wild or 'natural' Nature was now preferred to that which was cultivated and 'picturesque'. The essence of a personality tended to be more interesting than the generalities of society. Freedom of expression, individually and politically, was paramount.

Early manifestations of the romantic outlook can be seen variously in the writings of Gray, Cowper, Crabbe and Blake. Romanticism is anticipated in the cult of the exotic and supernatural in the Gothic novel. Wordsworth and Coleridge declared their determination to find a fresh vocabulary and insight for poetry – traditional Augustan diction had for them hardened into a literary mannerism that lacked creative vitality.

The Romantic developments in British poetry divided broadly into two generations: that of Blake, Wordsworth and Coleridge, followed by Byron, Shelley and Keats.

46

William Blake (1757–1827)

Vision

As a young boy, walking in Peckham Rye, Blake saw angels in a tree. That is what he told his parents. It was not a fantasy: the vision was real enough to him. On other occasions he saw the Old Testament prophet Ezekiel, brightly glowing in a field, and angelic figures moving among haymakers. Later, he saw "the prince of love".

He started writing poetry when he was about eleven, and before he was fourteen he had written this:

> *How sweet I roamed from field to field,*
> *And tasted all the summer's pride,*
> *Till I the prince of love beheld,*
> *Who in the sunny beams did glide.*

What we notice immediately about Blake is his extraordinary visionary power. As a child and as an adult writer he saw not simply into the heart of things, but beyond them. The opening lines of **"Auguries of Innocence"** suggest an excitingly sharp perception of that which is almost beyond words:

> *To see a world in a grain of sand*
> *And a Heaven in a wild flower,*
> *Hold Infinity in the palm of your hand*
> *And Eternity in an hour.*

Which is most real? The grain of sand or an imagined world? The wild flower or Heaven itself? For Blake the world of the imagination dominates.

He lived and died a Londoner. The Thames, the streets, the churches, the fields of London are a presence in much of his poetry. He probably spoke, we might remind ourselves, with what we would recognise as something of a Cockney accent. Try reading Cockney Blake aloud. The effect can be interestingly unexpected. Yet he does not simply describe London. Instead, the city becomes part of a nightmare vision of poverty and oppression, surreal in its images:

How the chimney-sweeper's cry
Every blackening Church appalls,
And the hapless Soldier's sigh
Runs in blood down Palace walls…   ('**London**')

Blake the visionary is also Blake the poet of social protest. The Church and the Palace are shamed and soiled by the anguish of the boy chimney sweep and the hurt of the powerless soldier.

Innocence

Blake was passionately angry about the exploitation of children. In '**Songs of Innocence**' (1789) he celebrates the inspiring innocence of the young and uncorrupted.

When the voices of children are heard on the green
And laughing is heard on the hill,
My heart is at rest within my breast
And everything else is still.   ('**Nurse's Song**')

These 'songs' have a ballad-like, lyrical simplicity in their form. They abound with images of security, peace, harmony and love.

Sweet dreams form a shade
O'er my lovely infant's head.   ('**A Cradle Song**')

In '**The Lamb**', one of his best-known poems, the child and the lamb both become identified with the infant Christ:

I a child and thou a lamb,
We are called by his name.

But for Blake, in the London of his time, the child is threatened, quite literally, by institutions and oppressiveness. The charity schools, the beadles and the priests regiment and stifle. Young boys are forced into becoming chimney sweeps. The pictures in the '**Songs of Innocence**' of "infant joy" – one of Blake's titles – slowly dissolve into images of children who are lost and weeping. (Read '**Holy Thursday**', in which Blake describes some six thousand of the poorest children from the charity schools being marshalled into St Paul's Cathedral for an annual service of thanksgiving. All appears sweetness and light until we begin to sense a chilling irony in the description of the "aged men, wise guardians of the poor", the "grey-headed beadles" who carry "wands as white as snow". This poem makes an interesting contrast with the poem of the same title in '**Songs of Experience**', written four years later.)

The '**Songs of Innocence**' celebrate childhood innocence. More profoundly, they affirm the values of "Mercy, Pity, Peace and Love" which adult humankind has betrayed, and which for Blake the established churches no longer represented. For him, Old Testament negatives had supplanted New Testament positives, as we see when we look at the '**Songs of Experience**'.

Experience

Blake did not go to school. He was self-taught. He read widely in the Bible, in the Greek and Roman classics, and in the mystical and psychic free-thinking which was popular amongst some contemporary intellectuals. All this finds a way into his work.

At 14 he was apprenticed to an engraver, and later set up his own engraving business which was to keep him only just above the poverty line for the rest of his life. The 'Songs of Innocence' and 'Experience' were published by him as engravings, in which the poetry and the illustrations are interwoven and are best seen together. (Most modern editions incorporate at least some of the plates; a selection of originals is on view at the Fitzwilliam Museum, Cambridge, and Tate Britain in London.)

The pictures are extraordinary, symbolic montages, with curling vegetation framing human and animal figures which are partly drawn from life and partly suggestive of states of mind.

The '**Songs of Experience**' create a vision of repressed lives and emotions.

> *How can the bird that is born for joy*
> *Sit in a cage and sing.*   ('**The Schoolboy**')

Selfishness and jealousy breed misery. '**The Garden of Love**' strikingly describes a visit to a chapel with "Thou shalt not, writ over the door",

> *And priests in black gowns, were walking their rounds,*
> *And binding with briars, my joys and desires.*

Blake is partly describing bleak social conditions, and partly a crippling of the imagination. The mind and the spirit are imprisoned by what Blake called "mind-forged manacles" – a mental oppressiveness generated by men themselves.

There is a strong suggestion, too, that sexual joys have become vulnerable to destructive emotional influences. 'The Sick Rose' expresses this powerfully. Read it as a fine example of a poem where it is impossible to separate the 'meaning' from the metaphor with which it is expressed.

In the midst of 'Songs of Experience' burns 'The Tyger', an irresistibly powerful poem whose interpretation has perplexed and excited readers since first publication. The poem evokes a threatening and frightening destructiveness, yet simultaneously an impressive and inspirational energy.

Revolution

Blake lived through the fervour and dislocation of the industrial revolution, the American Revolution of 1775, and the French Revolution of 1789 and its bloody aftermath. He was instinctively a radical. In his vision political, social and spiritual liberation become one.

His enemies are the institutions he regarded as oppressive (for example the Royal Academy, and especially its president, Joshua Reynolds) and figures whom he saw as materialistic or negative, such as the Old Testament Jehovah and – perhaps surprisingly – Isaac Newton, the scientist, who for Blake personified anti-imaginative ways of thinking and feeling.

He expresses his revolutionary values not only in the 'Songs' but in the so-called "prophetic books" – massive poems, often obscure, in which he invents his own mythical figures such as fiery Orc, who stands for Energy and the spirit of Revolution. (Try sampling 'America: A Prophecy' (1793), 'The Book of Urizen' (1794) and 'The Four Zoas' (1797).)

Blake's writings are scattered with memorably provocative, almost proverbial, sayings. (The very title of his prose work, 'The Marriage of Heaven and Hell', has this challenging quality.)

Consider, for example, the impact of these:

  – *Energy is eternal Delight*

— He who desires but acts not, breeds pestilence

— All deities reside in the human breast

— Everything that lives is Holy

— He who binds to himself a Joy
   Doth the winged life destroy;
   But he who kisses the Joy as it flies
   Lives in Eternity's sunrise

He was 13 years older than Wordsworth, and we would see him now as one of the early English Romantics. He was part of that wider blossoming of ideas in late Eighteenth Century Europe which re-emphasised the individual, the subjective, the imaginative and the visionary. But he founded no movements, attracted no popular following, and was buried, largely unknown, in a common grave. Blake is one of those geniuses whose time came after his own had passed away.

Blake's biography has been written by Peter Ackroyd. 'William Blake' by Jacob Bronowski has been long out of print, but is worth tracking down. 'William Blake: the complete Illuminated Books' is edited by David Bindman.

47
Robert Burns (1759–1796)

Burns became a cult figure even within his brief lifetime, and there has always been a risk of his being sentimentalised or patronised as "the ploughman poet". Despite his humble origins he was in fact shrewd and well-read.

He had an energetic comic vision. His poetry and songs have a sinewy and sure rhythmic feel and vary widely in tone, from gentle, warm-hearted, passionate and sad to red-blooded, satirical and rumbustious. (Ian McIntyre has written that "much of Burns's thinking was done below the neckline, and a good deal below the waist".) Byron admired the richness and vigour of Burns' output: "What an antithetical mind! – tenderness, roughness – delicacy, coarseness – sentiment, sensuality – soaring and grovelling, dirt and deity – all mixed up in one compound of inspired clay!"

Burns was one of seven children born to an Ayrshire small farmer. His father ensured for him a decent schooling which included a broad acquaintance with literature. The farming was tough and there were inevitable hardships. After his father's death in 1784 Burns and his brother tried to carry on the family tradition, but things went badly. He was seriously considering emigration to Jamaica when in 1786 a publisher accepted 'Poems, chiefly in the Scottish Dialect'. They brought him immediate celebrity.

Burns' writing belongs to the Scottish folk tradition of songs and ballads. He collected old songs, reworked some of them, and wrote his own. He freely uses and subtly adapts colloquial rhythms and vocabulary.

'To a Louse' begins with a comic challenge:

> Ha! whare ye gaun, ye crawlin ferlie!
> Your impudence protects you sairly;
> I canna say but ye strunt rarely,
>   Owre gauze and lace;
> Tho', faith, I fear ye dine but sparely
>   On sic a place.

The louse continues to ascend the fine clothes of Jenny, who in her vanity is quite unaware:

> O, Jenny, dinna toss your head,
> An' set your beauties a' abread!
> Ye little ken what cursed speed
>   The beastie's makin'!

The moral arrives with deft inevitability:

> O wad some Pow'r the giftie gie us
> To see oursels as others see us!

Among his best and most popular songs are 'John Anderson, my Jo', 'Ye Banks and Braes o' bonnie Doon', 'O my luve's like a red, red rose' and 'Scots wha hae wi Wallace bled'. 'Auld Lang Syne' he tells us he revised from words taken down from an old man. The title and first line are to be found in one of the poems of **Allan Ramsay** (1686–1758), whose collected Scottish ballads were for Burns a strong inspiration.

His finest poems include '**The Jolly Beggars**', his only narrative poem; '**Tam o' Shanter**'; '**To a Mouse**'; and '**Holy Willie's Prayer**', satirical of a self-regarding Calvinist.

Much of Burns' poetry was produced in his annus mirabilis of 1785. By the time of his death of rheumatic heart disease at the age of 37 his reputation was firmly established.

There are biographies of Burns by Catherine Carswell and Hugh Douglas. Also of interest is 'Understanding Robert Burns' by George Scott Wilkie.

48
William Cobbett (1763–1835)

>-+>-0-<+-<

Cobbett's '**Rural Rides**' (1830) is a fine example of Radical journalism and what Hazlitt called "plain, broad, downright English".

From 1802–1835 Cobbett produced the '**Political Register**', a political, campaigning weekly. It began with Tory sympathies, but after two years Cobbett's views began to change and the 'Register' adopted a still patriotic but now Radical stance.

Cobbett determined to see for himself the state of the kingdom's agricultural distress and rural living conditions, and from 1821 set out on a series of horseback journeys, primarily through the south and east of England. He printed his reflections in the 'Register'; they were later collected and published as '**Rural Rides**'. *"My object,"* he said, *"was not to see inns and turnpike roads, but to see the country: to see the farmers at home and to see the labourers in the fields."*

As an example of his vivid and direct style, this extract sees him at the sale of a certain Squire Charington's farm in Surrey in 1825:

This Squire Charington's father used, I dare say, to sit at the head of the oak - table along with his men, say grace to them, and cut up the meat and the pudding. He might take a cup of strong beer to himself, when they had none; but that was pretty nearly all the difference in their manner of living. So that all lived well. But the Squire had many wine-decanters and wine-glasses and a 'dinner-set' and a 'breakfast-set' and 'dessert-knives'; and these evidently imply carryings on and a consumption that must of necessity have greatly robbed the long oak table if it had remained fully tenanted. That long table could not share in the work of the decanters and the dinner set. Therefore, it became almost untenanted; the labourers retreated to hovels, called cottages; and instead of board and lodging, they got money; so little of it as to enable the employer to drink wine; but that he might not reduce them to quiet starvation they were enabled to come to him, in the king's name, and demand food as paupers…This is not only the natural progress, but it has been the progress in England. The blame is not justly imputed to Squire Charington and his like; the blame belongs to the internal stock-jobbing system. There was no reason to expect that farmers would not endeavour to keep pace, in point of show and luxury, with fund-holders, and with all the tribes that war and taxes created. Farmers were not the authors of the mischief; and now they are compelled to shut the labourers out of their houses, and to pinch them in their wages, in order to be able to pay their own taxes.

In 1823, happening upon the fortifications at Dover against French invasion, he hits a note of scandalised incredulity. It is an opinionated piece – he may well have been wrong – but it is splendidly entertaining:

Here is a hill containing, probably, a couple of square miles or more, holllowed like a honeycomb. Here are line upon line, trench upon trench, cavern upon cavern, bomb-proof upon bomb-proof; in short the very sight of the thing convinces you that either madness the most humiliating, or profligacy the most scandalous must have been at work here for years. The question that every man of sense asks is: What reason had you to suppose that the French would ever come to this hill to attack it, while the rest of the country was so much more easy to assail?…Let the French or let the devil take us, rather than let us resort to means of defence like these. This is, perhaps, the only set of fortifications in the world ever framed for mere hiding. There is no appearance of any intention to annoy an enemy. It is a parcel of holes made in a hill, to hide Englishmen from Frenchmen. Just as if Frenchmen would come to this hill! Just as if they would not go (if they came at all) and land in Romney Marsh, or on Pevensey Level, or anywhere else, rather than come to this hill; rather than crawl up Shakespeare's Cliff. All the way along the coast, from this very hill to Portsmouth, or pretty nearly all the way, is a flat. What the devil should they come to this hill for, then? And when you ask this question, they tell you that it is to have an army here behind the French, after they had marched into the country! And for a purpose like this; for a purpose so stupid, so senseless, so mad as this, and withal, so scandalously disgraceful, more brick and stone have been buried in this hill than would go to build a neat cottage for every labouring man in the counties of Kent and Sussex!

Cobbett was the son of a small farmer, and largely self-educated. He bought himself out of the army, accusing some of his officers of corruption, and fled first to France and then to America to avoid his own prosecution. In later life he became MP for Oldham. His many publications included what came to be called '**Hansard**', the formal record of London's parliamentary proceedings. '**Rural Rides**' is his master work.

There is a biography of Cobbett by Anthony Burton.

49

William Wordsworth (1770–1850)

Wordsworth and memory

In 1790, aged 20 and on a walking tour of Europe, Wordsworth is told by a local that he has just crossed the Alps. Inexplicably to him, he feels emotionally "lost". Over ten years later, he records the disturbance in his autobiographical poem '**The Prelude**'. He looks back on the confusing mix of exhilaration and disappointment he felt at the shock of realising he was travelling away from the summits; he explains in the poem that he now understands that he was experiencing the triumph of fulfilling an ambition, but simultaneously an unconscious sadness that the ambition, once fulfilled, could never happen again.

It is a characteristically Wordsworthian moment, worth dwelling upon because it illustrates a central feature of much of his poetry. This is that only rarely was he simply evoking first-hand experiences. More usually, he is reflecting upon an earlier experience, and *understanding it more deeply*. The emotions of the original moment are overlaid by the different emotions involved in *the act of remembering*.

The famous daffodils poem ('**I wandered lonely as a cloud**' – 1802) in a simple way is a case in point. His pleasure in the dancing flowers moves towards the reflection that (inevitably) he did not at the time appreciate their full significance for him, which was to be in frequently remembering them:

> *I gazed – and gazed – but little thought*
> *What wealth the show to me had brought.*

> *For oft, when on my couch I lie*
> *In vacant or in pensive mood,*
> *They flash upon that inward eye*
> *Which is the bliss of solitude;*
> *And then my heart with pleasure fills,*
> *And dances with the daffodils.*

Readers new to Wordsworth can sometimes be perplexed as they seek an immediacy which they do not always find. He can indeed be ponderously analytical in his less successful writing. However, when Wordsworth is at his reflective best, the immediacy lies in his excitement at setting his memories thoughtfully in motion.

He famously wrote of poetry both as "the spontaneous overflow of powerful feeling" and as "emotion recollected in tranquillity". The lines have been often misunderstood. There is no contradiction. He meant that poetry is a reflective activity, not an off-the-cuff affair. The "powerful feelings" are not the original ones, but those that arise from the act of remembering intense experiences from the past.

Wordsworth and nature

Wordsworth recalled sensing as a boy a fearful presence in the natural world. Nature's influence had for him a restorative and moral power. He describes this memorably in **'Lines composed a few miles above Tintern Abbey'** (1798). To his memories of the beauties of the River Wye and the surrounding landscape he ascribes:

> *That serene and blessed mood,*
> *In which the affections gently lead us on -*
> *Until, the breath of this corporeal frame*
> *And even the motion of our human blood*
> *Almost suspended, we are laid asleep*
> *In body, and become a living soul:*
> *While with an eye made quiet by the power*
> *Of harmony, and the deep power of joy,*
> *We see into the life of things.*

It is a mystical sensation – a feeling of being joined with an ultimate and transcendent reality, which is "the soul" of all his "moral being". It will often be a solitary experience, too – Wordsworth valued "the self-sufficing power of solitude".

And I have felt
A presence that disturbs me with the joy
Of elevated thoughts; a sense sublime
Of something far more deeply interfused,
Whose dwelling is the light of setting suns,
And the round ocean and the living air,
And the blue sky, and in the mind of man:
A motion and a spirit, that impels
All thinking things, all objects of all thought,
And rolls through all things.

In '**The Prelude**' he writes similarly of the meditation inspired by a moonlit landscape:

and it appeared to me
The perfect image of a mighty Mind,
Of one that feeds upon infinity,
That is exalted by an underpresence,
The sense of God, or whatso'er is dim
Or vast in its own being…

Wordsworth was not a nature poet in a simply descriptive way. He writes of the beauties and fears which he absorbed from the natural world, which impassioned him, and whose earliest origins, imperfectly understood, he finds in his childhood. "The Child", he wrote, in words which are almost proverbial, "is father to the Man".

Wordsworth and language

We may note in the extracts quoted that the blank verse lends weight and dignity to words which are unforced, and follow naturally the contours of the thought. In their joint enterprise of 1798, the '**Lyrical Ballads**', Wordsworth and Coleridge as a matter of principle aimed to break away from what they perceived to be the dead and artificial diction of recent contemporaries – what the 1800 Preface called "the gaudiness and inane phraseology of many modern writers". Wordsworth's declared aim was to use "the language really used by men". This meant not colloquialism, but an avoidance of literary veneer.

When his language is moving freshly, Wordsworth's poetry develops a moving power. His '**Ode: Intimations of Immortality from Recollections of Early Childhood**' (1802–4), a memorable celebration of childhood bliss, has this supple strength:

Our birth is but a sleep and a forgetting:
The Soul that rises with us, our life's Star,
Hath had elsewhere its setting,
And cometh from afar:
Not in entire forgetfulness,
And not in utter nakedness,
But trailing clouds of glory do we come
From God who is our home:
Heaven lies about us in our infancy!
Shades of the prison-house begin to close
Upon the growing Boy,
But He
Beholds the light, and whence it flows,
He sees it in his joy.

The poem concludes with the poignant and well-known affirmation:

Thanks to the human heart by which we live,
Thanks to its tenderness, its joys, and fears,
To me the meanest flower that blows can give
Thoughts that do often lie too deep for tears.

A landmark life

Wordsworth had a defining influence upon English Romanticism and subsequent poetry.

He was one of five children born in Cockermouth, Cumberland. His mother died when he was 8 and his father when he was 13. (This may partly explain why in subsequent life he was not always comfortable with himself.) He enjoyed the open country. Academic life at Cambridge (he was at St John's College) was uncongenial. His time in post-revolutionary France in the early 1790s was famously inspiring: "Bliss was it in that dawn to be alive..." As the early Revolution turned into the Terror, and England went to war with France in 1793, Wordsworth's disappointment and divided loyalties caused him great unhappiness.

Assisted by a timely legacy in 1795, he settled with his sister Dorothy first at Racedown in Dorset and then Alfoxden in Somerset – near his new friend Coleridge, living at Nether Stowey in the Quantocks, who had first met Wordsworth that same year. Wordsworth had already written some poems, but now began his greatest creative period. Collaboration with Coleridge over the '**Lyrical Ballads**' gave English poetry decisive new directions. Wordsworth's role was "to make incidents of common life interesting by tracing in them the primary laws of our nature". In 1799 he completed his first, two-part, '**Prelude**', which by 1805 he was reading to Coleridge in a revised and extended form, though it was not published in his lifetime. As an examination of the roots of personality and creativity '**The Prelude**' broke new ground.

Wordsworth moved to Dove Cottage in Grasmere in 1799, and remained in Cumbria for the rest of his life – at Allan Bank from 1808 and Rydal Mount from 1813. He married in 1802 Mary Hutchinson, who had been at infant school with him. '**Poems in Two Volumes**', his last significant publication, appeared in 1807.

In 1810 there was a rift with Coleridge. Attempts were later made to patch things up, but the original harmony was never restored. From this period onwards his poetic strengths went into decline. Politically he moved steadily into a more conservative position. In later years his public role became that of the Grand Old Man of English letters – he was made Poet Laureate in 1843 at age 73 – but he had long since forfeited the approval of many of the younger generation of Romantics. Browning was to call him the "Lost Leader". Meanwhile, Coleridge's tribute to his earlier poems – "a union of deep feeling with profound thought" – is a good description of his legacy.

*Poems particularly worth further reading include '**The Old Cumberland Beggar**'; '**Two April Mornings**' (a poem which much impressed Thomas Hardy); '**Michael**'; the '**Lucy**' poems – among the best of his shorter lyrics; '**Resolution and Independence**'; '**My Heart Leaps Up**' and the sonnet '**On Westminster Bridge**', which like a Turner painting takes a particular pleasure in the qualities of light.*

There is a scholarly biography of Wordsworth by Stephen Gill, and an accessible popular version by Hunter Davies.

50

Walter Scott (1771–1832)

Sir Walter Scott's poetry and his novels are informed by a sweeping vision of Scottish and English history. He devoured the old ballads and folk stories, especially of the Borders, and his detailed knowledge owed much to his antiquarian interests and a prodigious memory. He filed away the stories he picked up from people he met when travelling as a lawyer.

He was called to the bar in 1792, having been born in Edinburgh, the son of a Writer to the Signet, and educated at Edinburgh University. He married in 1797, and in 1799 was appointed sheriff-depute of Selkirkshire. In 1811 he bought the land at Abbotsford near Galashiels where he built the residence with which he became famously associated. He produced a huge output of literary studies, histories and essays. Of his major work the poetry was written first. Scott the novelist took over from 1814, when the poetry sales began to falter, possibly in competition with the popularity of Byron.

The poetry

The great three-volume collection, '**Minstrelsy of The Scottish Border**', appeared in 1802–03, and in 1805, to immense acclaim, Scott's own '**The Lay of the Last Minstrel**'. The verse is vigorous and colourful. Scott handles stirring and chivalric themes with a sure and undemanding rhythmic fluency. A secret of his wide contemporary appeal was that he appeared to confirm Scottish continuity with a romantic and legendary past. His stance is proud and uncomplicated.

> *Breathes there the man, with soul so dead,*
> *Who never to himself hath said,*
> *This is my own, my native land!*
> *Whose heart hath ne'er within him burned,*
> *As home his footsteps he hath turned,*
> * From wandering on a foreign strand!…*
>
> *O Caledonia! Stern and wild,*
> *Meet nurse for a poetic child!*
> *Land of brown heath and shaggy wood,*
> *Land of the mountain and the flood,*
> *Land of my sires! What mortal hand*
> *Can e'er untie the filial band,*
> *That knits me to thy rugged strand!*   ('**Patriotism**')

Occasionally, as in the last lines here, the tone approaches the bombastic. At his best Scott sustains a dashing, broadbrush narrative:

> *O, young Lochinvar is come out of the west,*
> *Through all the wide Border his steed was the best;*
> *And save his good broadsword he weapons had none,*
> *He rode all unarmed, and he rode all alone.*

So faithful in love, and so dauntless in war,
There never was knight like the young Lochinvar. ('**Lochinvar**')

Some of the novels include poems. Madge Wildfire's death-bed ballad from '**The Heart of Midlothian**' is a good example of Scott's sympathetic imitation of the elemental simplicities of the old songs:

Proud Maisie is in the wood,
Walking so early;
Sweet Robin sits on the bush,
Singing so rarely.

'Tell me, thou bonny bird,
When shall I marry me?'
– 'When six braw gentlemen
Kirkward shall carry ye.'

Scott was offered, but turned down, the Poet Laureateship in 1813.

The novels

Scott's novels may be called the first historical novels. He is not concerned in his fiction to analyse historical forces, but to draw characters shaped by events in Highland, Lowland and English history. The characterisations range easily from the highest to the lowest of society. Some are engagingly individual and eccentric. The settings and landscapes often have a romantic and legendary feel, in which the actuality of history is spilling over into the excitements of historical fantasy. He is especially strong with dialogue, which is where his characters live. The linking narrative prose explains and comments, though it rarely becomes an interestingly creative medium. Scott is not a polemical writer: there is no social or political agenda. The narrative momentum is all.

The breadth and colour of Scott's imagination gave him a powerful reputation in Europe throughout the Nineteenth Century. He was one of the first best-sellers on a modern scale. He was an influence on Stendhal and Balzac, and in England on the Brontes, George Eliot, and Elizabeth Gaskell. More recently there has been a fairly pointless debate over whether Scott is truly a Romantic or an Augustan, and there have been criticisms of clumsy plots and thin characters. E.M.Forster in his '**Aspects of the Novel**' (1927) bluntly criticised Scott for "a trivial mind and a heavy style". In truth Scott wrote a huge amount at great speed, in later years under the pressure of a large debt which burdened his bookselling and publishing partnership. In the final period he was also labouring under illness and stress. It was probably inevitable that his output would be uneven. He knew that neither temperament nor circumstances allowed him to give his work sufficient time; in 1826 he acknowledged there was in his poetry and prose "a hurried frankness of composition".

Amongst his finest achievements are the short stories, 'The Two Drovers' and 'The Highland Widow', where the sense of tragedy benefits from the compressed narrative form.

The successful novels – he did not until 1827 identify himself as the author – include 'Ivanhoe' (1819), 'Kenilworth' (1821), 'Quentin Durward' (1823) and 'Redgauntlet' (1824). The best are his first Scottish novels, the so-called 'Waverley' group – 'Waverley' itself (1814), 'Guy Mannering' (1815), 'The Antiquary' and 'Old Mortality' (1816), 'Rob Roy' (1817), and – perhaps best of all – 'The Heart of Midlothian' (1818).

'The Heart of Midlothian' tells the story of Jeanie Deans. Jeanie refuses to perjure herself in the trial of her half-sister, Effie, for allegedly murdering her own child. Effie is (wrongly) convicted and receives the death sentence. Jeanie journeys to London and with the help of the Duke of Argyle is granted an audience with Queen Caroline, with whom she successfully pleads for the pardon of Effie, who is imprisoned in the 'Heart of Midlothian', the old Edinburgh Tolbooth.

At the opening of the novel, Scott vividly describes the Porteous riots of 1736. Captain Porteous, commander of the Civil Guard, fires on the crowd protesting at the hanging of a robber, and some are killed. Porteous is condemned to hang, but on the appointed day there arrives a stay of execution from the Queen in London. Frustrated and outraged, a mob storms the Tolbooth, seizes Porteous and lynches him. Scott's impressive evocation of the mood of the crowd is caught in this extract, which comes shortly before Porteous' reprieve is announced:

> *On the day when the unhappy Porteous was expected to suffer the sentence*
> *of the law, the place of execution, extensive as it was, was crowded almost to*
> *suffocation...The area of the Grassmarket resembled a huge dark lake or sea*
> *of human heads, in the centre of which dangled the deadly halter. Every*
> *object takes an interest from its uses and associations, and the erect beam*
> *and empty noose, things so simple in themselves, became, on such an*
> *occasion, objects of terror and solemn interest.*

Amid so numerous an assembly there was scarcely a word spoken, save in whispers. The thirst of vengeance was in some degree allayed by its supposed certainty; and even the populace, with deeper feeling than they are wont to entertain, suppressed all clamorous exultation, and prepared to enjoy the scene of retaliation in triumph, silent and decent, though stern and relentless. It seemed as if the depth of their hatred to the unfortunate criminal scorned to display itself in anything resembling the more noisy current of their ordinary feelings. Had a stranger consulted only the evidence of his ears, he might have supposed that so vast a multitude were assembled for some purpose which affected them with the deepest sorrow, and stilled those noises which, on all ordinary occasions, arose from such a concourse; but if he had gazed upon their faces, he would have been instantly undeceived. The compressed lip, the bent brow, the stern and flashing eye of almost everyone on whom he looked, conveyed the expression of men come to glut their sight with triumphant revenge. It is probable that the appearance of the criminal might have somewhat changed the temper of the populace in his favour, and that they might in the moment of death have forgiven the man against whom their resentment had been so fiercely heated. It had, however, been destined that the mutability of their sentiments was not to be exposed to this trial.

In the stage management of a dramatic occasion, Scott comes into his own.

Biographers of Scott include Hesketh Pearson, A.N. Wilson and Rosemary Ashton.

51
Samuel Taylor Coleridge (1772–1834)

Coleridge suffered. Gifted with one of the finest intellects of his time, he was smitten with self-doubt. A loving man who craved friendship, he often faltered in his relationships. Most particularly his marriage failed, and his love for Sara Hutchinson, Wordsworth's sister-in-law, was ruined by unhappiness. He worried over his writing: some of his best poems are unfinished. The opium he took for depression and illness became a crippling addiction. In 1816, when he was broken by a sense of crisis in his inner being and his relationships, a London surgeon, Dr James Gillman, took him in and gave him sanctuary for the rest of his life. He is one of the saddest figures in our literature.

Charles Lamb, a good friend to this likeable and fragile man, described him as "an archangel slightly damaged". William Hazlitt, always sharp and caustic when roused, viewed Coleridge's life as a waste, and a betrayal of his early promise as a figurehead for the new Romantic generations. "Frailty, thy name is Genius!"

Meanwhile by the age of 30 he had written lastingly great poetry. As a lecturer and critic he was outstanding, especially on Shakespeare. His philosophical theories on literary creativity and intuition were of deep interest: he was the first to develop the idea that good writing has an organic kind of unity. His intellectual activity and appetite was huge. He was celebrated for his stimulating talk.

Coleridge and the supernatural

Coleridge was constantly fascinated by abnormal states of mind that moved beyond immediate experience, often induced by solitary silence. A random selection of phrases from the poems reflect this interest: "the influxes of shapes and sounds"; "strange and extreme silentness"; "so calm that it disturbs and vexes meditation"; "silent with swimming sense".

He agreed with Wordsworth, as they planned the '**Lyrical Ballads**', that his particular contribution would capitalise on this interest. While Wordsworth wrote of incidents from "ordinary" life, Coleridge would explore the supernatural. '**The Ancient Mariner**' was born.

The poem tells the tale (perhaps prophetically) of a suffering man. The Mariner sins by killing the albatross at sea. The ship and crew are stricken and he is cursed. The spell of the curse breaks as he involuntarily blesses some living sea creatures, but his lonely penance is to endure periodic recurrences of his soul's agony. These can be relieved only by his retelling of his tale.

Coleridge brilliantly recreates a balladic narrative style in sparse and haunting language.

> *And now there came both mist and snow,*
> *And it grew wondrous cold:*
> *And ice, mast-high, came floating by,*
> *As green as emerald.*
>
> *And through the drifts the snowy clifts*
> *Did send a dismal sheen:*

Nor shapes of men nor beasts we ken -
The ice was all between.

The ice was here, the ice was there,
The ice was all around:
It cracked and growled, and roared and howled,
Like noises in a swound!

The incantatory rhythms and simple, almost naïve, vocabulary create a sense of uncanny, primal myth. Later in the poem the laws of nature are suspended and time is foreshortened as the Mariner's torture intensifies. Skilfully, Coleridge's narration allows us intermittently to see the Mariner through the eyes of the alarmed wedding guest, whom he has compulsively transfixed with his story. This heightens our impression of the Mariner's frightening derangement.

'Kubla Khan' and 'Christabel' were both unfinished, both written in 1797 but not published until 1816. 'Christabel' has a pseudo-medieval, Gothic setting, in which the lovely Christabel is tantalised and threatened by Geraldine, an enigmatic *femme fatale*. Less intense than 'The Ancient Mariner', the poem still conjures a surreal atmosphere of trance and dream. The brief fragment which is all we have of the strange and visionary 'Kubla Khan' exerts a powerful spell, though the poem is often upstaged by Coleridge's note about how its opium-induced composition was interrupted by a visitor at the door from Porlock. (He records that after the interruption he was unable to recapture his inspiration and so 'Kubla Khan' remained forever incomplete.) What survives describes the "sunny pleasure-dome with caves of ice" miraculously created for the legendary Kubla Khan. The fragment ends with a hypnotic image which it is tempting to see as Coleridge's vision of his ideal self as an inspired and god-like creator:

I would build that dome in air,
That sunny dome! Those caves of ice!
And all who heard should see them there,
And all should cry, Beware! Beware!
His flashing eyes, his floating hair!
Weave a circle round him thrice,
And close your eyes with holy dread,
For he on honey-dew hath fed,
And drunk the milk of Paradise.

The conversational poems

In total contrast, Coleridge wrote poems which have all the feel of spontaneous, conversational reflection – most notably **'This Lime Tree Bower'** (1797), **'Frost At Midnight'** (1798) and **'Dejection: an Ode'** (1802).

'This Lime Tree Bower' begins with the relaxed sigh of "Well…" – Coleridge is one of the few poets who more than once has succeeded in making creative use of this ordinarily so empty word:

> *Well, they are gone, and here I must remain,*
> *This lime-tree bower my prison!*

Because of a scalded foot, he is unable to accompany on a walk in the Quantocks his visiting friends, Lamb and the Wordsworths. Consequently he imagines the beauties they will see, and then applies this heightened perception to his immediate surroundings outside the cottage:

> *A delight*
> *Comes sudden on my heart, and I am glad*
> *As I myself were there! Nor in this bower,*
> *This little lime-tree bower, have I not marked*
> *Much that has soothed me. Pale beneath the blaze*
> *Hung the transparent foliage; and I watched*
> *Some broad and sunny leaf, and loved to see*
> *The shadow of the leaf and stem above*
> *Dappling its sunshine! And that walnut-tree*
> *Was richly tinged, and a deep radiance lay*
> *Full on the ancient ivy, which usurps*
> *Those fronting elms, and now, with blackest mass*
> *Makes their dark branches gleam a lighter hue*
> *Through the late twilight…*

This gentle and affectionate mood leads to the affirmation that Nature keeps "the heart awake to Love and Beauty".

A similar reflective love informs another masterpiece, **'Frost At Midnight'**. Coleridge's baby son sleeps in his cradle. Outside –

Sea, hill, and wood,
This populous village! Sea, and hill, and wood,
With all the numberless goings on of life,
Inaudible as dreams! The thin blue flame
Lies on my low burnt fire, and quivers not...

Coleridge is thrilled to reflect that his son, upon whom he looks with "tender gladness", will grow up to enjoy the "eternal language" of Nature.

Therefore all seasons shall be sweet to thee...

The whole poem is beautifully shaped. It ends as it begins with the workings of the frost, and the loving descriptions of nature – as in 'This Lime Tree Bower' – become inseparably part of Coleridge's human love.

This "shaping spirit of Imagination" Coleridge prized as his greatest human and poetic gift. In the grief of his unhappinesses with Sara Hutchinson, it is the faculty which he has lost. 'Dejection: an Ode' expresses the acuteness of the loss. Of the clouds, stars and moon, he writes: *"I see, not feel, how beautiful they are."*

It is his last great poem.

Disappointment and crisis

The son of a Devon vicar, Coleridge did not complete his degree at Jesus College, Cambridge. Depressed while a student, he enlisted in the army under a false name, but was bought out two months later by his brother. He met the poet **Robert Southey** in Oxford and with him drew up plans for a new political system to be established in New England. It came to nothing. As with Wordsworth, his enthusiasm for the French Revolution waned into disenchantment. He met Wordsworth and his sister Dorothy, and with his wife Sara Fricker (Southey's sister-in-law) enjoyed living near them in his cottage at Nether Stowey in Somerset. He published 'Poems on Various Subjects' in 1796, which ushered in a golden and happy creative period of six years or so. He collaborated with Wordsworth in the landmark 'Lyrical Ballads' of 1798, and visited Germany with Wordsworth, extending his interest in German philosophy.

In 1800 he moved to the Lake District to continue to be near the Wordsworths. His marriage was not working well; he fell in love with Sara Hutchinson; his addiction to opium had begun. In 1804, leaving Southey to look after his family, he went to be secretary to the governor of Malta. By 1807 he was separating from his wife and moving to live again with the Wordsworths and Sara. Both relationships foundered: he split with Sara and quarrelled with Wordsworth. He returned to London, suicidal, and in spiritual and medical crisis. In his later years, sheltered by Gillman, he reaffirmed his Christianity, continued lecturing on poetry and drama, and busied himself with further writing. But the great period was over.

*His **Notebooks**, and his medley of literary essays '**Biographia Literaria**' (1817), are of continuing and often moving interest. Coleridge's biography has recently been completed in two volumes by Richard Holmes.*

52
Charles Lamb (1775–1834)

Lamb was a lifelong friend to Coleridge, and played host to Wordsworth, Hazlitt and many others on the London literary scene. He wrote poems, stories and literary criticism, but is best remembered for his essays.

He was a dedicated Londoner, employed briefly at South Seas House and then at East India House until he retired in 1825. His life was dominated by a dreadful family tragedy: his sister Mary, mentally disturbed, murdered their mother. She was eventually released from an asylum into Lamb's permanent care. Lamb himself suffered from a period of mental illness. Mary collaborated with Charles in the writing of '**Tales From Shakespeare**' (1807), a simplified and still accessible version for children.

The '**Essays of Elia**' appeared in 1823 – a collection of pieces first published in the 'London Magazine' over the previous three years. ('Elia' was a former Italian clerk at South Seas House; Lamb borrowed the name to give a fictional identity to his eccentric and whimsical narrator.)

The essays, with titles like 'A Dissertation on Roast Pig' and 'A Chapter on Ears', are curiosities – slight, inconsequential, and amusing in a self-indulgent kind of way. A tongue-in-cheek Hazlitt praised Lamb's "arch piquancy" and "picturesque quaintness". Here is an extract from 'In Praise of Chimney-Sweepers':

I am by nature extremely susceptible of street affronts; the jeers and taunts of the populace; the low-bred triumph they display over the casual trip, or splashed stocking, of a gentleman. Yet can I endure the jocularity of a young sweep with something more than forgiveness. In the last winter but one, pacing along Cheapside with my accustomed precipitation when I walk westward, a treacherous slide brought me upon my back in an instant. I scrambled up with pain and shame enough – yet outwardly trying to face it down, as if nothing had happened – when the roguish grin of one of these young wits encountered me. There he stood, pointing me out with his dusky finger to the mob, and to a poor woman (I suppose his mother) in particular, till the tears for the exquisiteness of the fun (so he thought it) worked themselves out at the corners of his poor, red eyes, red from many a previous weeping, and soot-inflamed, yet twinkling through all with such a joy, snatched out of desolation, that Hogarth – but Hogarth has got him already (how could he miss him?) in the 'March to Finchley', grinning at the pie-man – there he stood, as he stands in the picture, irremovable, as if the jest was to last for ever – with such a maximum of glee, and minimum of mischief, in his mirth – for the grin of a genuine sweep hath absolutely no malice in it – that I could have been content, if the honour of a gentleman might endure it, to have remained his butt and his mockery till midnight.

Something is made out of nothing. As Emrys Williams put it: "His subject is a pretext rather than an assignment". The entertainment is simply in the dextrous handling of the prose.

Lamb's fanciful imagination can be enjoyed at first-hand in his **letters**, *many of which have been preserved.*

53
Jane Austen (1775–1817)

➤──┤◆─◯─◆├──◄

The famous opening of '**Pride and Prejudice**' alerts us immediately to the brilliance and subtlety of Jane Austen's skills:

It is a truth universally acknowledged, that a single man in possession of a good fortune must be in want of a wife.

The statement is poised, authoritatative and satisfyingly crisp. And it is untrue. We pick up a dry suggestion that while there may indeed be those for whom this assertion would have been a universal truth, they do not include the writer.

After the elegant joke of the first sentence, the second sentence of the novel speaks more directly. A society in which this "universal truth" prevails is brought into view:

> *However little known the feelings or views of such a man may be on his first entering a neighbourhood, this truth is so well fixed in the minds of the surrounding families, that he is considered as the rightful property of some one or other of their daughters.*

In the third sentence, we enter the household of one such "surrounding family". A particular person speaks, on one particular day:

> *"My dear Mr Bennet," said his lady to him one day, "have you heard that Netherfield Park is let at last?"*

With superbly precise technique, Jane Austen has progressively identified a setting, a situation and a character (Mrs Bennet), and given a clear signal of the satiric amusement with which all three are to be viewed.

The six great novels

The beginning of 'Pride and Prejudice' illustrates in miniature the consummate artistry we find in the six major novels: 'Sense and Sensibility' (1811), 'Pride and Prejudice' itself (1813), 'Mansfield Park' (1814), 'Emma' (1816), and 'Persuasion' (like 'Northanger Abbey', published in 1818 after Jane Austen's death).

She tells a good story. The plots are meticulously designed and manipulated. The narrative voice is shrewdly and entertainingly judgmental. Not a word is out of place.

Walter Scott praised in Jane Austen "that exquisite touch which renders ordinary commonplace things and characters interesting". There have alternatively been criticisms of an alleged narrowness in her portrayal of a provincial middle class world, a lack of worldly experience, and the near total absence from the novels of the great historical events of the day. These comments are surely misconceived. She writes of provincial attitudes, but she does not share them. Nor are her settings insulated from the wider world: characters travel in and out from London, from Bath, or wherever, bringing with them a changing perspective. In '**Mansfield Park**' Sir Thomas Bertram's visit to the West Indies adds to his characterisation. In the same novel, Fanny Price's visit to her noisy family home in Portsmouth, and to her coarsely disquieting father, sets up a social milieu in great contrast to the gentility of Mansfield Park itself. Jane Austen's concentrated focus on one primary social location allows for a closer scrutiny of the human comedy, informed as it is by her wise and knowing perspective.

For instance, the comfortable narrowness of Emma Woodhouse's existence in '**Emma**' is early identified as the source of her defects in character:

> *The real evils indeed of Emma's situation were the power of having too*
> *much her own way, and a disposition to think a little too well of herself;*
> *these were the disadvantages which threatened alloy to her many enjoyments.*
> *The danger, however, was at present so unperceived, that they did not by*
> *any means rank as misfortunes with her.*

Emma's story is of her growth in self-knowledge.

In '**Mansfield Park**', Fanny Price walks in Portsmouth High Street with the debonair Henry Crawford, who hopes for their marriage as she does not. They bump into her dishevelled father. She is mortified at the thought that her father's crudeness will offend Crawford. Jane Austen's description of this class contretemps beautifully balances sympathy for Fanny with amusement at her confused dilemma:

> *She could not have a doubt of the manner in which Mr Crawford must be*
> *struck. He must be ashamed and disgusted altogether. He must soon give her*
> *up, and cease to have the smallest inclination for the match; and yet, though*
> *she had been so much wanting his affection to be cured, this was a sort of*
> *cure that would be almost as bad as the complaint; and I believe, there is*
> *scarcely a young lady in the united kingdoms, who would not rather put up*
> *with the misfortune of being sought by a clever, agreeable man, than have*
> *him driven away by the vulgarity of her nearest relations.*

The characterisations of the novels are memorably rich and wittily observed. Here is Mr Collins in '**Pride and Prejudice**', whose mincing and smug pomposity is caught in his manner of speech:

> *"I am by no means of opinion, I assure you," said he, "that a ball of this*
> *kind, given by a young man of character, to respectable people, can have any*
> *evil tendency; and I am so far from objecting to dancing myself that I shall*
> *hope to be honoured with the hands of all my fair cousins in the course of*

the evening, and I take this opportunity of soliciting yours, Miss Elizabeth, for the first two dances especially, a preference which I trust my cousin Jane will attribute to the right cause, and not to any disrespect for her."

Jane Austen's assured sentences are masterly. A satiric touch is often held back until the choicest moment:

...Mrs Grant having by this time run through the usual resources of ladies residing in the country without a family of children, having more than filled her favourite sitting-room with pretty furniture, and made a choice collection of plants and poultry, was very much in want of some variety at home. The arrival, therefore, of a sister whom she had always loved, and now hoped to retain with her as long as she remained single, was highly agreeable... (**'Mansfield Park'**)

Irony is sometimes singled out as Jane Austen's main device, though this can be misleading, implying as it may a collection of ironic remarks. What we find, rather, is the constant play of an ironic intelligence, a distancing which 'places' the narrative for us as it describes.

Charlotte Bronte's 'attack'

In her letters Charlotte Bronte faulted Jane Austen as a novelist for lack of passion and imagination:

She does her business of delineating the surface of the lives of genteel English people curiously well...She ruffles her reader by nothing vehement, disturbs him by nothing profound. The passions are perfectly unknown to her...what throbs fast and full, though hidden, what the blood rushes through, what is the unseen seat of life and the sentient target of death – this Miss Austen ignores...

It is an interesting attack, and it has had its supporters. However, the view that the Austen novels merely describe a surface gentility can easily be refuted. The characters do have their passions: the dispassion is in the narrator's viewpoint and in her moral insight. And here we begin to see the real difference between the two novelists. Jane Austen is no part of the Romantic movement and its celebration of individual emotion. Despite her dates, she belongs to the sceptical and rational world of Samuel Johnson and the Augustans. Charlotte Bronte was born over forty years later than Jane Austen; her antipathy is understandable, but misconceived.

Jane Austen's creative scope is sometimes seen as the more remarkable in the light of her own allegedly quiet and cloistered life. (She was educated by her father, the rector of Steventon in Hampshire, moved to Bath in 1801 upon his retirement, and back to Hampshire with her mother and sister four years later, after his death: first to Southampton, and finally to Chawton in 1809.) Such assumptions about her life may be quite wrong; in any case, there can of course be no staple recipe for a creative genius such as hers.

*There is useful further reading in Jane Austen's biographies by Claire Tomalin and Carol Shields, and 'Jane Austen: A Companion' by Josephine Ross. Her **letters** are of great interest, and reveal a sharpness about her contemporaries that sometimes borders on contempt.*

54
Thomas De Quincey (1785–1859)

Laudanum, a tincture of opium, and opium powder itself, were during the nineteenth century easily and cheaply available from chemists. Opium, and the syrups in which it was included, was commonly regarded as a valuable analgesic, and as both a tranquillizer and a stimulant. It was also sought as a liberator of the imagination. As De Quincey was to write: *"Happiness might now be bought for a penny, and carried in the waistcoat pocket"*. Thus often began a dizzying and painful spiral into addiction.

Thomas De Quincey first took opium to fight severe neuralgia when he was a nineteen-year-old Oxford student. By the age of 28 he was addicted. He tried to fight it, but with only limited success. Part of his problem was that the opium experience was as pleasurable as it was painful. '**Confessions of an English Opium Eater**', his autobiography, appeared in two parts in The London Magazine in 1821, and made him instantly famous.

He writes in translucent prose, fluid and articulate, and what emerges is an open, sensitive and appealing personality. Part of this relatively short work has nothing to do with opium, and interestingly describes his experiences, first in Wales and then in London, after he had at 17 run away from Manchester Grammar School. His platonic friendship with Ann, a 15-year-old London prostitute, her care for him, and his failure later to rediscover her, make a touching vignette which reads almost like an episode from a Victorian novel.

But it is his ambivalent relationship with opium that dominates. *"Opium! Dread agent of unimaginable pleasure and pain!... What solemn chords does it now strike upon my heart! what heart-quaking vibrations of sad and happy remembrances!"*

The virtue of the drug for De Quincey was that it *"brightened and intensified the consciousness"*. Opium stimulated dream images – he describes them powerfully – which symbolically enacted significant moments from childhood. (This over fifty years before Freud.) The negative effects, however, were frightening: *"I seemed every night to descend – not metaphorically but literally to descend – into chasms and sunless abysses, depths below depths, from which it seemed hopeless that I could ever re-ascend"*.

'**Confessions**' was to become a cardinal influence upon many nineteenth century writers, such as Baudelaire and Edgar Allen Poe, who sought to experiment with opium as a literary stimulus. It was also to alienate De Quincey from his hero, Wordsworth. We can never know for certain how far opium was a decisive factor in their creativity, but we do know that Coleridge, Wilkie Collins and George Crabbe were opium addicts for long periods of their lives, and that opium was also taken intermittently by Walter Scott, Keats, Dickens, Elizabeth Barrett Browning and others. It was of course a common medicinal remedy for the times.

De Quincey's other writing was almost exclusively journalism, produced either in Edinburgh or London to keep his head above water when his limited funds ran out. (His father, "a plain English merchant", died when he was seven.) 'On The Knocking at the Gate in "Macbeth"' (1823) is a famous and excellent essay, and 'The English Mail Coach' (1849) is an interesting prose-poem made up of dream images. On the vexed relationship between opium and literature, read Alethea Hayter, 'Opium and the Romantic Imagination'.

55

Thomas Love Peacock (1785–1866)

>∙◄►∙◄►∙⊙∙◄►∙◄►∙◄

Peacock is a civilised and sophisticated satirist, whose best work is in his four satirical novels: '**Headlong Hall**' (1816), '**Nightmare Abbey**' (1818), '**Crotchet Castle**' (1831) and '**Gryll Grange**' (1860–1).

All use the device of a house party gathering of figures who each represent a personality type or fashionable idea. Headlong Hall, for example, is Squire

Headlong's Welsh country house, where his Christmas guests include Mr Foster, who takes a totally optimistic view of human progress; Mr Escot, the opposite; Mr Jenkinson, who looks at it both ways; Mr Milestone, a landscape gardener; Dr Cranium, a phrenologist; and the Rev Gaster, a clergyman with gastronomic enthusiasms who has published a learned discourse on the art of stuffing a turkey.

There is a slight plot of a pseudo-romantic kind, but the heart of the novels is in the mock-scholarly dialogues in which each protagonist argues his case to comic extremes. Dr Cranium, surrounded by an array of skulls, gives a lecture:

> *Here is the skull of a beaver; and that of Sir Christopher Wren. You observe, in both these specimens, the prodigious development of the organ of constructiveness.*

> *This is the skull of a bullfinch; and that of an eminent fiddler. You may compare the organ of music…*

> *Here is the skull of a Newfoundland dog. You observe the organ of benevolence, and that of attachment. Here is a human skull, in which you may observe a very striking negation of both these organs; and an equally striking development of those of destruction, cunning, avarice and self-love. This was one of the most illustrious statesmen that ever flourished in the page of history…*

> *It is obvious from what I have said, that no man can hope for worldly honour or advancement, who is not placed in such a relation to external circumstances, as may be consentaneous to his peculiar cerebral organs; and I would advise every parent, who has the welfare of his son at heart, to procure as extensive a collection as possible of the skulls of animals, and, before determining on the choice of a profession, to compare with the utmost nicety their bumps and protuberances with those of the skull of his son.*

Such send-ups are mixed with farcical incidents and comic by-play. Later in **'Headlong Hall'**, Squire Headlong listens seriously to the advice of the landscape gardener, Mr Milestone, blows up part of his garden, and nearly kills two of his guests. In **'Crotchet Castle'**, Mr Crotchet and the Rev Dr Folliott earnestly discuss whether women should pose nude for artists ('crotchet' means 'prejudice'):

Mr Crotchet:	*Well, sir, the Greeks: why do we call the Elgin marbles inestimable? Simply because they are true to nature. And why are they so superior in that point to all modern works, with all our greater knowledge of anatomy? Why, sir, but because the Greeks, having no cant, had better opportunities of studying models.*
The Rev Dr Folliott:	*Sir, I deny our greater knowledge of anatomy. But I shall take the liberty to employ, on this occasion, the argumentum ad hominem. Would you have allowed Miss Crotchet to sit for a model to Canova?*
Mr Crotchett:	*Yes, sir.*

"God bless my soul, sir!" exclaimed the Reverend Doctor Folliott, throwing himself back into a chair, and flinging up his heels, with the premeditated design of giving emphasis to his exclamation: but by miscalculating his impetus, he overbalanced his chair, and laid himself on the carpet in a right angle, of which his back was the base.

It is clever fun. With his instinct for absurdity, Peacock would not have been out of place scripting radical television comedy in the 1960s and 1970s.

His main targets, what he called "the array of false pretensions, moral, political, and literary", include most fashionable and 'progressive' ideas, affectations of melancholy, scientific optimism, materialistic political economics, Toryism, and contemporary culture. (Coleridge is gently ridiculed as Mr Flosky in '**Nightmare Abbey**' and also as Mr Skionar in '**Crotchet Castle**'; Peacock's good friend Shelley appears as Scythrop Glowry in '**Nightmare Abbey**' and Byron as Mr Cypress.)

The novels are leisurely, and create a convivial and relaxed society that perhaps emanates naturally from Peacock, whose inheritance allowed him to live as a writer (he also wrote poems and essays) until he joined the East India Company in 1819. But intellectually he is always agreeably sharp and well-informed.

Unlike many of his Eighteenth Century satiric predecessors, Peacock's position is neutral, grinding no axes. The satire is good-humoured, and he develops considerable empathy for the cranks he caricatures. For this reason especially he remains very readable, even though many of the causes he picks up on have long since faded.

56

George Gordon, Lord Byron (1788–1824)

Byron as a man and a legend is possibly better known that his actual poetry. This is not surprising, given that he cultivated his public image, and that his poetry itself projects aspects of that image. He was very popular in England, but in the rest of Europe he has held mythical stature as a hero of Romanticism, and the champion of political freedom in Greece and Italy.

His life was chequered, colourful, and touched by scandal. He was sexually profligate – probably bisexual – and relished his pose of intelligent and dashing disdain. In some sections of society he was vilified, in others lionised. He loved to provoke, but in 1816, finding himself the focus of rumours concerning an incestuous relationship with his half-sister, Augusta, and embroiled in debt, he left England for good.

Until he was ten he was brought up in Aberdeen, the child of Captain 'Mad Jack' Byron and his second wife, the Scottish heiress Catherine Gordon. His father, having squandered the inheritance, died in 1791. His mother was eccentric and hysterical. Their lodgings were menial. This difficult childhood, and the lameness deriving from the club foot with which he was born, play their part in various theories about the development of Byron's personality.

In 1798 he inherited his title and Newstead Abbey in Nottinghamshire. His student life in Cambridge was more decadent than academic. In 1807 he published a collection of early poems, '**Hours of Idleness**', which was savaged by the *Edinburgh Review*. In retaliation, he wrote '**English Bards and Scots Reviewers**' (1809), a swingeing satirical romp in the style of Pope, which was his first major poetic success. It attacks everybody in sight on the cultural scene.

He embarked later that year on extensive travels in Europe. Supposedly based on those travels, but largely fictional, '**Childe Harold's Pilgrimage**' appeared in its first two parts in 1812, and the rest by 1818. It was a triumphant success. He became highly sought-after in society circles.

'**Childe Harold**' is a long, first-person description of experiences and thoughts, but the narrator is more of an invented personality – or **persona** – than Byron himself.

(Byron denied any link.) Nevertheless, the poem was rapidly taken to identify Byron as a melancholy and moody outcast, sophisticated but disillusioned. It was a character type that, despite his denials, probably involved a degree of self-dramatisation. He was later to regret what he called "the false, exaggerated style of youth". But thus began the legend of the so-called "Byronic hero", part self and part a manipulated public and literary personality.

We see the characteristic note, the angst of the world-weary and self-pitying artist, in these two stanzas (a form which he borrowed from Spenser):

Of its own beauty is the mind diseased,
And fevers into false creation: – where,
Where are the forms the sculptor's soul hath seized?
In him alone. Can nature show so fair?
Where are the charms and virtues which we dare
Conceive in boyhood and pursue as men,
The unreached Paradise of our despair,
Which o'er-informs the pencil and the pen,
And overpowers the page where it would bloom again?…

We wither from our youth, we gasp away -
Sick – sick; unfound the boon, unslaked the thirst,
Though to the last, in verge of our decay,
Some phantom lures, such as we sought at first -
But all too late – so are we doubly curst.
Love, fame, ambition, avarice – 'tis the same,
Each idle, and all ill, and none the worst -
For all are meteors with a different name,
And Death the sable smoke where vanishes the flame.

In 1814 Augusta had a daughter, most probably Byron's. In 1815 he married Annabella Milbanke, but within a year was legally separated from her. From England in 1816 he went to the Shelleys' villa in Geneva, where Claire Claremont became his mistress and bore him a daughter the following year. He moved on to live it up in Venice. The sale of Newstead freed him from money worries.

1819 saw the first two cantos of '**Don Juan**', which he completed by 1824. Here was a different kind of Byronic 'hero'. There is a swashbuckling, adventure narrative, but the point is not so much the story as the jaunty satire, whose targets include social hypocrisy, conventional sexual attitudes, and many contemporary writers and politicians. '**Don Juan**' was condemned by Blackwood's Magazine as "a filthy and impious poem", but it became rapidly popular for the vigorous and witty openness of its style:

> *Most epic poets plunge 'in medias res'*
> *(Horace makes this the heroic turnpike road),*
> *And then your hero tells, whene'er you please,*
> *What went before – by way of episode,*
> *While seated after dinner at his ease,*
> *Beside his mistress in some soft abode,*
> *Palace, or garden, paradise, or cavern,*
> *Which serves the happy couple for a tavern.*
>
> *That is the usual method, but not mine -*
> *My way is to begin with the beginning;*
> *The regularity of my design*
> *Forbids all wandering as the worst of sinning,*
> *And therefore I shall open with a line*
> *(Although it cost me half an hour in spinning)*
> *Narrating somewhat of Don Juan's father,*
> *And also of his mother, if you'd rather.*

This Italian eight-lined stanza – **ottava rima** – lends itself particularly well to the debunking, informal tone Byron adopts, with its brisk anti-sentimentality and comic rhymes:

> *It was upon a day, a summer's day; -*
> *Summer's indeed a very dangerous season,*
> *And so is spring about the end of May;*
> *The sun, no doubt, is the prevailing reason;*
> *But whatsoe'er the cause is, one may say,*
> *And stand convicted of more truth than treason,*
> *That there are months which nature grows more merry in, -*
> *March has its hares, and May must have its heroine.*

In 1821 the Countess Guiccioli left her husband for Byron. He picked up again with Shelley in Pisa. He associated himself with Italian patriotic movements. He wrote **'The Vision of Judgment'**, a devastating send-up of Robert Southey's 'A Vision of Judgment', an obsequious elegy on George III.

He had for some years enthusiastically embraced the Greek campaign for independence from Turkey. He aimed to become a partisan in the Greek cause as he moved to Missolonghi in 1824 to form 'Byron's Brigade', but after a soaking in an open boat he died of rheumatic fever before seeing action.

In many ways his literary identity was manufactured. The casual, dashed-off feel of much of the poetry was part of the pose. As a satirist he had no moral mission beyond the ridiculing of cant. Within the great variety of his work, the shorter lyrical poems – such as **'She Walks in Beauty'** and **'So We'll Go No More a Roving'** – are more attractive to those who tire of the self-dramatising monologues. '**The Prisoner of Chillon'** has a sombre narrative and a less 'Byronic' style.

Byron's heart was buried in Greece. The rest of his remains were buried near Newstead, having been refused by both Westminster Abbey and St Paul's.

There is a biography of Byron by Fiona MacCarthy.

57
Percy Bysshe Shelley (1792–1822)

Shelley described himself as *'a nerve o'er which do creep / The else unfelt oppressions of this earth'.* He responded with intensity to his sense of the world's wrongs, both politically and personally. In his personal life he experienced deep depressions, passions and traumas. There is in Shelley's quintessentially Romantic poetry a remarkable transparency of emotion. Unlike Byron, he never poses. In him, with an often brilliant and beautiful honesty, ideals and passions yearn and ache.

In some ways he is a young person's poet. (The great poetry is written in his twenties.) He wrote in his essay 'On Life': *"Let us recollect our sensations as children. What a distinct and intense apprehension had we of the world and of ourselves!...There are some persons who, in this respect, are always children."* Such is Shelley. Young, he continually looks to the future: to a perfected humanity, in both political health and in soul.

The son of an MP, he was a gifted, hyperactive child. At school at Eton he was nicknamed "Mad Shelley" and "the Eton Atheist". His radical sympathies had him devouring Tom Paine's 'The Rights of Man' (1792), and the views of his future father-in-law, William Godwin, on man's perfectibility. He was expelled from University College, Oxford, for writing with his friend Thomas Hogg a pamphlet,

'The Necessity of Atheism'. He eloped with 16-year-old Harriet Westbrook, and married her in 1811 in Edinburgh. His sending down from Oxford and his elopement created a rift with his father; he gave up his inheritance.

There followed a free-wheeling period in which he championed various causes, including vegetarianism, free love, and a free press. He started a commune of radical kindred spirits in Lynmouth, Devon, but abandoned it when he discovered he was being watched by government spies. His marriage failed in 1814 and for a period he was suicidal. Abandoning Harriet, he eloped again, this time with Mary Godwin and her stepsister companion Claire Clairmont (who was later to have a liaison with Byron).

After travels in Europe he settled with Mary in Windsor, where their son William was born. Mary started writing 'Frankenstein'. In 1816 he wrote **'Alastor'**, which was well-received. Subtitled 'The Spirit of Solitude', the poem evokes the sense of lonely destiny which was to haunt Shelley for the rest of his life.

> *When early youth had passed, he left*
> *His cold fireside and alienated home*
> *To seek strange truths in undiscovered lands.*

He picked up the theme two years later, in **'Julian and Maddalo'**, when writing of Byron's visit to him in Geneva:

> *I love all waste*
> *And solitary places; where we taste*
> *The pleasure of believing what we see*
> *Is boundless, as we wish our souls to be.*

In 1816 Harriet drowned herself in the Serpentine. Shelley at once married Mary, and sued for custody of his two children by Harriet. He lost the case and was shattered. Meanwhile friendships had been developing with Hazlitt, Keats and Peacock. He moved to Marlow. Debts and illness pursued him and in 1818 he decamped with Mary to Italy, and was never to return to England. He was to stay variously in Tuscany, Rome, Florence and Pisa.

Then began the highpoint of his creativity, a fertile year (1819-1820) in which he produced much of his finest work, including **'The Mask of Anarchy'**, **'Ode to the West Wind'**, **'To Liberty'**, and **'To A Skylark'**.

'The Mask [or masque] **of Anarchy'** is a chilling and surreal work, unpublished in

Shelley's lifetime. It is a ballad-like poem of protest, written in response to the Peterloo Massacre:

I met Murder on the way –
He had a mask like Castlereagh –
Very smooth he looked, yet grim;
Seven bloodhounds followed him.

The impermanence of tyranny had been the subject of his earlier sonnet **'Ozymandias'**, whose wrecked statue in the desert is massively mocked by the words on the pedestal. Shelley's rhythms are superbly modulated:

'My name is Ozymandias, king of kings:
Look on my works, ye Mighty, and despair!'
Nothing beside remains. Round the decay
Of that colossal wreck, boundless and bare
The lone and level sands stretch far away.

While in Rome, Shelley was devastated by the death of his son William. He wrote **'Ode to the West Wind'** under the pressure of this tragedy. In the poem he seeks to be symbolically swept up like a dead leaf before an autumn storm and translated into a new birth:

Oh, lift me as a wave, a leaf, a cloud!
I fall upon the thorns of life! I bleed!
A heavy weight of hours has chained and bowed
One too like thee: tameless, and swift, and proud.

We catch here a glimpse of the self-pity which demeans Shelley at his worst. But there is also his characteristic questing vision:

If Winter comes, can Spring be far behind?

Walter Bagehot in 1856 wrote persuasively of Shelley's **'To a Skylark'** that we hear in it "a clear single ring of penetrating melody". His best poetry lifts towards music. He does not describe the things of the actual world, but ideas, symbols, impressions, dreams and states of mind. Swinburne was to praise his reaching for "the soul and spirit of life rather than the living form, the growth rather than the thing grown". This is as Shelley saw his art; poetry, he wrote in **'A Defence of Poetry'** (1821) "strips the veil of familiarity from the world, and lays bare the naked and sleeping beauty which is the spirit of its forms".

In '**Epipsychidion**', written in 1821 as an evocation of ideal feminine beauty, we hear this transcendent note:

> *And from her lips, as from a hyacinth full*
> *Of honey-dew, a liquid murmur drops,*
> *Killing the sense with passion; sweet as stops*
> *Of planetary music heard in trance...*
> *The sweetness seems to satiate the faint wind;*
> *And in the soul a wild odour is felt,*
> *Beyond the sense, like fiery dews that melt*
> *Into the bosom of a frozen bud.*

Shelley was in the same year moved by the death of Keats to write his elegy '**Adonais**', which he regarded as "the least imperfect of my compositions":

> *He will awake no more, oh never more! -*
> *Within the twilight chamber spreads apace*
> *The shadow of white Death, and at the door*
> *Invisible Corruption waits to trace*
> *His extreme way to her dim dwelling-place...*

In 1822 Shelley died, drowned while boating in a summer squall. His voice was an original one. He had a brilliant ear for verbal sound. His happinesses were perpetually interrupted by disappointments, but he retained a spiritual optimism. In Matthew Arnold's famous description, he was *"a beautiful and ineffectual angel, beating his wings in a luminous void in vain"*. His style was much imitated by lesser Nineteenth Century poets, which did not help his Twentieth Century reputation, but more recently there has been a revival of interest in his delicate mastery.

*Other poems worth pursuing include '**When the Lamp is Shattered**' (1822), '**The Revolt of Islam**' (1818) and his huge lyrical drama '**Prometheus Unbound**' (1820). Also see '**Shelley: The Pursuit**' by Richard Holmes.*

58
John Clare (1793–1864)

John Clare has sometimes been called a "peasant poet", but it is a patronising and unhelpful description. Clare was not consciously in any particular poetic tradition. He wrote of his beloved Northamptonshire countryside around Helpston, and his anguished responses to its changing history.

He was the son of an agricultural labourer, who afforded him what little education he could. He worked variously as a farm labourer, a thresher, a hedge-setter and a gardener. He was moved by the poetry of Oliver Goldsmith and, particularly, James Thomson, and began writing poetry somewhat in imitation of them. He found, however, that their Eighteenth Century literary diction was an encumbrance, and dropped this for the natural vocabulary of his own region.

His main collections are 'Poems Descriptive of Rural Life and Scenery' (1820), 'The Village Minstrel' (1821), 'The Shepherd's Calendar' (1827), and 'The Rural Muse' (1835). His reputation did not firm until the Twentieth Century (some further poems were published in 1979). In his day he was celebrated in some circles and introduced in London to other writers, but sales were sluggish.

To his distress, the close-knit village community grew away from him as he became 'adopted' by literary friends and patrons. This insecurity was added to by other factors: he pined after his first love, Mary Joyce (he had married Martha Turner instead), and he could not settle happily in 1832 into a new cottage and environment three miles north of Helpston. His move there had been dictated by the steady drive towards enclosure of open farming land, a national development which dismayed him.

Many of his poems, including probably his best known, 'I Am', were written while he was in the Northamptonshire County Asylum. He was diagnosed as mentally ill in 1837. He was first committed to an asylum in Epping, from which he absconded in 1841, walking back to Northamptonshire under the sad delusion that he would there be reunited with his "wife", Mary Joyce. He spent the remainder of his life in the County Asylum. No doubt his problems were attributable in part to the stresses of having nine dependants.

I am! Yet what I am who cares, or knows?
My friends forsake me like a memory lost.

I am the self-consumer of my woes;
*   They rise and vanish, an oblivious host,*
Shadows of life, whose very soul is lost.
*   And yet I am – I live – though I am tossed*

Into the nothingness of scorn and noise,
*   Into the living sea of waking dream,*
Where there is neither sense of life, nor joys,
*   But the huge shipwreck of my own esteem*
And all that's dear. Even those I loved the best
*   Are strange – nay, they are stranger than the rest.*

This is affecting in its dignified hurt. But the really moving surprise comes with the imaginative leap of the last verse:

I long for scenes where man has never trod -
*   For scenes where woman never smiled or wept -*
There to abide with my Creator, God,
*   And sleep as I in childhood sweetly slept,*
Full of high thoughts, unborn. So let me lie -
*   The grass below; above, the vaulted sky.*

Clare wrote a revealing comment on Keats: *"He often described Nature as she appeared to his fancies and not as he would have described her had he witnessed the things he described."* His own poetry describes what he knows and sees, and the losses he regrets:

In unchecked shadows of green brown and grey
Unbounded freedom ruled the wandering scene
Nor fence of ownership crept in between
To hide the prospect of the following eye.
Its only bondage was the circling sky.
One mighty flat undwarfed by bush and tree
Spread its faint shadow of immensity...   (**'The Mores'**)

The bleak flatness was his love. At his best, he is unrivalled as a sharp-eyed recorder of rural detail. In a poem like **'Remembrances'** his lament for the beauties damaged by enclosure is traced with deceptive artlessness:

Where bramble bushes grew and the daisy gemmed with dew
And the hills of silken grass like to cushions on the view,
Where we threw pismire [ants] crumbs when we'd nothing else to do –
All levelled like a desert by the never weary plough...

And Crossberry Way and old Round Oaks narrow lane
With its hollow trees like pulpits I shall never see again.
Enclosure like a Bonaparte let not a thing remain
It levelled every bush and tree and levelled every hill
And hung the moles for traitors – though the brook is running still.
It runs a naked stream, cold and chill…

The rhythms are strong. The combination of nostalgia and anger is characteristic of this unassuming master.

Jonathan Bates' absorbing biography of Clare is illustrated with generous extracts from the poems. His appendix on 'Clare's text' incidentally gives an excellent insight into the problems facing editors of poetry. Read too Seamus Heaney's inspiring lecture on Clare in 'The Redress of Poetry'.

59
John Keats (1795–1821)

"I am certain of nothing but of the holiness of the heart's affections and the truth of imagination." (22 November, 1817)

"Poetry should be great and unobtrusive, a thing which enters into one's soul, and does not startle or amaze it with itself, but with its subject." (3 February, 1818)

"If poetry come not as naturally as the leaves to a tree it had better not come at all." (27 February, 1818)

"I feel more and more every day, as my imagination strengthens, that I do not live in this world alone but in a thousand worlds." (31 October, 1818)

Keats' **Letters** to his friends and family, from which these extracts are taken, are rich in interest. From them emerges a revealing impression of Keats' personality – loving, generous, insatiably intense about the world, and passionately committed to a quest for poetry which liberates the imagination.

The letters (fortunately over 200 have survived) are fascinating in their glimpses of people and places, and Keats' animated responses to matters great and (mostly) small in the life of the times. They are tinged with the sadness of his failing health, about which he is on the whole marvellously uncomplaining. And they set in motion challenging insights into the very nature of poetry.

They show us that what Keats especially celebrated in Shakespeare, whom he revered, was the capacity to be imaginatively open to everything. A poet's imagination *"lives in gusto, be it foul or fair, high or low, rich or poor, mean or elevated – it has as much delight in conceiving an Iago as an Imogen"*. It is this quality of non-judgmental imaginative acceptance (Keats called it 'negative capability') which Keats places at the centre. But we have to be careful not to let this emphasis mislead us into thinking that Keats is all for emotion and sensation – a misunderstanding that took hold in the later Nineteenth Century, when Keats was often approvingly identified with self-indulgence. Keats was one of the most intelligent of our poets. It is a kind of mind which he cultivates, not mindless sensation-seeking.

"Such miseries to bear"

Keats' father died when he was eight, and his mother when he was fourteen. For a while he was looked after by his grandmother. He was intensely devoted to his younger brothers, George and Tom, and his sister Fanny. Money had been left, but there were complications and life was not easy. At fifteen Keats was apprenticed to a surgeon-apothecary, and qualified as an apothecary six years later, but he opted instead to become a full-time writer. Always a Londoner, he moved to Hampstead in 1819 upon the death of Tom after a long struggle with tuberculosis. He met and fell in love with Fanny Brawne, to whom he was later engaged, but the relationship was not always easy and became a source of some unhappiness. By the winter of 1819 his financial problems and his health were worsening considerably. He died in Rome, also of tuberculosis, while travelling with his friend the artist Joseph Severn.

He was encouraged into poetry by Leigh Hunt, the editor of 'The Examiner', who kept a fatherly eye on him. 1819 was his great creative year, with the publication of most of his finest poetry following in 1820. The volume was better received than '**Endymion**' had been in 1818: the virulent hostility of some of the 'Endymion' reviews almost certainly wounded him more than he admitted. He took a pride in his poetic achievement, though he was never confident that he had realised his finest ambitions. A year before he died he wrote to Fanny Brawne: "If I should die, I have left no immortal work behind me – nothing to make my friends proud of my memory – but I have loved the principle of beauty in all things, and if I had had time I would have made myself remembered". He was not to know how high his star was to rise.

The five great odes

'Ode to a Nightingale', 'Ode on a Grecian Urn', 'Ode to Psyche', and 'Ode on Melancholy' were all written in early 1819, and followed later in the year by 'To Autumn'.

The song of a nightingale heard one evening was probably Keats' initial inspiration for the 'Nightingale Ode'. Within the poem the bird and its song have become an image of transcendent and timeless perfection. As he listens to the bird's "full-throated ease", he yearns to bond with its happiness, and with it "fade away into the forest dim":

> *Fade far away, dissolve, and quite forget*
> *What thou among the leaves hast never known,*
> *The weariness, the fever, and the fret*
> *Here, where men sit and hear each other grown;*
> *Where palsy shakes a few, sad, last grey hairs,*
> *Where youth grows pale, and spectre-thin, and dies;*
> *Where but to think is to be full of sorrow*
> *And leaden-eyed despairs;*
> *Where Beauty cannot keep her lustrous eyes,*
> *Or new Love pine at them beyond tomorrow.*

In the course of the poem the nightingale is further identified with an eternal, magical song, as of poetry itself. Keats suggests he cannot achieve the communion he seeks with this perfection, not even through poetic inspiration. Plaintively, in beautifully modulated lines, the poem ends, as the nightingale flies away, with self-questioning:

> *Was it a vision, or a waking dream?*
> *Fled is that music – do I wake or sleep?*

Keats' *imagination* has afforded him a brief glimpse of ethereal beauty, but his *mortality* constrains him from union with it. Perfection is apprehended by and through the imperfect. Life's very transience gives us our sense of the transcendent: such is the paradox.

'Ode on a Grecian Urn' explores similarly tantalising conundrums. The Greek Urn is beautiful but cold. The figures portrayed upon it tell a story that is captivating but enigmatic.

> *Bold Lover, never, never cans't thou kiss,*
> *Though winning near the goal – yet, do not grieve;*
> *She cannot fade, though thou hast not thy bliss,*
> *For ever wilt thou love, and she be fair.*

The frieze is both warmly alive and coldly dead. The urn, like the nightingale, has a timeless beauty, but its perfections are tantalisingly elusive.

> *Thou, silent form! dost tease us out of thought*
> *As doth eternity. Cold Pastoral!*

Keats ends the poem with words attributed to the urn itself:

> *'Beauty is truth, truth beauty – that is all*
> *Ye know on earth, and all ye need to know.'*

These lines have been much discussed. The urn's message is superficially reassuring, but baffling when pressed. Some readers find the words meaningless. Has Keats failed? Was he through the urn asserting something unambiguously profound? Or does he teasingly continue to play with the enigma that haunts the whole poem?

In both the '**Nightingale Ode**' and the '**Grecian Urn Ode**' Keats engages with themes of time, beauty, and mortality. In '**To Autumn**' they are not referred to so directly, but they are implicit. Keats brilliantly evokes a sense of Autumn's processes. We move through hot summer to late summer, through harvesting to the sights and sounds of autumn's "soft-dying day". The seasons are seen as part of a continuity, and there is a deeper sense of a cyclical movement of harvest and renewal which triumphs over time's ravages. (Keats' positive enthusiasm contrasts interestingly with many more conventional autumn poems, in which a sense of melancholy pervades the fall.)

The other poems

Among his fine early work is the sonnet '**On First Looking into Chapman's Homer**'. Keats' 1820 volume also includes the longer narrative poems '**Isabella**', '**Lamia**' and '**The Eve of St Agnes**'. Keats was himself dissatisfied with '**Isabella**', a love story derived from Boccaccio, as showing "too much inexperience of life". '**Lamia**', taking its story from Robert Burton's 'Anatomy of Melancholy' (1621), tells of the serpent-sorceress Lamia, disguised as a beautiful maiden, successfully capturing the affections of Lycius. At a wedding feast the sage Apollonius exposes Lamia's deception. She vanishes and Lycius dies. The poem is especially interesting for Keats' presentation of the ambiguities of Apollonius' 'truth' – which is destructive – and Lamia's 'beauty', which is subversive. This ambivalence is caught in the lines:

> *Philosophy will clip an Angel's wings,*
> *Conquer all mysteries by rule and line,*
> *Empty the haunted air, and gnomed mine -*
> *Unweave a rainbow, as it erewhile made*
> *The tender-personed Lamia melt into a shade.*

'**The Eve of St Agnes**' is magnificently entrancing. Set in a wintry baronial hall, the tale is of Madeline, who retires to bed believing that on St Agnes' Eve she will have a vision of her future lover. Porphyro, son of the baron's deadly enemy, has himself smuggled into Madeline's chamber, where he hides. She emerges from her dreams to find him there. They banquet on exotic delicacies, and melt away into the storm outside.

The story is brilliantly heightened by an atmospheric and dramatic narrative, mixing suspense, danger, and rich contrasts between the cold outside and the warmth of Madeline's room, and between the youthful lovers and the aged beadsman and lady-in-waiting. Keats' language, in the stanza form he borrowed from Spenser's 'Faerie Queene', is colourful, evocative and sensuous:

> *And still she slept an azure-lidded sleep,*
> *In blanched linen, smooth, and lavendered,*
> *While he from forth the closet brought a heap*
> *Of candied apple, quince, and plum, and gourd*
> *With jellies soother then the creamy curd,*
> *And lucent syrops, tinct with cinnamon;*
> *Manna and dates, in argosy transferred*
> *From Fez; and spiced dainties, every one*
> *From silken Samarcand to cedared Lebanon.*

When Keats died at the early age of 25, the loss to literature was incalculable. On his grave in Rome appear the words: 'Here lies one whose name was writ in water'. It is an epitaph that perhaps captures the purity – but not the passion.

There are biographies of Keats by Stephen Coote and Andrew Motion.

The Victorians

60
William Barnes (1801–1886)

Little known, and deserving of a wider audience, William Barnes started writing poems in the dialect of Dorset in 1833. A collected edition in 1879 appeared under the title '**Poems of Rural Life in the Dorset Dialect**'.

Proud of his Dorset background, in 1862 he became for the rest of his life rector of Winterbourne Came near Dorchester. A philological scholar with knowledge of scores of languages, he was strongly opposed to foreign and Latinate influences on English. He believed Dorset speech to be the best survivor of the pure Anglo-Saxon English he prized; it was, he said, "my mother tongue", and "the only true speech" of the world his poetry described.

While he wrote some poems in standard English – he called it "common English" – the dialect poems remain uniquely attractive. Barnes' admirers included Tennyson (who was to write some fine poems in the Lincolnshire dialect), Hopkins (influenced by his Anglo-Saxon-style word inventions), and Thomas Hardy, another Dorset friend, whose moving poem 'The Last Signal' was written at the time of Barnes' funeral.

'**Woak Hill**' is representative of Barnes at his best. In simple, economical rhythms and with the power of skilled understatement, the poem describes how a countryman moving house keeps alive his loving memories of the wife who died:

When sycamore leaves were a-spreaden
Green-ruddy in hedges,
Bezide the red doust o' the ridges,
A-dried at Woak Hill;

I packed up my goods, all a-sheenen
Wi' long years o' handlen,
On dousty red wheels ov a waggon,
To ride at Woak Hill.

The brown thatchen ruf o' the dwellen
I then wer a-leaven,
Had sheltered the sleek head o' Meary,
My bride at Woak Hill.

But now vor zome years, her light voot-vall
'S a-lost vrom the vlooren.
To soon vor my jay an' my childern,
She died at Woak Hill.

But still I do think that, in soul,
She do hover about us;
To ho vor her motherless childern,
Her pride at Woak Hill.

Zoo – lest she should tell me hereafter
I stole off 'ithout her,
An' left her, uncalled at house-ridden,
To bide at Woak Hill -

I called her so fondly, wi' lippens
All soundless to others,
An' took her wi' air-reachen hand
To my zide at Woak Hill.

An' that's why vo'k thought, vor a season,
My mind wer a-wandren
Wi' sorrow, when I wer so sorely
A-tried at Woak Hill.

On the road I did look round, a-talken
To light at my shoulder,
An' then led her in at the doorway,
Miles wide vrom Woak Hill.

But no; that my Meary mid never
Behold herzelf slighted,
I wanted to think that I guided
My guide vrom Woak Hill.

Other poems worth discovering include *'The Broken Heart'*, *'The Wife a-Lost'*, *'The Wind at the Door'*, and *'The Common A-Took In'* (like John Clare, Barnes was upset at the hardships brought about by the enclosures of common land).

61
Benjamin Disraeli (1804–1881)

Before Disraeli entered national politics as a Member of Parliament in 1837 he had published nine works, including five novels. (He inherited a literary background from his father, Isaac D'Israeli, who studied and published literary history and literary theory.) A recurrent theme in the early writing is that of a young man making his way in the world.

By 1842 Disraeli had become the leader of the 'Young England' group of Tories, looking to redefine Tory politics and attack the perceived injustices of Whig policies towards the poor and the franchise. Then came the trilogy of political novels for which he is best known: **'Coningsby'** (1844), **'Sybil'** (1845) and **'Tancred'** (1847). **'Sybil'** in particular is a novel of political mission, designed to highlight the imperative of dealing with the national divide between rich and poor – the **'two nations'** of the novel's sub-title.

It is one of the first Victorian novels to describe the squalor in which the larger part of the nation lived and worked. Sybil is the daughter of a Chartist, living in an industrial town. Charles Egremont is the younger brother to Lord Marney, the heartless master of a neighbouring grand estate. Egremont falls in love with Sybil and, moved by the social conditions in which she lives, campaigns in parliament for reform. The less successful parts of a complex novel creak with improbabilities, but its heart is in the shocking depravity it depicts, and the recognition that in cities men were *"not in a state of co-operation, but of isolation...modern society acknowledges no neighbour".*

Egremont naively asserts in his chance meeting with the Chartist Stephen Morley:

> *"...say what you like, our Queen reigns over the greatest nation that ever existed."*
> *"Which nation?" asked the younger stranger, "for she reigns over two."*
> *The stranger paused; Egremont was silent, but looked inquiringly.*
> *"Yes," resumed the younger stranger after a moment's interval. "Two nations; between whom there is no intercourse and no sympathy; who are as ignorant of each other's habits, thoughts and feelings, as if they were dwellers in different zones, or inhabitants of different planets; who are formed by a different breeding, are fed by a different food, are ordered by different manners, and are not governed by the same laws."*
> *"You speak of – " said Egremont, hesitatingly.*
> *"The Rich and the Poor."*

In his public life and his lighter writing, Disraeli cultivated a flourishing wit and a certain flamboyance. But it is the sobering perceptions of '**Sybil**' that still surprise and impress us.

62
Elizabeth Barrett Browning (1806–1861)

>─┤◆─○─◆├─◄

Edward Moulton Barrett made his money in Jamaican plantations. He was a formidable father, doting possessively on Elizabeth, the eldest of his twelve children. She was a studious child (reading Homer in Greek at the age of 10) who endured serious illness in her teens. In her early thirties she convalesced in Torquay after a lung haemorrhage, but was devastated when her brother Edward, in Torquay at her request as her companion, was killed in a sailing accident. Grief and guilt pursued her for the rest of her life. She returned as an invalid to the family home at 50 Wimpole Street in London. (Edward kept his family about him into their adulthood, as he moved from Durham to Hope End near Ledbury to Sidmouth and finally to Wimpole Street.)

From an early age Elizabeth wrote poetry. The first volumes of juvenilia were privately printed. 'Poems' of 1844 brought her wide public admiration, including that of Robert Browning, who wrote to her. He met her the next year, their love thrived, and for fear of her father's reaction they were secretly married in 1846 and eloped to Italy. She never returned to England and her father never forgave her.

It is a well-known story. Because of it Elizabeth Barrett has long been a pitiable figure in public sentiment, and that sentiment has infused attitudes to her poetry. 'How Do I Love Thee', in a recent BBC poll, was voted Britain's favourite love poem. It is one of the 'Sonnets from the Portuguese' (1850), which are not the translations implied by the intentionally misleading title but love poems which passed from Elizabeth to Robert Browning. (He called her his "little Portuguese".)

> *How do I love thee? Let me count the ways.*
> *I love thee to the depth and breadth and height*
> *My soul can reach, when feeling out of sight*
> *For the ends of Being and ideal Grace.*
> *I love thee to the level of every day's*
> *Most quiet need, by sun and candle light.*
> *I love thee freely, as men strive for Right;*
> *I love thee purely, as they turn from Praise.*
> *I love thee with the passion put to use*
> *In my old griefs, and with my childhood's faith.*
> *I love thee with a love I seemed to lose*
> *With my lost saints – I love thee with the breath,*
> *Smiles, tears, of all my life! – and, if God choose,*
> *I shall but love thee better after death.*

In 1851 she published from her base in Florence 'The Casa Guidi Windows', in which she describes her enthusiasm for Italian unity. 'Aurora Leigh' (1856), which she called "a novel in verse", is an extraordinary endeavour of over eleven thousand lines, the purported narrative of a woman writer, in the course of which she writes of the place of women in society, the role of the poet, and other social issues. Browning organised a posthumous collection, 'Last Poems', in 1861.

A particularly striking poem in the 1844 collection is 'The Cry of the Children', which deals with the plight of the young in factory employment. It begins:

> *Do you hear the children weeping, O my brothers,*
> *Ere the sorrow comes with years?*
> *They are leaning their young heads against their mothers,*

And that cannot stop their tears.
The young lambs are bleating in the meadows,
The young birds are chirping in the nest,
The young fawns are playing with the shadows,
The young flowers are blowing toward the west -
But the young, young children; O my brothers,
They are weeping bitterly!
They are weeping in the playtime of the others,
In the country of the free.

It is interesting to compare this with William Blake, writing on a similar theme in his **'Songs of Innocence and Experience'**. Blake works economically with beguilingly simple symbols. Elizabeth Barrett uses an accumulation of more conventional images. The images are trite, but despite that the structure develops a plaintive accusatory tone. Blake is the greater poet, but Elizabeth Barrett has a distinctive integrity and sharpness that is at the centre of a current revival of interest in her work. Perhaps because of the pressures of her personal life, she was not only of her age, but saw beyond it.

There is a biography by Margaret Forster. Also see 'Elizabeth Barrett Browning and Robert Browning' by Martin Garrett.

63
Edward Fitzgerald (1809-1883)

It is for one poem (and his letters) that Edward Fitzgerald is remembered. 'Fitz' was an amiable and well-liked eccentric – an important friend to Tennyson (whom with Thackeray he had met at Cambridge). He was born wealthy and lived, mostly at Woodbridge in Suffolk, as a country gentleman of leisure.

'The Rubaiyat of Omar Khayyam of Naishapur' – a frequently abbreviated title – was published in 1859, anonymously at first, and after three revisions emerged in its final form in 1879. It is a loose translation from the Persian of Omar Khayyam, a Twelfth Century poet and astronomer. ('Rubaiyat' means 'sequence of quatrains'.)

Fitzgerald had taken to oriental studies in the 1850s. There was a renewed interest in the orient in Victorian times, and works as dissimilar as Fitzgerald's **'Rubaiyat'** and '**Woak Hill**' by William Barnes are based on the authors' familiarity with the ancient Persian.

> *Here with a Loaf of Bread beneath the Bough,*
> *A Flask of Wine, a Book of Verse – and Thou*
> *Beside me singing in the Wilderness -*
> *And Wilderness is Paradise enow…*
>
> *The Worldly Hope men set their Hearts upon*
> *Turns Ashes – or it prospers; and anon,*
> *Like Snow upon the Desert's dusty Face*
> *Lighting a little Hour or two – is gone…*
>
> *Ah, my Beloved, fill the Cup that clears*
> *Today of past Regrets and future Fears -*
> *Tomorrow? – Why, Tomorrow I may be*
> *Myself with Yesterday's Sev'n Thousand Years…*
>
> *The Moving Finger writes; and, having writ,*
> *Moves on: nor all thy Piety nor Wit*
> *Shall lure it back to cancel half a Line,*
> *Nor all thy Tears wash out a Word of it…*

The poem was slow to succeed. Only 250 copies were printed of the original version. It began to take off as it received praise from the so-called **Pre-Raphaelite** writers such as Swinburne and Dante Gabriel Rossetti. For them, as for subsequent enthusiasts, there was an appeal in the poem's sensuous atmosphere, turning away from ordinary life's preoccupations into a mood of relaxed self-indulgence, tinged with a pleasantly fatalistic melancholy.

64
Alfred Lord Tennyson (1809–1892)

Tennyson was the Victorian poet par excellence. In a huge career which spanned the Victorian period, he had Queen Victoria's accolade and was universally respected. Following his appointment as Poet Laureate in 1850 in succession to Wordsworth, he was one of the most successful figures in that strange and difficult role. He refused a baronetcy in 1865, but was eventually persuaded to take his seat in the House of Lords in 1883. His major poetry chimed with the sentiments of the time. He belonged to his age. After his death his reputation waned and his appeal has never fully recovered.

He was a shy and introspective man, whose work owed a great deal to the loving support, encouragement and management of his wife Emily, whom he married in 1850 after a long engagement. His early personal life was unhappy and difficult; his father, the rector at Somersby in Lincolnshire, suffered from epilepsy and was an alcoholic. His rages tormented the young Tennyson, and there were histories of mental instability elsewhere in the family. Throughout his life he was fearful of the 'black blood' in the Tennyson line.

While at Trinity College, Cambridge, he met Arthur Hallam who became a close friend, and whose devastating early death in 1833 launched Tennyson into the sequence of poems which eventually was published as 'In Memoriam' in 1850 – a climactic year in his life. At Cambridge he won the Chancellor's Gold Medal for English Verse. Early volumes in 1830 and 1832 included 'Mariana' and 'The Lady of Shalott'. The breakthrough to widespread acclaim arrived in 1842 with 'Morte D'Arthur', 'Locksley Hall', 'Ulysses' and revisions of some of the earlier poems.

Three years later he was awarded a civil list pension, which helped significantly to lift a burden of financial worries. In 1853 the Tennysons moved to Farringford in the Isle of Wight; they moved on to Aldworth in Surrey in the 1860s. In addition to 'In Memoriam', there were major publications in 1847 ('The Princess'), 1854 ('The Charge of the Light Brigade'), 1855 ('Maud') and in 1859 the first four 'Idylls of the King', which pursued Tennyson's cherished project of a sequence based on the life and legends of King Arthur. These poems, completed in the early 1870s, contained an allegorical critique of materialistic values, but it was the romantic Arthurian story which accorded them a popular triumph. Some of Tennyson's most interesting dialect poems were included in 'Enoch Arden' (1864). His poignant last poem, 'Crossing The Bar', appeared in 1889.

Tennyson's best strength lay in his lyrics, rather than his narrative poems and his plays. (He wrote a number of long-forgotten verse dramas, of which only 'Becket', performed by Sir Henry Irving and Ellen Terry in 1893, briefly prospered.) The lyrical poems develop a strain of melancholy nostalgia. 'Break, Break, Break' is characteristic:

> Break, break, break,
>   On thy cold gray stones, O Sea!
> And I would that my tongue could utter
>   The thoughts that arise in me.

O well for the fisherman's boy,
  That he shouts with his sister at play!
O well for the sailor lad,
  That he sings in his boat on the bay!

And the stately ships go on
  To their haven under the hill;
But O for the touch of a vanish'd hand,
  And the sound of a voice that is still!

Break, break, break,
  At the foot of thy crags, O Sea!
But the tender grace of a day that is dead
  Will never come back to me.

World-weariness, loss, and hints of a 'Truth' that is mystically hidden are common elements. *"Not wholly in the busy world, nor quite / Beyond it, blooms the garden that I love"*, he writes in **'The Gardener's Daughter'**; and in **'The Two Voices'**:

Moreover, something is or seems,
That touches me with mystic gleams,
Like glimpses of forgotten dreams.

Tennyson was a supreme melodist. The 130 poems which together make up **'In Memoriam'** demonstrate his versatility in metrical skills, though the tone is consistently wistful and elegaic:

Dark house, by which once more I stand
  Here in the long unlovely street,
  Doors, where my heart was used to beat
So quickly, waiting for a hand,

A hand that can be clasp'd no more -
  Behold me, for I cannot sleep,
  And like a guilty thing I creep
At earliest morning to the door.

He is not here; but far away
  The noise of life begins again,
  And ghastly thro' the drizzling rain
On the bald street breaks the blank day.

Within his vast output Tennyson was neither a philosopher nor an intellectual, but he touched contemporary concerns in voicing Victorian doubts about religion, about materialism, and about science. (Darwin's **'Origin of Species'**, to be published in 1859, was to bring to a head for many Victorians a gathering crisis of religious faith.)

> *I stretch lame hands of faith, and grope,*
> *And gather dust and chaff, and call*
> *To what I feel is Lord of all,*
> *And faintly trust the larger hope.* (**'In Memoriam'**)

Despite his public role he was essentially a very private man, and he seems to have felt beleaguered as an artist. Like the Lady of Shalott, he gazes into the mirror, and at life only unwillingly and indirectly. Gone is that confidence of the younger romantics about the poet's mission. Perhaps the narrator in 'Maud' speaks for Tennyson himself in his darker moments:

> *At war with myself and a wretched race,*
> *Sick, sick to the heart of life, am I.*

The dialect poems in their humour and vitality are entertainingly different from the more solemn Tennyson; it is almost as if he felt such lightness inappropriate in the mainstream material that was expected of him. Try especially **'The Northern Farmer: Old Style'** and **'The Northern Farmer: New Style'** .

Footnote: One of the very first sound recordings made by Thomas Edison is of Tennyson. Edison wanted to preserve for posterity the voices of some of the great Victorians. Queen Victoria declined, but Tennyson (and others) agreed. Some of the old wax cylinders perished long since, but if you hunt for it it is possible still to hear the voice of the grand old man, rattling through "The Charge of the Light Brigade" at such an increasingly high-pitched speed that you imagine, frivolously no doubt, that he is accelerating in panic to fit it all in.

The memoir of Tennyson by his son, Hallam, is of interest, and also 'Emily Tennyson: the Poet's Wife', by Ann Thwaite. There are biographies by Norman Page and R.B.Martin.

65

Elizabeth Gaskell (1810–1865)

➤⫯◆⫯⚬⫯◆⫯⫷

As the wife of a Unitarian minister in Manchester, Elizabeth Gaskell saw at first hand the problems of the poor, the unemployed, and the uneducated. She was one of a growing cluster of novelists – Dickens and Disraeli amongst them – who were stirred by the increasingly urgent distresses of the urban poor.

'**Mary Barton**', published anonymously in 1848, is subtitled 'A Tale of Manchester Life', and documents the privations of textile workers in the "hungry forties". Mary Barton is the daughter of a trade unionist, John Barton, who, amid mounting industrial unrest, shoots his employer, Henry Carson. Carson had initiated an affair with Mary, who had meanwhile rejected the attentions of a young engineer, Jem Wilson. Following the murder, Mary is torn between loyalty to her father and her obligation to defend Jem against suspicions that he was the killer of his rival. This somewhat melodramatic plot is in some ways the least successful aspect of the novel, whose real interest lies in Elizabeth Gaskell's concerned descriptions of the squalid working and living conditions.

It was unpaved; and down the middle a gutter forced its way, every now and then forming pools in the holes with which the street abounded. Never was the old Edinburgh cry of 'Gardez l'eau' more necessary than in this street. As they passed, women from their doors tossed household slops of every description into the gutter; they ran into the next pool, which overflowed and stagnated. Heaps of ashes were the stepping-stones, on which the passer-by, who cared in the least for cleanliness, took care not to put his foot. Our friends were not dainty, but even they picked their way till they got to some steps leading down …into the cellar in which a family of human beings lived. It was very dark inside. The window panes were many of them broken and stuffed with rags, which was reason enough for the dusky light that pervaded the place even at mid-day…The smell was so foetid as almost to knock the two men down. Quickly recovering themselves, as those inured to such things do, they began to penetrate the thick darkness of the place, and to see three or four little children rolling on the damp, nay wet, floor, through which the stagnant, filthy moisture of the street oozed up.

(Such conditions Elizabeth Gaskell also saw in Haworth, where she visited her great friend Charlotte Bronte, whose biography she was later to write.)

Through '**Mary Barton**' Gaskell came to the attention of Dickens, who serialised '**North and South**' (1855) in his periodical 'Household Words'. '**North and South**' tells the story of Margaret Hale, the daughter of a Hampshire vicar, who upon moving to the industrial north of England slowly discards her prejudices about it.

Elizabeth Gaskell was brought up by an aunt in the small town of Knutsford in Cheshire, upon which she based the setting for '**Cranford**' (1853) and '**Wives and Daughters**' (1866). These novels offer a quite different social scene. '**Cranford**', always the most popular of her stories, is a warm and gentle comedy. Largely plotless, it describes the lives of the mostly genteel ladies who form the social circle of Miss Matty, a kindly spinster in an 1830s community. '**Wives and Daughters**', essentially the love story of the surgeon's daughter Molly Gibson and the squire's son, Roger Hamley, has a stylish prose and structure which approaches the sophistication of Jane Austen, and is regarded by some as her masterpiece. The dialogue is particularly accomplished; she is especially good at the importance of what is *not* said. Not quite finished when the author died of a sudden heart attack, the novel was serialised in 'The Cornhill Magazine', edited by Thackeray. Here is Elizabeth Gaskell on Molly's step-sister Cynthia:

> *A schoolgirl may be found in every school who attracts and influences all the others, not by her virtues, nor her beauty, nor her sweetness nor her cleverness, but by something that can neither be described nor reasoned upon…A woman will have this charm, not only over men but over her own sex; it cannot be defined, or rather it is so delicate a mixture of many gifts and qualities that it is impossible to decide on the proportions of each. Perhaps it is incompatible with very high principle; as its essence seems to consist in the most exquisite power of adaptation to varying people and still more varying moods; 'being all things to all men'. At any rate, Molly might soon have been aware that Cynthia was not remarkable for unflinching morality; but the glamour thrown over her would have prevented Molly from any attempt at penetrating into and judging her companion's character, even had such processes been the least in accordance with her own disposition.*

Mrs Gaskell, as she is still rather quaintly styled, started writing at the age of 35 to occupy her mind while she was grieving for the death of her young son, William. She wrote in all six novels and a number of short stories. The modest integrity of her writing attracts a widening readership.

Further reading: 'Elizabeth Gaskell – A Habit of Stories' by Jenny Uglow.

66
William Makepeace Thackeray (1811–1863)

The title of **'Vanity Fair'** came to Thackeray in the middle of the night, and he walked round repeating it until he could write it down. Taken from Bunyan, it perfectly caught his intentions: this fast-moving comic panorama was to resemble a puppet show, with the characters his puppets. The fairground-like spectacle was to function as a mockery of Vanity – the inflated egos of the upper stretches of English society in the generation previous to Thackeray's own, at the time of the wars with Napoleon.

The last paragraph of the novel summarises the concept:

> *Ah! Vanitas Vanitatum! Which of us is happy in this world? Which of us has his desire? Or, having it, is satisfied? Come, children, let us shut up the box and the puppets, for our play is played out.*

The foolishness of human expectations has been the theme of the show.

In the tradition of Fielding, Thackeray in the role of author-entertainer addresses his reader directly from time to time, sometimes with a confiding comment, sometimes drawing attention to the props and mechanisms of the story-telling. As, for example, at the beginning of Chapter 50:

> *The Muse, whoever she be, who presides over this Comic History, must now descend from the genteel heights in which she has been soaring, and have the goodness to drop down upon the lowly roof of John Sedley at Brompton, and describe what events are taking place there.*

'Vanity Fair', subtitled by Thackeray "a novel without a hero", tells the story of the totally unscrupulous but dazzlingly winning Becky Sharpe, and her trusting and unworldly friend Amelia Sedley. A complex but seamlessly-developed plot covers a vast range of events, circling around the battle of Waterloo half-way through the book. Despite Thackeray's whimsical description of what he is about, the characters are in fact anything but puppets. They are richly alive. The entertainingly drawn gallery includes Amelia's bovine brother, Jos, the gauche but likeable army officer

William Dobbin, the ravaged old baronet, Sir Pitt Crawley, and the deviously nasty Lord Steyne (modelled by Thackeray on Lord Hertford, upon whom Disraeli had also based a character, his Lord Monmouth in '**Coningsby**'). This description of Lord Steyne illustrates Thackeray's gift for character vignettes:

> *The candles lighted up Lord Steyne's shining bald head, which was fringed with red hair. He had thick bushy eyebrows, with little twinkling bloodshot eyes, surrounded by a thousand wrinkles. His jaw was underhung, and when he laughed, two white buck-teeth protruded themselves and glistened savagely in the midst of the grin. He had been dining with royal personages, and wore his garter and ribbon. A short man was his Lordship, broad-chested, and bow-legged, but proud of the fineness of his foot and ankle, and always caressing his garter-knee.*

'**Vanity Fair**' was published in instalments from 1847–1848, and to immediate acclaim. Thackeray was made. Previously he had eked out a living from journalism and periodic articles in Paris and London. (He gambled away some of his inheritance, and left Cambridge without taking his degree. In the 1830s collapsed investments disposed of the rest of the money.)

From 1842 he had been a significant contributor to the satirical magazine Punch, with which he remained associated until 1854. While with Punch he wrote his '**Book of Snobs**', exercising his dislike of social pretentiousness, and he parodied several contemporary novels, including '**Coningsby**'. He also wrote a pastiche of Tennyson's prize-winning Cambridge poem, '**Timbuctoo**'. Later novels include '**Pendennis**' (1848–50), '**The History of Henry Esmond**' (1852), and '**The Newcomes**' (1853–55). In '**Henry Esmond**', set in the period of Marlborough's European campaigns, Thackeray aimed to "make history familiar rather than heroic"; **Henry Esmond**' and '**Vanity Fair**' have been generally regarded as his finest work.

Charlotte Bronte paid Thackeray a colourful and fulsome tribute after she had read '**Vanity Fair**': *"I think I see in him an intellect profounder and more unique than his contemporaries have yet recognised…his wit is bright, his humour attractive, but both bear the same relation to his serious genius that the mere lambent sheet-lightning playing under the edge of the summer cloud does to the electric death-spark hid in its womb."* To him she dedicated the second edition of '**Jane Eyre**'.

There is a biography of Thackeray by D.J. Taylor.

67
Robert Browning (1812–1889)

➤─┤◆──○──◇─┤─<

Browning's poetry is a curiosity. Readers are often perplexed by his tortured expression and seeming obscurity, and find it difficult to work out his 'philosophy'. During his own lifetime he was paradoxically ignored when he was at his best, and celebrated as a sage when his writing was in decline. In his later years he was a revered figure in London society, awarded an honorary degree at Oxford, and made an honorary fellow of Balliol College. He is buried in Poets' Corner in Westminster Abbey.

He wrote a number of poems which are remembered with affection, and many more which are difficult or impenetrable. Snatches from some of the poems have entered the language: "the best is yet to be"; "God's in his heaven / All's right with the world"; "never glad confident morning again" (the latter in **'The Lost Leader'**, who is not named but was later admitted to be Wordsworth).

He wrote some fine lyrical poems and love poems. He made a speciality of the dramatised verse monologue, in which he adopts the personality of a historical or pseudo-historical figure. The best of these are remarkably skilful and effective, and 'modern' in their complex originality.

One of his best poems is **'Two in the Campagna'**, in which a lover tries unsuccessfully to pin down quite why it is that the loving relationship contains hurt and pain, and is not quite perfect. Here is the poem's ending:

> *No. I yearn upward, touch you close,*
> *   Then stand away. I kiss your cheek,*
> *Catch your soul's warmth – I pluck the rose*
> *   And love it more than tongue can speak -*
> *Then the good minute goes.*
>
> *Already how am I so far*
> *   Out of that minute? Must I go*
> *Still like the thistle-ball, no bar,*
> *   Onward, whenever light winds blow,*
> *Fixed by no friendly star?*

Just when I seemed about to learn!
Where is the thread now? Off again!
The old trick! Only I discern -
Infinite passion, and the pain
Of finite hearts that yearn.

In the subtle modulations of the speaking voice, and the sensitivity with which the elusiveness of the feeling is caught, this is beautifully done.

Such poetry makes nonsense of Oscar Wilde's quip that Browning "used poetry as a medium for writing in prose". Wilde may have been foxed by the unromantic novelty of lines like the beginning of '**The Bishop Orders His Tomb at St Praxed's Church**', in which Browning conjures the personality of a crotchety, vainglorious and worldly Renaisssance cleric:

Vanity, saith the preacher, vanity!
Draw round my bed: is Anselm keeping back?
Nephews – sons mine…ah God, I know not! Well -
She, men would have to be your mother once,
Old Gandolf envied me, so fair she was!
What's done is done, and she is dead beside,
Dead long ago, and I am Bishop since,
And as she died so must we die ourselves,
And thence ye may perceive the world's a dream.
Life, how and what it is?…

Such lines struck a new note in English poetry – we have to go back to Chaucer to find a similar creation of fictional personality in verse. Browning's sentences flick from one thing to another as the old man's mind darts and wanders. Again we see Browning's cultivation of an individual speaking voice.

These dramatic monologues, mostly based on Italian Renaissance personalities, were one of Browning's specialities. We read them for the characterisation, or, as in Browning more generally, the story they tell. Those who seek for a philosophy or theme will not find it, though there is occasional interest in the nature of art and the artist. Some critics have faulted Browning for evasiveness, for wearing 'masks' and failing to commit himself, but after all a poet is not obliged to develop a world view. We must take what we find. (Thomas Hardy, finding in Browning an occasional note of forgiving positiveness, smacked him down for "a smug Christian optimism worthy of a dissenting grocer"!)

However, it remains the case that much of Browning is obscure and hard going. The syntax becomes awkward and contorted. Sometimes the poetry is pleasing in patches, but the poem as a whole lacks structure and drifts away from us. 'The Ring and the Book' (1868–9), an epic Roman murder story in verse, popular in its day and regarded by some as Browning's masterpiece, deters those who find it forbiddingly complicated.

The most available of Browning is in 'Men and Women' (1855) and poems published in pamphlets in the 1840s. Here we will find the popular 'Home Thoughts From Abroad', 'How They Brought the News from Ghent to Aix' and 'The Pied Piper of Hamelin'. Also try 'Love Among the Ruins' and, among the character monologues, 'My Last Duchess', 'Fra Lippo Lippi', 'Andrea del Sarto', and 'A Toccata of Galuppi's'.

Browning's poetry was for him a gentle leisure activity. He never had to earn a living. His father, a Bank of England clerk, was an artistic intellectual whose large library gave Browning a mostly informal education. It was in the library as a teenager that he came to admire Shelley. His mother was a strong nonconformist; he attended London University. He lived in London with his parents until he married (see **Elizabeth Barrett Browning**). His travels, particularly in Italy, informed his poetry. After Elizabeth's death he returned to England. He died in Venice.

See 'Robert Browning: His Life and Work' by F.E.Halliday, 'Browning: The Private Life' by Iain Finlayson, and 'Elizabeth Barrett Browning and Robert Browning' by Martin Garrett. An interesting approach is to be found in 'Robert Browning – A Life After Death' by Pamela Neville-Singleton.

68
Edward Lear (1812–1888)

Lear was in the first instance an artist and draughtsman: the famous nonsense poetry happened almost incidentally. A Londoner, the youngest of 20 children, he came to the attention of the Earl of Derby, who commissioned him to do colour drawings of the animals he kept in his menagerie at Knowsley Hall. Lear was later to give drawing lessons to Queen Victoria. He travelled extensively in three continents (partly under Derby's patronage), and produced a collection of travel books accompanied by sketches and oils.

His first '**Book of Nonsense**', with his own illustrations, was put together for the Earl of Derby's grandchildren, and initially published anonymously in 1845. It was followed by three enlarged editions, and collections of new nonsense verse in 1862, 1871, 1872, and 1877. Lear popularised (though did not invent) the limerick. His staple nonsense ingredients were easy rhymes and rhythms, animals, invented words, and a memorably dotty and exotic sense of fantasy.

He celebrates the long-postponed marriage of '**The Owl and the Pussy-Cat**' in the land where the Bong-tree grows:

'Dear Pig, are you willing to sell for one shilling
    Your ring?' Said the Piggy, 'I will.'
So they took it away, and were married next day
    By the Turkey who lives on the hill.
They dined on mince, and slices of quince,
    Which they ate with a runcible spoon;
And hand in hand, on the edge of the sand,
    They danced by the light of the moon,
        The moon,
        The moon,
They danced by the light of the moon.

Sadly Lear suffered from loneliness and fits of depression, perhaps partly attributable to his epilepsy. He did not lack for friends, and was close to the Tennysons, particularly Emily, with whom he corresponded prolifically. (He set some of Tennyson's poems to music.) For a total of 27 years he preferred to live in Italy, where he died at San Remo. Meanwhile the Pobble who has no toes, the Jumblies, the Dong with the luminous nose, and the Yongy-Bonghy-Bo have passed into our folklore.

69
Charles Dickens (1812–1870)

Dickens was a showman of genius. He stands in the forefront of British novelists for the breadth of his creative imagination, and the exciting exuberance of his output. He wrote fifteen great novels. At the centre of each his presence radiates the confident glow of the successful public entertainer. His vision, sometimes comic and sometimes tragi-comic, has entered the national consciousness.

Traditionally we ascribe to him a profound insight into the nature of his times. From Dickens we rightly derive much of our grasp of the Victorian period. But we should recognise that in his fiction his instinct is not to record and describe in documentary fashion. He is not a social historian. He has a transforming poetic imagination, and it is this which underpins the memorability of his work.

The intensity of a life

Dickens' writing is rooted in his experiences. He was born in Portsmouth, but his home in the early years alternated between London and Chatham in Kent. Two childhood afflictions were particularly formative. At the age of 12 he started in a blacking factory, working long hours in grim conditions for a mere pittance. Then his father was imprisoned in the Marshalsea for debt. The family joined him there, but not Charles, who morning and night trudged the four miles between the factory and his lodgings in Camden Town. He visited his parents only for some meals and on Sundays. After John Dickens was released, Charles' mother insisted that he continue at the factory. The misery for him of her attitude must have bitten deep.

Meanwhile he read extensively, and especially in the novels of Smollett and Fielding. As a young man he started to write reports of parliamentary debates and political meetings, and in 1836–37 a collection of early pieces was republished as '**Sketches by Boz, Illustrative of Everyday Life and Everyday People**'. In 1836 he married Catherine Hogarth, and met John Forster, who was to be a lifelong friend and confidant, and eventually his first biographer. In the same eventful year he launched upon the first instalments of '**The Pickwick Papers**'. Publication by instalments was to be his standard system. He was rarely more than four or five instalments ahead of his readers, and always felt free to adapt his plots and characters in the light of public responses. (The harmony between Pip and Estella at the end of '**Great Expectations**' was one such emendation, replacing the gloomy disappointment which he originally planned for Pip.)

'**Pickwick**' was a huge success, and financially Dickens never looked back. Work on '**Oliver Twist**' (1837) and '**Nicholas Nickleby**' (completed 1839) overlapped. It is remarkable that throughout his life Dickens was often handling several projects simultaneously. '**The Old Curiosity Shop**' (1840–41) introduced one of his most popular heroines in Little Nell, whose death scene, often criticised for mawkish sentiment, became one of the most celebrated episodes in Victorian fiction. 1841 also saw Dickens complete '**Barnaby Rudge**'. By 1843 he had produced 'A **Christmas Carol**' and begun the serialisation of '**Martin Chuzzlewit**'. This was something of a turning point. Compared with the earlier works sales were disappointing. Having recently visited America, Dickens diverted the plot of 'Chuzzlewit' to include an American sequence, but neither this nor the glorious characterisations of Mrs Gamp and Mr Pecksniff rescued the book's popularity; the satirical presentation of America went down very badly in that country.

Henceforth, while serial publication continued, the novels were more thoroughly planned, and the concerns of the books more seriously considered. This phase began with 'Dombey and Son (1848) and 'David Copperfield' (1849–50), which in parts draws directly on Dickens' early life. From 1850 he began to edit the weekly he called 'Household Words', which became 'All The Year Round' in 1859 and continued until his death. Then began the great sequence of 'Bleak House' (1852–3), 'Hard Times' (1854), 'Little Dorrit' (1855–57), 'A Tale of Two Cities' (1859), 'Great Expectations' (1860–61) and 'Our Mutual Friend' (1864–65). Publication of 'The Mystery of Edwin Drood' had begun when Dickens died in 1870, and the novel remained tantalisingly unfinished.

Towards the end personal stresses accumulated. In the 1850s there developed Dickens' passion for the young actress Ellen Ternan. His marriage had been weakening for some time, and in 1858 he and Catherine separated. (Peter Ackroyd, one of today's foremost interpreters of Dickens, in his biography and his broadcasts speaks illuminatingly of the dark night of Dickens' soul, the guilts, fears and secrets from his past which surface in his writings.) Dickens loved the theatre – in an already crowded life he found time both to act and to arrange a series of amateur productions – and he took great pleasure in public readings from his works. These performances became an increasingly important part of his life, but the second American tour in 1867 took a tremendous toll on his health. The trauma of his involvement in a railway accident in 1865 never left him. He died in his favourite home, Gad's Hill Place near Rochester, having the previous day persisted with his writing despite feeling seriously unwell. He was buried with much public grief in Westminster Abbey.

A poetic inspiration

Dickens has been much adapted for film and television, often with great popular appeal and artistic success. But many aspects of his writing do not translate easily or at all into a *visual* medium. The theatrical element in the characterisations will often transfer well, and superficial aspects of his rich descriptions can be caught, but his narratives frequently generate an intensity of symbolism or surrealism which only live in the original words.

Consider, for example, the huge dustheaps in **'Our Mutual Friend'**, which become symbolic of greed, money and corruption. In the same novel garbage, human degradation and the Thames intermingle at Rotherhithe, *"down by where the accumulated scum of humanity seemed to be washed from higher grounds, like so much moral sewage, and to be pausing until its own weight forced it over the bank and sunk it in the river"*. The Thames, in which bodies mingle among the filth, has a sinister predatoriness which keys in with the wider themes of the story:

> *Not a ship's hull, with its rusty iron links of cable run out of hawse-holes long*
> *discoloured with the iron's rusty tears, but seemed to be there with a fell intention.*
> *Not a figure-head but had the menacing look of bursting forward to run them*
> *down. Not a sluice gate, or a painted scale upon a post or wall, showing the depth of*
> *water, but seemed to hint, like the dreadfully facetious Wolf in bed in*
> *Grandmamma's cottage, 'That's to drown you in, my dears!' Not a lumbering black*
> *barge, with its cracked and blistered side impending over them, but seemed to suck*
> *at the river with a thirst for sucking them under. And everything so vaunted the*
> *spoiling influences of water – discoloured copper, rotten wood, honey-combed stone,*
> *green dank deposit – that the after-consequences of being crushed, sucked under, and*
> *drawn down, looked as ugly to the imagination as the main event.*

The celebrated opening of **'Bleak House'** describes a grim London November assailed by mud, drizzle, "the death of the sun" and fog – at the very heart of which sits the Lord High Chancellor in his High Court of Chancery. Thus, brilliantly, Dickens links fog to the processes of the law, which metaphorically it surrounds:

> *Never can there come fog too thick, never can there come mud and mire too*
> *deep, to assort with the groping and floundering condition which this High*
> *Court of Chancery, most pestilent of hoary sinners, holds, this day, in the*
> *sight of heaven and earth. On such an afternoon, if ever, the Lord High*
> *Chancellor ought to be sitting here – as here he is – with a foggy glory round*
> *his head, softly fenced in with crimson cloth and curtains, addressed by a*
> *large advocate with great whiskers, a little voice, and an interminable brief,*
> *and outwardly directing his contemplation to the lantern in the roof, where*
> *he can see nothing but fog. On such an afternoon, some score of members of*
> *the High Court of Chancery bar ought to be – as here they are – mistily*
> *engaged in one of the ten thousand stages of an endless cause, tripping one*
> *another up on slippery precedents, groping knee-deep in technicalities,*
> *running their goat-hair and horse-hair warded heads against walls of words,*
> *and making a pretence of equity with serious faces, as players might.*

The fog, we notice, not only encircles but occupies the courtroom.

Similarly charged pictures are to be found throughout Dickens – in the overpowering savagery of industrial Coketown in '**Hard Times**', out of whose chimneys *"interminable serpents of smoke trailed themselves for ever and ever, and never got uncoiled"*; in the urban wasteland detailed in '**The Old Curiosity Shop**', where *"on mounds of ashes by the wayside, sheltered only by a few rough boards, or rotten penthouse roofs, strange engines spun and writhed like tortured creatures, clanking their iron chains, shrieking in their rapid whirl from time to time as though in torment unendurable, and making the ground tremble with their agonies"*; in the railway building site of '**Dombey and Son**', with its *"carcasses of ragged tenements, and fragments of unfinished walls and arches, and piles of scaffolding, and wildernesses of bricks, and giant forms of cranes, and tripods straddling above nothing"*.

The coming of the railway is alarming and intimidating, but it is also – with an ambivalence characteristic of Dickens – exciting and exhilarating : *"To and from the heart of this great change, all day and night, throbbing currents rushed and returned incessantly like its life's blood…Night and day the conquering engines rumbled at their distant work, or, advancing smoothly to their journey's end, and gliding like tame dragons into the allotted corners grooved out to the inch for their reception, stood bubbling and trembling there, making the walls quake, as if they were dilating with the secret knowledge of great powers yet unsuspected in them, and strong purposes not yet achieved"*.

Character and caricature

The novels bustle with memorable figures, some identified with one particular physical trait or habit of mind as in a cartoon, and others whose psychology is more complicated and more deeply etched, such as Bradley Headstone in '**Our Mutual Friend**', Pip in '**Great Expectations**', or the title character in the eerie short story '**The Signalman**'. The simply sketched figures are a stock-in-trade, especially where comedy or villainy is the keynote. Uriah Heep in '**David Copperfield**' has his catchphrase – *"Be umble"* – but is also frightening: *"I'm very umble to the present moment, Master Copperfield, but I've got a little power."* The sting is in the tail.

Sometimes Dickens' characterisations are drawn so economically and neatly that they at first appear two-dimensional, but they rapidly grow. One such is Jeremiah Flintwinch in '**Little Dorrit**':

> He was a short, bald old man, in a high-shouldered black coat and
> waistcoat, drab breeches, and long drab gaiters. He might, from his dress,
> have been either clerk or servant, and in fact had long been both. There was

nothing about him by way of decoration but a watch, which was lowered into the depths of its proper pocket by an old black ribbon, and had a tarnished copper key moored above it, to show where it was sunk. His head was awry, and he had a one-sided, crab-like way with him, as if his foundations had yielded at about the same time as those of the house, and he ought to have been propped up in a similar manner…

His neck was so twisted, that the knotted ends of his white cravat usually dangled under one ear; his natural acerbity and energy, always contending with a second nature of habitual repression, gave his features a swollen and suffused look; and altogether, he had a weird appearance of having hanged himself at one time or other, and of having gone about ever since, halter and all, exactly as some timely hand had cut him down.

Frequently, as here, characters are developed almost as an extension of the buildings or environment to which they belong. Dickens is superb at linking rooms with those who inhabit them – Krook's shop in '**Bleak House**', or the rooms of Mr Jaggers and Miss Havisham in '**Great Expectations**'.

Man and society

Within his plots Dickens is typically concerned with social injustice. The institutions and the machinery of state are frequently seen as the oppressors of ordinary people. The law's delays, problems of money and inheritance, hypocrisy in figures of power, the sinister and mad aspects of the political world – all aroused his anger. He was especially sensitive to the sufferings of children – as orphans, in so-called 'schools', and as victims of the world of work. (Some of his children we find sentimentalised, but who could fail to be touched, for example, by '**Nicholas Nickleby**'s Smike?) He had profoundly mixed feelings about cities, and in particular London; he loved the busy turmoil and the maze of streets and yards, but he hated the ways in which the teeming life of the multitude could isolate and destroy the lonely and the weak. Images abound in Dickens of the lives of those who are trapped and stunted.

Dickens' friend the writer Wilkie Collins described the novelist's task as to "make 'em laugh, make 'em cry, make 'em wait". Dickens is outstandingly skilled in his manipulation of the reader, in the best sense. The surest guarantee of his continuing power to absorb us is the sheer energy of his invention.

See the biographies of Dickens by Jane Smiley and Peter Ackroyd, and the shorter 'Dickens: Public Life and Private Passion' also by Peter Ackroyd.

70
Anthony Trollope (1815–1882)

Trollope's literary output was prodigious: 47 novels, and a range of short stories, travel books, biographies, and other publications. His **'Autobiography'** (1883) is one of the fullest accounts we have of a Victorian writing life, and particularly interesting in its description of his writing routines. He had a daily set plan, writing from 5.30am until breakfast time, aiming for 250 words each quarter of an hour, leading to approximately 10,000 words per week. Each novel would be about the same length, and he took pleasure in meeting his publisher's commissioned word length and deadline almost exactly. For some time after these details became public Trollope was despised by those who saw revealed in them a merely mechanical approach to literature. It is equally possible, of course, to view his method as no more than a sensible discipline.

He stated plots to be uninteresting and unimportant. (We may take this with a little pinch of salt.) Character was all:

> *I have never troubled myself much about the construction of plots…The novelist has other aims than the elucidation of his plot. He desires to make his readers so intimately acquainted with his characters that the creations of his brain should be to them speaking, moving, living human creatures. This he can never do unless he knows those fictitious personages himself, and he can never know them well unless he can live with them in the full reality of established intimacy…He must learn to hate them and to love them. He must argue with them, quarrel with them, forgive them, and even submit to them…On the last day of each month recorded, every person in his novel should be a month older than on the first…It is so that I have lived with my characters…There is a gallery of them, and of all in that gallery I know the tone of the voice, and the colour of the hair, every flame of the eye, and the very clothes they wear.*

The novel for Trollope was "a picture of common life enlivened by humour and sweetened by pathos". Accordingly he offers his readers not excitement and surprise, but an easy-paced immersion in a carefully and divertingly detailed world, usually an upper-middle-class world. He is the first of the English novelists to devise sequences of novels in which certain characters recur.

He wrote two major sequences of this kind. The first, the so-called 'Barchester' novels, were inspired by his strolling one summer evening in the close of Salisbury Cathedral. (Barchester is the county town of Trollope's Barset, in the West Country.) The novels develop a gentle comedy of (largely) genteel folk. There are 'plots', involving misjudgments, rivalries, and manoeuvrings for power within the clergy. The unctuously ambitious and unpleasant chaplain, Mr Slope, is seen off at the end of '**Barchester Towers**'. Other memorably crafted characters include the Bishop's thrusting wife, Mrs Proudie, and Septimus Harding, the mild but troubled warden of 'Hiram's Hospital'. The sequence begins with '**The Warden**' (1855), and continues with '**Barchester Towers**' (1857), '**Dr Thorne**' (1858), '**Framley Parsonage**' (1861), '**The Small House at Allingham**' (1864) and '**The Last Chronicle of Barset**' (1867).

Trollope's second thematic group is the 'Palliser' novels, centring upon the political world of Plantagenet Palliser and his wife, Lady Glencora. (Trollope tried unsuccessfully for Parliament as a Liberal candidate in 1868.) The sequence is not written with the crusading zeal of a Dickens (Trollope regarded Thackeray as his master), but the novels quietly unpick the unscrupulousness of designing politicians. Palliser appears in each book of the series: '**Can You Forgive Her?**' (1864), '**Phineas Finn**' (1869), '**The Eustace Diamonds**' (1873), '**Phineas Redux**' (1876), '**The Prime Minister**' (1876) and '**The Duke's Children**' (1880).

Also of note is '**The Way We Live Now**', Trollope's satirical novel of 1875, which targets "the commercial profligacy of the age" and includes the monstrous figure of the corrupt financier, Augustus Melmotte.

Until his resignation in 1867, Trollope from 1834 worked for the London Post Office, eventually reaching a senior administrative level. (It was he who introduced the pillar-box.) Hence for over half of his literary life he was reconciling the needs of his art with the demands of the working day. The unpressured and leisurely feel of his prose was a hard-won skill.

Trollope's autobiography is still in print, and there are biographies by James Pope-Hennessey and R.H.Super.

71

The Brontes

Charlotte Bronte (1816–1855)
Emily Bronte (1818–1848)
Anne Bronte (1820–1849)

Haworth Parsonage today, despite alterations made since the early 1800s, still evokes the intensity of the isolation in which the imaginations of the Bronte sisters flourished. Overlooking the old graveyard and in close proximity to the wild moors, the small house was home for almost all of their lives. All three had brief and unhappy spells away at boarding schools – Emily especially was afflicted by homesickness – and neither Charlotte nor Anne settled well as governesses with distant families. Charlotte, who was the most outgoing of the three, spent some months studying languages in Brussels, where she was joined briefly by Emily. Unlike her sisters Charlotte developed a small circle of friends and correspondents, but after the tragically early deaths of Emily and Anne from tuberculosis life remained difficult and often lonely.

Haworth was their world. Their father, Patrick Bronte, took up the Church of England living at Haworth as perpetual curate in 1820. (His name was originally 'Brunty', which he changed in 1799 when his admired Lord Nelson was made Duke of Bronte.) His wife died in 1821, and her sister, Elizabeth Branwell, came to look after the household. There were two elder sisters, Maria and Elizabeth, whose deaths in 1825 are attributed to the conditions of the boarding school they attended, and one brother, Branwell, who died in 1848 after a troubled and directionless life of drink, opium, and adultery. In the face of her father's disapproval Charlotte in 1854 married his curate, but died while pregnant a few months later. Patrick Bronte, the last to survive of the stricken family, died in 1861.

As children the Brontes pursued a lively fantasy life of stories written up in tiny notebooks. Mr Bronte's present to Branwell of twelve wooden soldiers prompted a series of extensively detailed romances about imaginary countries and kingdoms, which nourished their appetite for fiction. They educated themselves in the wide range of literature and reviews available on their father's shelves. All wrote poetry. All felt bound to publish at first under male pseudonyms – Currer, Ellis and Acton Bell.

Charlotte Bronte

In 1845 Charlotte stumbled across Emily's poems, which prompted a joint edition of the three sisters' poetry in 1846. Virtually none were sold, and Charlotte turned to fiction. '**The Professor**', loosely based on her unreciprocated infatuation with the principal of the academy in Brussels, was written in 1847 but not published until 1858 after her death. Her triumph, '**Jane Eyre**', appeared in 1847; its success was immediate. '**Shirley**', set at the time of the Luddite riots in Yorkshire, was published in 1849, and her last novel, '**Villette**', also related to the Brussels experiences, appeared in 1853. Her first meeting with Elizabeth Gaskell in 1850 led to a strong friendship. She also met Thackeray and George Eliot's husband G.H.Lewes.

'**Jane Eyre**' is one of the first novels to convey sexual passion. Jane, a spirited and independent young girl, attends a restrictive and debilitating school, Lowood, which is no doubt based on Charlotte's own time at Cowan Bridge near Kirkby Lonsdale. She is appointed governess at Thornfield Hall to the illegitimate daughter of Mr Rochester, with whom she falls passionately in love.

Charlotte Bronte's narration – Jane's account presented in the first person – is strongly directed and emotionally open. In Chapter 18 we find Jane mistakenly under the impression that Rochester has designs on one of his house guests, Mary Ingram. Jane struggles with her feelings:

> *I have told you, reader, that I had learnt to love Mr Rochester: I could not unlove him now, merely because I found that he had ceased to notice me – because I might pass hours in his presence, and he would never once turn his eyes in my direction – because I saw all his attentions appropriated by a great lady, who scorned to touch me with the hem of her robes as she passed; who, if ever her dark and imperious eye fell on me by chance, would withdraw it instantly as from an object too mean to merit observation. I could not unlove him, because I felt sure he would soon marry this very lady – because I read daily in her a proud security in his intentions respecting her – because I witnessed hourly in him a style of courtship which, if careless and choosing rather to be sought than to seek, was yet, in its very carelessness, captivating, and in its very pride, irresistible.*

> *There was nothing to cool or banish love in these circumstances, though much to create despair. Much too, you will think, reader, to engender jealousy: if a woman, in my position, could presume to be jealous of a woman in Miss Ingram's. But I was not jealous: or very rarely; – the nature*

of the pain I suffered could not be explained by that word. Miss Ingram was a mark beneath jealousy: she was too inferior to excite the feeling. Pardon the seeming paradox; I mean what I say. She was very showy, but she was not genuine: she had a fine person, many brilliant attainments; but her mind was poor, her heart barren by nature: nothing bloomed spontaneously on that soil; no unforced natural fruit delighted by its freshness. She was not good; she was not original: she used to repeat sounding phrases from books: she never offered, nor had, an opinion of her own. She advocated a high tone of sentiment; but she did not know the sensations of sympathy and pity; tenderness and truth were not in her.

This is very revealing, both of Jane's emotional turmoil and of Charlotte Bronte's skills and values. Jane's intelligence, her frustrations, her amusing touches of self-deception (*"I was not jealous: or very rarely"*), her evident determination to let nothing stand in her way, and her almost wilful trick of interpreting things to her own disadvantage – all are brilliantly caught. And the second paragraph makes very clear Charlotte Bronte's evaluation of what should constitute character, and her implicit rejection of an inferior status for Jane or any other woman. Throughout '**Jane Eyre**' there is a sometimes unspoken assertion of feminine equality, and of a woman's right to her passions.

A further source of the novel's appeal has been the captivating enigma of Rochester, with his dark eyes, Byronic attractiveness, and hints of a secret past. The success with which Charlotte Bronte establishes the turbulent power of Jane's relationship with Rochester allows readers to overlook various improbabilities and coincidences in the plot. Some of its elements – such as the mad wife concealed in the attic, and the conflagration in which she perishes – would have seemed mere gothic melodrama had it not been for the emotional conviction with which the novel is handled.

(For an example of the kind of excess which Charlotte Bronte usually avoided, but which she has sometimes been criticised for, we may look briefly at the closing paragraphs of '**Villette**': *"That storm roared frenzied for seven days. It did not cease till the Atlantic was strewn with wrecks; it did not lull till the deeps had gorged their fill of sustenance. Not till the destroying angel of tempest had achieved his perfect work would he fold the wings whose waft was thunder, the tremor of whose plumes was storm. Peace; be still! Oh! a thousand weepers, praying in agony on waiting shores, listened for that voice; but it was not uttered…"* This is an inflated flourish, though in mitigation we perhaps may note that when Charlotte Bronte first saw the sea, she was moved to tears.)

Emily Bronte

Emily Bronte is celebrated for her only novel, '**Wuthering Heights**' (1847), and for her lyrical poetry – she was the best poet of the three. Charlotte described her poetry as "condensed and terse, vigorous and genuine". Her poems have a quality of tough self-sufficiency that also characterised her life.

> *But when the days of golden dreams had perished,*
> *And even Despair was powerless to destroy,*
> *Then did I learn how existence could be cherished,*
> *Strengthened, and fed without the aid of joy;*
>
> *Then did I check the tears of useless passion,*
> *Weaned my young soul from yearning after thine;*
> *Sternly denied its burning wish to hasten*
> *Down to that tomb already more than mine!*
>
> *And, even yet, I dare not let it languish,*
> *Dare not indulge in Memory's rapturous pain;*
> *Once drinking deep of that divinest anguish,*
> *How could I seek the empty world again?*   ('**Remembrance**')

We cannot be certain how autobiographical is the loss described here, but the words remain movingly powerful. In the last poem that she wrote, the consolations of faith are asserted with a lean and confident authority:

> *Though earth and man were gone,*
> *And suns and universes ceased to be,*
> *And thou were left alone,*
> *Every existence would exist in thee.*
>
> *There is not room for Death,*
> *Nor atom that his might could render void:*
> *Thou – thou art being and Breath,*
> *And what thou art may never be destroyed.*

One of the best commentators on '**Wuthering Heights**' was Charlotte. Using the metaphor of the novel as a statue hewn from a rock on the moors, she wrote:

> *With time and labour, the crag took human shape; and there it stands*
> *colossal, dark, and frowning, half-statue, half rock: in the former sense,*

terrible and goblin-like; in the latter, almost beautiful, for its colouring is of
mellow grey, and moorland moss clothes it; and heath, with its blooming
bells and balmy fragrance, grows faithfully close to the giant's foot.

Emily loved the moors in their wildness and bleakness. She loved them in all seasons, and Charlotte's comment usefully reminds us that the moods and settings of **'Wuthering Heights'** have their beauties as well as their darknesses. There is nevertheless something of primal myth about this story, with overtones that are stark and sinister. Over it, says Charlotte in her biographical note of 1850, there broods "a horror of great darkness…We seem at times to breathe lightning".

Heathcliff, the demonic figure with whom Catherine Earnshaw falls into a passionate and doomed love, causes the housekeeper Nelly Dean, one of Emily Bronte's narrators, to comment: *"I did not feel as if I were in the company of a creature of my own species".* But Heathcliff, unearthly and strange though he seems, is very much a tortured and destructive *human being.* It is one of Emily Bronte's masterstrokes that she uses as narrators Nelly Dean and Mr Lockwood, Heathcliff's tenant, neither of whom can comprehend the violent and cruel events that surround them. Elemental and terrifying forces appear to erupt from the depths of Heathcliff's very nature.

The novel is brilliantly plotted, with its two narrators, interweaving timeshifts, colourful and intense settings, and the contrasting worlds of Wuthering Heights and Thrushcross Grange and their two families. In Chapter 15, after an absence of three years, Heathcliff returns to find a seriously ill Catherine who is now married to Edgar Linton. He had left in the mistaken belief that she was abandoning him. Nelly Dean is the narrator:

With straining eagerness Catherine gazed towards the entrance of her
chamber. He did not hit the right room directly; she motioned me to admit
him; but he found it out, ere I could reach the door, and in a stride or two
was at her side, and had her grasped in his arms.

He neither spoke, nor loosed his hold for some five minutes, during which
period he bestowed more kisses than ever he gave in his life before, I dare
say; but then my mistress had kissed him first, and I plainly saw that he
could hardly bear, for downright agony, to look into her face! The same
conviction had stricken him as me, from the instant he beheld her, that
there was no prospect of ultimate recovery there – she was fated, sure to die.

"O Cathy! Oh, my life! How can I bear it?" was the first sentence he
uttered, in a tone that did not seek to disguise his despair.

And now he stared at her so earnestly that I thought the very intensity of his gaze would bring tears into her eyes; but they burned with anguish, they did not melt.

She taunts him bitterly for the sufferings he has caused her. He kneels on one knee to embrace her. She seizes his hair, keeps him down, and speaks of her imminent death.

"Don't torture me till I'm as mad as yourself," cried he, wrenching his head free, and grinding his teeth.

The two, to a spectator, made a strange and fearful picture. Well might Catherine deem that heaven would be a land of exile to her, unless, with her mortal body, she cast away her mortal character also. Her present countenance had a wild vindictiveness in its white cheek, and a bloodless lip, and scintillating eye; and she retained, in her closed fingers, a portion of the locks she had been grasping.

If we reduce this tableau to its elements, it would be easy to ridicule it as empty melodrama: the five-minute embrace, the charged language, the teeth grinding, the lock of hair, and so on. What is extraordinary about this extraordinary novel is that in context this scene and others like it assume a primitive and disturbing power. It is as if Catherine and Heathcliff are possessed, and there is a dark ambiguity about this love which is so full of hatred. The stylised simplicities of the scene are not those of melodrama, but of symbolism and myth.

'**Wuthering Heights**' had little success in Emily Bronte's brief lifetime. More recently it has developed an imaginative appeal which for many readers is paradoxically stronger insofar as the story defies rational explanation.

Anne Bronte

Anne, who was particularly close to Emily, perhaps achieved less than her two sisters. '**Agnes Grey**' (1847), clearly drawing on strands in Anne's own life, tells of a rector's daughter who becomes a governess. '**The Tenant of Wildfell Hall**' (1848) includes a character who is obviously based on her drunken brother Branwell. Charlotte Bronte thought it "a mistake".

We have to grant that Anne's work may not have become known at all were it not for her situation and the fame of her sisters. What is still truly remarkable is that the novels of the three were written at the same time in the same place within the same family, and that two of the most popular achievements in English literature came from that family in the same year.

Elizabeth Gaskell's biography of Charlotte is an interesting document, as is 'The Bronte Myth' by Lucasta Miller. There is also a biography by Lyndall Gordon. Emily's life has been written by Edward Chitham.

72
George Eliot (1819–1880)

The Nineteenth Century was a flourishing period for English novelists, and George Eliot is a supremely distinguished member of that company. (Oddly, perhaps, the pseudonym 'George Eliot' is still used, though we know her to have been Mary Ann Evans.) She is unrivalled in her especial strength of fine intellect deployed with searching compassion. Her characters are presented in convincing psychological depth. She places them securely within their times, tracing their attempts to shape their own destinies in the face of sometimes obstructive circumstances.

'Middlemarch'

'**Middlemarch**' (1871–72), her masterpiece, paints a superb picture of provincial Midlands society set in the period of agitation which preceded the 1832 Reform Act. The novel traces the detailed history of four marriages, interwoven with each other amid the wider panorama of the town and the countryside.

In Chapter 39, the central character Dorothea Brooke chides her uncle for his lacklustre and neglectful management of the estate he is responsible for. (Originally brought up in Mr Brooke's care, Dorothea is now unhappily married to an elderly pedantic scholar who cannot keep up with her youthful idealism.) Brooke tells her that he will never let himself be pushed around, but he has plans…

> *'Yes,' said Dorothea, with characteristic directness, ' Sir James* [the squire] *has been telling me that he is in hope of seeing a great change made soon in your management of the estate – that you are thinking of having the farms valued, and repairs made, and the cottages improved, so that Tipton may*

look quite another place. Oh, how happy!' – she went on, clasping her hands, with a return to that more childlike impetuous manner which had been subdued since her marriage. 'If I were at home still, I should take to riding again, that I might go about with you and see all that! And you are going to engage Mr Garth, who praised my [designs for] cottages, Sir James says.'

'Chettam is a little hasty, my dear,' said Mr Brooke, colouring slightly. 'A little hasty, you know. I never said I should do anything of the kind. I never said I should not do it, you know.'

'He only feels confident that you will do it,' said Dorothea, in a voice as clear and unhesitating as that of a young chorister chanting a credo, 'because you mean to enter Parliament as a member who cares for the improvement of the people, and one of the first things to be made better is the state of the land and the labourers. Think of Kit Downes, uncle, who lives with his wife and seven children in a house with one sitting-room and one bed-room hardly larger than this table! – and those poor Dagleys, in their tumble-down farmhouse, where they live in the back kitchen and leave the other rooms to the rats! That is one reason why I do not like the pictures here, dear uncle – which you think me stupid about. I used to come from the village with all that dirt and coarse ugliness like a pain within me, and the simpering pictures in the drawing-room seemed to me like a wicked attempt to find delight in what is false, while we don't mind how hard the truth is for the neighbours outside our walls. I think we have no right to come forward and urge wider changes for good, until we have tried to alter the evils which lie under our own hands.'

All this is beautifully captured – Brooke's ineffectual embarrassment, Dorothea's impassioned zeal tinged with impatient naivety, and the sense that she is alive with feeling here as she is not in her marriage – which, as George Eliot tells us, *"had been a perpetual struggle of energy with fear"*. The passage makes vivid the contrast between Brooke's grange and the farmhouses beyond. Dorothea's dislike of the *"simpering pictures in the drawing-room"* tellingly reflects George Eliot's own view that many contemporary paintings of rural scenes lied, in their cosmetic picturesqueness, about the ugly realities.

Another dimension to the novel is the responses to the young Dorothea of the men about her. Will Ladislaw, the cousin of Dorothea's husband, is present with Mr Brooke during this conversation. When she first enters the room his deep affection for her is clear:

...he started up as from an electric shock, and felt a tingling at his finger-ends. Any one observing him would have seen a change in his complexion, in the adjustment of his facial muscles, in the vividness of his glance, which might have made them imagine that every molecule in his body had passed the message of a magic touch. And so it had...Dorothea's entrance was the freshness of morning.

But after her outburst his emotions are subtly changed:

For the moment, Will's admiration was accompanied with a chilling sense of remoteness. A man is seldom ashamed of feeling that he cannot love a woman so well when he sees a certain greatness in her: nature having intended greatness for men. But nature has sometimes made sad oversights in carrying out her intentions; as in the case of good Mr Brooke, whose masculine consciousness was at this moment in rather a stammering condition under the eloquence of his niece.

The ironies here are subtly handled. Neither Will nor Brooke, in their different ways, can quite cope with an intelligent woman who speaks her own mind.

Later in the same chapter Mr Brooke visits Mr Dagley's farm in order to make a gentle point about Dagley's son having poached a leveret. George Eliot describes the distressed conditions of the farm – *"the very pigs and white ducks seeming to wander about the uneven neglected yard as if in low spirits from feeding on a too meagre quality of rinsings".* Dagley, fired by drink, unleashes a torrent of abuse at Brooke. The contrast with the earlier scene is compelling in its bleak revelation of Dagley's "midnight darkness".

'Adam Bede'

In her first full-length novel, **'Adam Bede'** (1859), George Eliot draws on the account her aunt, a Methodist preacher, had given her of a night she spent in the condemned cell of Nottingham gaol, accompanying a girl sentenced to death for the murder of her child. The novel works towards a climax in which Hetty Sorrel, similarly condemned, is visited by her comforter Dinah Morris, also a Methodist preacher.

After a moment's pause, Hetty lifted her head slowly and timidly from her knees, and raised her eyes. The two pale faces were looking at each other: one with a wild hard despair in it, the other full of sad, yearning love. Dinah unconsciously opened her arms and stretched them out.

'Don't you know me, Hetty? Don't you remember Dinah? Did you think I wouldn't come to you in trouble?'

Hetty kept her eyes fixed on Dinah's face — at first like an animal that gazes, and gazes, and keeps aloof.

'I'm come to be with you, Hetty — not to leave you — to stay with you — to be your sister to the last.'

Slowly, while Dinah was speaking, Hetty rose, took a step forward, and was clasped in Dinah's arms.

They stood so a long while, for neither of them felt the impulse to move apart again. Hetty, without any distinct thought of it, hung on this something that was come to clasp her now, while she was sinking helpless in a dark gulf; and Dinah felt a deep joy in the first sign that her love was welcomed by the wretched one. The light got fainter as they stood, and when at last they sat down on the straw pallet together, their faces had become indistinct.

Not a word was spoken. Dinah waited, hoping for a spontaneous word from Hetty; but she sat in the same dull despair, only clutching the hand that held hers, and leaning her cheek against Dinah's. It was the human contact she clung to, but she was not the less sinking into the dark gulf.

The power of this scene derives from George Eliot's restraint. The tableau is real and not contrived, and makes an interesting contrast with the deathbed scenes in Dickens, which he often heightens into theatrical melodrama.

We do not find in George Eliot the poetic fantasies of Dickens or the passionate romanticism of the Brontes. She writes with a controlled and sensitive realism. Her descriptions remind us of the delicate care in the paintings of the old Dutch masters, whose "truthfulness" she applauds in the narration of **'Adam Bede'**. Here, from that novel again, is the Poysers' dairy:

…such coolness, such purity, such fresh fragrance of new-pressed cheese, of firm butter, of wooden vessels perpetually bathed in pure water; such soft colouring of red earthenware, and creamy surfaces, brown wood and polished tin, grey limestone and rich orange-red rust on the iron weights and hooks and hinges.

Mary Ann Evans

'George Eliot' came from a cultivated background. As a child she learnt German, Italian and music. She read widely. In the early 1850s she became the partner of G.H.Lewes, philosopher, essayist, and scientist, until his death in 1878. (They were unable to marry as he had condoned the adultery of the wife from whom he had separated. It was, for the times, a notably unconventional arrangement.) In social and religious matters she became a free thinker, having rejected her early evangelicalism. Two years after Lewes' death she married John Walter Cross, but herself died within seven months and is buried beside him in Highgate Cemetery.

She started writing for London's 'Westminster Review', of which she became assistant editor in 1851. The first of her '**Scenes of Clerical Life**' appeared in 'Blackwood's Magazine' in 1857. '**Adam Bede**' was warmly received on its publication in 1859. It was closely followed by '**The Mill on the Floss**' (1860), '**Silas Marner**' (1861) and – following her visit to Florence – '**Romola**'. '**Felix Holt**' (1866) and '**Middlemarch**' (serially published in 1871–72), like '**The Mill on the Floss**', drew in part on her memories of childhood around the Warwickshire estate for which her father was the agent. The first part in particular of '**The Mill on the Floss**' is one of the most sensitive and joyous evocations we have of a country childhood. Her last great novel, '**Daniel Deronda**' (1874–76), in which a young English gentleman discovers his Jewishness, consolidated for many of her contemporaries her standing as the greatest living English novelist.

In the decades after her death there was some reaction against her novels, on the curious grounds that they were too thoughtful. Among her champions was Virginia Woolf, who in 1919 described '**Middlemarch**' as "one of the few English novels written for grown-up people".

There is a biography of George Eliot by Rosemary Ashton.

73

Matthew Arnold (1822–1888)

>–!◆→–O–←◆!–◄

"This iron time" – Arnold's description of his age (it comes in his memorial poem on Wordsworth) captures his sad disenchantment with high Victorian Britain. There were, he thought, two central wrongs: an unthinking and unspiritual materialism, which he called 'Philistinism'; and, related to this, a personal and national loss of religious certainty.

Arnold was one of the great Victorian 'thinkers'. The son of Dr Thomas Arnold, the famous headmaster of Rugby, he won the Newdigate Prize for poetry while at Balliol College, Oxford, and became a distinguished inspector of schools and – simultaneously – Professor of Poetry at Oxford. Like Wordsworth, whom he greatly admired, he wrote his best poetry when young. (Collected volumes were published in 1849, 1853 and 1867). His literary criticism advocated a quest for "the best that has been thought and said in the world" as an antidote to the cultural disarray of the times. (His influential essay '**Culture and Anarchy**' appeared in 1869.) He was *European* in his instincts.

His gravity can be forbidding, but the most attractive lyrics have a clarity and sometimes an intimacy that makes them moving in their honest dismay. '**Dover Beach**' is one of the great Victorian poems: some would say the greatest. Written partly on his honeymoon, it is a remarkable fusion of a love poem, a landscape (or seascape) and a brooding reflection on an unpromising world. We hear the simple strength of a troubled speaking voice:

> *The sea of faith*
> *Was once, too, at the full, and round earth's shore*
> *Lay like the folds of a bright girdle furl'd;*
> *But now I only hear*
> *Its melancholy, long, withdrawing roar,*
> *Retreating to the breath*
> *Of the night-wind down the vast edges drear*
> *And naked shingles of the world.*
>
> *Ah, love, let us be true*
> *To one another! For the world, which seems*
> *To lie before us like a land of dreams,*
> *So various, so beautiful, so new,*
> *Hath really neither joy, nor love, nor light,*
> *Nor certitude, nor peace, nor help for pain;*
> *And we are here as on a darkling plain*
> *Swept with confused alarms of struggle and flight,*
> *Where ignorant armies clash by night.*

That closing image is astonishingly dramatic, engulphing the two figures, as they gaze upon a tranquil moonlit sea, in a vision of apocalyptic disaster.

Arnold valued in Wordsworth his 'healing power', a joyful freshness of response to nature which the world has lost. He felt himself, meanwhile, to be

> *Wandering between two worlds, one dead,*
> *The other powerless to be born.*   ('**The Grande Chartreuse**')

"Genuine poetry", Arnold wrote, "is conceived and composed in the soul". His limpid and solemn sadness cannot easily be taken in large quantities, but at his best he disarms us.

There is a biography of Arnold by Nicholas Murray.

Towards the Turn of the Century

74

The Beginnings of Crime Fiction

Wilkie Collins (1824–1889)
Arthur Conan Doyle (1859–1930)

The first significant appearance of an investigating policeman in English fiction is that of Inspector Bucket in Dickens' **'Bleak House'**. The first full-length crime fiction came within the next twenty years from **Wilkie Collins**. He wrote twenty novels (not all of them crime mysteries) of which the best remembered are two: **'The Woman in White'** (1860) and **'The Moonstone'**(1868).

Both are told through the various narrative voices of eye-witnesses to strange events. **'The Woman in White'** tells a sinister tale of murder, switched identities, and the haunting figure of the title, an escapee from a mental asylum. **'The Moonstone'** centres on a diamond stolen from a Hindu shrine at the siege of Seringapatam. Like **'The Woman in White'**, it succeeds through a particularly ingenious plot, powerful atmospherics, and skilful suspense. The melancholy but sharp Sergeant Cuff is the first of the long line of characterful policemen that stretches down to Colin Dexter's Morse, Ruth Rendell's Wexford, and P.D.James' Dalgliesh.

Collins trained as a lawyer, though he never practised. He was a close friend of Dickens, with whom he collaborated as a frequent contributor to **'Household Words'** and **'All The Year Round'**, in which both novels were serialised. Sales were strong in the 1860s, but Collins' popularity and powers waned thereafter – maybe because of his growing addiction to laudanum, and the death of Dickens in 1870.

Sir Arthur Conan Doyle's Sherlock Holmes makes his first appearance in **'A Study in Scarlet'** in 1887. This was followed by a series of short stories in **'The Strand Magazine'** from 1891, which launched the huge popularity of this unconventional private detective, gifted with lightning lateral thinking. Conan Doyle's attempt to kill off Holmes caused a public outcry. And the characterisation was so convincingly rounded that many readers have assumed him to be a real person. (He was possibly modelled on Dr Joseph Bell, who lectured on medicine to Conan Doyle when he was a student at Edinburgh University.) The myth has bred its own legends: Conan Doyle never actually wrote the words *Elementary, my dear Watson*.

Next in the tradition was G.K.Chesterton's unassuming Catholic priest, Father Brown. '**The Innocence of Father Brown**' (1911) became the first of a series. In the 1920s and 1930s crime fiction evolved into the 'whodunnit'. **Agatha Christie** owed her success to the ingenuity of her puzzles: her stories are largely devoid of characterisation and style. Writing more interestingly, **Dorothy Sayers** developed her Lord Peter Wimsey into a rounded figure: '**The Nine Tailors**' is one of the best 1930s crime stories.

Crime fiction as a largely Anglo-American genre (with the Belgian **Simenon** a notable exception) has long since broken free from the artificial settings which dominated in the inter-war years. Occasionally, despite self-imposed restrictions in scope, it reaches the heights of the best mainstream fiction.

There have been a number of biographies of Conan Doyle, among the most recent those by Daniel Stashower and Hesketh Pearson.

75

The Pre-Raphaelites and After

Dante Gabriel Rossetti (1828–1882)

Christina Rossetti (1830–1894)

Algernon Charles Swinburne (1837–1909)

>-+-<+>-+-O-+-<+-+-<

In the 1840s a group of poets, painters and critics banded together in rebellion against the ugliness of modern life as they saw it, and specifically the style and values of conventional Victorian painting, the tradition stemming from Sir Joshua Reynolds, and the veneration of Raphael as the greatest of artists. The 'Pre-Raphaelite Brotherhood' valued more highly the pre-Renaissance painters of Fourteenth Century Italy. In technique they were to put a strong emphasis on bright intensity of colour and freshness of detail, especially in the decorative use of flowers and plants; thematically they were drawn to ethereal beauty, mystical and religious subjects, occult symbolism and medievalism. The Brotherhood, founded in 1848, was dissolved in the 1850s, but its influence lived on.

The Rossettis were the children of an Italian patriot who had come to England in 1824. **Dante Gabriel** was one of the founders of the movement, together with his mentors, the painters Sir John Millais and Holman Hunt. His sister **Christina** was briefly engaged to the painter James Collinson, one of three other foundation members.

Throughout his life, in addition to painting, **Dante Gabriel** wrote poetry – technically accomplished, but vague and over-indulged in its search for purity of sensation. His best-known poem, '**The Blessed Damozel**', mixes the erotic and the divine with a strange preciousness:

> *And still she bowed herself and stooped*
> *Out of the circling charm;*
> *Until her bosom must have made*
> *The bar she leaned on warm,*
> *And the lilies lay as if asleep*
> *Along her bended arm.*

Christina was the better poet, though her elegiac themes range narrowly over tragic love and death. Her predominant note is wistful sadness, as in *"When I am dead, my dearest, / Sing no sad songs for me"* and in the sonnet *"Remember me when I am gone away, / Gone far away into the silent land"*. We also owe to her the words that have become the carol *"In the bleak midwinter"*.

A number of other poets shared in these trends: **Coventry Patmore** (1823–1896); **William Allingham** who wrote *'The Fairies'* (1824–1889); **George Meredith** (1828–1909); and **William Morris** (1834–1896), who favoured medievalism in his poetry, but is better known as a pioneer of socialism and a champion of fine craftwork in furniture, fabrics, wallpaper and stained glass.

Swinburne, while an undergraduate at Balliol, became friendly with Rossetti and his Pre-Raphaelite associates who were engaged in painting with frescoes the walls of the Oxford Union (unsuccessfully, as the walls had not been properly prepared). He followed their rebellious stance and adopted many of their aesthetic principles. However, while he was a versatile and skilled poet, with a huge output, his work descends into decadent artificiality – poetry with no end other than itself. Elements of paganism, atheism, and lush sexuality in his poems offended Victorian middle class taste, and like the Pre-Raphaelites themselves, he was attacked for immorality.

There is a biography of D.G.Rossetti by Jan Marsh.

76
Lewis Carroll (1832–1898)

Charles Lutwidge Dodgson (alias Lewis Carroll) lectured in Mathematics at Christ Church, Oxford, from 1855. He had the kind of mind that enjoyed all kinds of puzzles: logic games, board games, acrostics and numbers, puns and paradoxes.

His two famous 'Alice' books (**'Alice in Wonderland'**, 1865, and **'Through The Looking Glass'**, 1871) came like a breath of fresh air into the world of children's books because they had no moral and did not moralise. They began life as fantasies improvised to entertain the three young daughters of the Dean of Christ Church during a series of boating trips on the Isis. Later Dodgson wrote them down, expanded them, and dedicated them to Alice Liddell, who was ten at the time. (The Alice of the stories is seven.) **'The Hunting of the Snark'**, a long nonsense poem of 1876, is the best survivor of his other writings.

'Alice in Wonderland' (originally 'Alice Under Ground') introduces the imperishable comedy of the Mad Hatter's tea party and the Lobster Quadrille, and a host of unforgettably zany characters such as the March Hare and the King and Queen of Hearts. **'Through the Looking Glass'** creates a back-to-front mirror image world in which Dodgson's love for inversions and chop logic flourishes. There is a kind of twinkling sense in the nonsense which distinguishes it from Edward Lear's dreamy diversions. Along the way, as in 'Wonderland', there are parodies of songs and poems, and the brilliantly inventive **'Jabberwocky'**, one of the finest nonsense poems in the language.

Martin Gardner's **'The Annotated Alice'** is the definitive modern edition, with scores of unobtrusively entertaining footnotes. It includes **'The Wasp in a Wig'**, first published in 1977, which was originally set in type as part of 'Through the Looking Glass', but deleted by Dodgson at the last minute at the suggestion of his illustrator Tenniel, who couldn't see the point of it.

Dodgson was particularly shy, had a severe stammer, and never married. His fondness for the innocent company of young girls has excited various psychological theories. Meanwhile the Alice books have been phenomenally successful in many languages. He would have enjoyed the conundrum of how one sets about translating nonsense into nonsense.

There is a biography by Stephanie Lovett Stoffel. Also see 'In The Shadow of the Dreamchild' by Karoline Leach.

77
Thomas Hardy (1840–1928)

"What I value most in Hardy", said W.H.Auden, "is his hawk's vision, his way of looking at life from a very great height." It is his huge perspectives of time and landscape that give Hardy's novels and poetry their characteristic feel of man's tiny destinies being played out against a vast and indifferent backdrop. Some readers have reacted against what they perceive as Hardy's gloomy pessimism. He lost his Christian faith in early life, and there is always that sense in Hardy that hope has to be balanced against the prospect of disappointment, and that love and ambition may be thwarted or unfulfilled.

Nevertheless, that which is pessimism to some is realistic resignation to others. Hardy values stoical fortitude, and the wry adaptability he found in rural life. He admired what he called "that curious, mechanical regularity of country people in the face of hopelessness". There is a warm regard for the rootedness of a man who is at one with his work and his place. At the same time, and increasingly in his later work, Hardy records the increasing difficulties of maintaining that rooted security. He is partly reflecting a social change – the vanishing during the Nineteenth Century of a particular style of rural living – and partly responding to broody unhappinesses in his own life.

Dorset, where he was born (at Higher Bockhampton, near Dorchester) was the county he made his own, and the wider south-west of 'Wessex' the setting for most of his fiction and his poetry. His father was a master mason, and Hardy trained locally as an architect. After a spell in London, he returned to an architectural practice in Dorchester in 1867. The next year, while surveying the church at St Juliot in Cornwall, he met Emma Gifford whom he was to marry seven years later. Apart from brief spells in London, Dorset was their home – in Swanage, Sturminster Newton, Wimborne and finally Dorchester. It was not a happy marriage, and when Emma died in 1912 it left Hardy racked with guilt and grief, and produced in **Poems of 1912–13** one of the most remarkable collections of love poems in the language. He was married again, to Florence Dugdale, in 1914. After his death, Florence's name appeared as the author of his biography, though in fact Hardy wrote it himself.

The novels

Hardy loved stories, particularly those old country stories of passion, betrayal and tragedy reminiscent of the ancient ballads. He wrote in his notebooks: "Though a good deal is too strange to be believed, nothing is too strange to have happened". This is the spirit in which the twists and coincidences of his plots have to be seen.

The sequence of his major novels begins with '**Under The Greenwood Tree**' in 1872, and continues with '**Far From The Madding Crowd**' (1874) – which was sufficiently successful to enable him to give up architecture for full-time writing – '**The Return of the Native**' (1878), '**The Mayor of Casterbridge**' (1886), '**The Woodlanders**' (1887), '**Tess of the D'Urbervilles**' (1891) and '**Jude The Obscure**' in 1896. '**Wessex Tales**' (1888) is a collection of short stories. Of his shorter pieces, '**The Withered Arm**' and '**Tryst at an Ancient Earthwork**' are especially attractive.

The novels do not moralise: Hardy called his 'philosophy' but 'a confused heap of impressions'. What we find, darkening as the sequence proceeds, is the progressive and tragic isolation of each of the central characters. This process is partly the result of social forces: Henchard, the mayor of Casterbridge, yielding to a 'new' agriculture which he does not understand; Tess, in '**Tess of the D'Urbervilles**', the victim of a destructive hostility to 'fallen women'; Sue and Jude, social outcasts because they are not married. In parallel to these external threats, the characters suffer emotional turmoil which Hardy explores with great psychological sensitivity. And beyond all this there is the timeless continuity of nature, sometimes restorative and sometimes ungiving – like Egdon Heath in '**The Return of the Native**', which is "a face on which time makes but little impression".

We find also in Hardy an attempt to treat aspects of sexuality which the conventions of the time were not ready for. '**Jude the Obscure**' in particular outraged some sections of society. One bishop publicly burned it. Hardy wrote no more novels.

Within this difficult context, nevertheless, Hardy creates episodes of real beauty and joy. Tess is one of the very few fictional characters of innocent goodness who is not insipid or unconvincing. She is "a mere vessel of emotion untinctured by experience". There is a fine description of her on a summer evening, approaching the window of an attic in which Angel Clare, with whom she is falling in love, is playing the harp:

> *The outskirt of the garden in which Tess found herself had been left*
> *uncultivated for some years, and was now damp and rank with juicy grass*
> *which sent up mists of pollen at a touch; and with tall blooming weeds*
> *emitting offensive smells – weeds whose red and yellow and purple hues*

formed a polychrome as dazzling as that of cultivated flowers. She went stealthily as a cat through this profusion of growth, gathering cuckoo-spittle on her skirts, cracking snails that were underfoot, staining her hands with thistle-milk and slug-slime, and rubbing off upon her naked arms sticky blights which, though snow-white on the apple-tree trunks, made madder stains on her skin; thus she drew quite near to Clare, still unobserved of him.

Tess was conscious of neither time nor space. The exaltation which she had described as being producible at will by gazing at a star, came now without any determination of hers; she undulated upon the thin notes of the second-hand harp, and their harmonies passed like breezes through her, bringing tears into her eyes.

The last chapter of 'Tess' is a masterpiece of tragic stillness. Tess's death, anticipated throughout the novel, is part of a seemingly inevitable process of growth through suffering. She is not crushed: she dies happy.

The poems

Hardy thought of himself as primarily a poet. He wrote over 900 poems, which are extraordinarily consistent in style. The first published volume, 'Wessex Poems', appeared in 1898, and was followed by seven further collections.

The poems display his acute visual eye, his shrewd wisdom, and his sardonic humour. He notes the harsher ironies of existence, and the poetry occasionally reflects, though it does not always directly describe, the melancholy and pain of his personal life. Some poems have a cosmic scale (like 'At A Lunar Eclipse' or 'The Convergence of the Twain', which relates to the sinking of 'The Titanic'); others are close to the detail of nature ('The Darkling Thrush'; 'Weathers'). Some have a ballad-like narrative ('The Trampwoman's Tragedy'), others dwell on a single moment ('I Look Into My Glass'). Everywhere we notice Hardy's mastery of a speaking voice, expressed in a virtuoso range of subtle rhythms and modulations.

'At Castle Boterel' is characterisic of Hardy at his best. One of the anguished and nostalgic poems released by Emma's death, it shows Hardy remembering a moment years back when he and Emma walked up a hill near 'Castle Boterel' (Boscastle) in Cornwall. He revisits the scene in the rain, an old man aware that he will never repeat the visit. He and Emma were part of the transitory history of the place, long since erased by "Time's unflinching rigour". Now he sees a vision of her, but receding as his wagonette carries him away.

I look and see it there, shrinking, shrinking,
  I look back at it amid the rain
For the very last time; for my sand is sinking,
  And I shall traverse old love's domain
    Never again.

Hardy's poetry too is unflinching, and unsentimental when wounded. Perhaps surprisingly, it was little regarded in his own time.

When in a group of people, Hardy enjoyed pretending that he wasn't really there, but watching like a kind of ghost. That tells us a great deal about the nature of his artistic vision.

In addition to the 'biography' by Florence Hardy, there is a study of Hardy's life and work by F.E.Halliday. See also 'Thomas Hardy – Behind the Inscrutable Smile' by Andrew Norman. Editions of Hardy's novels and poems are published by Macmillan, Penguin, Everyman and Wordsworth.

78
Gerard Manley Hopkins
(1844–1889)

In his notebook for September, 1870, Hopkins records his experience of first sighting the Northern Lights. He is awestruck by this "busy working of nature independent of the earth", which is separated from human time. The spectacle is "like a new witness to God". It "filled me," he writes, "with delightful fear."

Having got a First in Classics at Oxford, Hopkins joined the novitiate of the Society of Jesus in 1868, and was ordained in 1877. His poems were in effect celebratory prayers, many only written when authorised by his superiors, and circulated in letters to his friends. None were published in his lifetime.

For Hopkins true poetry was the language of divine inspiration, a capturing of "delightful fear", as distinct from poetry which was merely a decoration of prose thought. (The latter was what he found in the worst of Wordsworth and Tennyson.) To write this inspired poetry Hopkins broke with poetic conventions in remarkable ways, developing new kinds of rhythms, words and word-combinations. His mission was to capture the live energy of God's revelation, especially in the beauties of the natural world, as in the opening of '**Pied Beauty**':

> *Glory be to God for dappled things -*
> *For skies of coupled-colour as a brinded cow;*
> *For rose-moles all in stipple upon trout that swim;*
> *Fresh-firecoal chestnut-falls; finches' wings;*
> *Landscape plotted and pieced – fold, fallow, and plough;*
> *And all trades, their gear and tackle and trim.*

More complicatedly, '**The Windhover**' in its surging rhythms identifies the beauty of the bird's flight with a vision of Christ:

> *I caught this morning morning's minion, kingdom of daylight's dauphin,*
> *dapple-dawn-drawn Falcon, in his riding*
> *Of the rolling level underneath him steady air, and striding*
> *High there, how he rung upon the rein of a wimpling wing*
> *In his ecstasy! Then off, off forth on swing,*
> *As a skate's heel sweeps smooth on a bow-bend: the hurl and gliding*
> *Rebuffed the big wind. My heart in hiding*
> *Stirred for a bird – the achieve of, the mastery of the thing!*

This kind of writing, when it was finally published in 1918 by Hopkins' friend the poet Robert Bridges, was extraordinarily modern, appearing as it did at a time when the forms of poetry were changing radically – in 1918 T.S.Eliot's poetry was already appearing. There is a difficulty in Hopkins: at his most intense the words begin to collapse under the pressure of what he intends. If the meaning is beyond words, the words and the meaning cannot finally fuse. But it is worth persevering with his unique and rewarding voice.

*Try particularly '**Hurrahing in Harvest**', '**God's Grandeur**', '**Felix Randal**', '**Harry Ploughman**', '**The Starlight Night**', the two sonnets '**No worse there is none**' and '**Thou art indeed just, Lord**', and the long poem '**The Wreck of the Deutschland**', written after the drowning of five Franciscan nuns in the Thames estuary in 1875.*

*'**Landscape and Inscape**', by Peter Milward with photographs by Raymond Schoder, is a helpful commentary on Hopkins' life and poetry.*

79

Oscar Wilde (1854–1900)

'**The Importance of Being Earnest**' (1895), one of the most dazzlingly brilliant comedies in the language, is wholly frivolous entertainment. The language and the plot are delightfully ingenious, and the behaviour of the high society characters is elegantly absurd. (The forbiddingly preposterous Lady Bracknell, one of the great comic characters, is a grande dame so amusingly ridiculous that her bombast threatens no-one.) The play is a dance of wit. In this extract, Jack Worthing and Algernon Moncrieff fence verbally as they discuss the deceptions they have invented to pursue their courtships. Algernon has devised a fictitious country friend called Bunbury, whose 'illnesses' give him the excuse to pursue his fancies out of town.

Jack	*This ghastly state of things is what you call Bunburying, I suppose?*
Algy	*Yes, and a perfectly wonderful Bunbury it is. The most wonderful Bunbury I ever had in my life.*
Jack	*Well, you've no right whatsoever to Bunbury here.*
Algy	*That is absurd. One has a right to Bunbury anywhere one chooses. Every serious Bunburyist knows that.*
Jack	*Serious Bunburyist! Good heavens!*
Algy	*Well, one must be serious about something, if one wants to have any amusement in life. I happen to be serious about Bunburying. What on earth you are serious about I haven't got the remotest idea. About everything, I should fancy. You have such an absolutely trivial nature.*
Jack	*Well, the only small satisfaction I have in the whole of this wretched business is that your friend Bunbury is quite exploded. You won't be able to run down to the country quite so often as you used to do, dear Algy. And a very good thing too.*
Algy	*Your brother is a little off colour, isn't he, dear Jack? You won't be able to disappear to London quite so frequently as your wicked custom was. And not a bad thing either.*
Jack	*As for your conduct towards Miss Cardew, I must say that your taking in a sweet, simple, innocent girl like that is quite inexcusable. To say nothing of the fact that she is my ward.*
Algy	*I can see no possible defence at all for your deceiving a brilliant, clever, thoroughly experienced young lady like Miss Fairfax. To say nothing of the fact that she is my cousin.*

| Jack | *I wanted to be engaged to Gwendolen, that is all. I love her.* |
| Algy | *Well, I simply wanted to be engaged to Cecily. I adore her.* |

Wilde's comedy here is built on the epigrams, on the parallels between the two men's situations, and on the balancing symmetries of their words. The play generates a sequence in which seemingly unanswerable 'last words' are wittily capped, and seemingly deadlocked situations escaped from.

'**The Importance of Being Earnest**' was appropriately Oscar Wilde's greatest success, for it perfectly accords with his often-repeated view that exquisite style is the only end of art. *"Art never expresses anything but itself"* he wrote in '**The Decay of Lying**' (1891); *"There is no such thing as a moral or immoral book. Books are well-written or badly written. That is all"* he declared in his preface to '**The Picture of Dorian Gray**' (1891).

There is of course an element of deliberate provocation in such statements. Wilde's favourite form of wit, the epigram or paradox, depends on reversing expectation and challenging orthodoxy. Like Byron, he cultivated an image of himself as independent of convention. *"I have put my genius into my life; all I have put into my works is my talent,"* he said to André Gide. As an Oxford undergraduate he wore velvet knee breeches and collected peacocks' feathers and blue china. He embraced the late Nineteenth Century **aesthetic movement** (a successor to the Pre-Raphaelite Brotherhood) whose adherents fostered an art-for-art's sake philosophy and a lifestyle that appeared decadent and offensive to mainstream taste.

Born in Dublin, Wilde attended Trinity College before he went to Oxford, where he won the Newdigate poetry prize. He was a fine classicist. Before he achieved success as a dramatist, he wrote poetry and fairy stories. (The tales in '**The Happy Prince**' of 1888, though said to be written for his two sons – he was married in 1884 – are in fact rather grim allegories, appropriate he said for "childlike people from 18 to 80".)

The winning series of comedies began in 1892 with '**Lady Windermere's Fan**', continuing with '**A Woman of No Importance**' (1893) and '**An Ideal Husband**' (1895). '**The Importance of Being Earnest**' was three months into its run when Wilde was jailed for two years for homosexual offences. His trial was precipitated by his failed libel action against the Marquess of Queensbury. Queensbury had publicly pilloried Wilde, angry at Wilde's association with his son, Lord Alfred Douglas. '**The Ballad of Reading Gaol**' (1898) reveals a different, compassionate and disturbed side to Wilde. The poem is centred on the hanging of a murderer during Wilde's time in prison, but the line *'Yet each man kills the thing he loves'* is probably an embittered reference to Douglas. Wilde went to France upon his release. A broken man, he died in Paris.

There are biographies by H.Montgomery Hyde, Barbara Belford and Richard Ellman. Also of interest is 'The Secret Life of Oscar Wilde' by Neil McKeane.

80

Drama at the Turn of the Century

Arthur Wing Pinero (1855–1934)

George Bernard Shaw (1856–1950)

John Galsworthy (1867–1933)

John Millington Synge (1871–1909)

❯━╋━❯━O━❮━╋━❰

In the 1890s **Shaw**, Dublin-born but now in London, was writing articles condemning the artificiality of the London theatre, and campaigning for plays that dealt with contemporary social problems. (In this he was much influenced by his Norwegian contemporary **Henrik Ibsen**, though as we can now see he took a very one-sided view of that great dramatist.)

An early move in this direction was made by **Pinero**, who attempted to create a tragic mood in '**The Second Mrs Tanqueray**' (1893). The play centres on the respectably married Paula Tanqueray, who commits suicide after confessing that her step-daughter has become engaged to her own father, Paula's seducer. With his 'social problem' plays, particularly focused on the plight of women, Pinero tried to keep a toehold in a theatre that was changing with the new ideas, but ironically he is best remembered for his comedies and farces. He did not have Wilde's gifts of language, but the strong situational comedy of '**The Magistrate**' (1885) and '**Trelawny of the Wells**' (1898) has ensured a long life for both plays.

Meanwhile Shaw's free-thinking socialism, embracing women's rights and the abolition of private property, led him to dramatise conflicts of ideas in such plays as '**Man and Superman**' (1903) and '**Major Barbara**' (1907). 'Man and Superman' debates his idea that humanity needed a willed act of determination to evolve beyond war and disease – he called it the 'Life Force' – but the surreal Act Three which develops this was omitted from the first London production, which concentrated on the surrounding comedy of the pursuit by a 'New Woman' of a 'New Man'. 'Major Barbara' uses the contexts of the Salvation Army and an armaments factory to dramatise the tensions between spiritual and material values.

Shaw's problem was that despite his wit his plays are too cerebral: he tends to dramatise ideas rather than people. He had more success with the relatively lighter

'Androcles and the Lion' and 'Pygmalion' (both 1913), and the popular dramatic treatment of 'Saint Joan' (1923). These were nevertheless more substantial than many popular diversions of the pre-war theatre, such as the dramatisation of **James Barrie**'s 'Peter Pan' of 1904.

Galsworthy also wrote plays which handled the iniquities of conventional attitudes and practices (which he would pursue in his Forsyte Saga novels of the 1920s). In the solidly-structured dramas of '**The Silver Box**' (1906), '**Strife**' (1909) and '**Justice**' (1910) he deals respectively with problems of crime and the poor, industry, and the law's inhumanities.

In contrast the Abbey Theatre in Dublin, which opened in 1904 with **Yeats**, **Synge** and **Lady Gregory** as directors from 1906, was the venue for an exciting renaissance of poetic drama. The most durable work came from Synge. He had spent the summers of 1898 to 1902 studying the way of life in the Aran Islands, and realised the lyrical and tragic possibilities there might be in adapting the islanders' modes of speech. His one-act '**Riders to the Sea**' (1904) memorably presents the desolate tragedy of Maurya. Lonely in her cottage by the shore, she learns that her last son has followed her other four sons, her father and her grandfather in perishing in the waves. '**The Playboy of the Western World**' (1907) is a delightful, whimsical comedy. It provoked riots on its first performances in Dublin and New York because of its allegedly insulting portrayal of the Irish peasantry, and a mention of girls' "shifts" too indelicate for the times.

There is a biography of Shaw by Michael Holroyd.

The Twentieth Century and After

"It took me nearly ten years to learn that I couldn't write."
"I suppose you gave it up then?"
"Oh, no! By that time I had a reputation established."

PUNCH, 1924

81
Joseph Conrad (1857–1924)

At the age of 23 Conrad spoke fluent French in addition to his native Polish. He knew no English, and started then to learn it. Fifteen years later, remarkably, he published his first novel in English and went on to become a major figure in the English literary tradition.

He was born into the Polish aristocracy as Jozef Konrad Korzeniowski. Both his parents were dead by the time he was 11 and he was brought up by an uncle. The sea was in his blood, and was to become a mainspring of his fiction. His early life was in turn colourful, adventurous and stressful. He travelled the world on cargo boats, becoming especially familiar with the Far East and Africa. (He was to use his experience of sailing a river steamer in the Belgian Congo in the 1902 story '**Heart of Darkness**'.) At one point he got involved in gun-running. He attempted suicide. He sailed in French vessels before adopting English ships in 1878. In 1886 he was awarded his Master's certificate and became a British citizen. In 1896 he married and settled near Canterbury.

His themes are sombre: man's vulnerable attempts to shape his own destiny are seen as threatened by corruption, with man either resisting evil or succumbing to it. In one of his finest novels, '**Nostromo**' (1904), we find the following characteristic exchange:

> *"That man is calmness personified…He must be extremely sure of himself."*
> *"If that's all he is sure of, then he is sure of nothing," said the doctor. "It is the last thing a man ought to be sure of."*

Conrad's settings are sometimes maritime and sometimes political. They include an imaginary South American republic in the epic '**Nostromo**'; Russia and the world of Russian emigrés in Geneva in '**Under Western Eyes**' (1911); and revolutionary anarchists in contemporary London in '**The Secret Agent**' (1907). His characters often lead lives which are lonely and morally bleak. In '**The Heart of Darkness**' the narrator Marlow tells of his increasingly disturbing and nightmarish voyage to reach a seriously ill ivory trader in the heart of colonial Africa. This man turns out to be a figure of diabolical cruelty. Marlow's journey has reached the darkest areas of the human soul. As he finishes his tale he looks from his drifting boat towards the Thames estuary: *"…and the tranquil waterway leading to the uttermost ends of the earth flowed sombre under an overcast sky – seemed to lead into the heart of an immense darkness".*

This kind of symbolism is typical. Conrad's technique is not to tell a conventional story in which description and commentary make everything clear. He makes use of symbolic and poetic suggestiveness. There are time shifts. Different characters and narrators present different points of view. In all this he speaks to our sub-conscious. His aim, he wrote, was *"to address the secret springs of responsive emotions"*.

As an example of Conrad's masterfully controlled power, we might take, from '**The Secret Agent**', the murder of the double-agent Mr Verloc by his long-suffering wife:

> *'Come here,' he said in a peculiar tone, which might have been the tone of brutality, but was intimately known to Mrs Verloc as the note of wooing.*

> *She started forward at once, as if she were still a loyal woman bound to that man by an unbroken contract. Her right hand skimmed slightly the end of the table, and when she had passed on towards the sofa the carving knife had vanished without the slightest sound from the side of the dish. Mr Verloc heard the creaky plank in the floor, and was content. He waited. Mrs Verloc was coming…He was lying on his back and staring upwards. He saw partly on the ceiling and partly on the wall the moving shadow of an arm with a clenched hand holding a carving knife. It flickered up and down. Its movements were leisurely. They were leisurely enough for Mr Verloc to recognise the limb and the weapon.*

> *They were leisurely enough for him to take in the full meaning of the portent, and to taste the flavour of death rising in his gorge. His wife had gone raving mad – murdering mad. They were leisurely enough for the first paralysing effect of this discovery to pass away before a resolute determination to come out victorious from the ghastly struggle with that armed lunatic. They were leisurely enough for Mr Verloc to elaborate a plan of defence involving a dash behind the table, and the felling of the woman to the ground with a heavy wooden chair. But they were not leisurely enough to allow Mr Verloc the time to move either hand or foot. The knife was already planted in his breast. It met no resistance on its way. Hazard has such accuracies.*

We look for the moment when the murder actually happens – and we do not find it. And Conrad is not simply teasing us. The way in which the plunge of the knife creeps up on us (and on Mr Verloc) refocuses our attention on the ironies in the situation: that this arrogant and seemingly untouchable man is actually very vulnerable; that his murder enigmatically seems both inevitable and the product of chance; that, tragically, Winnie Verloc has come to be sucked into the criminality which was his world, and which – as we see in the wider story – led to the death of her brother, which she now avenges.

For further reading in Conrad, try 'Lord Jim' (1900); the short stories 'Youth' and 'Typhoon' (1902); 'Chance' (1913) – his first financial success; and 'Victory' (1915). There is a biography of Conrad by Norman Sherry.

82
Contrasts in Englishness

A.E.Housman (1859–1936)
Rudyard Kipling (1865–1936)

Housman's poetry was enormously popular at the time of the First World War. (First a clerk at the London Patent Office, he was Professor of Latin at London University from 1892, and then at Cambridge from 1911.) His 67 poems in **'A Shropshire Lad'** (1896) are set in a nostalgically-created pastoral shire which is largely a fantasy world. It is inhabited by ploughmen, milkmaids, and soldiers going to the wars. The simple lyric forms offer lines which are stark and often memorable. Housman had a gift for musicality.

> *Into my heart an air that kills*
> *From yon far country blows*
> *What are those blue remembered hills*
> *What spires, what farms are those?*
>
> *That is the land of lost content,*
> *I see it shining plain,*
> *The happy highways where I went*
> *And cannot come again.* ('Blue Remembered Hills')

There is a sense of pessimism and pain that is not explicitly rooted in recognisable experience (unlike Hardy's poetry). Many of the poems have a rather cloying approach, a self-indulged loneliness. But they can be at the least interesting because they spoke so strongly in their day, and there is still a sad power in poems such as **'Epitaph on an Army of Mercenaries'** and **'Is My Team Ploughing?'**

The writings of Housman's contemporary **Rudyard Kipling** were also extremely popular. Both were of their time, but in quite different ways. Kipling is cosmopolitan as Housman is provincial. He grew up in India until the age of 6, and returned from London to India as a journalist for seven years in his twenties. He married an American and lived in Vermont for two years before settling in Sussex in 1896. He travelled extensively, especially in South Africa. He was the first Englishman to receive, in 1907, the Nobel Prize for Literature.

Kipling loved India – his novel '**Kim**' (1901) celebrates the life of the continent. He coined the phrase *"the white man's burden"*, but he is not the crude imperial jingoist he has often been painted. His poem '**Recessional**' (1897), which became a kind of Empire hymn, called for an allegiance to Christian duty to replace power mania. The perspective he usually adopts is that of the civil servant or ordinary soldier, of dedicated responsibilities well managed. There are in Kipling words and sentiments which grate now, but in '**Barrack-Room Ballads**' (1892) particularly we find poems that can still impress in their vigorous and satirical championing of the rank and file. The robust colloquial rhythms – Cockney, Scottish and Irish – owe much to the traditions of music hall and street ballad. Poems like '**Mandalay**' and '**Danny Deever**' are essentially Kipling's impersonations of a popular entertainer, brilliantly done.

There is another quite different Kipling in quieter poems like '**The Way Through The Woods**', whose nostalgia is wholly unsentimental (unlike Housman's):

> *Yet, if you enter the woods*
> *Of a summer evening late,*
> *When the night-air cools on the trout-ringed pools*
> *Where the otter whistles his mate,*
> *(They fear not men in the woods,*
> *Because they see so few)*
> *You will hear the beat of a horse's feet,*
> *And the swish of a skirt in the dew,*
> *Steadily cantering through*
> *The misty solitudes,*
> *As though they perfectly knew*
> *The old lost road through the woods...*
> *But there is no road through the woods.*

Kipling made a virtue of plainness. His temperament was independent. While lionised in London, he revealingly declined the award of the Order of Merit, and turned down the Laureateship when Tennyson died.

He also wrote for children; 'The Jungle Book' (1894) and 'Stalky and Co' (1899), while dated, are still readable. 'Stalky and Co', based on Kipling's time at the United Services College in Devon, predates Frank Richards' school stories about 'Billy Bunter', and is much better done.

Housman's "A Shropshire Lad' and 'Collected Poems' are published by Penguin. Publishers of Kipling's poems include Everyman, Penguin and Wordsworth. His fiction is published by Penguin, Oxford and Wordsworth. His biography has been written by David Gilmour.

83

William Butler Yeats (1865–1939)

>─┤─◆>─○─<◆├─<

On his tombstone at Drumcliffe in County Sligo are words taken from Yeats' last poem, '**Under Ben Bulben**':

> *Cast a cold eye*
> *On life, on death.*
> *Horseman, pass by!*

He wrote the lines explicitly for his grave. In their spare, almost frightening dignity they tell us a great deal about him – about his fierce integrity, about his respect for dedicated heroism, about lonely idealism. For Yeats, the horseman was a symbolic image of perfect Renaissance man, reborn in modern times. The lines have the ring of great poetry – captivating and unalterable. It is appropriate that they are chiselled in stone.

Yeats is one of the great figures, difficult but rewarding. His mature poetic voice is unique. He was a *public* poet in the sense that he resurrected the Bardic tradition of the poet as a visionary, declaiming for the community. When we read a Yeats poem, it is as if we are hearing a public performance.

He played a crucial role in a revival of interest in Irish literature and Irish national consciousness. He wrote about and rewrote Irish folklore. He was active in founding the Irish Literary Society and an Irish national theatre, based at the Abbey Theatre in Dublin of which he became a director, and for which he wrote poetic dramas. He was a senator of the Irish Free State from 1922 to 1928. (**Hugh Macdiarmid**, 1892–1978, taking Yeats as a model, became the most significant writer in the Twentieth Century movement to revive *Scottish* culture.)

In his three years at the School of Art in Dublin Yeats developed an interest in mysticism and the supernatural. In later life he became fascinated by the esoteric and the occult, and developed his own visionary system. He had a literal belief in magic. Georgie, whom he married in 1917, encouraged his experimentation in spiritualism. These preoccupations inform his work but fortunately do not for the most part obscure it for us.

His early poetry is strongly influenced by the Pre-Raphaelites – there is an atmosphere of romantic Celtic dreaminess. (We find it, for example, in '**The Lake Isle of Innisfree**', a poem whose great popularity exasperated the older Yeats, who felt it no longer represented him.) Later this is replaced by a lean poetry of direct assertion. He was progressively shedding "poetic" embroiderings and subjects, learning to 'walk naked'. Throughout he cultivates in his poetry the power of symbolism, just as in the plays he was heavily influenced by the formal stylisation of the ancient Noh theatre of Japan.

His poetic reputation was established by '**The Wanderings of Oisin**' (the folk hero of Irish legend) in 1889. A succession of volumes followed, culminating in '**Last Poems**' (1936–39). He was awarded the Nobel Prize for Literature in 1923.

His themes are of Ireland, and the traditional strengths of aristocracy and peasantry; his contempt for bourgeois values and the undervaluing of high art; civilisation centred on beauty and the values of the artist (for which he found a symbol in Byzantium); old age strengthened by intellect; and the natural cycle of birth and death to which he links the great cyclical movements of history. There is, too, a sense of the artist as an embattled and isolated figure.

In '**The Second Coming**', published in his 1921 collection, we can see some of these themes working together:

> *Turning and turning in the widening gyre*
> *The falcon cannot hear the falconer;*
> *Things fall apart; the centre cannot hold;*
> *Mere anarchy is loosed upon the world,*
> *The blood-dimmed tide is loosed, and everywhere*
> *The ceremony of innocence is drowned;*
> *The best lack all conviction, while the worst*
> *Are full of passionate intensity.*

In some ways these lines may seem prophetic of the dark crises of world history to come later in the century. Yeats' vision embraces that, but is wider still: the whole of human history seems to have spiralled out of control. The breaking of the accord between the falcon and the falconer symbolises the breakdown of order in a characteristically Yeatsian way, in an image that is part feudal and part heraldic. Yeats built a vocabulary of 'gyres', 'vortexes' and spiralling circles to represent patterns of ideal order; here the patterns are breaking down. It is an impassioned vision; the charged words have a terrifying precision.

Yeats repays careful reading. Here, in the order in which they were published, is a very short list of some of his major poems: 'The Wild Swans at Coole', in which the swans symbolise solitary souls; 'An Irish Airman Foresees His Death' – an image of modern heroism; 'Easter, 1916'; 'The Second Coming'; 'A Prayer for My Daughter'; 'Sailing to Byzantium'; 'Leda and the Swan'; 'Among Schoolchildren'; 'Byzantium'; 'Long-Legged Fly'; and 'The Circus Animals' Desertion', in which the old poet movingly reviews his career.

Read, too, W.H.Auden's fine poem of tribute, 'In Memory of W.B.Yeats', written upon Yeats' death in January, 1939.

There is a biography by Roy Foster. Yeats is published by Macmillan, Penguin, Faber and Oxford.

84

Science Fiction and Urban Realities

H.G.Wells (1866–1946)
Arnold Bennett (1867–1931)

➤·┼◆➤·◦·◄◆┼·◄

H.G.Wells was fascinated by the possibilities of science. Trained as a zoologist at London's Normal School of Science (later Imperial College), where he gained a First Class degree under T.H.Huxley, he lectured at the University Tutorial College before he turned to writing. **'The Time Machine'** (1895), **'The War of the Worlds'** (1898) and **'The First Men in the Moon'** (1901), all still eminently readable, convey the excitement of the possibilities of space exploration, and the drama of an invasion of the earth by Martians. **'The Time Machine'** is a short fable anticipating the extinction of mankind. In these and other novels and **short stories** he is one of the first in the field of English science fiction. He foresaw the invention of aeroplanes, tanks, and nuclear bombs.

At the same time his socialist instincts and his lower middle class background (his father was an unsuccessful shopkeeper) prompted his comic novels of suburban provincial life, of which the best are **'Love and Mr Lewisham'** (1900), **'Kipps'** (1905) and **'The History of Mr Polly'** (1910). All three record the trials and tribulations of the little man attempting to make his way in the world, where class and money are obstacles to realising ambition and romance. Anger lurks in the background of these stories – *"the stupid little tragedies of these clipped and limited lives"* – but the predominant tone is of gentle humour, and the pathos of uneducated characters like Kipps who had a dim awareness of *"the wonder of life"* which *"never reached the surface of his mind"*.

Wells' fictional world is in London and the southern counties of England; **Arnold Bennett** describes middle class society in the industrial Midlands of Stoke-on-Trent and the Potteries, where he was brought up. The central novels are **'Anna of the Five Towns'** (1902), **'The Old Wives' Tale'** (1908), and the trilogy **'Clayhanger'** (1910), **'Hilda Lessways'** (1911) and **'These Twain'** (1916). As in Wells we find characters attempting to escape from the confines of a narrow world, particularly Anna, and Edwin Clayhanger. Bennett left the Potteries when he was 21, and lived in France (he married a Frenchwoman) from 1902 to 1912. In his approach he is influenced by the documentary realism of French novelists such as Zola and Flaubert. But while Bennett is not at all blind to the ugly aspects of this environment, he describes it with affection and compassion (his word).

The techniques of Wells and Bennett in describing unfulfilled lives irritated some of their successors. For Virginia Woolf, from a lofty and rather rarefied perspective, both failed to capture 'ordinariness'; for her the "myriad impressions" received by a mind each day would make that day, in fact, something other than ordinary. D.H.Lawrence, lamenting the absence of passion, wrote in a letter: *"I hate Bennett's resignation. Tragedy really ought to be a great kick at misery. But 'Anna of the Five Towns' seems like an acceptance"*.

In their day both Wells and Bennett found large and loyal audiences, which they also cultivated in their journalism. In his last months, while dying of typhoid, Bennett was looked after by Wells. In later years Wells moved in new directions, including a popular **'Outline of History'** in 1920, a self-portrait in **'Experiment in Autobiography'** (1934), and a despairing last work, **'Mind At The End of its Tether'** (1945).

There is a biography of Arnold Bennett by Alexander Games.

Wells' fiction is published by Everyman and Oxford, and Bennett's by Phoenix, Penguin and Wordsworth.

85

Classic Literature for Children

Kenneth Grahame (1859–1932)

Beatrix Potter (1866–1943)

A.A.Milne (1882–1956)

>-!-<>-·O-·<+!-<

The years from 1900 to 1928 were a golden age for children's literature. From 'The Wind in the Willows' (1908) to 'The House at Pooh Corner' (1928), from 'The Tale of Peter Rabbit' (1900) to 'Cecily Parsley's Nursery Rhymes' (1922), the writing offered both a remarkable instinct for what would appeal to a young imagination, and an enduring appeal to adults which depends on literary quality at least as much as it does on nostalgia.

Kenneth Grahame worked for the Bank of England. He wrote, in essays published in 'The Golden Age' (1895) and 'Dream Days' (1898), of adults who were depressingly out of touch with children. (His own childhood had been troubled.) 'The Wind in the Willows' began life as bedtime stories and letters for his son Alastair over a four-year period. Eventually published in revised and extended form, the book triumphed with its colourful animal characterisations: the loud and scoundrelly Toad, Ratty and Badger, and Mole, whose gentle timidity is reminiscent of Grahame himself. They are types of English gentlemen. Arnold Bennett, reviewing the first edition, wrote of Grahame's "irony at the expense of the English character". The first illustrator was E.H.Shephard. The dramatised version by A.A.Milne adds the character of the horse: under the title 'Toad of Toad Hall' it was first produced in 1930.

Like Grahame, **Beatrix Potter** had not enjoyed her childhood, which was quiet and lonely. Born into a wealthy family in Kensington, she spent most of her girlhood in the hands of governesses. The first two stories, 'Peter Rabbit' and 'The Tailor of Gloucester' (1902), she wrote for the child of one of these governesses and published at her own expense. The sequence that followed created the first classic tales to be written for the very young, with recognisably human animals such as Benjamin Bunny, Jemima Puddle-Duck and Mrs Tiggy-Winkle. There is no talking down to young readers. In some of the stories, mysterious and potentially frightening adventure is contained by a narration which is warm and reassuring (but never sentimental). As in Lewis Carroll, there is a fine relish for words – *'It is said that the effort of eating too much lettuce is 'soporific''* ('The Tale of the Flopsy Bunnies') – and the vocabulary is both

adult ('*improvident*', *frivolity*', '*deplorable*') and skittish ('*the most beautifullest coat*').
Beatrix Potter's own superb illustrations draw on the Lake District landscapes which
she had loved from childhood holidays and in which she eventually settled.

A.A.Milne was the son of a Scottish teacher whom he much admired. After a happy
boyhood, the youngest of three brothers, he read Maths at Cambridge and aimed for
a career in writing. At the age of 24 he was appointed assistant editor of 'Punch',
where he stayed until 1914. He wrote many novels, stories and plays (encouraged by
James Barrie). His four best-remembered works are his children's poetry – '**When
We Were Very Young**' (1924), which sold half a million copies in its first ten years,
and '**Now We Are Six**' (1927) – and '**Winnie-the-Pooh**' (1926) and '**The House at
Pooh Corner**'. Pooh, "a bear of no brain at all", was invented for Milne's son
Christopher, who was included in the stories as Christopher Robin. (The poem
'Vespers', beginning "*Hush, hush, whisper who dares / Christopher Robin is saying his
prayers*", Milne wrote when Christopher was three.) Milne's famously original
creations include the comically morose donkey, Eeyore; Piglet, who like Pooh and
Eeyore was based on Christopher's toys; the game of Poohsticks; and the heffalump
trap. The original illustrations were, like Kenneth Grahame's, by E.H.Shephard, who
worked with Milne at 'Punch'. The Pooh fantasy is particularly appealing because it
is firmly and wittily rooted in the idiosyncracies of all childhood imaginations.

*There is a biography of Kenneth Grahame by Peter Green and of Beatrix Potter by
Margaret Lane. A.A.Milne's autobiography, '**It's Too Late Now**', appeared in 1939. See
also Anne Thwaite's 'The Brilliant Career of Winnie-the-Pooh', and Elspeth Grahame's
'First Whisper of "The Wind in the Willows"'. An entertaining anthology is 'So I Shall
Tell You a Story…: Encounters with Beatrix Potter' edited by Judy Taylor. Beatrix Potter's
coded '**Journals**' were transcribed and published by Leslie Linder in 1966. Enthusiasts
may also enjoy the Little Grey Rabbit stories of **Alison Utley** (1884–1976).*

*Kenneth Grahame is published by Walker Books, Chrysalis Children's Books, Harper
Collins and Everyman. Beatrix Potter's '**Tales**' are published by Frederick Warne and
A.A. Milne's work by Methuen, Hamlyn and Hodder.*

86
E.M.Forster (1879–1970)

⊱⊶⊷⊙⊷⊶⊰

Forster was one of the Twentieth Century's most respected humanists in the English
liberal tradition. He champions the values of tolerant intelligence, civility and art.

His essays, lectures and reviews – there is an excellent selection in 'Two Cheers for Democracy' (1951) – are witty and stimulating. (It is a kind of writing which has fallen out of fashion in recent years, but is worth sampling.)

In his earlier years, as one of what came to be called the Bloomsbury Group, he shared in the intellectual excitement of a new wave of thinkers and artists who were reacting against Victorianism. He had no religious faith – his "motto", he says, is "Lord, I disbelieve. Help thou my unbelief" – and the developing century confirmed his distrust of all absolutist moral creeds and political platforms. At times, and we can find this in his greatest novels, 'Howard's End' (1910), and especially 'A Passage to India' (1924), he touches on a profound sense of darkness, of the void which replaces certainties. *"Everything exists, nothing has value"*, says a disturbed Mrs Moore in 'A Passage to India'.

In an unhappy schooling at Tonbridge, Forster came to detest the old public school ethic. The open intellectual society of King's College, Cambridge, he found much more congenial. After university he travelled in Italy and Greece, and visited India in 1912–13. He returned in 1921–22, as the personal secretary to a maharajah. He hated imperialism. His first short story appeared in 1904 and his first novel, 'Where Angels Fear To Tread', in 1905. 'The Longest Journey' (1907) attacks the public school ethos. In 1908 came 'A Room With A View', a lightly ironic period piece set scrupulously in Florence. 'Maurice', a novel with a homosexual theme, was completed in 1913 but not published until 1971.

After the success of his last novel, 'A Passage to India', he wrote, broadcast and lectured on literature. In 1934 he became the first president of the National Council of Civil Liberties. He campaigned against censorship, appearing for the defence in the 'Lady Chatterley's Lover' trial in 1961. In 1949 he turned down a knighthood.

'Howard's End' explores the tensions between the civilised and humane values of the Schlegel sisters, Margaret and Helen, and the more philistine and worldly practicality of the Wilcox family with whom the sisters become involved. An exception is the dying Mrs Wilcox, the owner of the house Howard's End, whose spirit presides over the novel with a sympathetic and wise dignity. (There are parallels with Mrs Moore in 'A Passage to India'.) Margaret Schlegel's passion is to bridge the two habits of mind: *"Only connect!... Only connect the prose and the passion, and both will be exalted, and human love will be seen at its height...But she failed."*

'A Passage to India' brilliantly evokes the atmosphere of relationships between the British and the Indians in imperial India. But it is about much more than that. Forster wrote: "It's about the search of the human race for a more lasting home, about the universe as embodied in the Indian earth and the Indian sky, about the horror lurking in the Marabar Caves and the release symbolised by the birth of Krishna. It is – or rather desires to be – philosophic and poetic."

"The horror lurking in the Marabar Caves" refers to a central incident, one of the great moments in English fiction. Adela Quested, an earnest but unimaginative Englishwoman in pursuit of 'the real India', wanders alone into the Caves. Then, after a highly charged experience which Forster presents with deliberate ambiguity as neither quite reality nor fantasy, she asserts that she has been followed into the Caves by the Indian Dr Aziz, who has attempted to sexually assault her. Aziz (assistant to the British Civil Surgeon) is put on trial. Adela Quested later withdraws the charge. The episode is highly symbolic. The "horror" is not only the alleged attack, but the echo in the Caves which appears to reduce everything to nothingness.

The **Bloomsbury Group** was not a formal society, but the name that came to be given to a loose association of like-minded friends who kept in touch from about 1905 until the 1930s. They met originally in London's Bloomsbury at the home of Virginia Woolf and her elder sister Vanessa Bell, both then unmarried.

What mattered most to them were personal relationships, 'the enjoyment of beautiful objects', and the arts, especially literature and painting. They constituted a kind of intellectual avant-garde, and were to be criticised later as being élitist.

The members of the company varied from time to time. In addition to Virginia Woolf and Forster, they included Lytton Strachey, David Garnett, the economist J.M.Keynes, the philosopher G.E.Moore, and the artists Roger Fry and Clive Bell.

The elderly Mrs Moore is Miss Quested's travelling companion. She has a much deeper feel for India, and develops a close friendship with Aziz. She has heard the echo, is profoundly upset and never recovers. She returns to England before the trial, but without enthusiasm:

> *She had come to that state where the horror of the universe and its smallness are both visible at the same time – the twilight of the double vision in which so many elderly people are involved. If this world is not to our taste, well, at all events there is Heaven, Hell, Annihilation – one or other of those large things, that huge scenic background of stars, fires, blue or black air. All heroic endeavour, and all that is known as art, assumes that there is such a background, just as all practical endeavour, when the world is to our taste,*

assumes that the world is all. But in the twilight of the double vision a spiritual muddledom is set up for which no high-sounding words can be found; we neither act nor refrain from action, we can neither ignore nor respect Infinity. Mrs Moore had always inclined to resignation.

There is a great deal of Forster here – in the narrative comment, in which he virtually speaks through Mrs Moore, and in the "spiritual muddledom". For him, as for Mrs Moore, India had aroused the beautiful goal of being "at one with the universe". But the press of practicalities (and the symbolic booming echo of the Caves) gets in the way. *"There was always some little duty to be performed first, some new card to be turned up from the diminishing pack…"*

There are biographies of Forster by P.N.Furbank and Nicola Beauman. The books are published by Penguin.

87
Sean O'Casey (1880-1964)

Sean O'Casey in the 1920s was one of the first dramatists to use what were called **expressionist** techniques. He occasionally departed from realism into a poetic heightening of both words and visual presentation.

'**The Silver Tassie**', first produced in London in 1928, is a vividly powerful treatment of the First World War, highly regarded in its day. The first act, staged conventionally, shows a soldier on leave from the war leading his Dublin tenement football team to a cup victory – hence the title. The original set designer for the second act, Augustus John, created a stylised montage of battlefield devastation, incorporating a leaning crucifix, a ruined monastery, and silhouetted shapes of broken trees and buildings. Returning to realism, the last two acts confirm the message that the war achieved little at huge cost.

The Dublin Abbey Theatre at first refused to stage the play (they eventually relented in 1935), which precipated O'Casey's moving to England – permanently as it turned out. He was born in Dublin into a poor Protestant family, and brought up without a formal education in the physical rough-and-tumble of the streets. He soon became an Irish Nationalist. His first plays were rejected by the Abbey, but they took '**The Shadow of a Gunman**' (1923), '**Juno and the Paycock**' (1924) and '**The Plough and the Stars**' (1926). All are tragi-comedies, dealing with the despairing plight of the poor in Dublin during the violence and political upheaval of the times.

'The whole counthry's in a state of chassis' – Boyle in **'Juno'**.

O'Casey championed Irish patriotism, but the comic elements in the plays grated on some contemporary audiences. **'The Plough and the Stars'** provoked riots from those who took offence at his supposedly unsympathetic portrayal of participants in the Easter Rising of 1916.

There is a biography by Garry O'Connor. Penguin publish the plays.

88
James Joyce (1882–1941)

Joyce is the ultimate wordsmith, the genius who has been the most versatile and brilliant experimenter with the language. Imagine for a moment an impossibility, the total pun – one word that contains all meanings and all possibilities. Unrealisable, of course, but it is as if Joyce's dazzling virtuosity, when he pushes language to its frontiers, seems to toy with that teasing ambition.

His early short stories, **'Dubliners'** (1914), are conventionally written in comparison with what is to come later, but these explorations of the lives of various Dublin characters have a beautiful delicacy and poetry to them. Take for example Mr Duffy, who has just alighted from a train:

> *He turned back the way he had come, the rhythm of the engine pounding in his ears. He began to doubt the reality of what memory told him. He halted under a tree and allowed the rhythm to die away. He could not feel her near him in the darkness nor her voice touch his ear. He waited for some minutes listening. He could hear nothing: the night was perfectly silent. He listened again: perfectly silent. He felt that he was alone.*

That is the ending of the story called **'A Painful Case'**. 'She' has died, and we do not need to go into the detail of Mr Duffy's sad story to sense Joyce's gift for capturing a piercing moment.

The opening of his next novel, **'A Portrait of the Artist as a Young Man'** (1914–15), which is partly autobiographical, astonishes with its playful inventiveness:

Once upon a time and a very good time it was there was a moocow coming down along the road and this moocow that was coming down along the road met a nicens little boy named baby tuckoo...

His father told him that story: his father looked at him through a glass: he had a hairy face.

He was baby tuckoo. The moocow came down the road where Betty Byrne lived: she sold lemon platt.

> *O, the wild rose blossoms*
> *On the little green place.*

He sang that song. That was his song.

> *O, the green wothe botheth.*

When you wet the bed first it is warm then it gets cold. His mother put on the oilsheet. That had the queer smell.

His mother had a nicer smell than his father. She played on the piano the sailor's hornpipe for him to dance.

The perceptions of early childhood: the random, inconsequential thinking – barely 'thinking' at all; the lisping song ('O the green rose bushes'); the remembered sensations of touch and smell – they are all here. And the way the child sees but does not understand the world. The father looks at him 'through a glass'. Presumably it is a monocle, but our own momentary incomprehension mimics the child's inability to interpret what he sees.

In 1922 comes the great novel '**Ulysses**'. It tells the story of one day in Dublin – 16th June, 1904. There are four main characters: Leopold Bloom, an advertising canvasser; Molly, his unfaithful wife; and Stephen Dedalus, a young poet, who was the central figure in 'Portrait of the Artist'. The fourth character is the city itself. Bloom and Dedalus wander the city, and eventually meet. In the course of the day – Bloomsday – we visit a newspaper office, the National Library, several pubs and shops, a brothel, a maternity hospital, the public baths, the seashore, a funeral.

It is an ordinary day of banal and mundane routines, of sleep, food, and sex. Nothing dramatic happens. Joyce loosely models the day upon Homer's '**Odyssey**', the heroic Greek epic which follows the adventures of Odysseus – Ulysses in the

Latin. Odysseus/Ulysses is shadowed by Bloom. Molly is Penelope. Stephen is Telemachus. (In Homer, Telemachus is Odysseus' son; in Joyce, Stephen is the son that Bloom never had.) But the doings of Joyce's characters are not at all heroic: theirs is a *mock* epic. Ulysses has an adventure with cannibals: Bloom goes to lunch. The epic parallel works in two ways. It reduces the events of the day to comic ordinariness, but it simultaneously does the opposite, giving the events a universal scale and significance: all human life is there. One day in the life of Dublin is the history of the world.

This extraordinary novel, both comic and tragi-comic, both workaday and transcendent, intellectually stimulating and profoundly moving, is written in extraordinary ways. Joyce delights in wordplay – puns, parodies, jokes, allusions. He poetically creates what he called 'epiphanies', those "most delicate and evanescent" of moments, like Mr Duffy's, when we have an intense revelation, and perhaps a sense of the wholeness of the universe. (Joyce owed much here to his readings of St Thomas Aquinas.) Parts of the novel are written realistically, other parts are surreal fantasy. The episode in the maternity hospital, where a baby is being born, is written in a brilliant montage of the changing historical styles of English prose.

Frequently Joyce employs a **stream of consciousness** technique, replicating the unedited, casual flow of thoughts and sensations as they pass through a person's mind. Joyce had met this experiment in the French novel '**Les Lauriers Sont Coupées**' (1888) by Edouard Dujardin, and became its master. '**Ulysses**' ends with the stream of Molly's consciousness as her mind meanders over her life, her marriage and her sexual encounters: 20,000 remarkable words without a full stop.

Here is Leopold Bloom, walking in the early morning through the Dublin streets. Watch how Joyce has Bloom's mind flick from Dublin to his imaginings of exotic places abroad:

> *He crossed to the bright side, avoiding the loose cellarflap of number seventyfive. The sun was nearing the steeple of George's church. Be a warm day I fancy. Specially in these black clothes feel it more. Black conducts, reflects (refracts is it?), the heat. But I couldn't go in that light suit. Make a picnic of it. His eyelids sank quietly often as he walked in happy warmth. Boland's breadvan delivering with trays our daily but she prefers yesterday's loaves turnovers crisp crowns hot. Makes you feel young. Somewhere in the east: early morning: set off at dawn, travel round in front of the sun, steal a day's march on him. Keep it up for ever never grow a day older technically. Walk along a strand, strange land, come to a city gate, sentry there, old ranker too, old Tweedy's big moustaches leaning on a long kind of a spear.*

Wander through awned streets. Turbaned faces going by. Dark caves of carpet shops, big man, Turko the terrible, seated crosslegged smoking a coiled pipe. Cries of sellers in the streets. Drink water scented with fennel, sherbet. Wander along all day. Might meet a robber or two. Well, meet him.

When he wrote 'Ulysses' Joyce was living in Paris where his novel was first published. Early copies imported to England were seized by the customs. The book was (unsuccessfully) prosecuted in the United States for obscenity. It did not appear in England until 1936.

Joyce was born in Dublin where he had a Jesuit education. He was a brilliant linguist – he studied modern languages at University College, Dublin. He came to be frustrated by the bigotries of Irish religious life as he found it, and in 1903 with Nora Barnacle he left Ireland more or less permanently for Europe, living variously in Zurich, Trieste and Paris. He just about kept poverty at bay through literary grants, and struggled for most of his life with glaucoma and incipient blindness.

His last novel, '**Finnegans Wake**' (1939), takes his punning adventure with language to daunting heights. The book centres on a Dublin innkeeper, Earwicker, and his family asleep during one night, but there is no narrative and no plot. The novel is formidably obscure and yet wonderfully entertaining taken in small doses. It is probably impossible to grasp it wholly. Some advocates claim it as Joyce's greatest work; others are content with the wonders of '**Ulysses**'. There are two giants in Twentieth Century English literature, Joyce and T.S.Eliot. It is idle but interesting to speculate that in the years to come it may well be Joyce who will tower above them all.

Joyce also wrote poems and a play, 'Exiles' (1918). His biography is written by Richard Ellmann. Joyce is published by Everyman, Oxford, Penguin and Wordsworth.

89
Virginia Woolf (1882–1941)

Virginia Woolf was one of the first to state vigorously the modern feminist case. In her extended essay '**A Room of One's Own**' (1929), which has become a feminist classic, she writes that England has been under the rule of a patriarchy. A huge block on the development of women's writing, she argued, had been a male view that women are intellectually inferior; what women writers have lacked is the practical independence symbolised by having money and a room of their own.

She was a Londoner who was educated at home. Her house in Gordon Square became a centre for meetings of the **Bloomsbury Group**. Her writing career began with anonymous contributions to the 'Times Literary Supplement' in 1905, which continued throughout her life. With her husband Leonard she founded in 1917 the Hogarth Press, which was later to publish important work by T.S.Eliot, E.M.Forster and others. She suffered from recurrent spells of mental illness; a final attack drove her to drown herself in the Ouse near her home in Sussex.

Her novels experimented with the new techniques of **stream of consciousness** which she admired in Joyce's **'Ulysses'** (though she was less enthusiastic about its content). She was impatient with realism in the novel as pursued by Arnold Bennett and H.G.Wells. For her the art of fiction was to recreate, in prose that had a delicate poetic suggestiveness, the complex passage of ordinary experience – a continuous flux without any plot. The author was to be as discreetly withdrawn a presence as possible.

Her major work is in **'To The Lighthouse'** (1927), **'Mrs Dalloway'** (1925) and **'The Waves'** (1931). In general she was well received, though some were critical of the rarefied atmosphere and a hint of snobbery. Her best seller, **'Orlando'** (1928), dedicated to her close friend Victoria Sackville-West, is a light fantasy tracing the life of a sometimes male and sometimes female Orlando from Elizabethan times to the 1920s. The book makes fun of traditional attitudes to gender.

Here, in an extract from **'To The Lighthouse'**, she is working with her common themes of beauty and time. The ethereal loveliness of the empty house is interrupted by the prosaic arrival of Mrs McNab:

Now, day after day, light turned, like a flower reflected in water, its clear image on the wall opposite. Only the shadows of the trees, flourishing in the wind, made obeisance on the wall, and for a moment darkened the pool in which light reflected itself; or birds, flying, made a soft spot flutter slowly across the bedroom floor.

So loveliness reigned and stillness, and together made the shape of loveliness itself, a form from which life had parted; solitary like a pool at evening, far distant, seen from a train window, vanishing so quickly that the pool, pale in the evening, is scarcely robbed of its solitude, though once seen. Loveliness and stillness clasped hands in the bedroom, and among the shrouded jugs and sheeted chairs even the prying of the wind, and the soft nose of the clammy sea airs, rubbing, snuffling, iterating and reiterating their questions – "Will you fade? Will you perish?" – scarcely disturbed the peace, the indifference, the air of pure integrity, as if the question they asked scarcely needed that they should answer: we remain.

*Nothing it seemed could break that image, corrupt that innocence or disturb
the swaying mantle of silence which, week after week, in the empty room,
wove into itself the falling cries of birds, ships hooting, the drone and hum
of the fields, a dog's bark, a man's shout, and folded them round the house
in silence. Once only a board sprang on the landing; once in the middle of
the night with a roar, with a rupture, as after centuries of quiescence a rock
rends itself from the mountain and hurtles crashing into the valley, one fold
of the shawl loosened and swung to and fro. Then again peace descended;
and the shadows wavered; light bent to its own image in adoration on the
bedroom wall; when Mrs McNab, tearing the veil of silence with hands that
had stood in the wash-tub, grinding it with boots that had crushed the
shingle, came as directed to open all windows, and dust the bedrooms.*

The leisurely unfolding of these sentences becomes part of the peacefulness which
Mrs McNab shatters. Readers of a passage like this will ask themselves whether the
images are successfully created, or whether the style becomes too self-conscious. It
could be argued that the style *is* the subject.

*Virginia Woolf's **diaries** and **letters** are of interest. There is a biography by her nephew,
Quentin Bell. Her niece Angelica Bell has written about her in 'Deceived with Kindness'.
The novels are published by Everyman, Oxford, Penguin and Wordsworth.*

90
D.H.Lawrence (1885–1930)

Opinions have always been sharply divided on Lawrence: he tends to excite either
deep loyalty or hostility. The truth is that he could write superbly well, but he could
also be hectoringly off-putting. He became a powerful influence throughout the
Twentieth Century.

He passionately advocated the individual's uniqueness, which he felt to be under
threat from the ugly, mechanical and desensitising aspects of modern life. *"My great
religion"*, he wrote, *"is a belief in the blood, the flesh, as being wiser than the intellect.
We can go wrong in our minds. But what the blood feels, and believes, and says, is always
true."* While he rejected many aspects of Freud's theory, he recognised what Freud
called the 'subconscious' as the driving force in the depths of the psyche. He believed
every person's moral being and inner life required expression through their sexuality,
and through the immediacy of their response to the natural world.

Lawrence was born in the coal-mining district of Eastwood, Nottinghamshire. The family was poor. His father was a miner (and former teacher); his mother, from a more genteel background, was determined that Lawrence should prosper beyond his class. He taught briefly in Croydon, but it was clear that despite the financial insecurities writing was to be his mission. In 1912 he met Frieda Weekley, a married woman with three children. They eloped to Germany, returning during the war years. It was an intense and often stormy relationship. Frieda was divorced in 1914, and they spent the rest of their lives in a nomadic kind of existence, travelling in England, Ceylon, Australia, America, Mexico and Italy. Lawrence suffered from ill-health throughout; his condition kept him from taking part in the 1914–18 War.

His first major novel (and maybe his best) is 'Sons and Lovers' (1913). There are strong autobiographical elements in the story of Paul Morel, the sensitive child in a mining family who is oppressed by a brutish though not unloving father and a possessive mother. (Lawrence later thought that he had been too tough on the father.) The novel is brilliantly descriptive of the Nottinghamshire countryside, the tough but resourceful living, and the tensions, fears and embarrassments that engulf Paul as he grows up. In his early love affairs there is a fierce conflict, characteristic of Lawrence himself, between the compulsion to love and the need to retain emotional independence.

'The Rainbow' (1915) and 'Women in Love' (written in 1916 but not published until 1920 in New York) pursue this theme. The two main characters, the sisters Ursula and Gudrun, appear in both books, which explore the depths and complexities of the emotional relationships across three generations of a Nottinghamshire family. There is a scene in 'Women in Love' where Gerald Critch, the son of the local colliery owner, is watched with appalled fascination by Ursula and Gudrun as he forces his horse close to a train at a level crossing:

> "The fool!" cried Ursula loudly. "Why doesn't he ride away till it's gone by?"

> Gudrun was looking at him with black-dilated, spellbound eyes. But he sat glistening and obstinate, forcing the wheeling mare, which spun and swerved like a wind, and yet could not get out of the grasp of his will, nor escape from the mad clamour of terror that resounded through her, as the trucks thumped slowly, heavily, horrifying, one after the other, one pursuing the other, over the rails of the crossing.

> The locomotive, as if wanting to see what could be done, put on the brakes, and back came the trucks rebounding on the iron buffers, striking like horrible cymbals, clashing nearer and nearer in frightful strident concussions. The mare opened her mouth and rose slowly, as if lifted up on a wind of

terror. Then suddenly her fore-feet struck out, as she convulsed herself utterly away from the horror. Back she went, and the two girls clung to each other, feeling she must fall backwards on top of him. But he leaned forward, his face shining with fixed amusement, and at last he brought her down, sank her down, and was bearing her back to the mark. But as strong as the pressure of his compulsion was the repulsion of her utter terror, throwing her back away from the railway, so that she spun round and round on two legs, as if she were in the centre of some whirlwind. It made Gudrun faint with poignant dizziness, which seemed to penetrate to her heart.

The train, the horse, the moment of crisis – all are caught with graphic vividness. At the same time Lawrence suggests the sexual undercurrents: Gerald's sadistic self-assertion, and Gudrun's turmoil of captivation despite herself, in contrast with Ursula's more controlled antipathy. This kind of writing, alive with immediate detail and at the same time symbolically suggestive, was distinctively new in the English novel.

In Lawrence's writing at its best we find a poetic luminosity. He has the committed urgency of a visionary, and sometimes – at his worst – of a propagandist. The real problem with '**Lady Chatterley's Lover**' (1928) is that he wrote it too much as a manifesto for emancipated attitudes to twentieth century living (in which sex is a central feature but by no means the only one.) In this extract he powerfully condemns the deadening effect of urban ugliness, but there are moments in it when his anger risks becoming a numbing rant. It was not an easy balance to keep:

The car ploughed uphill through the long squalid straggle of Tevershall, the blackened brick dwellings, the black slate roofs glistening their sharp edges, the mud black with coal-dust, the pavements wet and black. It was as if dismalness had soaked through and through everything. The utter negation of natural beauty, the utter negation of the gladness of life, the utter absence of the instinct for shapely beauty which every bird and beast has, the utter death of the human intuitive faculty was appalling. The stacks of soap in the grocers' shops, the rhubarb and lemons in the greengrocers! The awful hats in the milliners! All went by ugly, ugly, ugly......

Throughout his life, and afterwards, Lawrence's work has been much misunderstood. It is extraordinary that the puritanical zeal with which he campaigned for a wholesome view of sexuality should have been mistaken for the prurience of obscenity and pornography. His novels and paintings, including '**The Rainbow**' and '**Women in Love**', were subject to a string of prosecutions. After their acquittal at the Old Bailey in 1960 of publishing an obscene article, '**Lady Chatterley's Lover**', Penguin Books published a transcript of the trial edited by

C.H.Rolph. (The evidence incidentally constitutes a searching study of Lawrence.) The trial was fascinating for its revelation of contemporary attitudes, not least in the prosecuting counsel's memorable question to the jury: "Is this a book that you would wish your wife or your servants to read?"

Lawrence wrote many short stories. Two striking examples, **'Odour of Chrysanthemums'** and **'The Rocking Horse Winner'** show in quite different ways his mastery of the form. In his poems he preferred the spontaneity of free verse, with no regular patterns of rhyme or rhythm. (Particularly rewarding are **'Piano'**, **'Snake'** and **'Bavarian Gentians'**.) His neglected play, **'The Daughter-in-Law'**, is a sensitive work of social realism. His **essays** have a lively and unliterary directness. He believed urgently in the liberating influence of literature. "The novel," he wrote, "can help us live as nothing else can."

Lawrence's biography is written by Brenda Maddox. The novels are published by Penguin. There is a Wordsworth edition of the poems.

91
Poets of the First World War

Edward Thomas (1878–1917)

Siegfried Sassoon (1886–1967)

Rupert Brooke (1887–1915)

Isaac Rosenberg (1890–1918)

Wilfred Owen (1893–1918)

Robert Graves (1895–1985)

Charles Sorley (1895–1915)

Edmund Blunden (1896–1974)

To Germany

You are blind, like us......

When it is peace, then we may view again
With new-won eyes each other's truer form
And wonder. Grown more loving-kind and warm
We'll grasp firm hands and laugh at the old pain,
When it is peace. But until peace, the storm
The darkness and the thunder and the rain.

Charles Sorley, *killed at Loos, aged 20*

How was it that the carnage of 1914–1918 came to provoke such an abundance of strong and memorable poetry? The question is often asked. Part of the answer may be that most of the major poets of the war were writing poetry of a kind before the war began. Several of them encouraged each other's writing about the war. For most of them experience of the trenches precipitated a decisive change in the way they wrote.

This could not be said, however, of **Rupert Brooke**, who died of blood poisoning on his way to the Dardenelles. Brooke was unfairly vilified in the later Twentieth Century for welcoming the war as an opportunity for patriotic duty – a view that many shared, especially before they encountered the realities of modern warfare. His five 'war sonnets' of 1915 included his famous '**The Soldier**' (*'If I should die, think only this of me......'*). He was a romantic hero in his day, and celebrated for the pre-war English pastoral lyricism of '**Grantchester**'.

Edward Thomas was killed at Arras. A writer of books about literature, travel in England, and nature, he had been encouraged into poetry by Robert Frost, the American poet who was living in England at the time. From Frost he learnt how to use the natural rhythms of speech in poetry, and his austere, understated words – all his poems were written in his last two and a half years – have come to be highly regarded in recent years. '**As The Team's Head Brass…**' is one of the century's finest poems, beautifully structured as a conversation about the war between the poet and a man ploughing. Also read '**This is no Case of Petty Right or Wrong**' (*'I hate not Germans, nor grow hot / with love of Englishmen'*) and '**No One Cares Less Than I**'. Like Rupert Brooke and **Edmund Blunden**, he also writes poems that look back to the solace offered by pastoral England, as in the well-known '**Adlestrop**'.

Before he saw action, **Siegfried Sassoon**'s attitude was similar to Brooke's. But to the caustic sarcasm of his anti-war poetry we owe some of the most graphic images of the horror and the psychological stress. He threw away his Military Cross. He had no respect for the politicians or the military leaders, and was publicly critical. **Robert Graves** intervened so that instead of being disciplined he was sent by a medical board to Craiglockhart Hospital, Edinburgh, where he met **Wilfred Owen**, whom he strongly influenced and encouraged. It is interesting to compare his dramatically vivid poem **'The Rear-Guard'**, where he stumbles across the dead body of a German, with his prose account of the same event in **'Memoirs of an Infantry Officer'** (1930) – one of the books in his semi-autobiographical trilogy. We find his characteristic voice in **'Christ and The Soldier'**, **'The Redeemer'** and **'The General'**. **'Everyone Sang'**, which he wrote suddenly, speedily and without any revision, captures his heady sense of release at the ending of the war. *'Everyone suddenly burst out singing; / And I was filled with such delight / As prisoned birds must find in freedom......'*

The Jewish family of **Isaac Rosenberg** held pacifist views, but he signed up and reached the trenches in 1916. He was killed on the Somme. Sassoon has praised the effect of the mingling of Hebraic and English traditions in his poetry. His touch is astonishingly mature; he mixes disturbing images with poignantly restrained detail. See his **'Dead Men's Dump'** and **'Louse Hunting'**. **'Break of Day in the Trenches'** is one of the finest poems of the time:

> *The darkness crumbles away -*
> *It is the same old druid Time as ever.*
> *Only a live thing leaps my hand -*
> *A queer sardonic rat -*
> *As I pull the parapet's poppy*
> *To stick behind my ear......*

Most of the poems of **Wilfred Owen** were written from 1917–18. Concussion and shell-shock saw him invalided out to Craiglockhart, where he met and was urged into poetry by **Sassoon**, who later introduced him to **Graves**. He returned to the front in 1918, when he was awarded the Military Cross. He was killed one week before the armistice. Before he joined up in 1915 he had been the lay assistant to the vicar of Dunsden in Oxfordshire, and his parents were deeply religious. The bitter realism of his writing is sometimes interwoven with dark symbolism and Christian imagery. He has been widely regarded as the outstanding poet of the many who wrote of the war. **'Anthem for Doomed Youth'** in its elegiac sadness, and **'Dulce et Decorum Est'** in its haunted anger, are famously representative. Read also **'Strange Meeting'** and **'Futility'**. He wrote of "the pity" of war, and said that his poetry was "in no sense consolatory".

Amongst many memoirs of the war, 'Testament of Youth' by Vera Brittain (1893–1970) has been much acclaimed. In the first of her three autobiographical 'testaments', she writes movingly from the perspective of a volunteer wartime nurse. Her fiancé Roland Leighton died in France.

Robert Graves' 1929 autobiography 'Goodbye to All That' (Penguin), is absorbingly and sometimes revoltingly detailed in the sections where he documents life at the front, perhaps more effectively than in his war poems. He describes his friendships with Sassoon and Owen. Having been seriously wounded, he was at a camp in Wales when the armistice was announced:

> *The news sent me out walking alone along the dyke above the marshes of*
> *Rhuddlan (an ancient battlefield, the Flodden of Wales), cursing and sobbing and*
> *thinking of the dead. Siegfried's famous poem celebrating the Armistice began:*
> *'Everybody suddenly burst out singing…' But 'everybody' did not include me.*

There are several anthologies of 1914–18 poetry in print; there is a biography of Wilfred Owen by Dominic Hibberd, and of Rupert Brooke by Nigel Jones. Edmund Blunden's autobiography, 'Undertones of War', is finely written.

92
T.S.Eliot (1888–1965)

Eliot is a defining influence in Twentieth Century literature. His poem 'The Waste Land' (1922) is in its radical style a landmark of modernism. It speaks powerfully for a post-war mood of disillusionment and depression.

Eliot was born in St Louis, Missouri. After studying at Harvard, he came on a travel scholarship to Europe and eventually settled in London, where he taught and reviewed. From 1917 he worked as a banker, and then from 1925 as a director of the publishers Faber and Faber. His first marriage, to Vivien in 1915, was marred by her mental illness and their separation in the early 1930s. He married Valerie Fletcher in 1957. He became a British citizen in 1927; he won the Nobel Prize in 1948.

In addition to 'The Waste Land' Eliot's major poetry includes 'The Love Song of J. Alfred Prufrock' (1917), written while he was at Harvard, 'The Hollow Men' (1925), 'The Journey of the Magi' (1927), 'Ash Wednesday' (1930) and 'Four Quartets' (1935–1942).

Modernism is the broad term used for a wide range of innovations in the arts in the early Twentieth Century. It includes any experimentation which was reacting against traditional forms. In the visual arts and architecture there was a vogue for daring abstract shapes and geometrically clean lines: anything which was self-consciously futurist and 'new'.

In modernist literature we see an abandonment of traditional ways of ordering and structuring poems, novels and plays (though European drama was more strongly affected than British theatre). New techniques developed, including stream of consciousness writing, a breakdown into fragmentary impressions (imagism), and a collage or montage effect incorporating references, allusions and quotations from other writers. Some writers were influenced by anthropology and psychology. The tone was often – not always – intellectual rather than emotional. Key figures included T.E.Hulme, Ezra Pound, Wyndham Lewis, Yeats, Joyce, Conrad, Virginia Woolf and Eliot.

In the early poems there is a strong anti-romantic and disparaging tone. Prufrock is an unheroic modern 'hero', given away by his name, comically inadequate in life and in love, and endlessly postponing the big (and little) decisions. *"Shall I part my hair behind? Do I dare to eat a peach?"* He is mocked as a suburban nonentity, socially pretentious and drably embarrassing. *"I have measured out my life with coffee spoons."*

The light satire of 'Prufrock' darkens into bleakness with 'The Waste Land'. Eliot gives us a depressing impression of a civilisation which is empty and soulless. It is an *impression*, not a picture. The long poem, in five sections, does not tell a story or give a conventional description. Eliot works through a collage of random images, snatches of conversation, and a kaleidoscope of references to other civilisations and other writers. The total effect is to suggest the barrenness and sterility of modern times.

> *What are the roots that clutch, what branches grow*
> *Out of this stony rubbish?*

London is an "unreal City" deadened in fog. The second section, 'A Game of Chess', parodies the baroque vanities of upper class wealth and titivation (the parallels with Pope's 'Rape of the Lock' and Shakespeare's 'Cleopatra' are interesting) and follows this with the banalities of dead-end conversation in a Cockney pub. A brief flurry of jazz rhythms captures an empty-headed and frantic pursuit of culture, meaning and purpose:

O O O O that Shakespeherian Rag -
It's so elegant
So intelligent
'What shall I do now? What shall I do?'
'I shall rush out as I am, and walk the street
'With my hair down, so. What shall we do tomorrow?
'What shall we ever do?'

'The Waste Land' defines a doomed civilisation, a doomed planet:

What is that sound high in the air
Murmur of maternal lamentation
Who are those hooded hordes swarming
Over endless plains, stumbling in cracked earth
Ringed by the flat horizon only
What is the city over the mountains
Cracks and reforms and bursts in the violet air
Falling towers
Jerusalem Athens Alexandria
Vienna London
Unreal

Gradually Eliot's politics moved to the right (putting him out of step with the majority of poets of the Thirties). He joined the Church of England in 1927, and developed a very private kind of High Anglican mysticism. (At Harvard he had begun a continuing interest in Buddhism.) His vision of communal emptiness (*"We are the hollow men / We are the stuffed men / Leaning together / Headpiece filled with straw"* – **'The Hollow Men'**) is succeeded by an emphasis upon the *"intolerable wrestle"* of an individual in expressing meaning through words:

Words strain,
Crack, and sometimes break, under the burden,
Under the tension......   (**'Burnt Norton'**, in **'Four Quartets'**)

This quest for a certainty of meaning is resolved as nearly as Eliot can resolve it in **'Four Quartets'**. *'Human kind cannot bear very much reality'*, he writes, but in consolatory fashion various places and landscapes in the poem come to symbolise moments where time intersects with the timeless, and spiritual harmony is achieved – where music is *"heard so deeply / That it is not heard at all, but you are the music / While the music lasts"*.

Eliot's lighter verse is at its best in 'Old Possum's Book of Practical Cats' (1939), which has been popular with both children and adults and provided the somewhat unexpected basis for the successful musical. He was distinguished not only as a poet but as a critic and a dramatist. 'Murder in the Cathedral' (1935), his most successful play, handles in dignified formal verse the theme of the martyrdom of Thomas a' Becket. Eliot's essays crystallised many influential ideas, in particular his view that a writer can never be wholly original, but is a recipient of all that has been written previously.

Eliot cultivated impersonality and anonymity, which is one reason why his poetry is difficult. Another difficulty lies in the complexity of his themes, one of which is the loss of coherence in his time. Paradoxically his poetic voice is instantly recognisable, and dominated the century. It is the voice we hear in 'Prufrock':

> *On Margate Sands.*
> *I can connect*
> *Nothing with nothing.*

There are biographies of Eliot by Peter Ackroyd and Lyndall Gordon. There are also fascinating recordings of both Sir Alec Guinness and Eliot himself reciting his poetry. Guinness is the more attractive reader. Eliot is published by Faber.

93
J. R. R. Tolkien (1892–1973)

'The Hobbit' (1937) and 'The Lord of the Rings' (1954–55) are imaginatively driven by two things: Tolkien's scholarly love of ancient languages, and his affection for a fast-diminishing rural England.

Tolkien was brought to England from South Africa at the age of three. His early childhood was happily spent in rural Warwickshire to the south of Birmingham (where he was to go to school). While still a schoolboy he invented a new language, and his mature university studies firmed his enthusiasm for Old Norse, Anglo-Saxon, and the Icelandic sagas. His philological scholarship led to his appointment at Oxford University to professorships in English Language and Literature and Anglo-Saxon from 1925–1959.

For him his major work was not the epic fantasies which have had worldwide success, but 'The Silmarillion', in which single-handedly he attempted to replace the lost mythology of England, destroyed by the Norman Conquest. This dense and extraordinarily detailed work reached its first draft in 1925, but was finally assembled for publication only in 1977 by Tolkien's son Christopher.

The concept of 'The Hobbit' and 'The Lord of the Rings' is at once fantastically vast and surprisingly specific. "Middle Earth" is conceived as planet Earth at an earlier stage of evolution, and the shire of the Hobbits is pastoral England, in retreat before the ravages of industrialism and suburbia. Tolkien always denied that his tale of the struggle to rescue Middle Earth from the evil intentions of Sauron had any allegorical meaning, though some readers have been tempted to see the evils of Mordor as representative of actual Twentieth Century horrors: the 1914–18 war (in which Tolkien fought), Nazism, or the threat of nuclear annihilation. It has also been suggested that 'The Lord of the Rings' symbolically tells of the journey from childhood to adulthood.

Meanwhile his graphic narrative has powerfully caught imaginations. The changing landscapes are beautifully detailed; the unfolding adventure is structured with skilful suspense. And there is the undoubted appeal – virtually an escapist one – of an entire invented world, down to the detail of the maps, the folkloric illusion of the songs, the undergrowth of mythic reference, and the created languages. Tolkien's style is strongly influenced by the old sagas and by the Bible: it reads in places as if it were a translation from an ancient original.

The almost obsessive subtlety of Tolkien's imagination is caught in a detail of his introduction to 'The Hobbit', in which he distinguishes carefully between the brutish "Orcs" in his story and 'our' word "orc", meaning a dolphin-like sea animal. As we read Tolkien we take possession of an intricate, sophisticated fantasy that is at root related to a simple nostalgia for a lost England, "long ago" – as he writes in 'The Hobbit' – "in the quiet of the world, when there was less noise and more green......"

Tolkien is published by Allen and Unwin; there are biographies by Humphrey Carpenter and Michael White.

94
Two Prophetic Novelists

Aldous Huxley (1894–1963)
George Orwell (1903–1950)

The title of **Huxley**'s '**Brave New World**' (1932) is taken ironically from Shakespeare's 'Tempest'. The novel describes his appalling vision of a future in which independence of spirit is literally bred out of human beings. Scientific breeding and conditioning of people by the state is designed to achieve a robotic kind of harmony. A state-controlled drug, 'Soma', acts to induce passivity. The potential for scientific manipulation of people Huxley thought posed a greater threat than political totalitarianism.

He was progressively disillusioned with his times. His underlying theme is that human intellect is in excess of human achievement. Earlier novels – '**Crome Yellow**' (1921), '**Antic Hay**' (1923) and '**Point Counter Point**' (1928) – take a satirical view of contemporary intellectual and social life. In parallel with Eliot's poetry, they catch a hollowness at the heart of things. (The character of Mark Rampion in '**Point Counter Point**' is, interestingly, a portrait of Huxley's friend D.H.Lawrence.)

There are many autobiographical elements in '**Eyeless in Gaza**' (1936), in which the central character Anthony Beavis is possessed by the meaninglessness of western life, and adopts a form of pacifist mysticism. In 1937 Huxley moved to California, where his experiments with mescalin as a route to mystical being are documented in '**The Doors of Perception**' (1954) and '**Heaven and Hell**' (1956). His concerns for the future continued in '**Ape and Essence**' (1948), which describes the degenerative behaviour of survivors of an atomic war, and in the utopian vision of '**Island**' (1962).

Had it not been for an eye disease which prevented him from studying biology at Oxford (he chose English instead) Huxley's path might have been more concentratedly towards science. As it was, literature benefited from his scientific acumen.

*Huxley also wrote **short stories**, and while in California wrote the scripts for Hollywood versions of 'Pride and Prejudice' and 'Jane Eyre'. There is a biography by Nicholas Murray.*

George Orwell (his real name was Eric Blair) was educated, as was Huxley, at Eton. He was born in India and from 1922 to 1927 served in Burma with the India

Imperial Police. Like E.M.Forster he came to hate imperialism. Back in England, motivated by a keen sense of social justice and equality, he became preoccupied with what he called "the submerged working class". He adopted the life of a tramp to discover at first hand what deprivation meant, and published his findings in '**Down and Out in London and Paris**' (1933). A commission to investigate living conditions in the industrial north of England, especially among the unemployed, produced '**The Road to Wigan Pier**' (1937). A democratic socialist, avoiding party ties, he consolidated a career in writing, journalism and broadcasting. (His essays are full of interest: '**Shooting an Elephant**' is a small masterpiece.) He served in the Home Guard during the Second World War.

During the 1930s Orwell increasingly focused on the threat of totalitarianism. Unlike Huxley, who thought it would be defeated, Orwell saw it as a profound danger. He fought for the Republicans in the Spanish Civil War, and saw what he felt was a prospect of real socialism crushed by Stalin's intervention. He describes his experiences in '**Homage to Catalonia**' (1938). His two most famous novels, '**Animal Farm**' (1945) and '**1984**' (published in 1949), picked up the theme. '**Animal Farm**', which he described as 'a fairy tale', was inspired by the Russian Revolution and the tyranny of Stalinist Russia, particularly the Moscow 'purges' of the 1930s. But as a political fable it works as an analysis of how generally revolutions can become dictatorships.

His pessimism about the evolution of totalitarian systems is extended forbiddingly in '**1984**'. The famous opening sentence – *"It was a bright cold day in April, and the clocks were striking thirteen"* – alerts us to a world where the familiar and reassuring has shifted. The state disciplines the workers through brainwashing and thought control. Orwell's terminology, some of which has passed into common usage, chillingly defines the techniques of the regime: "doublethink", "Newspeak", "thoughtcrime", "The Anti-Sex League", "The Two Minute Hate", "Room 101", "Big Brother is Watching You". The dehumanised populace become "proles". (It is not Orwell's purpose to speculate about future technological developments, but Big Brother's two-way television screens, spying at will on every household, are an inspired detail.)

Has **Huxley**'s vision of the future turned out to be more accurate than **Orwell**'s? In a sense the question is irrelevant to both of them. To more sinister effect than the science fiction crystal-gazing of H.G.Wells, both created powerful nightmare scenarios, which retain their alarming effect long after the years that provoked them have passed.

There are biographies of Orwell by Bernard Crick, Gordon Bowker and D.J. Taylor. Huxley is published by Flamingo, and Orwell by Penguin.

95

L.P.Hartley (1895–1972)

Hartley was part of the artistic and literary set associated from 1908 to the late 1920s with Lady Ottoline Morrell, and meeting at first in London and then at her country house, Garsington Manor near Oxford. Overlapping the Bloomsbury Group, its members included Virginia Woolf, T.S.Eliot and Aldous Huxley.

He is best remembered for two prize-winning works of fiction: the '**Eustace and Hilda**' trilogy, completed in 1947, and '**The Go-Between**' (1953).

Both contain compelling studies of adolescence. '**The Shrimp and the Anemone**' (1944), the first unit of the trilogy, describes the Edwardian childhood of Eustace, who is trusting, fragile, an innocent hedonist, and his loving but dominating older sister, Hilda. The trilogy takes us through his schooldays, his student days at Oxford, and beyond. The present is constantly shaped by the past, and the trilogy ends with Eustace's death at the rock pool where the story began. Hartley writes with meticulous clarity, in a slow-paced narrative that is impeccably structured.

'**The Go-Between**' creates a beautifully evocative picture of Edwardian England. The heart of the story is in 12-year-old Leo's holiday at a rich school friend's house in Norfolk during the hot summer of 1900. He becomes the innocent go-between in an affair between his friend's older sister and a local farmer – an affair which is doomed to end in disaster. The manner of Leo's initiation into adult sexuality results in an emotional scarring which is to persist throughout his life. The story is told in flashback by the elderly Leo, and begins with the famous sentence: *"The past is a foreign country; they do things differently there."*

Hartley's biography is written by Adrian Wright. He is published by Faber and Penguin.

96
Social Comedy

Evelyn Waugh (1902–1966)
Anthony Powell (1905–2000)

In his first novel, 'Decline and Fall' (1928), Evelyn Waugh offered elegant absurdity, entertainingly light frivolity at the expense of the professional classes and high society. 'Decline and Fall' traces the comic disasters that befall Paul Pennyfeather, first as an Oxford undergraduate, then as a teacher in a small and bizarre boarding school, followed by tutoring in a wealthy Mayfair family and finally a spell in prison. 'Vile Bodies' (1930) and 'A Handful of Dust' (1934) deal similarly with the intrigues and sillinesses of upper class life in the 1920s and 1930s. 'Scoop' (1938) wittily sends up the world of Fleet Street magnates and ruthless newspaper rivalries. (Waugh draws on his own social world, and his experiences as a teacher and a journalist.)

But there is also a darker, sadder strain in Waugh. It shows itself briefly in the character of Tony Last in 'A Handful of Dust', when Waugh describes the lonely pathos of this victim of adultery. *"For a month now he had lived in a world suddenly bereft of order; it was as though the whole reasonable and decent constitution of things, the sum of all he had experienced or learned to expect, were an inconspicuous, inconsiderable object mislaid somewhere on the dressing table."* Ultimately this is still a comic world – the dressing table simile tells us that – but by the time we get to 'Brideshead Revisited' (written on military sick leave and published in 1945) the mood has changed. While we still have the background of country-house wealth and what Waugh once called *"beautiful high-born people"*, there is now a powerful sense of social decay, of the collapse of a brittle world. An important element in the story is the testing of Catholic faith. Waugh became a Catholic in 1928, and there are autobiographical aspects to 'The Ordeal of Gilbert Pinfold' (1957), which in whimsical fashion describes a writer's breakdown followed by a spiritual healing.

Possibly Waugh's best work lies in the 'Sword of Honour' trilogy – 'Men at Arms' (1952), 'Officers and Gentlemen' (1955) and 'Unconditional Surrender' (1961). Guy Crouchback, the central character and a Catholic, embarks in his Second World War military service on a vividly described journey of self-discovery. Some of the earlier episodes are farcically amusing, but the sequence modulates into a sombre sense of disaster and waste.

Waugh's high comedy makes an interesting contrast with the world of **P.G. Wodehouse** (1881–1975), best known for his Jeeves and Wooster novels. Though these elegantly trivial comedies of an upper-class toff and his witty, long-suffering butler have an Edwardian setting, they are essentially sanitised and timeless. The unpleasantnesses of the real world do not intrude.

Anthony Powell was a contemporary of Waugh and Orwell at Oxford. Like Waugh he belonged to the well-connected, clubbish society which his fiction describes. He is a master of social comedy, brilliantly funny, with a gift for eccentric characterisations. His major work, **'A Dance to the Music of Time'**, unwinds a huge satirical panorama of upper middle class English lives from the 1920s to the 1970s. In four trilogies of twelve novels – written from 1951 to 1975 and published as **'Spring'**, **'Summer'**, **'Autumn'** and **'Winter'** – the inter-weaving lives of over three hundred characters are observed through the narrative eyes of a novelist, Nicholas Jenkins. The sheer scale of the enterprise has prompted comparisons with Proust.

Powell takes his title from the allegorical painting of the same name by Poussin (1594–1665), which is displayed in London's Wallace Collection. The picture shows the personified figures of the four seasons dancing to a lyre. A satyr-like face in a cloud, the master of the dance, looks enigmatically down on the scene. **'A Dance to the Music of Time'** echoes the picture's suggestion of people dancing to a pattern which they do not control. Destinies criss-cross in the flickering fortunes of chance events. A recurring character is the comic and slightly sinister Kenneth Widmerpool, son of a manufacturer of liquid manure, arch plotter and manipulator, a splendidly created example of ruthless successful man.

Powell weaves into his – or his narrator's – superbly structured prose a lattice of literary allusions which enrich the civilised tone. Jenkins is often slightly unsure, slightly on the defensive, as in the wonderfully comic episode in 'The Valley of Bones' (**'Autumn'**) when his wartime commanding officer grills him on why he does not enjoy reading Trollope. The narrative is tinged with melancholy and powerlessness: *"As in musical chairs, the piano stops suddenly, someone is left without a seat, petrified for all time in their attitude of that particular moment. The balance sheet is struck there and then, a matter of luck whether its calculations have much bearing, one way or the other, on the commerce conducted......it was no good battling against Fate, which, seen in the right perspective, almost always provides a certain beauty of design, sometimes even an occasional good laugh."*

There are biographies of Evelyn Waugh by Christopher Sykes, David Wykes, Douglas Patey and Selina Hastings. Waugh is published by Penguin, and Powell by Heinemann and Random House.

97
Graham Greene (1904-1991)

Around his twentieth birthday, Graham Greene played Russian roulette six times within six months. At school, where his father was the headmaster, persecution by the other boys made him attempt his life. As his novels show, he had an instinctive sympathy with the outcast and the underdog, those who lived close to danger and to failure.

After graduating from Oxford he worked in journalism and as a reviewer and film critic. He travelled extensively, often to unglamorous or troubled parts of the globe. During the war he worked for the Foreign Office. His first novel to sell well was the thriller 'Stamboul Train' (1932). Somewhat arbitrarily he divided his fiction into the serious novels and the "entertainments"; of the latter, there were further successes with 'The Third Man' (adapted in 1950 from his 1949 screenplay for the Carol Reed film) and 'Our Man in Havana' (1958). Of his 28 novels, the outstanding achievements are 'Brighton Rock' (1938) and 'The Power and the Glory' (1940).

His conversion to Catholicism in 1926 was highly significant for his writing. His particular kind of faith led him to make a central theme of what in 'Brighton Rock' he called *"the appalling strangeness of the mercy of God"*. His major characters are haunted by depression, guilt, and betrayal. Often portrayed as pathetic or tragi-comic, they come from the seedier reaches of a hostile society – rejects, criminals, men on the run. Greene quoted, as "an epigraph for all the novels I have written", these lines from Browning's 'Bishop Blougram's Apology':

> *Our interest's on the dangerous edge of things,*
> *The honest thief, the tender murderer,*
> *The superstitious atheist......*

In 'Brighton Rock' the racked character of Pinkie, the violent Brighton gangster, comes as a real shock. The victim of an unhappy childhood, he has a disturbingly raw bitterness about life:

> *"I'll tell you what life is. It's jail. It's not knowing where to get some money.*
> *Worms and cataract, cancer. You hear 'em shrieking from the upper*
> *windows – children being born. It's dying slowly."*

Greene treats Pinkie, dying slowly, as a kind of martyr. At the end of the story the old priest finds a parallel for Pinkie in a man *"who lived in sin all through his life, because he couldn't bear the idea that any soul could suffer damnation".*

(Readers of '**Brighton Rock**' will find an interesting comparison in '**A Clockwork Orange**' (1962) by **Anthony Burgess** (1917–1993). Here too is a study of violence and evil, experimentally written using an invented slang to reflect the desensitised young gangsters. As in Greene the villains, while not vindicated, are made sympathetic.)

'**The Power and the Glory**' follows the flight from the authorities of a Mexican priest who is determined still to practise, despite the state's persecution of the church. A shabby and unheroic alcoholic, Greene's "whisky priest" is given to giggling fatalistically at his plight. *"He could never take the complications of destiny quite seriously......He felt like a man without a passport who is turned away from every harbour."* As we follow his adventures, and his moments of tenderness and love, we warm to this wreck of a man. Finally captured, and facing execution, he felt *"only an immense disappointment because he had to go to God empty-handed, with nothing done at all".* It is a powerful story, distinguished by Greene's remarkable evocation of a sour and down-at-heel country where the vultures continuously circle "like indigestion spots". Chapter One, for example, is a masterly conjuring of heat, lassitude and degeneration. The distinction between serious writing and 'entertainments' dissolves before this gripping and moving novel.

Graham Greene also wrote travel books and plays. Other novels worth pursuing are 'The Heart of the Matter' (1948), 'The End of the Affair' (1951), 'The Quiet American' (1955), set in 1952 war-time Saigon, and, in lighter vein, 'Monsignor Quixote' (1982). Greene wrote autobiographical essays. His biography has been written by Norman Sherry. The novels are published by Vintage Classics and Penguin.

98
John Betjeman (1906–1984)

➤─┤◆➤─◯─◀┤─◆─◀

As a poet and as a personality, an eccentric who celebrated eccentricity, Betjeman has been immensely popular with the English, with whom his humour and his foibles strike a deep chord. Critical opinion rather condescended to him in his lifetime. He was sometimes dismissed as a lightweight rhymer whose very popularity – he could be easily understood! – seemed to disqualify him from serious consideration in an age that affected to value complexity in verse.

His qualities were recognised by fellow practitioners such as Auden and Larkin. His metrics are subtle and witty. He has a gift for unexpected and often outrageous rhymes (*"I put my final shilling in the meter / And only made my loneliness completer."*) Some of his poems affectionately evoke a long-vanished country-house Englishness, but it would be wrong to identify him with simple nostalgia. He has an alert eye for comic detail and absurdity, not least his own. Flights of lustful fancy directed at muscular sporting girls are developed with a twinkle that quickly becomes self-parody. The later poems are haunted by a melancholy sense of bodily decay hurrying near (as in **'Late Flowering Lust'**, 1954); his Anglicanism mixes with an insistent fear of death.

He brought into poetry a memorable evocation of a middle-class world that fondly amused him: a world of cruets and gymslips, fish knives and tennis clubs, *"the six o'clock news and a lime juice and gin"*. He creates strong impressions of houses, streets and landscapes, and had a genius for recognising the period suggestiveness of the names of products and places – Home and Colonial Stores, radiograms, plimsolls; Upper Lambourne, Beaulieu water, and Marchmont Avenue. **'A Lincolnshire Tale'** is a good example of how Betjeman used and enjoyed place names – the plangent effect of their sound and the pictures they create.

> *A whacking great sunset bathed level and drain*
> *From Kirkby with Muckby to Beckby-on-Bain,*
> *And I saw as I journeyed, my marketing done*
> *Old Caistorby tower take the last of the sun.*

(The unliterary enthusiasm of that *"whacking great sunset"* is characteristic, and as impishly calculated as it appears casual.)

Betjeman's cherishing of arcane detail, Victoriana, London's metropolitan railway, church history and gothic architecture, in his writings and in his broadcasts, opened a generation's eyes to the need to preserve and restore an architectural heritage. He was a prominent campaigner against the march of tarmac and concrete. *"Come friendly bombs and fall on Slough / It isn't fit for humans now..."*

Betjeman sometimes seems to be travelling towards a merely conventional sentiment and then startles us with a telling word or image. **'Death of King George V'**, which draws on a newspaper headline 'New King Arrives in his Capital By Air', describes the late king's stamp collection *"with mounts long dry"*, and closes with a picture of old men in country houses staring with incomprehension as *"a young man lands hatless from the air"*. The passing of an era is beautifully caught. In another short poem, '**In a Bath Tea Shop**', a *"very ordinary little woman"* and *"a thumping crook"* are glimpsed holding hands. They are, for a moment, *"little lower than the angels"*.

His first collection of poems appeared in 1931. The blank verse autobiography, '**Summoned by Bells**', was published in 1960. He was knighted in 1969 and appointed Poet Laureate in 1972. The **Collected Poems** (1958, with subsequent editions) were a huge popular success. He can be very amusing. His comedy combines a cheerful recapturing of a disappearing society with a wistful and hurt response to life's disappointments:

> *...Time, bring back*
> *The rapturous ignorance of long ago,*
> *The peace, before the dreadful daylight starts,*
> *Of unkept promises and broken hearts.*   '**Norfolk**'

Betjeman's biography has been prepared in three volumes by Bevis Hillier. The poetry is published by John Murray.

99
Samuel Beckett (1906–1989)

There is no reason why bleakness should not be entertaining. If you take the absolute view, as Beckett does, that life is meaningless, then your sense of absurdity is duly heightened. In his plays and his fictions Beckett is gripping, absorbing, and often very funny.

Beckett was born in Dublin where he had a Protestant upbringing. He studied English, French and Italian at Trinity College, and spent the five years after his graduation as a lecturer, mostly in Dublin, London and Paris. Like James Joyce, another Irishman who was self-exiled, he settled in Paris more or less permanently in 1932. He had met Joyce in Paris in 1928, and for a while he became a kind of honorary secretary to Joyce, and a lasting friend. He shared Joyce's obsession with words. But whereas in Joyce the excitement of words is a liberation, in the mouths of Beckett's characters words are often minimal and inadequate tools, groping to map out illogicality and meaninglessness, and sometimes collapsing into total inconsequentiality or silence. His creations are suffering, isolated figures – outcasts, misfits, tramps, clowns.

The major novels are 'Watt' (1953), and the trilogy 'Molloy', 'Malone Dies' and 'The Unnameable', first published in French and appearing in English in 1955, 1956 and 1958. His triumphant and ground-breaking play, 'Waiting For Godot', was produced in Paris in 1953 and in London in 1955. The classic radio play 'All That Fall' was first broadcast by the BBC in 1957. Later plays include 'Endgame' (1958), 'Krapp's Last Tape' (also 1958), and 'Happy Days' (1961).

The novels take the form of interior monologues, in which the narrators document struggle and despair, sometimes with dogged black humour. 'Malone Dies' ends with the words *"...where I am I don't know, I'll never know, in the silence you don't know, you must go on, I can't go on, I'll go on"*. The plays were revolutionary, extending the possibilities of theatre towards a new kind of minimalism. In 'Endgame', a blind and paralysed man communes with his parents, both of whom are senile and confined in dustbins. Winnie, the sole character in 'Happy Days', is buried in sand up to her neck. In 'Krapp's Last Tape' the stage is exclusively occupied by an old man listening to tapes of his younger self. 'Breath' (1970) has no characters at all; the stage is empty save for a pile of rubbish. On the soundtrack we hear one sigh. The play lasts for thirty seconds.

In the two acts of 'Waiting for Godot', two clown-like figures await an appointment with Godot, who never comes. The wait is interrupted only by a bullying brute pulling a broken companion on a rope, and a boy bearing the message that Godot is on his way. In the second act the bare and solitary tree which is the set has grown leaves, and the bully reappears, now blind, and dependant on his slave as on a guide-dog. Nothing else changes. As a critic said of the two acts, "Nothing happens, twice". But nothing happens brilliantly. The play's dialogue draws on the knockabout style of music hall and vaudeville, and the mild diversions created by the two main figures to entertain themselves as they wait are painfully comic. After one such episode we have this exchange:

- *That passed the time.*
- *It would have passed in any case.*
- *Yes. But not so rapidly.*

The play has been variously interpreted, both as a nihilistic statement of the folly of awaiting Christian salvation, and as a Christian affirmation of hope. Both extremes are possibly wide of the mark. If, as Beckett once said, life is but a brief interval between the forceps and the grave, then waiting is the only meaning. What briefly flickers, in this challenging and touching play, is the humanity of the central companionship.

In 1956 Beckett stated that "at the end of my work there's nothing but dust". Out of that dusty nothing he has made compelling art.

There is a biography of Beckett, "Damned to Fame", by James Knowlson. His plays are published by Faber and the novels by Calder.

100
W.H.Auden (1907–1973)

In the 1930s, a deeply troubled and self-aware decade, English poetry was dominated by W.H.Auden. His first collection had been published in 1930; he authoritatively shaped the left-wing agenda for many of his contemporaries. (T.S.Eliot, who did not follow a radical and politically committed route, meanwhile became for some of the new generation of writers a lost leader, rather as Wordsworth had done a hundred years before.)

For Auden poetry was not a matter of self-expression. Disliking emotional indulgence, he preferred an austere strength. He gives us an unsentimental, unremittingly honest vision of life, death, and the evil, cruelty and threat of the times. It is of course a personal vision – how could it be anything else? – but it commands respect through its uncompromising intelligence.

Stylistically his range is remarkable. He had a musical ear (he was to collaborate later with both Britten and Stravinsky) and his rhythmical sureness is felt alike in traditional forms, ballad metres and jazz-like improvisation. His carefully wrought lines have an appearance of spontaneity, which is a key to their memorability. (It is a distinctive voice: his recorded readings can be quite mesmerising.) This stanza from a later poem, '**The Shield of Achilles**' (1955), has a characteristic directness:

> *A ragged urchin, aimless and alone,*
> *Loitered about that vacancy, a bird*
> *Flew up to safety from his well-aimed stone:*
> *That girls are raped, that two boys knife a third,*
> *Were axioms to him, who'd never heard*

Of any world where promises were kept,
Or one could weep because another wept.

The same poem illustrates his distrust of the state within which citizens are impersonally manipulated – *"Out of the air a voice without a face / Proved by statistics that some cause was just…"* He later wrote: *"Whoever rules, our duty to the City / Is loyal opposition".*

As a bulwark against political darkness Auden affirms a beacon in beauty, 'faultless love', and humanity. There is a controlled lyricism in **'Seascape'** (*"Look, stranger, on this island now"*) and **'Lullaby'** (*"Lay your sleeping head, my love / Human on my faithless arm"*).

Wystan Hugh Auden was at prep school with **Christopher Isherwood**, whose 'Goodbye to Berlin' (1939) was later to inspire the musical 'Cabaret', and with whom Auden was co-author of three plays. At Oxford he was an influence upon **Stephen Spender**, **Louis MacNeice**, **Cecil Day-Lewis** and **Rex Warner**, all of whom were to be significant writers in the 1930s and beyond. His anti-fascist sympathies took him to Spain in 1936, where he was an ambulance driver for the Republicans. In 1939, with Isherwood, he emigrated to the United States, and became an American citizen in 1946. In the 1940s his Christian faith strengthened. He discarded his Marxism and repudiated some of his earlier poems. A homosexual relationship with Chester Kallman, met in America, became central to his life. From 1956–1960 he was Professor of Poetry at Oxford. Most of his time from 1958 was spent in Austria with Kallman, but in 1972 he accepted the invitation to return to a living in Christ Church, his old college. He died in Vienna.

Throughout his work Auden maintains a cool detachment, as if he is living through a warp in a much broader historical continuum. He frequently refers to 'Time' with a sense of sweep that he may have got from Hardy, whom he admired. This, and his related interest in geology, informs one of his best poems, **'In Praise of Limestone'**.

Among other poems worth sampling are **'Night Mail'** (a simple but engaging piece written for the soundtrack of a short documentary film, and an early example of Auden's rhythmic versatility), **'Roman Wall Blues'**, **'One Evening'**, **'Autumn Song'**, **'The Quarry'**, **'Musée des Beaux Arts'** and **'Gare du Midi'**. The ballads **'Victor'** and **'Miss Gee'** have a skittish, undergraduate humour about them. Auden was a fine writer of obituary poems: **'Stop All The Clocks…'** has had a recent revival in popular appeal, and **'In Memory of W.B. Yeats'** is especially impressive. Its last section, about the surviving value of poetry, has an appropriateness to his own best work:

In the deserts of the heart
Let the healing fountain start,
In the prison of his days
Teach the free man how to praise.

Auden's biography has been written by Humphrey Carpenter. The poetry is published by Faber and Penguin.

101

The Human Condition

William Golding (1911–1993)
Charles Causley (1917–2003)

>─┤─◆>─◦─<◆┤─<

At the opening of **William Golding**'s '**Pincher Martin**' (1956) a man is struggling against drowning in the sea. At the close of the novel, he drowns. We realise that the duration of the novel, in which a series of anguished memories make him question the moral bases of his life, has coincided with the terrifying seconds of his drowning.

It is Golding's favourite strategy as a novelist to place his characters in an extreme and testing situation. How they cope has things to tell us about human nature and the human condition. The novels take on the qualities of allegory or myth. At the same time Golding has descriptive powers of a very high order; the crises are not merely fables – they live, often with captivating and disturbing immediacy.

These are the threads which bind his writing, from his first novel and outstanding success, '**Lord of the Flies**' in 1954, and on through '**The Inheritors**' (1955), '**Pincher Martin**', '**Free Fall**' (1959), '**The Spire**' (1964), '**The Pyramid**' (1967), '**Darkness Visible**' (1979) and the trilogy which begins with '**Rites of Passage**' (1980).

While at Oxford Golding switched from a science degree to English Literature. During the Second World War he served in the Royal Navy, and then taught English at Bishop Wordsworth's School in Salisbury from 1945–1961. A group of young boys, marooned on a tropical island during a nuclear war, are the subject of '**Lord of the Flies**'. Golding's book was partly a response to '**The Coral Island**' (1857), one of over eighty adventure stories by R.M.Ballantyne, in which three boys, also abandoned on a tropical island, survive by developing skills of cooperation and dependency. At the end of Ballantyne's narrative the boys are imprisoned by 'savages', but rescued when a missionary comes to the island and converts the natives to Christianity. Golding's story, in contrast, questions Ballantyne's implicit assumption that human nature is essentially good, rational and benevolent (and that 'savages' will bow to a higher law). In a Conrad-like moment Golding's central figure, Ralph, glimpses "the darkness of man's heart". Despite Ralph's attempts as elected leader, the rival 'tribe' of Jack progressively dominates the island as the boys deteriorate, in a dark and thrilling sequence of events, into a violent savagery of their own, which mimics the nuclear contest in the world beyond the island. A fascinating and rather ominous gloss on the novel is provided by Peter Brook's story of how, when he was filming **'Lord of the Flies'**, his boy actors became so caught up in their violence that they would ignore the call of "cut", and it became difficult for the film crew to snap them out of it.

In this brief extract, where a fire has got out of control, we see Golding's vivid power.

> *The flames, as though they were a kind of wild life, crept as a jaguar creeps on its belly towards a line of birch-like saplings that fledged an outcrop of the pink rock. They flapped at the first of the trees, and the branches grew a brief foliage of fire. The heart of flame leapt nimbly across the gap between the trees and then went swinging and flaring along the whole row of them. Beneath the capering boys a quarter of a mile square of forest was savage with smoke and flame. The separate noises of the fire merged into a drum-roll that seemed to shake the mountain.*

> *"You got your small fire all right."*

> *Startled, Ralph realised that the boys were falling still and silent, feeling the beginnings of awe at the power set free below them. The knowledge and the awe made him savage.*

'Rites of Passage' won the Booker Prize, and in 1983 Golding received the Nobel Prize for Literature.

There are interesting parallels between the career of William Golding and that of **Charles Causley**. Causley, too, served in the Royal Navy, and was a teacher in Launceston in Cornwall until he retired. He wrote a series of collections of poetry, many of the poems about and for children. The **Collected Poems** of 1975 was added to in 1992.

Causley's vision of children is intriguingly different from what we see in 'Lord of the

Flies'. (But we must be careful: Causley's children are real, whereas Golding's, while fleshed out, are figures in a parable.) Causley portrays innocence. Not a sentimentalised innocence – it has its upsets, fears and mysteries – but underpinned by a pulsating sense of childhood energy and delight. He often uses traditional ballad forms, and John Clare and Blake have been a particular inspiration. Here he is, in buoyant mood, in part of '**Timothy Winters**':

> *Timothy Winters comes to school*
> *With eyes as wide as a football pool,*
> *Ears like bombs and teeth like splinters:*
> *A blitz of a boy is Timothy Winters.*
>
> *His belly is white, his neck is dark,*
> *And his hair is an exclamation mark.*
> *His clothes are enough to scare a crow*
> *And through his britches the blue winds blow.*

Causley does not only write of children. Like Golding, he is also drawn to the sea, and there are religious themes in his work. His poetry deserves to be better known, both in its own right, and as a companion to '**Lord of the Flies**', which in a curious way it complements.

Golding's novels are published by Faber, and Causley's poetry by Macmillan.

102

Distinctive Welsh Voices

R.S.Thomas (1913–2000)

Dylan Thomas (1914–1953)

In the poetry of **R.S.Thomas**, Wales is a land snarled up in its history, unromantic but bleakly attractive. '**Welsh Landscape**' gives us his metaphorical perspective:

> *There is no present in Wales,*
> *And no future;*
> *There is only the past,*
> *Brittle with relics...*

Thomas was ordained a clergyman in the Church of Wales in 1937, and practised in a series of rural parishes. He was born in Cardiff and studied at University College, Bangor. While at university he learnt Welsh, but wrote his poems in English. He married the painter Mildred Eldridge. His spiritual home is "the bald Welsh hills" of his parishes, where he identifies a dogged kind of heroism in the unsung and imperfect men who farm the uplands. Iago Prytherch, in 'A Peasant', is *"half-witted"*. *"There is something frightening in the vacancy of his mind"*, but he is valued as a *"prototype"*, admirable in his natural fortitude. 'The Face' hymns the memory of a ploughman who becomes an icon of uncelebrated stoicism. *"His hands are broken / But not his spirit. He is like bark / Weathering on the tree of his kind."*

Thomas's first collection, 'Song At The Year's Turning', appeared in 1955. His later poetry, from 'H'm' (1972), is more complex and difficult, and develops his religious themes. As a poet he was a solitary and independent figure. He did not court popularity. (I remember him at a public poetry reading appearing indifferent and almost grudging that an audience had appeared expecting him to read his poems!) In a defiant-seeming way his verses speak from a deeply-entrenched tradition of rural values.

His Collected Poems, 1945–1990, are published by Phoenix.

Dylan Thomas enjoyed assuming the public mantle of 'Poet'. His readings have a quality of bardic proclamation (though he knew no Welsh). There has been criticism that he is in love simply with the colour and sound of words and has no regard for meaning, though we know that in fact he took great care in his revisions. Poetry as a transforming celebratory vision *mattered* to him. He was a late romantic, singing the vigour and glory of life and landscape, particularly the Taff estuary that was overlooked by his home at Laugherne.

Born in Swansea, he moved to London in 1934 to a life of journalism, broadcasting, poetry and stories. Some of his broadcast stories, particularly 'A Child's Christmas in Wales' and 'Conversation about Christmas' from 'A Prospect of the Sea', have a Dickensian humour and richness. In 1937 he married Caitlin; in 1949 they settled in Laugherne, where he is buried.

The frenzied American lecture tours in the 1950s (reminiscent again of Dickens), and the alcohol poisoning which contributed to his final collapse in New York, have perhaps over-dominated our picture of him, suggesting a careless bohemianism. In the writing itself there is at its best an uplifting gusto, especially when he fondly recalls his boyhood. We find it in the lyric excitement of 'Poem in October', when he looks back at the age of thirty:

...And I saw in the turning so clearly a child's
Forgotten mornings when he walked with his mother
 Through the parables
  Of sun light
 And the legends of the green chapels

And the twice told fields of infancy
That his tears burned my cheeks and his heart moved in mine.
These were the woods the river and sea
 Where a boy
  In the listening
Summertime of the dead whispered the truth of his joy
To the trees and the stones and the fish in the tide.
 And the mystery
  Sang alive
Still in the water and the singingbirds.

For Dylan Thomas the mysterious cycle of life and death is a constant reference point – *"Time held me green and dying."*

Other poems to seek out are '**Fern Hill**', '**The Force that through the green fuse...**', '**The Hand that Signed the Paper**', '**And Death Shall Have No Dominion...**' and the touching elegy for his father, '**Do not go gentle into that good night...**'

One of his best-remembered works is '**Under Milk Wood**', the radio play first broadcast by the BBC in 1954. Produced by Douglas Cleverdon, it was immediately acclaimed as a classic. With 69 voices and two narrators, '**Under Milk Wood**' gives a comic fantasy impression of one day in the fictional village of Llareggub. (The name is Thomas' little joke, revealed when the letters are reversed.) The language is alive, and Thomas has a superb grasp of radio's potential:

Mrs Pugh	*Persons with manners,*
Second Voice	*snaps Mrs cold Pugh,*
Mrs Pugh	*do not nod at table.*
First Voice	*Mr Pugh cringes awake. He puts on a soft-soaping smile: it is sad and grey under his nicotine-eggyellow weeping walrus Victorian moustache worn thick and long in memory of Doctor Crippen.*
Mrs Pugh	*You should wait until you retire to your sty,*
Second Voice	*says Mrs Pugh, sweet as a razor. His fawning measly quarter-smile freezes. Sly and silent, he foxes into his*

> *chemist's den and there, in a hiss and prussic circle of*
> *cauldrons and phials brimful with pox and the Black*
> *Death, cooks up a fricassee of deadly nightshade,*
> *nicotine, hot frog, cyanide and bat-spit for his needling*
> *stalactite hag and bednag of a pokerbacked nutcracker*
> *wife.*

Mr Pugh *I beg your pardon, my dear,*
Second Voice *he murmurs with a wheedle.*

*The **Collected Poems** are published by Dent / Everyman and Weidenfeld & Nicholson.*
There are biographies of Dylan Thomas by Paul Ferris, Andrew Lycett and Andrew Sinclair.
His widow, Caitlin, has written 'Double Drink Story: My Life with Dylan Thomas'.

103
Patrick O'Brian (1914–2000)

Many devotees of modern fiction have yet to discover Patrick O'Brian. His sequence of twenty novels following British naval exploits during the wars with Napoleon's France appeared from 1969 onwards (he was three chapters into the twenty-first when he died). But it was not until the 1990s that his reputation began to soar. He is now rightly celebrated as one of the finest – if not the very best – of historical novelists.

What do we expect of a *historical* novel? – the evocation of a living past in all its fascinating detail, certainly; and also a perspective upon the reciprocal shaping of people and events. Historical 'truth' may well be an illusory goal, but paradoxically writers of fiction have as good a chance as historians of persuading us that they have captured the character and characters of an epoch. O'Brian is brilliant in his use of meticulous research, yet at the same time he makes free with facts and invents his key personalities in order to paint a rich and compelling canvas. (His sequence covers the years from 1801–1815.) Revealingly, he has recorded that after writing his biography of Picasso he was "glad to get back to my naval tales, where I could say what I liked, and control rhythm and events, if not the course of history".

Two superbly-drawn characters bestride the novels – Captain Jack Aubrey and his surgeon friend Stephen Maturin. Aubrey is warm-hearted, inspirational to his crews, professional to his fingertips when on deck, proud and ambitious as a sailor, and a Jack the Lad when in foreign ports. He enjoys a good (and bad) pun. He is amusingly much less a man of the world when he attempts to do battle with the sharks and manipulators of Whitehall and Regency society. In contrast Maturin, while innocent of the naval life to which he is introduced by Aubrey, is wily and shrewd as befits his secret role as a British agent. Expert in medical matters (he performs some extraordinary shipboard operations), he also entertains us with his boyish and knowledgeable enthusiasm for natural history as he seizes every opportunity thrown up by their world-wide voyages to collect specimens. Both men share a love of music – play the violin and the cello together – and the ship's company rehearse the 'Messiah' as their vessel blockades Toulon.

O'Brian's fiction is cultivated and exciting. There's a wealth of knowledge to be gleaned from the novels about life aboard ship, naval strategies and naval politics. He has a fine ear for ways of speech, and the extensive vocabulary of a linguist. He is vivid and skilled in evoking the rawness and hazards of life with the elements: searing tropical heat, wind, storm, ice, fire at sea, sinkings, drowning. The sea battles are grippingly described. But he is equally compelling and subtle in his descriptions of life ashore, be it in exotic locations about the world or in the Admiralty in London, or Jack Aubrey's home in Hampshire. There are triumphant chapters where O'Brian ventures with great aplomb into Jane Austen territory – drawing room society, banquets, and delicate interplay between the sexes.

For these are not grown-up stories for boys. What distinguishes O'Brian from his predecessors in the tradition of naval historical fiction, writers such as Captain Marryat (1792–1848) and C.S.Forester (1899–1966), is his wit, his cultivated learning and the depth of his characterisations. He tells a rattling good yarn, but the appeal is as great in the quieter moments. Here he is in '**Treason's Harbour**' (1983), describing Jack Aubrey on shore in Valletta and about to improve his education:

> *When Laura Fielding came to give him his Italian lesson…she found him in a startlingly enterprising mood, despite a heavy day at the dockyard and a great deal of concern about his frigate's knees. Since Jack Aubrey had never deliberately and with malice aforethought seduced any woman in his life, his was not a regular siege of her heart, with formal lines of approach, saps and covered ways; his only strategy (if anything so instinctive and unpremeditated deserved such a name) was to smile very much, to be as agreeable as he could, and to move his chair closer and closer.*

> *Very early in their recapitulation of the imperfect subjunctive of the irregular verb* stare *Mrs Fielding saw with alarm that her pupil's conduct was likely to grow even more irregular than her verb. She was aware of his motions rather before they were quite clear in his own mind, for she had*

*been brought up in the free and easy atmosphere of the Neapolitan court,
and she had been accustomed to gallantry from a very early age; ancient
counsellors, beardless pages, and a large variety of gentlemen had attacked
her virtue, and although she had repulsed the great majority it was a subject
that interested her – she could detect the earliest symptoms of an amorous
inclination, and upon the whole she found they did not differ very much,
from man to man.*

Compare the leisurely comedy of this with the tight drama in the south Atlantic of
the pursuit of Aubrey's ship by a Dutch man-of-war. Notice how the technicalities
of sails and navigation expertly draw us in rather than deter:

*They raced furiously over the empty, heaving sea under a clear late evening
sky, both ships being driven very hard; and the first to lose an important
spar or sail would lose the race that night. The sun was setting; in an hour
and forty minutes the moon would rise, a little past her full. With the
afterglow and then the strong moonlight, there would be small chance of
jigging unperceived; yet half an hour before the moon he would bring the
wind a point or so on the quarter, just so that the jibs and forward staysails
would stand and give him another half knot or even more. And all things
being considered, hammocks might be piped down: the larboard watch
would turn in with all their clothes on in case of emergency, and there was
no point in keeping them at quarters, shivering behind their tight-closed
ports: the crisis, if it came to that, was some way off. Perhaps a great way to
the east. He had chased forty-eight hours before this.*

*In the darkened cabin he found Stephen with his 'cello' between his knees
and a soup-tureen at his side. 'Judas,' he said, lifting the lid and beholding
the emptiness.*

*'Not at all, my dear. More is on the brew; but I cannot recommend it. You
would be better with a glass of water, tempered with a few drops of wine, a
very few drops of wine, and a piece of biscuit.'*

*'What did you eat it for, then? Why did you not leave a scrap, not a single
scrap?'*

*'It was only that I felt my need was greater than thine, my business of
greater importance than your business. For whereas yours is concerned with
death, mine is the bringing forth of life. Mrs Boswell is in labour, and some
time tonight or tomorrow I think I may promise you an addition to your
crew.'*   ('**Desolation Island**', 1978)

O'Brian was born in England, though he later invented an Irish identity. Like his creation Maturin, he was fluent in French, Spanish and Catalan. He was an intelligence officer in World War Two. He wrote other novels, short stories, poetry, biography and translations. After the war, he moved with his second wife to France – where in Collioure he lived for the rest of his life. The cosmopolitan background invigorates the writing.

The Aubrey-Maturin novels, as they have come to be called, are published by Harper Collins. Also see 'Patrick O'Brian (A Life Revealed)' by Dean King, and 'Patrick O'Brian: The Making of a Novelist' by his step-son, Nikolai Tolstoy.

104
Experiment in the Modern Novel

Iris Murdoch (1919–1999)
John Fowles (1926–   )

John Bayley's '**Iris: A Memoir**', and the subsequent film '**Iris**', give a moving account of his marriage to **Iris Murdoch**, and her suffering from Alzheimer's Disease. Perhaps less well-known to many are her novels themselves. After '**Under the Net**' (1954), she wrote twenty-five further novels, in addition to plays and philosophical works. She won a number of literary awards and attracted a strong following as one of the most original and sophisticated of modern novelists.

She was born in Dublin of Anglo-Irish parents but brought up in London where she worked as a Treasury Civil Servant before becoming a lecturer in philosophy at Oxford University, where she was a fellow of St Anne's College from 1948–1963. She said that her plots were driven by "the energy of philosophical problems", though not in a dryly theoretical way – characters must not "think" too much. An unusual mix of psychological realism, poetic symbolism, mystery and humour, the novels defy traditional categorisations: they are sharp, stimulating and often comic.

The stories combine entertainingly shrewd observations of human nature with a sense of patterns and myths in human behaviour. The characters, twentieth century people who are usually self-aware and professional, seek in some bewilderment an understanding of their moral position, searching to take responsibility for themselves in fielding their sexual relationships and insecurities. Happiness, Iris Murdoch wrote, "is being busy and lively and unconcerned with self...to be damned is for one's ordinary everyday mode of consciousness to be unremitting, agonising preoccupation with self."

The four novels which between them constitute her most successful work are 'Under the Net'; 'The Bell' (1958), which is set in a lay religious community; 'The Black Prince' (1973), concerned with the gulf between great art and the fallible human beings who create it; and 'The Sea, The Sea' (1978), winner of the Booker Prize, which centres on a theatre director's childhood love.

John Fowles' fiction combines traditional features of the novel, such as gripping plots, suspense, and psychological journeys of discovery, with a bold experimentation that keeps the reader intrigued. His craft is informed by a deep interest in the novel as an art form, his knowledge of French literature (he read French at Oxford), and the philosophy of existentialism – which raises issues of individual identity and freedom. (One of 'Daniel Martin's characters is faulted for "her obsession with solitary independence".)

His first novel, 'The Collector' (1963), tells of a bizarre and sadistic kidnap. Fowles uses split narrative as we follow the compelling but unpleasant first-person account of an abductor, interspersed with the diary of his victim. 'The Magus' (1966, revised in 1977) is a more elaborate variation on the theme of manipulation. A tense, clever story, it tells of an English teacher on a Greek island whose life is mysteriously deceived and controlled by the strange Conchis, who presides over events rather like a mischievous novelist teasing his characters. This novel also sets in motion a favourite Fowles device, the *femme fatale*. Dangerous eroticism, another version of elusive teasing, becomes one of his favourite themes. 'The French Lieutenant's Woman' (1969) operates on two levels. Set in Lyme Regis in Dorset, Fowles' home since 1968, it consists of a remarkably dense imitation of the content and style of a Victorian novel, interwoven with Twentieth Century interpolations and commentary. There are two endings, leading in opposite directions.

'Daniel Martin' (1977) is more conventionally written. The opening chapter (interestingly written last) is a beautifully evocative description of a Devon harvest in 1942, and could stand alone as a short story in its own right. The novel also contains, in the Egyptian chapters, one of the best modern English recreations of the 'feel' of another country.

Also worth exploring is the richly descriptive story, 'The Ebony Tower' (1974). Iris Murdoch and John Fowles are both published by Vintage. See Peter J. Conrad, 'Iris Murdoch: A Life', and 'John Fowles – A Life in Two Worlds' by Eileen Warbutt.

105

Philip Larkin (1922–1985)

>·◆>·◒·<◆·<

Larkin once said in an interview that the arrival of the postman in the morning is consoling and healing. "It's a bad day when I don't get any post." So true, and so revealing – you warm to a poet who noticed the ordinary, caught the sense of failure and loneliness in the bad days, and yet had a witty self-awareness to carry him through.

Larkin's **Collected Poems** (1988) was a best-seller. Three volumes in three decades, some 85 poems, had established him as one of the most significant voices of his time: **'The Less Deceived'** (1955), **'The Whitsun Weddings'** (1964) and **'High Windows'** (1974). His poems describe people trapped in the banality of unfulfilled lives; his principal focus, in his words, was "the melancholy…frustrating, failing elements of life". Depressing material, maybe. But his wit, his humour and his supreme *skill* uplift and transform even as they define a downbeat stance.

> *Parting, after about five*
> *Rehearsals, was an agreement*
> *That I was too selfish, withdrawn,*
> *And easily bored to love.*
> *Well, useful to get that learnt.*
> *In my wallet are still two snaps*
> *Of bosomy rose with fur gloves on.*
> *Unlucky charms, perhaps.*
>
> [last verse of **'Wild Oats'** from **'The Whitsun Weddings'** (Faber)] ·

The words are carefully placed. The failure of the relationship is offset by the perceptive humour of the "five rehearsals", the ironic throwaway of the fifth line, and a conclusion whose wry judgement leaves no trace of self-indulgence. Social awkwardness and inadequacy with women are recurrent themes.

The poems are not all autobiographical. Larkin frequently put on the guise of personalities and speaking styles – *personae* – which allowed him to capture contemporary cynicisms in memorably defining words. He parodied blunt inelegance, as in *"Books are a load of crap"* (**A Study of Reading Habits'**). More subtly, and possibly recalling his parents' unhappinesses, he creates ironies in the vernacular directness of *"They fuck you up, your Mum and Dad"* (**'This Be The Verse'**). (There's an in-joke in the reference to books: after he graduated from Oxford, Larkin became a librarian, and from 1955 until retirement was Librarian for the University of Hull.)

In contrast, Larkin writing without irony can be astonishingly forceful in his choice of words: old photographs *"lacerate"* simply by being over (**'Lines on a Young Lady's Photograph Album'**); loneliness *"clarifies"* (like jam setting) in **'Here'**; a rapist's mind lies open *"like a drawer of knives"* (**'Deceptions'**).

Sometimes there is a beautiful, sad lyricism, in poems like **'Afternoons'**, **'At Grass'**, and **'An Arundel Tomb'**, where he contemplates the earl and countess lying in stone above their tomb:

> *Time has transfigured them into*
> *Untruth. The stone fidelity*
> *They hardly meant has come to be*
> *Their final blazon, and to prove*
> *Our almost-instinct almost true:*
> *What will survive of us is love.*

Almost true. At the last moment, the positive affirmation is held back.

Larkin's two finest poems are **'Church Going'** and **'The Whitsun Weddings'**. In the first, a cyclist stops to look inside a country church. A bored unbeliever, he fools around at the lectern, but despite himself he is drawn into the church by a seriousness in the place which he respects. *"It pleases me to stand in silence here."* (At the beginning of the poem, he removes his cycle-clips *"in awkward reverence"*; those cycle-clips have become a comic icon of the 1950s.)

'The Whitsun Weddings' pictures a railway journey to London in which at a sequence of stations newly-married couples are seen onto the train by wedding parties on the platforms. The poem is full of riches, not least in the description of a train journey as *"a frail travelling coincidence"*, and in the notion of the disappearing platform parties being *"out on the end of an event"*.

Larkin leavens his poems with wit (*"sexual intercourse began in 1963"*) and with plaintive epigrams (*"nothing, like something, happens anywhere"*). But there is a darker, persistent note in the fear of death that shadows a number of them. *"Nothing contravenes / The coming dark."* His vision, ultimately, was not so much depressed as stoic, and ruthlessly honest.

Larkin is sometimes castigated for unpleasantnesses of personality – alleged grouchiness or prurience. He has his defenders, but in any case we have to ask how far such considerations should influence our reaction to the poems. Larkin's biography has been written by Andrew Motion, the Poet Laureate. The **'Collected Poems'** *are published by Faber.*

106
Drama from Rattigan to Osborne

Terence Rattigan (1911–1977)

John Whiting (1917–1963)

N.F.Simpson (1919–   )

Brendan Behan (1923–1964)

Robert Bolt (1924–1995)

John Osborne (1929–1994)

John Arden (1930–   )

Arnold Wesker (1932–   )

>–‹•›–◉–‹•›–‹

1956 has been widely mythologised as a watershed year for the British theatre, in which one play, John Osborne's **'Look Back in Anger'**, radically transformed the style and the agenda. In a year of wider political upheavals (Suez, and the Hungarian uprising), Osborne was seen as the prototypical 'Angry Young Man' whose work would finally put an end to the outmoded theatre of playwrights such as Terence Rattigan.

Today, interestingly, it all looks very different. Osborne's play no longer looks like the significant pivotal event it seemed at the time. Osborne's stock has fallen, and Rattigan's plays are enjoying revivals and renewed respect.

Terence Rattigan dominated successful London theatre in the 1940s. His first play was light comedy (**'French Without Tears'**, 1937), but then came a succession of serious plays in which he showed great talent in developing taut, emotional crisis: **'Flare Path'** (1942), **'The Winslow Boy'** (1946), and **'The Browning Version'** (1948). These were to be followed by two one-act dramas, **'Separate Tables'**, in 1954, and his study of T.E.Lawrence (of Arabia) in **'Ross'** (1960). Rattigan is particularly strong in exploring the solitary anguish of unfulfilled individuals, like Andrew Crocker-Harris, the ageing classics teacher of 'The Browning Version'. He skilfully accelerates and decelerates his plots, deftly withholding and revealing information. The major problem for him in the 1960s was twofold. The middle or upper-middle class background of his characters was no longer theatrically fashionable, and his great skill in crafting traditional naturalistic theatre counted for less as the influence of the East German Berthold Brecht and the experimentation of the Berliner Ensemble took hold. The phrase "well-made play" was turned against him as a term of abuse.

Another original talent of Rattigan's vintage was **John Whiting**. 'A Penny for A Song' (1951) was an eccentric comedy based on England's preparations to meet the threat of Napoleonic invasion, with set designs by Rowland Emmet, the Punch cartoonist famous for his drawings of whimsically weird railways. Whiting never quite found the commercial success that Rattigan had; he came closest with '**The Devils**' (1961), based on Aldous Huxley's '**The Devils of Loudon**'.

John Osborne was working as an actor when he submitted his controversial script to London's Royal Court theatre. The opening production of '**Look Back in Anger**' excited impassioned responses. Kenneth Tynan in *The Observer* said, "I doubt if I could love anyone who did not wish to see *Look Back in Anger*." Eric Keown in *Punch* wrote, "John Osborne makes it clear from the start that he intends to kick us in the teeth, and go on kicking us…Having got this gall out of his system he should write a more interesting play." Osborne's central character, Jimmy Porter, dominates the play with vitriolic abuse of his wife, her genteel father, and the complacent English 'establishment'. Porter dramatises himself as a rebel against the drabness and deadweight of post-war England. Undoubtedly the character struck a chord, though he was more a simple iconoclast than the left-wing radical he was sometimes taken for. Osborne's next most successful plays were '**The Entertainer**' (1957) and '**Luther**' (1961) – 'The Entertainer', about a fading and unfunny music hall comedian, Archie Rice, is arguably his richest play.

'**Look Back in Anger**' created huge excitement and was thought to be ground-breaking, though curiously in its stage idiom it is much closer to the Rattigan tradition than was recognised at the time. Meanwhile more significant pioneering work had been going on since 1953 in **Joan Littlewood**'s Theatre Workshop company based at Stratford East. Developing Brechtian techniques and the **expressionist** tradition, her company evolved a style of theatre in which ensemble playing, improvisation, song and dance opened up fresh new possibilities. There was a pronounced left-wing slant to the material performed, and one of the great successes was Brendan Behan. Behan was born in Dublin and arrested for IRA activity in 1939. There are echoes of Sean O'Casey in '**The Quare Fellow**' (1954), set in an Irish prison prior to a hanging, and '**The Hostage**' (1958), where a kidnapped British soldier is captive in a Dublin brothel. The Theatre Workshop style achieved its greatest triumph with Charles Chilton's '**Oh What A Lovely War**' in 1963.

Meanwhile, untouched by the new experimentation, **N.F.Simpson** and **Robert Bolt** each made a mark with contrastingly different styles. Simpson's '**A Resounding Tinkle**' (1957) and '**One Way Pendulum**' (1959) appealed to the late-50s appetite for zany, surreal comedy in the style of radio's Goon Show, while Bolt had a huge success with his play about Thomas More, '**A Man For All Seasons**' (1960), originally a radio script, which used the distancing technique of a narrator-presenter who also takes part in the action.

Two other playwrights were notable for their distinctive and individual work in the late 50s and early 60s. In '**Serjeant Musgrave's Dance**' in particular, **John Arden** used songs, verse and flexibility of staging to advantage in an "unhistorical parable". Set in a late Nineteenth Century colliery town in the north of England, the play tells the story of an army deserter who arrives on a crusading pacifist mission, but himself succumbs to violence. At the end of the play he aims a gatling gun at the audience.

Arnold Wesker is most especially known for his trilogy, '**Chicken Soup With Barley**' (1958), '**Roots**' (1959) and '**I'm Talking About Jerusalem**' (1960). Spanning two generations, and moving from 1930s London to 1940s Norfolk, the plays dramatise in a convincingly realistic style a family's tensions as some of its members strive for socialist ideals in the changing pre- and post-war world.

Wesker has complained that his plays have in recent years been unduly neglected. Fashions in theatre come and go, with almost quirky unpredictability. The history of these years in London theatre confirms the general truth that commercial success and dramatic value tend not to walk hand in hand. Equally, however, they illustrate the more provoking fact that notions of what constitutes good drama are themselves constantly on the move.

107
Harold Pinter (1930–   )

>─◆>─◦─<◆─!─<

In a seaside boarding house two superficially affable but increasingly threatening strangers arrive in search of Stanley. Stanley is wrapped up in himself, on edge, and lies about his past. The two strangers accuse Stanley of having betrayed their organisation. In a bizarre sequence of accelerating vitriol and violence, climaxing with Stanley's birthday party, they break him down and take him away. By the end he is an inarticulate wreck. We never have a context that enables us to make full sense of all this. The play is at once comic, gripping and troubling.

The production of Pinter's 'The Birthday Party' in 1957 was a far more exciting turning point in modern British theatre than Osborne's 'Look Back in Anger' a year earlier. While initially derided by the critics, 'The Birthday Party' established a new idiom. Like all subsequent Pinter it was instinctively dramatic in its structure (Pinter trained as an actor) and compellingly fresh in the nature of the dialogue and the style of the characterisation.

Pinter's territory, then and since, has been psychological insecurity: the tentative but flawed steps we make towards self-possession and identity. We build a personality for ourselves to give us a form of protection, but that necessarily involves a degree of self-deception. Each dialogue, each exchange, is a negotiation of nerves, part of an attempt to create identity and assert control. Pinter's characters offer bogus assurances about themselves. Ben in 'The Dumb Waiter' (1960) says when challenged that he has got "interests", but is pushed to identify them; the tramp Davies in 'The Caretaker' (also 1960) mutters about his "papers" that are in Sidcup, but they never materialise; Max in 'The Homecoming' (1965) aggressively asserts the perfection of the marriage he had, but simultaneously vilifies his dead wife.

Characters do not so much have relationships as circle about each other. As they circle about their past. They have – or invent – memories, but memories are no guide to truth. In the compulsion to dominate, characters may be undone when their fantasies are exposed and their insecurities revealed. Ruth in 'The Homecoming' radiates a controlled eroticism which throws the normally brash and cocky Lenny. The wife of Lenny's brother, Ruth one night turns up unexpectedly from America at the family's London home. Lenny gets her a glass of water. He asserts himself, tries to impress:

Lenny	*And now perhaps I'll relieve you of your glass.*
Ruth	*I haven't quite finished.*
Lenny	*You've consumed quite enough, in my opinion.*
Ruth	*No, I haven't.*
Lenny	*Quite sufficient, in my own opinion.*
Ruth	*Not in mine, Leonard.*

Pause

Lenny	*Don't call me that, please.*
Ruth	*Why not?*
Lenny	*That's the name my mother gave me.*

Pause

	Just give me the glass.
Ruth	*No.*

Pause

Lenny	*I'll take it, then.*
Ruth	*If you take the glass...I'll take you.*

Pause

Lenny	*How about me taking the glass without you taking me?*
Ruth	*Why don't I just take you?*

Pause

Lenny	*You're joking.*

As often in Pinter, the comedy of this is charged with disquiet. Lenny's attempt at self-assurance dissolves before her poise. Enigmatically, Ruth plays with language as she plays with Lenny. The sexual advance is verbal, not real.

Pinter was born an East Londoner. In his reworkings of London speech patterns he brilliantly suggests that what is said is frequently not what is meant. Language both conceals and reveals. Words are not to be trusted. What is unspoken, in the 'pauses' and the 'silences', speaks volumes: silence is a necessary avoidance. "The more acute the experience," Pinter once said, "the less articulate its expression."

Various labels have been attached to Pinter's drama – 'psychological thriller', 'comedy of menace', 'theatre of the absurd'. None are especially helpful. There are echoes of Chekhov in his lost and self-deluding characters, but the gentility of Chekhov's world is far removed from the latent violence we find in Pinter. His style is unique, and the term "Pinteresque" now belongs to the language.

Pinter has directed plays and written screenplays (including 'The Servant' and 'Accident') and film adaptations (for example 'The Go-Between' and 'The French Lieutenant's Woman'.) His short story **'The Examination'** *(1955) tells of a student psychologically reversing roles with his teacher, and the radio play* **'A Night Out'** *(1960) portrays a mother, her son, and a prostitute all frightened by their own insecurities.*

The **Complete Works** *are published by Methuen and there is a biography by Michael Billington.*

108
Ted Hughes (1930–1998)

There is in Hughes' writing a remarkable closeness to natural forces, an instinctive rawness, which has separated him from those poets of his time whose world is urban and cerebral. His father was a survivor of Gallipoli, a carpenter and later a tobacconist. His childhood in the Calder Valley of Yorkshire, its mill towns surrounded by moors, gave him a visceral excitement in the mysteries of creation that became the driving force in his poems and stories.

There are two sides to his vision, one a sheer delight in the beauties and magnificence of nature, and the other a darker sense of nature's violence and anarchy. When we read his work, from '**The Hawk in the Rain**' (1957) through to the personal pain of '**Birthday Letters**' (1998), it is clear that these two aspects to his work are parts of one vision, the one embedded in the other. His sense of the precariousness of existence, of the threat of apocalypse just beyond the horizon, is implicit throughout.

When he describes the animal and natural world his words have a provoking originality. Daffodils are *"ballerinas too early for music"*; an eel's mouth is *"a grin long and perfunctory"*; birds in the branches of trees are *"a market of gossip"*. The details can be amusing, like these, but there is also an intimidatory sense that man is a fragile intruder in a timeless and menacing environment. (This powerful theme is sometimes underpinned by Hughes' interest in anthropology, which he studied as well as English at Cambridge University.)

In the early poem '**The Horses**', he watches dawn break over the moors. He comes upon ten horses, motionless and silent – *"megalith-still"* – who seem in that lonely place to belong to a wild and elemental reality that excludes him.

> *I listened in emptiness on the moor-ridge.*
> *The curlew's tear turned its edge on the silence.*

It is like the sharpening of a knife.

Another poem, '**Wind**', describes a huge storm. A house rings *"like some fine green goblet in the note / That any second would shatter it"*. Inside the house *"we grip our hearts"*

> *Seeing the window tremble to come in,*
> *Hearing the stones cry out under the horizons.*

The poems in 'Crow' (1970) present a symbolic, mythical creature which squawks raucous scorn at man; the contempt is enhanced by Leonard Baskin's striking illustrations which accompany the book. In 'Wodwo' (1967) the poem 'Ghost Crabs' contrasts the *"nothingness"* of mankind with sinister invading crabs, who are the real power of the world, associated by Hughes with turmoil and convulsion. It is in 'Wodwo', incidentally, where we find one of the most remarkable short stories of the century, 'The Rain Horse', in which a man walking in a rain-sodden landscape is panicked into terror when he thinks himself pursued by a strange horse.

Hughes' vast output includes much writing designed primarily for children, but there is a rich appeal for adults in books such as 'The Iron Man' (1968), 'Season Songs' (1976), 'Remains of Elnet' (1979), 'River' (1983) and 'Flowers and Insects' (1986), which is again illustrated by Leonard Baskin. (He collaborated too with photographers such as Fay Godwin and Peter Keen.) In these he conjures brilliant images, as in 'Big Poppy' from 'Flowers and Insects' (Faber):

> *She sways towards August.*
> *A Bumble Bee*
> *Clambers into her drunken, fractured goblet -*
>
> *Up the royal carpet of a down-hung,*
> *Shrivel-edged, unhinged petal, her first-about-to-fall.*
> *He's in there as she sways. He utters thin*
>
> *Sizzling bleats of difficult enjoyment.*

The anthology 'Poetry in the Making' (1967) includes Hughes' fine accounts of poetry and the nature of poetic composition, originally written for BBC schools' radio. He often recorded and broadcast his poems: the tapes make excellent listening.

Up until his death, responses to Hughes' writing were sometimes sidetracked by controversy about the extent of his responsibility for the suicide of his wife **Sylvia Plath** in 1963. (He met her while an undergraduate at Cambridge and they were married in 1956.) He endured strident criticisms to which he never publicly responded. Then in 1998 came 'Birthday Letters', a poetry collection written over the decades following the suicide. These open and hurt poems explore a relationship that is revealed to be complex and intensely moving. Hughes took the decision to publish only when he knew that he was dying of cancer.

He succeeded John Betjeman as Poet Laureate in 1984. He did not enjoy or seek public celebrity, but his role in educational broadcasting in the 1960s was significant, and in later years he took very seriously his work with the Arvon writing foundation based in Devon (he moved with Sylvia Plath to a Devon farmhouse in 1961). The lasting qualities of his poetry will survive the arguments about his personal life.

Hughes' 'Tales From Ovid' (1997) was received with great enthusiasm. The Collected Poems were published by Faber in 2003. A biography has been written by Elaine Feinstein.

109
Sylvia Plath (1932–1963)

She was born in Boston, Massachusetts. Her father, a German-born professor of entomology, had emigrated to America. He died when she was eight. She came to Cambridge on a Fulbright Scholarship, meeting Ted Hughes there, and marrying him in 1956. They lived for three years in America, then London, and in 1961 moved to Devon. In 1962 she separated from him, and the next year took her own life. Twice before, before coming to England, she had attempted suicide.

She wrote some of the century's most troublingly memorable poems, many of them born out of stress and suffering. She had a needle-sharp mind that blinked at nothing. Written with the intense self-scrutiny that derives from the so-called "confessional" poetry of 1950s America, her poems hold her fears and her anger in a bright, disturbing glare. In 'The Eye-Mote' a splinter, stuck in her eye and after a week still resisting all attempts to remove it, becomes a metaphor for a blight that has settled on her life. *"What I want back is what I was."*

There are, amid the angst, loving and joyous moments. In 'Morning Song' she celebrates her pregnancy (*"Love set me going like a fat, gold watch"*) and in 'You're' the child in the womb is *"O high-riser, my little loaf"*. Yet such moments are fragile and threatened. 'Watercolour of Grantchester Meadows' describes a pastoral pleasantness, but finishes with a jolt – *"The owl shall stoop from his turret, the rat cry out."* In 'Mirror', similarly, the poem's conclusion introduces a jarring note. Playful presentations of what the mirror sees are followed by:

In me she has drowned a young girl, and in me an old woman
Rises towards her day after day, like a terrible fish.

One of her best-known poems, '**Daddy**', is a searing exorcism, in which she grapples with the frustration of never having really known her father. She blames him for deserting her, and turns him into a Nazi monster.

Sylvia Plath's two principal collections, 'The Colossus' (1960) and the posthumous 'Ariel' (1965), are subsumed in **Collected Poems** *(Faber, 1981). Her novel 'The Bell Jar' is based on her student depression while at Smith College in New England. See 'Rough Magic', a biography of Sylvia Plath by Paul Alexander. The new (2004) edition of 'Ariel' includes poems omitted from the 1965 edition, restoring the volume to Sylvia Plath's original manuscript.*

110
Alan Bennett (1934–   )

"The world we have lost wasn't one in which I would have been happy, though I look back on it and read about it with affection. And from this affection stem both the parody and the nostalgia; they are very close together." ('Writing Home', Faber) Alan Bennett is writing about the England of 1900–1940, the background to his first stage play '**Forty Years On**' (1968, Faber). The remark points us towards the essence of Bennett's appeal as a writer. He is in love with Englishness, partly *because* of the absurdities which he so dryly identifies. His work abounds in a warmth for quirkiness. Anger rarely finds a place; his drollery and ironies reveal but do not destroy.

He was born and went to school in Leeds, helped in his father's butcher's shop, and won a scholarship to Oxford. The Yorkshire roots gave him a sharp eye for pretentiousness and any kind of silliness. He first caught the public eye in '**Beyond the Fringe**', the hugely successful satirical revue of 1960; even then it was clear that his kind of humour was distinctively different from the surreal flights of his contemporaries, albeit that they were for a time more fashionable.

One of his most successful inventions has been '**Talking Heads**' (BBC Books), a series of six dramatic monologues originally presented on BBC television in 1987, and subsequently on radio and in theatres. (A further six appeared in 1998.) In 'A Lady of Letters' Miss Ruddock addresses us from an easy chair:

> *Prison, they have it easy. Television, table tennis, art. It's just a holiday camp, do you wonder there's crime? And people say, "Well, what can you do?" Well,*

you can get on to your MP for a start. I do, regularly. Got a reply to one letter this morning. I'd written drawing his attention to a hitherto unnoticed factor in the rise of crime, namely the number of policemen these days who wear glasses. What chance would they have against a determined assailant? He noted my comments and promised to make them known in the proper quarter. He's Labour but it's always very good notepaper and beautifully typed.

When I'd dusted round and done my jobs I had a walk on to the end and bought a little packet of pork sausage and some Basildon Bond. Big black hair in the sausage. So I wrote off to the makers enclosing the hair. Stuck it under a bit of sellotape. Little arrow: 'This is the hair.' I emphasised that I didn't want a substitute packet, as it was plainly manufactured under unhygienic conditions, so would they send me a refund of the purchase price plus the cost of the postage. I don't want inundating with sausage.

The entertainment of this is enriched by Bennett's wonderful ear for speech mannerisms and his artful mix in Miss Ruddock's characterisation of a comic gentility and a vulgarity which exclude self-knowledge. As the monologue ends, we discover that she is now herself in prison, a persistent writer of nuisance letters.

Alan Bennett's scripts also include 'An Englishman Abroad' (1982 – for television, about the double agent Guy Burgess, in Moscow); 'A Question of Attribution' (1988, about the spy Sir Anthony Blunt); 'The Madness of King George' (1991); and 'The Lady in the Van' (1999, a play about the tramp whom he allowed to set up home in his garden for fifteen years.) Bennett's drama is published by Faber and BBC Audiobooks, and his biography is written by Alexander Games.

111
Tom Stoppard (1937–   )

From his first success, **'Rosencrantz and Guildenstern are Dead'** (1966), Stoppard has built a reputation for plays that fizz with mind games and bold theatricality. Some of them are extended intellectual jokes. When he probes philosophical and political issues, it is the sheer speed and versatility of his wit that delights.

He was born Tom Straussler in Czechoslovakia. His family, fleeing before the Nazis, went to Singapore. His mother took him to India to escape the Japanese invasion; his father, staying behind, was killed. His mother now married a British army major, and the family settled in England in 1946.

In the summer of 1979 Stoppard had four plays running simultaneously in London. His prolific output includes fiction, radio and television drama, and screenplays (with especially distinctive work for 'Empire of the Sun', 1987, and 'Shakespeare in Love', 1998.) His trademark is exuberant wordplay, and plots which confound expectation and turn conventions inside out. **'Rosencrantz and Guildenstern are Dead'** brilliantly inverts Shakespeare's 'Hamlet', so that the two courtiers, inept and bewildered, take centre stage. They are comically marooned in incomprehension while the great events of the play sweep around them. Similarly two theatre critics find themselves, in **'The Real Inspector Hound'** (1968), drawn into the action of the hackneyed murder mystery they are reviewing. The play is a superb send-up of the genre.

In **'Travesties'** (1974) Stoppard builds a dazzlingly ingenious comedy upon the fact that Lenin, James Joyce and the Dadaist artist Tristan Tzara chanced to be in Zurich in 1918, and that Joyce was the business manager of a company presenting Wilde's 'The Importance of Being Earnest'. Out of this Stoppard creates an anarchic pastiche of the philosophy of art, political theory, period nostalgia, and Oscar Wilde. (One scene is written entirely in limericks.)

How serious is Stoppard? Where is he coming from? There are 'issues' in the plays, such as free will, the meaning of meaning, the intersection of art and politics, and the nature of human rights, but overall if there is a central earnestness in Stoppard's plays it seems to be simply the excitement of thinking. As he has written: "The truth is always a compound of two half-truths, and you never reach it, because there is always something more to say." What we enjoy is the bubble of puns, paradoxes and teases.

Here, in **'The Real Thing'** (1982), Annie, an actress, asks her lover Henry, a professional playwright, to use his skills to 'improve' a play written by a soldier who has been imprisoned after an anti-war demonstration. Henry thinks the play is rubbish.

Annie	*You say he can't write, like a head waiter saying you can't come in here without a tie. Because he can't put words together. What's so good about putting words together?*
Henry	*It's traditionally considered advantageous for a writer.*
Annie	*He's not a writer. He's a convict. **You're** a writer. You write **because** you're a writer. Even when you write **about** something, you have to think up something to write about just so you can keep writing. More well-chosen words nicely put together. So what? Why should that be it? Who says?*
Henry	*Nobody says. It just works best.*
Annie	*Of **course** it works. You teach a lot of people what to expect*

> *from good writing, and you end up with a lot of people saying*
> *you write well......*

Henry   *Jesus, Annie, you're beginning to scare me. There's something*
scary about stupidity made coherent.

Stoppard's other plays include the farcical philosophical satire 'Jumpers', (1972) in which university philosophers appear as actual acrobats; 'Arcadia' (1993), which he described as "a thriller and a romantic tragedy with jokes"; 'The Invention of Love' (1997) about the unrequited homosexual love of A.E.Housman; and 'The Coast of Utopia' (2002), his most ambitious work to date – three linked three-hour plays set in mid-Nineteenth Century Russia. Stoppard's biography has been written by Ira Nadel, and the plays are published by Faber.

112
Seamus Heaney (1939–   )

He is the greatest living poet. The citation for his Nobel Prize for Literature in 1995 praised his "works of lyrical beauty and ethical depth, which exalt everyday miracles and the living past".

Seamus Heaney was born in County Derry, the eldest of nine, his father a farmer in Mossbawm. He was educated at a diocesan boarding school, St Columb's College in Derry, and at Queen's University, Belfast. He became a teacher, and later he lectured at Queen's. In 1972, with his wife and three children, he moved to County Wicklow. From 1976 his home has been Dublin. He has lectured at Carysfort, the college of education in Dublin, and for several years has spent an annual term teaching creative writing at Harvard. He was Professor of Poetry at Oxford from 1989–1994.

He was inspired to write by Ted Hughes' 'View of a Pig'. That poem, in its sensuous fascination with the "thick, pink bulk" of a dead pig, kindled in Heaney a liberating impulse. About a year later, he started to write poems. The spirit of his poetry is generous, warm and humane. His first collections, **'Death of a Naturalist'** (1966) and **'Door into the Dark'** (1969), marvellously evoke Mossbawm and its environment: his father ploughing and digging – *'the curt cuts / of an edge through living roots'*; the *'summer's blood'* in blackberries; the smells, anxieties and delights of childhood. There is in these poems a deep respect for craft – ploughman, thatcher, water diviner. Water divining gives Heaney an image for the revelatory role of the poet. In the early poem '**Personal Helicon**' he defines one of the functions of his poetry – '*I rhyme / To see myself, to set the darkness echoing*'.

From '**Wintering Out**' (1972) the context widens. We sense an implicit exploration of roots, in history, archaeology, and – literally – in fields and peat bogs. Poems, says Heaney, come to consciousness "like bodies surfacing in a bog" – Tollund man, Grauballe man. Words – Gaelic, English, Saxon – become objects, each with their own tactile history.

> *Kinned by hieroglyphic*
> *peat on a spreadfield*
> *to the strangled victim,*
> *the love-nest in the bracken,*
>
> *I step through origins* ...... ('**Kinship**')

Images of violence, from the primitive past and from the Northern Irish 'troubles' of the present, begin to appear in poems like '**Strange Fruit**', '**Casualty**' and '**Punishment**'. The poems express him caught between *"civilised outrage"* and an understanding of dark tribalism. Heaney has always avoided the role of political poet. While some have criticised him for that, his pained ambivalence is honourable rather than evasive. (He has quoted with approval Roy Foster's statement that "the notion that people can reconcile more than one cultural identity may have much to recommend it".)

For Heaney, poetry as "the imaginative transformation of life" is the means by which "we can most truly grasp and comprehend it". Poetry makes the reader *feel good* – fills us "with a momentary sense of freedom and wholeness". Of his own discoveries, he writes in one of the '**Squarings**' poems *"It steadies me to tell these things"*. Poetry, he says in his Nobel acceptance speech, has an order and a truth that *"satisfies all that is appetitive in the intelligence and prehensile in the affections"*.

'**Wheels Within Wheels**', a poem in the 1991 collection, '**Seeing Things**', describes Heaney's childhood love of pedalling a bike upside down, enjoying what is at first a physical and then an emotional excitement, *"like an access of free power"*. Seeking more satisfaction, he drags the bike to a water hole and runs the tyres through the water, showering himself in muck. Wheels within wheels. It is a perfect image of creativity, the fulfilling headiness of words. Elsewhere, Heaney approves Dylan Thomas, aged twenty-three, asserting that a poem should be a happening, not a still life.

The sequence of '**Squarings**' poems also appears in '**Seeing Things**'. ('Squarings',

Heaney explains, were *"all those anglings, aimings, feints and squints"* in the game of marbles which preceded the shooting – another image, if we like, of poetry making). One of these poems recounts the legend of a strange ship that appeared in the air above the monks of Clonmacnoise as they were at prayer. The anchor snags on the altar rails and one of the sailors "shins and grapples" down a rope to release the ship. When he fails, the abbot instructs the monks to help him because the sailor cannot survive in their world, and will drown. They do so, the ship sails on, and the man climbs back

Out of the marvellous as he had known it.

Heaney describes this splendid poem as a parable "about crossing from the domain of the matter-of-fact into the domain of the imagined" – as both the monks and the sailor have done.

A poem, for Heaney, taps into our primitive consciousness, a sense of connection with memory and the past. An instinctive imaginative sense is the origin, he argues, both of poetic creativity and of our response to a poem. We all have that sense but, we may add, it takes the rare genius of a wordsmith like Heaney to release it.

Collections not already mentioned include 'North' (1975), 'Field Work' (1979), 'Station Island' (1984), 'The Haw Lantern' (1987) and 'The Spirit Level' (1996). Heaney has himself made a comprehensive selection in 'Opened Ground: Poems 1966–1996'. His Oxford lectures, 'The Redress of Poetry' (1995), make rewarding reading, as, in a different vein, does his magnificent translation of 'Beowulf' (1999). All are published by Faber.

Afterword

Why stop there? There is admittedly some appeal in the symmetry whereby we close with Seamus Heaney, whose translation of *Beowulf* features in the very first section of this book. But in truth any ending to this particular story is necessarily arbitrary. The writing to which we have referred includes much that has been written in our own time, but it would have been impossible within the scope of this volume to do justice to the infinite variety of contemporary authors.

> *Our noisy years seem moments in the being*
> *Of the eternal Silence: truths that wake,*
> *To perish never.*   **Wordsworth**

Appendix on Reading

- the reading experience
- reading poetry
- reading plays
- reading novels

The reading experience

Reading is a creative skill. Disraeli's father, Isaac, put it exactly: 'There is an art of reading, as well as an art of thinking, and an art of writing'.

Reading is not a natural activity. We learn to do it, and with help from our teachers when we are still quite young we consolidate our skills. A minority of us struggle, and may continue to receive help into adulthood. But for most of us, that is the end of it. We do not review whether we have built up good or bad habits, or seek to refresh our talents. Generally speaking, we do not actively think about our reading at all: we just get on with it.

Consider two brief instances of how we might think further about our reading.

Some people read one word at a time, maybe through the lingering influence of how they learned to read in the very earliest days. A realisation that by doing this they may be slowing themselves down, *impeding* understanding instead of enhancing it – losing the thread of a sentence, for example – comes at first as something of a shock, but experimentation soon shows that a distinct advantage comes from *varying* the number of words one takes in 'at a glance', as well as adjusting reading speed to suit changes in the nature of what is read.

Take another example. Nowadays, as well as having books, we can with the aid of the internet rapidly conjure up the complete text of many major works. Yet it is actually quite difficult to read certain kinds of text on a computer screen, especially literary texts. We can get through them, but at times it becomes a frustrating exercise: we consciously or half consciously realise that we are fighting the material. Why is this? One reason may relate to the fact that when reading we constantly need to check back on what we have just read, or check ahead to see where things are leading. (This is normal and necessary, as we adjust to contexts and meanings.)

These 'checks' are done in mere flicks of the eye, lasting often no more than a fraction of a second. They may be done with text showing on screen as easily as with the printed page, but problems arise if we want to flick to what is beyond the screen, maybe a line or two forward, maybe whole paragraphs back. Of course there is no *mechanical* obstacle – we can scroll to where we want to be. But scrolling is slower. And – more significantly still – it is a deliberate act and not an involuntary or instinctive one. Making and implementing the decision to scroll may interfere with the fluency of our reading and comprehension, and an accumulation of such decisions can build frustration.

It is easy to assume that the faster we can read the better. There was in recent years a vogue for 'speed reading' courses, which encouraged techniques for increasing the number of words read per minute. (With remarkable success in some cases, as adults discovered that it was possible to double or even treble one's speed.) Clearly there is a very good case for increasing efficiency in handling reading material. If we can do this without sacrificing comprehension, and practise how to skim material rapidly in order to fillet out that which is of especial significance for us, and do all this without any loss of comprehension – then the benefit is substantial.

However, we perhaps think less frequently about the virtues of slow reading, reflective reading, and re-reading. This is where we can return specifically to the reading of *literature*. When we read literature, we savour it. It lingers on the palate. (And indeed there is an almost sensory experience in some kinds of reading. We have all succumbed at some time or other to *smelling* a new book! More complicatedly, the pleasure of remembering a book can be linked with its feel and its smell quite as much as it is with the more obvious verbal features. It is almost as if the sensory pleasures of a book metaphorically represent its complex appeal to us.)

Part of the enjoyment lies in *re*-reading a detail, *re*-reading a whole work. A novel, a poem, a play that has made an impression comes to possess the memory. When children re-read, there is comfort in the familiarity. When adults re-read, there is the opportunity for new discoveries, different experience. The literature will work for us on many different levels. Our mind and our memories move on, so we bring to our re-reading subtle shifts of perspective. Equally, in the subtlest of writing, the words on the page develop new associations, strike us afresh. (Is there an interesting contrast here with old photographs? They remain unalterably themselves, whereas good writing evolves for us as our lives evolve.)

Our reading is enriched by our dwelling not simply on *what* is said, but on *how* it is said. As we read we value the *thing made*, whichever way it may provoke us – whether it be to shock, to delight, to move or to disturb – and we are in parallel able to value *the way it is made*. The one is part of the other. When the minor Seventeenth Century poet Francis Quarles prefaced an edition of his intricate poems with the statement to the reader 'I wish thee as much pleasure in the reading, as I had in the writing', this was not a bland goodwill wish, but a specific invitation to explore pleasurably both the reader's and the poet's absorption in an artefact.

Language itself is constantly on the move, and attitudes to the importance of reading literature change through history. There is the view – found in Plato and the English Puritans – that imaginative writing is a self-indulgence, possibly untruthful and debasing. There is the contrasting opinion that literature has a high moral function in revealing 'truth' (whatever we may take 'truth' to mean.) At another extreme literature is seen as amoral, meaningful only in its own terms. In the English tradition, there is a contrast between those, especially in the Eighteenth Century and earlier, who placed an emphasis on the best writers providing illumination through reason and intellect, and those after 1800 or so who elevated the imagination and the emotions for giving the most reliable kind of insight. In the early Twentieth Century there was a fashionable – and very English – tendency to see literature as an agreeable appendage of gentlemanly leisure. Later came a stress on rigorous close reading, which linked back to a late Nineteenth Century conviction that great literature preserved essential civilised values. More recently, there has been a movement to look beyond the actual work, to focus instead on what the writing tells us about its historical context, about the writer's psyche, and how the way words are used defines the nature of a society.

In the second half of the Twentieth Century the highly influential and contentious 'deconstruction' movement built on the assumption that words are always inexact, and that meaning is necessarily imprecise and constantly changing. It follows, in this 'post-modern' view, that reading never reveals a finished text and meaning; the most we can do is peel away the layers of temporary 'meanings' that have gathered about the words. There can be no value judgments. Can there be such a thing, some would ask, as objectively great literature, or is our sense of the literary past merely an illusion, the product in each age of shifting tastes, of changing ways of seeing things?

Fortunately, most of the time, we don't need to be bothered by such issues. Our best approach must still be to read with an open mind, to adjust to what we find, and to take pleasure in the extraordinary variety and vitality of what lies before us.

Reading poetry

A poem should not mean
But be.

(Archibald MacLeish, *Ars Poetica*)

What is a poem? Archibald MacLeish gives us a good answer, one that deflects the question. A poem is itself. You can't 'translate' it into 'what it means': it is itself. If it is a good poem, that is. A good poem resonates, etches itself into our mind and our memory, because the way it is said is so perfectly its meaning that we cannot separate the two.

And this is fascinating. As we read a good poem, paradoxically, we instinctively look for how it is done, for the craft, for the skill. How does it work? – what is the trick? When we look for this, the art of the poem, are we guilty of murdering the very thing we are responding to, dissipating the magic? If we open up the watch to see how it works, can we any longer tell the time?

A consciousness of a poem's craft is surely a nourishing, not a dilution, of its importance for us. Because the craft is the poem. A poem should not mean, but be. Fine-tuning our sense of what is going on in the workings of the poem is fine-tuning our response to its very essence.

A simple way into every poem is to *listen* to it. Hear its speaking voice. Imagine it being read aloud. Read it aloud. (The best reason for advocating the memorisation of poems by school pupils, incidentally, is not that they thereby carry with them a living anthology – though that may be true – but that they are taken by the process into the heart of what a poem is.)

As we respond to the voice of a poem, we attune to its rhythm. Every poem has a rhythm.

'What are the bugles blowin' for?' said Files-on-Parade.
'To turn you out, to turn you out,' the Colour-Sergeant said.
'What makes you look so white, so white?' said Files-on-Parade.
'I'm dreading what I've got to watch,' the Colour-Sergeant said.
(Rudyard Kipling, *Danny Deever*)

The rhythm here is simple enough, but Kipling uses it in a sophisticated way. The spectacle which the Colour-Sergeant dreads is the hanging of a disgraced soldier, and as the poem develops (these are the opening lines) the insistent rhythm tightens the unpleasantness, the starkness and the sickly inevitability of the event.

If we read '*Danny Deever*' aloud, we will probably echo that forceful regularity of beat (though we will probably vary the pace at those moments where the enormity of it all sinks in). However, not all poems derive their strength from a single rhythmic thrust. Look, for example, at how Yeats begins his poem '*Byzantium*'. There is a rhythm, certainly; we hear its strong undertow. But we notice that there is a counter-rhythm, too. The speaking voice of the poem does not, if it is sensitive, follow the simple tee-tum-tee-tum of the opening lines:

> *The unpurged images of day recede:*
> *The Emperor's drunken soldiery are abed;*
> *Night resonance recedes, night-walkers' song*
> *After great cathedral gong;*
> *A starlit or a moonlit dome disdains*
> *All that man is,*
> *All mere complexities,*
> *The fury and the mire of human veins.*

There is a second rhythm here, a kind of counterpoint, overlaying the basic *tee-tum*. Yeats creates an authoritative dignity of tone which puts into perspective the drunkenness and the human 'complexities'. How many stresses or rhythmic emphases are there in the second line? In *tee-tum-tee-tum* terms there are five (Emp - drunk - sold - are - bed), but the contrapuntal rhythm gives us perhaps only two (Emp - bed) or maybe three (Emp - sold - bed). The speaking voice of the poem finds its own weight and pace, and when we reach the last four lines we are beyond simple repetitive patterns altogether. We balance whole cadences of phrases against each other.

And these rhythms *are* the meaning. We hear the inner soul of the poem. A poet whose 'ear' is sure will sometimes transcend simple rhythms altogether. In the opening to D.H.Lawrence's '*Snake*' the subtle modulations of the speaking voice have entirely taken over:

> *A snake came to my water-trough*
> *On a hot, hot day, and I in pyjamas for the heat,*
> *To drink there.*

(Other poets who are masters of an arrhythmical speaking voice include Thomas Hardy, W.H.Auden and the American poet Robert Frost.)

The rhythms will only work, of course, if the *words* are right. The words create the patterns; the patterns reinforce the words. And the whole poem will be shaped into a structure that honours the words and creates the meanings. Wilfred Owen's famous '*Anthem for Doomed Youth*' is written as a sonnet. (For a more detailed discussion of sonnets, see the section earlier in this book on Shakespeare's sonnets.) The poem sets against the brutality of anonymous death in war a series of funeral images – 'passing-bells', 'prayers', 'candles', 'pall' – and we progressively understand that these dead soldiers will have no funeral. They will be remembered and celebrated by their absence, mourned by the 'sad shires' and the 'patient minds'. We can sense as we read it that the poem moves ineluctably towards the wrenching images of the last two lines. [The hyphen in the first line, incidentally, directs us clearly towards a stress on 'passing' and not on 'bells', where it would otherwise be.]

> *What passing-bells for these who die as cattle?*
> *Only the monstrous anger of the guns.*
> *Only the stuttering rifles' rapid rattle*
> *Can patter out their hasty orisons.*
> *No mockeries now for them; no prayers nor bells,*
> *Nor any voice of mourning save the choirs -*
> *The shrill, demented choirs of wailing shells;*
> *And bugles calling for them from sad shires.*
>
> *What candles may be held to speed them all?*
> *Not in the hands of boys, but in their eyes*
> *Shall shine the holy glimmers of goodbyes.*
> *The pallor of girls' brows shall be their pall;*
> *Their flowers the tenderness of patient minds,*
> *And each slow dusk a drawing-down of blinds.*

In that arresting last line the under-rhythm would lead us from 'each' to 'dusk', but instinctively we realise that '*slow*' is a key word, and as we emphasise it it points up for us a complex suggestion, both a gentleness and softness – caught from the girls' brows and the tenderness of the preceding lines – *and* a pain, the pain of undiminishing, lingering grief. The savage energy of the guns and the rifles modulates into the haunting stillness and darkness of the ending. (If you press the penultimate line for its meaning, there is no easy answer; the meaning is the untranslatable image.) The power of the poem derives from Owen's sculpting of words and rhythms into an evolving shape – it is almost a musical movement – whose effect is greater than the mere sum of its parts.

Poems heighten our response to language. But they are not coded messages. We will set off on many false trails if we assume that a poet is concealing some loaded and hidden significance behind his words. Take a look at '*The Red Wheelbarrow*' by William Carlos Williams.

so much depends
upon

a red wheel
barrow

glazed with rain
water

beside the white
chickens.
    (*Collected Poems* published by New Directions)

In discussions of this poem with young students, it has been amusing to notice how some, initially baffled, take refuge in heavily complicated interpretations: it is 'about' the Russian civil war [the reds and the whites!], or communism, or conservation, or kindness to animals. Eventually we are able to recognise that the poem is delicately transparent. The poet invites us to 'picture' that wheel barrow, and respect it for what it is, an object separate from ourselves. The poem grammatically makes a simple statement, and that statement is enhanced by the clarity and unpretentiousness directness of the placing of the words on the page. The absence of capital letters serves that intention. (We would react very differently, perhaps, if we met the words merely as a continuous prose sentence.)

'The Red Wheelbarrow' shows us that there is no formulaic approach to impose on the reading of a poem. We need to take each on its own terms.

Reading plays

We don't, of course, read plays. We see plays. We *read* playscripts. And the first thing we have to appreciate when we read a script is that it is not a 'text' in the way that a novel or a poem is a text, in the sense of a finished artefact. It is a starting-off point.

The play is the thing – in the theatre, live, happening as an electric interaction of actor and audience, and carrying the intriguing possibility that each time the performance happens it may be a little different, or indeed surprisingly different. So when we read a script, we see it as an intermediary, the raw material from which the theatrical event will be fashioned. We read it with the eye of a director.

But how do we do that? – we may not be professionally trained, we may never have directed a play in our lives. Happily, it is not a problem. We are not, after all, going to take charge of an actual production. All we have to do is imagine possibilities. We are in the privileged position of wielding creative power without responsibility.

Antony Sher, in his autobiography 'Beside Myself', writes of the complications of acting Shakespeare: "I'm still not mature enough to play Shakespeare. He writes people and language in such complexity it's like the real thing. A mass of contradictions and layers. Every time I do one of the big roles I begin by becoming baffled by its inconsistencies and then, if I'm lucky, I learn to embrace these seemingly loose ends. Not by attempting to tie them up, just by holding on fast."

This is interesting from several points of view. Sher experiences Shakespeare's script as an unfinished thing – all those loose ends. But he is nonetheless content with that because it is apt. As in life, so in the theatre: we can never put too firm an interpretation on a personality, because human life isn't like that. What the actor will attempt to do – and this is the real challenge – is to create a convincingly complex being that resists definitive understanding.

But surely, we may ask, the dramatist isn't *that* 'vague'? It depends on the dramatist. It depends on the type of play. Of the good dramatists we may expect that they are not vague, only truthful. The weaker the playwright, the greater the risk that the script will fail to lift off the page in an exciting complexity: the characters will appear straitjacketed by a narrowness in their conception. (Meanwhile, of course, *some* perfectly successful plays, such as highly stylised comedies or sweeping pageants, will not present Sher with his problem, because in them the focus will be intentionally elsewhere.)

Reading a script with a director's eye, we know that we must pay attention to far more than the dialogue. Harold Pinter's 'The Caretaker' begins with a jumbled attic. A tramp-like figure is sitting alone on a bed. He moves about the room, examining its objects, before sitting again on the bed, and gazing expressionlessly out front for *thirty seconds* (as Pinter's stage directions suggest). He then leaves the room. Nothing has been said. In the theatre this opening can be riveting, establishing both a situation – though we are not quite sure what situation – and an unease. In the first London production I recall an audience moving through rapt attention to an anxiety as if something had gone wrong, then to some nervous laughter before the tension gripped again. Thirty seconds of silence is a long time in a theatre. When reading the script we cannot predict with certainty an audience's reactions, but we must open ourselves to the dramatic possibilities of what is *un*spoken, perhaps simply visual. A recent professional revival of R.C.Sheriff's 'Journey's End', set in the First World War trenches, ended with a stunning, profoundly moving montage in which the cast, 'dead' statuesque soldiers, stood facing the audience while on a backcloth behind them were projected in tiny print the unending names of the fallen. Sheriff has not scripted that ending; a director's inspiration saw the possibilities of realising the script in that particular way.

When reading plays we meet countless styles of language. Irrespective of whether we are reading, say, such contrasting forms as the heightened poetry of Christopher Marlowe's 'Dr Faustus' (1589) or the modern American prose of David Mamet, we should listen for the rhythms, which take us into the characters, the scenes, the play as a whole. Here is the Bad Angel in Marlowe, bullying Faustus with a vision of the Hell to which he is condemned:

> *Now, Faustus, let thine eyes with horror stare*
> *Into that vast perpetual torture-house.*
> *There are the furies, tossing damned souls*
> *On burning forks; their bodies boil in lead:*
> *There are live quarters broiling on the coals,*
> *That ne'er can die: this ever-burning chair*
> *Is for o'er-tortured souls to rest them in:*
> *These that are fed with sops of flaming fire*
> *Were gluttons and lov'd only delicates*
> *And laugh'd to see the poor starve at their gates.*
> *But yet all these are nothing; thou shalt see*
> *Ten thousand tortures that more horrid be.*

The intensity of this quickens as we listen. The sentences lengthen as the speech proceeds, until we reach the turn of the knife, 'But yet all these are nothing', and the clinching threat of the final couplet. As we 'hear' the sinew of the rhythms, the script begins to live for us. Compare this with David Mamet's 'Glengarry Glen Ross'(1984), which presents us with real estate salesmen whose moral emptiness is reflected in their language. The actual words are debased, charmless, barely articulate. Yet the rhythms of Mamet's dialogue brilliantly create theatre as the threadbare corruption of his characters is exposed. In this extract, Moss aims to persuade Aaronow to join him in stealing from their firm client information ('*leads*' on potential sales) and selling it to a rival:

AARONOW. You haven't talked to him.
MOSS. No. What do you mean? Have I talked to him about *this*?

Pause.

AARONOW. Yes. I mean are you actually *talking* about this, or are we just...
MOSS. No, we're just...
AARONOW. We're just '*talking*' about it.
MOSS. We're just *speaking* about it. (*Pause.*) As an *idea*.
AARONOW. As an idea.
MOSS. Yes.
AARANOW. We're not actually *talking* about it.
MOSS. No.
AARANOW. Talking about it as a ...
MOSS. *No.*
AARANOW. As a *robbery.*
MOSS. As a 'robbery'?! No.
AARANOW. *Well.* Well...
MOSS. *Hey.*

Pause.

AARANOW. So all this, um, you didn't actually, you didn't actually, go talk to Graff.
MOSS. Not actually, no.

Pause.

AARANOW. You didn't?
MOSS. No. Not actually.
AARANOW. Did you?
MOSS. What did I say?

AARANOW. What did you say?
MOSS. Yes. (*Pause.*) I said 'Not actually'. The fuck you care, George? We're just *talking*...
AARANOW. We are?
MOSS. Yes.

Pause.

AARANOW. Because, because, you know, it's a *crime*.
MOSS. That's right. It's a crime. It is a crime. It's also very safe.
AARANOW. You're actually *talking* about this?
MOSS. That's right.

Pause.

AARANOW. You're going to steal the leads?
MOSS. Have I said that?

Pause.

AARANOW. Are you?

Pause.

MOSS. Did I say that?
AARANOW. Did you talk to Graff?
MOSS. Is that what I said?
AARANOW. What did he say?
MOSS. What did he say? He'd *buy* them.

Pause.

AARANOW. You're going to steal the leads and sell the leads to him?

Pause.

MOSS. Yes.

The language here is clearly not a straight transcription from life. On the contrary, it is carefully plotted and patterned in ways that actual dialogue matches only rarely. Mamet's modulating rhythms explore the workings of the characters' minds. He generates black humour and a dramatic stimulus. Read carefully, the words lift our imagination into the theatre.

It is useful finally to remind ourselves that a play is not necessarily *dependent* on technical effects, on scenery, on lighting, and so forth. I remember a transfixing production of 'Waiting for Godot' that took place in a bare room with no technical resources of any kind. Beckett would have approved. Ask the question, what are the irreducible minimal conditions essential for drama to happen, and we may be surprised by the answers: an audience, presumably (will one person be enough?); but how many characters?; do we need a stage? Do we need a theatre? ...

Reading novels

'And what are you reading, Miss —— ?' 'Oh! It is only a novel!' replies the
young lady: while she lays down her book with affected indifference, or
momentary shame. 'It is only Cecilia, or Camilla, or Belinda:' or, in short,
only some work in which the most thorough knowledge of human nature,
the happiest delineation of its varieties, the liveliest effusions of wit and
humour are conveyed to the world in the best chosen language.

(Jane Austen, *Northanger Abbey*, 1818)

Thus Jane Austen deftly satirises her heroine's attitude to fiction and society's attitudes to novels (and women reading them), while at the same time eloquently championing the novelist's art.

Of course there are novels and novels. More novels of all kinds are published and read now than at any time in the novel's brief history. However, there is indeed an oddity about the view – we can still encounter it, in its death throes – that because novels are associated with leisure, there is something inherently trivial about them. On the contrary, the fact that reading fiction is a leisure activity takes us to the very heart of its importance. We *live* with the story. Reading a novel is a portable, interruptible, renewable experience. It happens for us over time, often a considerable time, in a way that is special amongst the arts. The imaginative experience is mellowed and matured. We carry a fantasy world about with us, which intensifies as we proceed. The novel then ripens in the memory, possibly to be renewed and enhanced in a second reading.

Prose fiction reaches us in an infinite variety of forms, from short story to novella, from so-called 'long short story' to 'three- or four-decker' novel, and it is pointless to theorise about where one begins and another ends. They are all points along a scale. There has been frequent experimentation with the medium. (The 'Fictions' for instance of the Argentinian writer Jorge Luis Borges are in the form of brief, stimulating puzzles, philosophical challenges, often with no 'characters' present at all.) Novelists may communicate through the device of letters, diaries, first person narration, third person narration and multiple narration. [A powerful example of the latter is the American William Faulkner's '*The Sound and the Fury*' (1930). Its first section narrates events through the eyes of a mentally disturbed young man. Subsequent sections retell the story, first as seen by another character and then in the authorial voice, so that our understanding progressively deepens.] There has been a novel with interchangeable pages and another with interchangeable chapters. In Lawrence Sterne's '*Tristram Shandy*' (1759+) we have a mock autobiography that plays games with the impossibility of ending and the near impossibility of beginning. (See pages 118–120.)

As we read fiction we do well to avoid preconceptions. We soon get a feel for the novelist's intentions. One of our first impressions is whether the writer is making a personal appearance. Some, like Fielding or Thackeray, make direct interventions in the narrative, addressing us, telling us what they think, inviting a kind of partnership with the reader. Others create a world apart, a self-sufficient 'reality' which sustains the illusion of an existence independent of ourselves and the author. There are novelists whose purpose, at however sophisticated or unsophisticated a level, is simply to entertain. There are others, more polemical, who aim to challenge, to take a moral stance, to change the way we view things. There are novelists who give us a sense of history, the authentic feel of a past or present world; in contrast there are those who sever all links with the known, whose mission is to generate myth or fantasy. (And we might distinguish between those who knowingly set out to evoke a time and a place, and others who only incidentally, yet fascinatingly, reveal to us aspects of a period, simply because *they themselves are of it.*)

As we settle into a novel, we start to notice how the novelist is weaving together its various strands. There is a satisfaction for us in the narrative dexterity. Dickens, usually handling a vast cast of characters and a complex of narrative threads, is an instructive master builder. Compare, for example, the relatively simple structure of his earliest novel '*Pickwick Papers*', which sets Pickwick off on his travels with a lightly uncomplicated series of adventures, with the later '*Our Mutual Friend*', in which Dickens introduces a number of apparently unrelated knots of characters whose lives begin to form a connecting pattern as the novel unfolds. Sinister drama, social satire, rich symbolism and a vivid evocation of locations almost imperceptibly combine to create a dazzling and compelling mix.

Opening chapters are in themselves a revealing study. Some novelists invite us in, immediately make us feel at home. Others like to play with us a little, teasingly withholding some of the cards in their hand. Some openings are flashbacks, or in other ways deliberately disconnected from what follows them. It can be entertaining and instructive to re-read an opening chapter while the first reading of the novel is fresh in our minds. Invariably, we see more than at the first encounter. By extension, of course, the whole novel yields more to us as we relive it. A second reading may beget a third, and the book becomes a companion that on each acquaintance entertains us with new insights.

There will be a story. As E.M.Forster famously and archly put it, "Yes – oh dear, yes – the novel tells a story". But the story may not be the heart of the matter. We must beware of slipping into the maybe unconscious habit of skipping or discarding those parts of the text that seem not to be advancing the plot. Only in the simplest novels is there one narrative spine to which are loosely attached various disposable appendages. The most basic of whodunits may be of this kind (there may be no appendages at all) but not the finer crime fiction of, say, P.D.James, or Ian Rankin, or Alexander McCall Smith. There are novels indeed in which the narrative spine is of subsidiary importance. One of the greatest of all novels, James Joyce's '*Ulysses*', tracks two men's journeyings through Dublin during one day, but the richness of the book is in the characters' musings, the digressions, the feel for place, time and history, and in the extraordinary poetry of the prose. In the best fiction the plot, the characters and the descriptive and narrative detail blend into an organic whole. You don't taste the cake if you try to pick out the currants. As we see in our opening extract from '*Northanger Abbey*', Jane Austen provokingly does not mention telling stories at all.

Bibliography

I have found the following works a helpful reference in the preparation of this book:

The Oxford Companion to English Literature, edited by Margaret Drabble

The Cambridge Guide to Literature in English, edited by Ian Ousby

Chambers Biographical Dictionary, edited by Magnus Magnusson

The Cambridge Illustrated History of British Theatre, Simon Trussler

The New Oxford Book of English Verse, edited by Helen Gardner

Lives of the Poets, Michael Schmidt

The Oxford Dictionary of Quotations

The Cambridge Encyclopedia of The English Language, David Crystal

The Oxford Companion to Children's Literature, Humphrey Carpenter and Mari Pritchard

The English Novel, Walter Allen

A Writer's Britain – Landscape in Literature, Margaret Drabble

Publishers of reprints and editions of texts include Penguin, Wordsworth, Everyman, Oxford, Cambridge, Norton, Faber and Carcanet

Index

A Mad World My Masters, 34
A Midsummer Night's Dream, 47
A Night Out, 300
A Penny for A Song, 297
Absalom and Achitophel, 90
Adam Bede, 219–220
Addison, Joseph, 79, 102, 104, 110
Adlestrop, 265
Adonais, 176
Advancement of Learning, 32
Adventures of Peregrine Pickle, 125
Adventures of Roderick Random, 125
aesthetic movement, 237
Afternoons, 295
Agnes Grey, 216
Alastor, 174
Alchemist, 60
Alice in Wonderland, 230
All for Love, 89
All That Fall, 281
All The Year Round, 205, 227
allegory, 13, 18, 29, 54, 86, 99, 193, 276, 284
Allingham, William, 229
alliterative verse, 6, 7
Amelia, 113
America: A Prophecy, 143
Among Schoolchildren, 249
Amoretti, 30
An Arundel Tomb, 295
Anatomy of Melancholy, The, 69–71, 182
Ancient Mariner, 157–158
And Death Shall Have No Dominion, 288
Andrea del Sarto, 202
Androcles and the Lion, 238–239
Animal Farm, 29, 273
Anna of the Five Towns, 250
Annotated Alice, 230
Anthem for Doomed Youth, 266, 316
Antic Hay, 272

Antiquary, 155
Antony and Cleopatra, 49, 50–51, 89
Ape and Essence, 272
Apology for the Life of Mrs Shamela Andrews, 112
Arcadia (Sidney), 26–27
Arcadia (Stoppard), 307
Arden, John, 298
Areopagitica, 80
Ariel, 304
Arnold, Matthew, 176, 221–223
Ars Poetica, 314
As the team's head brass…, 265
As You Like It, 47–49
Ash Wednesday, 267
Astraea Redux, 89
Astrophel and Stella, 26
At A Lunar Eclipse, 233
At Castle Boterel, 233
At Grass, 295
Auden, W.H., 231, 249, 279, 282–284, 315
Auguries of Innocence, 140
Augustan Age, 89, 108, 115, 134, 139, 165
Auld Lang Syne, 145
Aurora Leigh, 190
Austen, Jane, 132, 134, 162–166, 197, 323, 325
Autobiography (Trollope), 209
Autumn Song, 283

Bacon, Francis, 31–33, 70
ballad metre, 22
Ballad of Reading Gaol, 237
ballads, 20–22, 145, 152
Ballantyne, R.M., 284–285
Barchester Towers, 210
Barnaby Rudge, 204

Barnes, William, 187–188, 192

Barrack-Room Ballads, 246

Barrie, James, 239, 252

Bartholemew Fair, 60

Battle of the Books, 101

Bavarian Gentians, 264

Bayley, John, xi, 292

Beaumont, Francis, 34

Becket (Tennyson), 193

Beckett, Samuel, 280–282, 322

Beggar's Opera, 105–107, 110

Behan, Brendan, 297

Behn, Aphra, 93, 112

Bell, 293

Bell Jar, 304

Bennett, Alan, 304–305

Bennett, Arnold, 250, 260

Beowulf, 3–4, 5, 79, 309

Betjeman, John, 278–280, 302

Beyond the Fringe, 304

Bible: Authorised Version, 87–89

Big Poppy, 302

Billy Bunter, 247

Birthday Letters, 301–302

Birthday Party, 298

Bishop Blougram's Apology, 277

Bishop Orders His Tomb, 201

Black Prince, 293

Blake, William, 16, 79, 139, 140–144, 191, 286

blank verse, 26, 29, 35, 76, 130, 150

Bleak House, 205, 206, 208, 227

Blessed Damozel, 229

Bloomsbury Group, 253, 254, 260, 274

Blue Remembered Hills, 245

Blunden, Edmund, 265, 267

Boccacio, 11, 182

Bolt, Robert, 298

Borges, Jorge Luis, 323

Book of Nonsense, 203

Book of Snobs, 199

Book of Urizen, 143

Borough, 134

Boswell, James, 105, 115–116, 118

Brave New World, 272

Break of Day in the Trenches, 266

Break, Break, Break, 193

Breath, 281

Brecht, 42, 105, 297

Brideshead Revisited, 275

Bridges, Robert, 235

Brighton Rock, 277–278

Brittain, Vera, 267

Britten, Benjamin, 127, 135, 282

Broken Heart, 188

Bronte sisters, 154, 211–217, 220

Bronte, Anne, 211, 216–217

Bronte, Charlotte, 165, 196, 199, 211–217

Bronte, Emily, 211, 214–216

Brook, Peter, 285

Brooke, Rupert, 71, 265, 267

Browning Version, 296

Browning, Elizabeth Barrett, 167, 189–191

Browning, Robert, 152, 191, 200–202, 277

Bunyan, John, 29, 86–87, 99, 198

Burgess, Anthony, 278

Burke, Edmund, 116, 134, 135

Burney, Fanny, 132–133

Burns, Robert, 144–146

Burnt Norton, 269

Burton, Robert, 69–71, 182

Byron, Lord, 29, 133, 139, 144, 153, 170–173, 174, 237

Byzantium, 249, 315

Camilla, 133

Can You Forgive Her?, 210

Canterbury Tales, 12–14

Caretaker, 299, 319

Carroll, Lewis, 119, 230, 251

Casa Guidi Windows, 190

Castle of Otranto, 125

Casualty, 308

Causley, Charles, 284–286

Cecilia, 133

Cecily Parsley's Nursery Rhymes, 251
Centuries, 85
Cervantes, 113
Chance, 245
Charge of the Light Brigade, 193, 195
Chaucer, Geoffrey, 5, 8–14, 201
Chesterton, G.K., 228
Chicken Soup With Barley, 298
Childe Harold's Pilgrimage, 170
Child's 'Ballads', 20
Child's Christmas in Wales, 287
Chilton, Charles, 297
Christ and the Soldier, 266
Christabel, 158
Christie, Agatha, 228
Christmas Carol, 204
Church Going, 295
Church Music, 76
Church Porch, 76
Cider with Rosie, 100
Circus Animal's Desertion, 249
Clare, John, 177–179, 188
Clarissa, 111–112
Clayhanger, 250
Clockwork Orange, 278
Coast of Utopia, 307
Cobbett, William, 146–148
Coleridge, Samuel Taylor, 29, 130, 134, 139, 150, 151–152, 156–161, 167
Collar, 76
Collector, 293
Collier, Jeremy, 92
Collins, Wilkie, 167, 208, 227
Colossus, 304
Comedy of Errors, 39, 49
comedy of manners, 93
Common A-Took In, 188
Conan Doyle, Arthur, 227
conceit, 67, 75
Confessions of an English Opium Eater, 166–167
Congreve, William, 92, 94, 105, 107
Coningsby, 188, 199
Conrad, Joseph, 243–245, 268

Convergence of the Twain, 233
Conversation about Christmas, 287
Coral Island, 284
Corinna's Going a Maying, 74
Coriolanus, 52, 53
Country Wife, 94
Coverdale, Miles, 87
Cowper, William, 129–130, 139
Crabbe, George, 133–135, 139, 167
Cradle Song, 141
Cranford, 197
Crashaw, Richard, 84
Critic, 130
Crome Yellow, 272
Crossing the Bar, 193
Crotchet Castle, 167, 168, 169
Crow, 302
Cry of the Children, 190
Culture and Anarchy, 222
Cymbeline, 53

Daddy, 304
Daemonologie, 40
Dame Julian of Norwich, 16
Dance to the Music of Time, 276
Daniel Deronda, 221
Daniel Martin, 293
Danny Deever, 246, 314
Darkling Thrush, 233
Darwin, Charles, 195
Daugher-in-Law, 264
David Copperfield, 205, 207
Day-Lewis, Cecil, 283
Dead Men's Dump, 266
Death of a Naturalist, 307
Death of King George V, 279
Decay of Lying, 237
Deceptions, 295
Decline and Fall, 275
Defence of Poetry (Shelley), 175
Defence of Poetry (Sidney), 26, 27
Defoe, Daniel, 99–101, 105, 111

Dejection: an Ode, 159, 160

Dekker, Thomas, 33, 34

De Quincey, Thomas, 166–167

Deserted Village, 128

Devils, 297

Dickens, Charles, 13, 48, 114, 126, 167, 196, 203–208, 210, 220, 227, 287, 324

Dictionary of the English Tongue, 117

Disraeli, Benjamin, 188–189, 196, 199

Disraeli, Isaac, 311

Do not go gentle into that goodnight..., 288

Doctor Faustus, 36, 319

Dombey and Son, 205, 207

Don Juan, 171

Don Quixote, 34, 113

Donne, John, 32, 65–69, 75, 80, 82, 83, 89

Door into the Dark, 307

Doors of Perception, 272

Dover Beach, 222

Down and Out in London and Paris, 273

Dr Thorne, 210

Drink to me only..., 60

Dryden, John, 14, 65, 89–90, 102, 107

Dubliners, 256

Duchess of Malfi, 71

Duenna, 130

Dujardin, Edouard, 258

Duke's Children, 210

Dulce et Decorum Est, 166

Dumb Waiter, 299

Dunciad, 110

Easter, 1916, 249

Ebony Tower, 293

Ecstasy, 67

Elegy Written in a Country Churchyard, 123

Eliot, George, 154, 212, 217–221

Eliot, T.S., 29, 42, 71, 84, 235, 260, 267–270, 272, 274, 282

Elixir, 76

Elizabethan and Jacobean Theatre, 33–35

Emma, 163, 164

End of the Affair, 278

Endgame, 281

Endymion, 180

English Bards and Scots Reviewers, 170

Englishman Abroad, 305

Enoch Arden, 193

Entertainer, 297

epic, 79

Epicene, 59, 60

Epigram on the Collar of a Dog, 108

Epipsychidion, 176

Epistle to Dr Arbuthnot, 110

Epitaph on an Army of Mercenaries, 245

Epithalamion, 30–31

Essay in Criticism, 110–111

Essay on Man, 110

Essays of Elia, 161

Etherege, George, 93

Eustace and Hilda, 274

Eustace Diamonds, 210

Eve of St Agnes, 182–183

Evelina, 132

Every Man in his Humour, 60

Everyman, 18–19, 99

Everyone Sang, 266

Examination, 300

Expedition of Humphry Clinker, 125

expressionism, 255, 297

Eyeless in Gaza, 272

Eye-Mote, 303

Face, 287

Faerie Queene, 29, 79, 183

Far From The Madding Crowd, 232

Farquahar, George, 94

Faulkner, William, 323

Felix Holt, 221

Felix Randal, 235

Fern Hill, 288

Field Work, 309

Fielding, Henry, 113–115, 198, 204, 324

Finnegans Wake, 259

First Men in the Moon, 249

Fitzgerald, Edward, 191–192
Flare Path, 296
Flaubert, Gustave, 250
Flea, 67, 83
Fletcher, John, 34
Flowers and Insects, 302
Force that through the green fuse..., 288
Forced Marriage, 93
Forester, C.S., 290
Forster, E.M., 154, 252–255, 260, 273, 324
Forty Years on, 304
Four Quartets, 267, 269
Four Zoas, 143
Fowles, John, 292–293
Fra Lippo Lippi, 202
Framley Parsonage, 210
Frankenstein, 125, 174
Free Fall, 284
French Lieutenant's Woman, 293
French Without Tears, 296
Freud, 167, 261
Frost at Midnight, 159
Frost, Robert, 265, 315
Futility, 266

Galsworthy, John, 239
Garden, 83
Garden of Appleton House, 83
Garden of Love, 142
Gardener's Daughter, 194
Gare du Midi, 283
Garrick, David, 116, 132
Gaskell, Elizabeth, 154, 196–197, 212
Gather ye rosebuds..., 74
Gay, John, 102, 105–107, 110
General, 266
Gentleman's Magazine, 116
Ghost Crabs, 302
Glengarry Glen Ross, 320
Go-Between, 274
God moves in a mysterious way..., 130
God's Grandeur, 235

Goethe, 36
Golding, William, 284–285
Goldsmith, Oliver, 116, 127–129, 130, 177
Goodbye to All That, 267
Goodbye to Berlin, 283
Gormenghast, 125
gothic novel, 125, 139
Grace Abounding, 87
Grahame, Kenneth, 251
Grande Chartreuse, 223
Grantchester, 265
Graves, Robert, 266, 267
Gray, Thomas, 123–124, 139
Great Expectations, 204, 205, 207, 208
Greene, Graham, 277–278
Gregory, Lady, 239
Gryll Grange, 167
Gulliver's Travels, 101, 103
Guy Mannering, 155
Gwyn, Nell, 93

Hamlet, 34, 39, 42–43, 306
Hand That Signed the Paper, 288
Handful of Dust, 275
Hansard, 148
Happy Days, 281
Happy Prince, 237
Hard Times, 205, 207
Hardy, Thomas, 29, 74, 187, 201, 231–234, 245, 283, 315
Harry Ploughman, 235
Hartley, L.P., 274
Haw Lantern, 309
Hawk in the Rain, 301
Hazlitt, William, 108, 157, 161, 174
He Who Would Valiant Be, 87
Headlong Hall, 167, 168
Heaney, Seamus, 3–4, 307–309
Heart of Darkness, 243
Heart of Midlothian, 154, 155
Heart of the Matter, 278
Heaven and Hell, 272

Henry IV Parts 1 and 2, 53
Henry V, 38, 52
Herbert, George, 65, 74–76, 80, 82, 85
Here, 295
heroic couplet, 89, 107, 134
Heroic Stanzas, 89
Herrick, Robert, 73–74
Heywood, Thomas, 33, 34
High Windows, 294
Highland Widow, 155
Hilda Lessways, 250
History of Henry Esmond, 199
History of Mr Polly, 250
H'm, 287
Hobbes, Thomas, 93
Hobbit, 270
Hogarth, 113, 114
Holinshed's 'Chronicles', 40
Hollow Men, 267, 269
Holy Sonnets, 68
Holy Thursday, 141
Holy Willie's Prayer, 146
Homage to Catalonia, 273
Home Thoughts From Abroad, 202
Homecoming, 299–300
Homer, 11, 51, 79, 189, 258
Hopkins, Gerard Manley, 90, 187,
    234–235
Horatian Ode, 82–83
Horses, 301
Hostage, 297
House at Pooh Corner, 251–252
Household Words, 205, 227
Housman, A.E., 245–246
How Do I Love Thee, 190
*How They Brought the News from Ghent to
    Aix*, 202
Howard's End, 253
Hughes, Ted, 301–303, 307
Hunting of the Snark, 230
Hurrahing in Harvest, 235
Huxley, Aldous, 272, 274, 297
Hymn to Saint Teresa, 84

I Am, 177
I Look Into My Glass, 233
I wandered lonely as a cloud…, 148
iambic pentameter, 22, 35, 90
Ibsen, Henrik, 238
Ideal Husband, 237
Idler, 116
Idylls of the King, 193
I'm Talking About Jerusalem, 298
Importance of Being Earnest, 236–237, 306
In a Bath Tea Shop, 280
In Memoriam, 193, 194, 195
In Memory of W.B. Yeats, 249, 283
In Praise of Limestone, 283
In the bleak midwinter, 229
Inheritors, 284
Innocence of Father Brown, 228
Invention of Love, 307
Inviting a Friend to Supper, 59
Irish Airman Foresees His Death, 249
Iron Man, 302
Is My Team Ploughing?, 245
Isabella, 182
Isherwood, Christopher, 283
Island, 272
Ivanhoe, 155

Jabberwocky, 230
{James I of England,
{James VI of Scotland,   40, 60, 69, 88
James, P.D., 325
Jane Eyre, 199, 212–213, 272
Jew of Malta, 37
John Anderson, my Jo, 145
John Gilpin, 130
Johnson, Samuel, 46, 65, 70, 79, 104,
    107, 112, 115–118, 123, 126, 128,
    132, 165
Jolly Beggars, 146
Jonathan Wild, 113
Jonson, Ben, 34, 35, 37, 59–61, 73
Joseph Andrews, 113–115

Journal of the Plague Year, 99, 100
Journey of the Magi, 267
Journey's End, 319
Joyce, James, 119, 256–259, 260, 268, 306, 325
Jubilate Agno, 127
Jude the Obscure, 232
Julian and Maddalo, 174
Julius Caesar, 40, 52
Jumpers, 307
Jungle Book, 247
Juno and the Paycock, 255
Justice, 239
Juvenal, 117

Keats, John, 29, 139, 167, 174, 178, 179–183
Kempe, Margery, 14–16
Kenilworth, 155
Kim, 246
King Lear, 39, 45–47, 72
Kinship, 308
Kipling, Rudyard, 245–247, 314
Kipps, 250
Krapp's Last Tape, 281
Kubla Khan, 158
Kyd, Thomas, 34

Lady Chatterley's Lover, 263–264
Lady in the Van, 305
Lady of Shalott, 193, 195
Lady Windermere's Fan, 237
Lake Isle of Innisfree, 248
Lamb (Blake), 141
Lamb, Charles, 157, 159, 161–162
Lamia, 182
Langland, William, 4–6, 8
Larkin, Philip, 294–295
Last Chronicle of Barset, 210
Last Signal, 187
Late Flowering Lust, 279
Lawrence, D.H., 250, 261–264, 272, 315

Lay of the Last Minstrel, 153
Lear, Edward, 202–203, 230
Leda and the Swan, 249
Lee, Laurie, 100
Les Lauriers Sont Coupees, 258
Less Deceived, 294
Let us with a gladsome mind…, 77
Leviathan, 93
Lie, 27
Life of Addison, 104
Life of Johnson, 118
Life of Richard Savage, 116
Lincolnshire Tale, 279
Lines on a Young Lady's Photograph Album, 295
Little Dorrit, 205, 207
Littlewood, Joan, 105, 297
Lives of the Poets, 116
Lochinvar, 153–154
Locke, John, 119
Locksley Hall, 193
London (Blake), 140–141
London (Johnson), 117
Longest Journey, 253
Long-legged Fly, 249
Look Back in Anger, 296–297, 299
Lord Jim, 245
Lord of the Flies, 284–286
Lord of the Rings, 270–271
Lost Leader, 200
Louse Hunting, 266
Love, 75
Love Among the Ruins, 202
Love and Mr Lewisham, 250
Love Letters between Nobleman and Sister, 112
Love Song of Alfred J. Prufrock, 267–268
Lover's Infiniteness, 67
Love's Labour's Lost, 49
Lucy poems (Wordsworth), 152
Lullaby (Auden), 283
Luther, 297
lyrical ballads, 139, 150, 152, 157, 160

Macbeth, 40–42

Macdiarmid, Hugh, 247

MacFlecknoe, 90

MacLeish, Archibald, 314

MacNeice, Louis, 283

Madness of King George, 305

Magistrate, 238

Magnyfycence, 19

Magus, 293

Major Barbara, 238

Malone Dies, 281

Mamet, David, 319

Man and Superman, 238

Man For All Seasons, 298

Mandalay, 246

Mann, Thomas, 36

Mansfield Park, 163–165

Mariana, 193

Marlowe, Christopher, 35–37, 55, 319

Marriage of Heaven and Hell, 143

Marryat, Captain, 290

Martin Chuzzlewit, 204–205

Marvell, Andrew, 65, 74, 79, 82–83

Mary Barton, 196–197

Mask of Anarchy, 174–175

Maud, 193, 195

Maurice, 253

Mayor of Casterbridge, 232

McCall, Smith, Alexander, 325

Measure for Measure, 49

Meditations, 68

Memoirs of an Infantry Officer, 266

Men and Women, 202

Men at Arms, 275

Merchant of Venice, 49, 50

Meredith, George, 229

metaphysical poetry, 65

Michael, 152

Middlemarch, 217–219, 221

Middleton, Thomas, 34

Mill on the Floss, 221

Milne, A.A., 251–252

Milton, John, 29, 35, 76–81, 89

Minstrelsy of the Scottish Border, 153

Mirror, 303

Miss Gee, 283

modernism, 267–268

Modest Proposal, 101–103

Moll Flanders, 99

Molloy, 281

Monsignor Quixote, 278

Montaigne, 31

Moonstone, 227

morality plays, 18–19

Mores, 178

Morning Song, 303

Morrell, Lady Ottoline, 274

Morris, William, 229

Morte D'Arthur, 193

Mrs Dalloway, 260

Much Ado About Nothing, 48

Murder in the Cathedral, 270

Murdoch, Iris, 292–293

Musee des Beaux Arts, 283

My Heart Leaps Up, 152

My Last Duchess, 202

Mysteries of Udolpho, 125

Mystery of Edwin Drood, 205

mystery plays, 17–18

Newcomes, 199

Newton, Isaac, 143

Nicholas Nickleby, 204, 208

Night Mail, 283

Nightmare Abbey, 167, 169

Nineteen Eighty Four, 273

Nine Tailors, 228

No One Cares Less Than I, 265

No worse there is none…, 235

Nocturnal upon St Lucies Day, 67

Norfolk, 280

North, 309

North and South, 197

Northanger Abbey, 163, 323, 325

Northern Farmer: New Style, 195

Northern Farmer: Old Style, 195

Nostromo, 243

novel, 111
Now We Are Six, 252
Nurse's Song, 141

O my luve's like a red, red rose, 145
O'Brian, Patrick, 289–292
O'Casey, Sean, 255–256, 297
Ode on a Distant Prospect of Eton College, 123
Ode on a Grecian Urn, 181–182
Ode on Melancholy, 181
Ode on the Death of a Favourite Cat, 123, 124
Ode to a Nightingale, 181
Ode to Psyche, 181
Ode to the West Wind, 174, 175
Ode: Intimations of Immortality, 150–151
Odour of Chrysanthemums, 264
Odyssey, 257
Officers and Gentlemen, 275
Oh What A Lovely War, 297
Old Cumberland Beggar, 152
Old Curiosity Shop, 204, 207
Old Mortality, 155
Old Possum's Book of Practical Cats, 270
Old Wive's Tale, 250
Oliver Twist, 204
On First Looking into Chapman's Homer, 182
On his Mistress, 67
On My Son, 60–61
On Shakespeare, 81
On the Death of Dr Robert Levett, 117–118
On the Late Massacre in Piedmont, 81
On the Morning of Christ's Nativity, 81
On Westminster Bridge, 152
One Day I Wrote Her Name, 30
One Evening, 283
One Way Pendulum, 298
Ordeal of Gilbert Pinfold, 275
Origin of Species, 195
Orlando, 260
Orwell, George, 29, 272–273, 276

Osborne, John, 296–297
Othello, 43–45, 54
ottava rima, 172
Our Man in Havana, 277
Our Mutual Friend, 205, 206, 207, 324
Owen, Wilfred, 266, 267, 316
Owl and the Pussy-Cat, 203
Ozymandias, 175

Paine, Tom, 173
Painful Case, 256
Pamela, 111–112, 114
Paradise Lost, 77–80
Passage to India, 253–255
Passionate Man's Pilgrim, 28
Patmore, Coventry, 229
Patriotism, 153
Peacock, Thomas Love, 167–169, 174
Peake, Mervyn, 125
Peasant, 287
Pendennis, 199
Pepys, Samuel, 91–92, 93
Percy's 'Reliques', 20
Perfume, 67
Pericles, 53
Personal Helicon, 308
Persuasion, 163
Peter Pan, 239
Peter Rabbit, 251
Petrarch, 11, 25, 26, 55
Phineas Finn, 210
Phineas Redux, 210
Piano, 264
picaresque, 113, 125
Pickwick Papers, 204, 324
Picture of Dorian Gray, 237
Pied Beauty, 235
Pied Piper of Hamelin, 202
Piers the Plowman, 4–6, 8
Pilgrim's Progress, 29, 86–87, 99
Pincher Martin, 284
Pinero, Arthur Wing, 238
Pinter, Harold, 298–300, 319

Plath, Sylvia, 303–304

Plato, 313

Playboy of the Western World, 239

Plough and the Stars, 255

Poem in October, 287–288

Poems Descriptive of Rural Life, 177

Poems of 1912-13 (Hardy), 231

Poems of Rural Life in the Dorset Dialect,
187

Poems, Chiefly in the Scottish Dialect, 145

Point Counter Point, 272

Political Register, 146

Pope, Alexander, 107–110, 170, 268

Poplar Field, 130

Portrait of the Artist as a Young Man,
256–257

Potter, Beatrix, 251–252

Powell, Anthony, 276

Power and the Glory, 277–278

Prayer for My Daughter, 249

Preface to Shakespeare, 117

Prelude, 148, 150, 152

Pre-Raphaelite movement, 192, 228–229,
237, 248

Pride and Prejudice, 162–165

Prime Minister, 210

Princess, 193

Prisoner of Chillon, 173

Professor, 212

Prometheus Unbound, 176

Proust, Marcel, 276

Pulley, 76

Punishment, 308

Pygmalion, 239

Pyramid, 284

Quare Fellow, 297

Quarles, Francis, 313

quatrain, 22

Quarry, The, 283

Quentin Durward, 155

Question of Attribution, 305

Quiet American, 278

Radcliffe, Ann, 125

Rain Horse, 302

Rainbow, 262, 263

Rake's Progress, 115

Raleigh, Walter, 25, 27–28, 60

Rambler, 116

Ramsey, Allan, 145

Rankin, Ian, 325

Rape of the Lock, 108–110, 268

Rasselas, 117

Rattigan, Terence, 296–297

Real Inspector Hound, 306

Real Thing, 306–307

Rear-Guard, 266

Reasons Against the Succession, 99

Recessional, 246

Redeemer, 266

Redgauntlet, 155

Red Wheelbarrow, The, 317

Relapse, 94

Remains of Elnet, 302

Remember me when I am gone away…, 229

Remembrance (Emily Bronte), 214

Remembrance (Wyatt), 25–26

Remembrances (Clare), 178–179

Resolution and Independence, 152

Resounding Tinkle, 298

Restoration Comedy, 92–95, 104

Return of the Native, 232

Revelation of Divine Love, 16

Revenger's Tragedy, 34

Revolt of Islam, 176

Reynolds, Joshua, 116, 132, 143, 228

Richard II, 52

Richard III, 52

Richards, Frank, 247

Richardson, Samuel, 111–112, 113, 115,
125, 133

Riders to the Sea, 239

Ring and the Book, 202

Rites of Passage, 284

Rivals, 130, 131

River, 302

Road to Wigan Pier, 273

Rob Roy, 155
Robinson Crusoe, 99
Rochester, Earl of, 93
Rocking Horse Winner, 264
Roman Wall Blues, 283
Romanticism, 134, 139, 144, 151, 170, 173
Romola, 221
Room of One's Own, 259
Room With A View, 253
Roots, 298
Rosenberg, Isaac, 266
Rosencrantz and Guildenstern are Dead, 306
Ross, 296
Rossetti, Christina, 228–229
Rossetti, Dante Gabriel, 192, 228–229
Rover, 93
Rubaiyat of Omar Khayyam, 191–192
Rural Muse, 177
Rural Rides, 146–148

Sailing to Byzantium, 249
Saint Joan, 239
Sassoon, Siegfried, 266, 267
Sayers, Dorothy, 228
Scenes of Clerical Life, 221
School for Scandal, 130, 132
Schoolboy, 142
Scoop, 275
Scots wha hae wi Wallace bled, 145
Scott, Walter, 20, 134, 152–156, 163, 167
Seascape, 283
Season Songs, 302
Second Coming, 248–249
Second Mrs Tanqueray, 238
Secret Agent, 244–245
Seeing Things, 308
Sense and Sensibility, 163
Sentimental Journey, 120
Separate Tables, 296
Serjeant Musgrave's Dance, 298
Shadow of a Gunman, 255
Shakespeare, William, 34, 35, 37–58, 59, 72, 89, 157, 268, 272, 381

Shaw, George Bernard, 238–239
She Stoops to Conquer, 128–129
She walks in beauty…, 173
Shelley, Mary, 125
Shelley, Percy Bysshe, 139, 169, 171, 173–176
Shepherd's Calendar, 177
Sher, Antony, 318
Sheridan, Richard Brinsley, 130–132
Sheriff, R.C., 319
Shield of Achilles, 282–283
Shirley, 212
Shooting an Elephant, 273
Shortest Way with the Dissenters, 99
Shrimp and the Anemone, 274
Shropshire Lad, 245
Sick Rose, 143
Sidney, Philip, 25–27, 28
Signalman, 207
Silas Marner, 221
Silex Scintillans, 85
Silmarillion, 271
Silver Box, 239
Silver Tassie, 255
Simenon, Georges, 228
Simplex Munditiis, 59
Simpson, N.F., 298
Sir Charles Grandison, 111
Sir Gawain and The Green Knight, 6–8
Skelton, John, 19
Sketches by Boz, 204
Small House at Allingham, 210
Smart, Christopher, 126–127
Smollett, Tobias, 111, 125–126, 204
Snake, 264, 315
So We'll Go No More a Roving, 173
Soldier, 265
Song At The Year's Turning, 287
Song to David, 126
Songs and Sonnets, 66–67
Songs of Experience, 142–143
Songs of Innocence, 141–142, 191
sonnet, 26, 55–56
Sonnets from the Portuguese, 190

Sons and Lovers, 262
Sorley, Charles, 265
Sound and the Fury, The, 323
Southey, Robert, 160, 161, 172
Spenser, Edmund, 27, 28–31, 79, 171, 183
Spire, 284
Spirit Level, 309
Squarings, 308–309
Stalky and Co, 247
Stamboul Train, 277
Starlight Night, 235
Station Island, 309
Steadfastness, 25
Steele, Richard, 102, 104–105
Steps to the Temple, 84
Sterne, Laurence, 111, 118–120, 126, 323
Stop All The Clocks, 283
Stoppard, Tom, 305–307
Strange Fruit, 308
Strange Meeting, 266
Stravinsky, 282
stream of consciousness, 258, 260, 268
Strife, 239
Study in Scarlet, 227
Study of Reading Habits, 294
Summoned by Bells, 280
Sunne Rising, 67
Surrey, Earl of, 25–26, 35, 55
Sweetest love I do not go…, 66
Swift, Jonathan, 101–103, 106, 107, 110, 114
Swinburne, Algernon Charles, 175, 192, 228–229
Sword of Honour, 275
Sybil, 188–189
Synge, John Millington, 239

Tailor of Gloucester, 251
Tale of a Tub, 101
Tale of Peter Rabbit, 251
Tale of the Flopsy Bunnies, 251
Tale of Two Cities, 205

Tales From Ovid, 303
Tales from Shakespeare, 161
Talking Heads, 304–305
Tam o' Shanter, 146
Tamburlaine the Great, 36–37
Tancred, 188
Task, 129, 130
Tate, Nahum, 46
Teach me my God and King…, 76
Tempest, 53, 54, 272
Temple, 74
Tenant of Wildfell Hall, 216
Tennyson, Alfred Lord, 35, 187, 191, 192–195, 199, 203, 234, 246
Tess of the D'Urbervilles, 232–233
Testament of Youth, 267
Thackeray, William Makepeace, 191, 197, 198–199, 210, 212, 324
The Redress of Poetry (Heaney), 309
The Sea, The Sea, 293
These Twain, 250
Third Man, 277
This Be The Verse, 294
This Is No Case of Petty Right and Wrong, 265
This Lime Tree Bower, 159, 160
Thomas, Dylan, 287–289, 308
Thomas, Edward, 265
Thomas, R.S., 286–287
Thomson, James, 177
Thou art indeed just, Lord…, 235
Threepenny Opera, 105
Through the Looking Glass, 230
Timbuctoo, 199
Time Machine, 249
Timothy Winters, 286
Tintern Abbey, 149–150
Titus Alone, 125
Titus Groan, 125
To a Louse, 145
To a Mouse, 146
To a Skylark, 174, 175
To Autumn, 181, 182
To his Coy Mistress, 74, 83

To His Mistress Going to Bed, 67
To Liberty, 174
To the Immortal Memory…, 59
To The Lighthouse, 260
To The Memory of William Shakespeare, 59
To The Virgins, 74
Toad of Toad Hall, 251
Toccata of Galuppi's, 202
Tolkien, J.R.R., 270–271
Tom Jones, 113, 114, 115
Tom Thumb, 113
Tottel, Richard, 25
Tourneur, Cyril, 34
Traherne, Thomas, 84–85
Trampwoman's Tragedy, 233
Traveller, 128
Travels Through France and Italy, 126
Travesties, 306
Trelawny of the Wells, 238
Tristram Shandy, 118–120, 323
Troilus and Cressida (Shakespeare), 49, 51
Troilus and Criseyde (Chaucer), 11–12, 51
Trollope, Anthony, 209–210
Tryst at an Ancient Earthwork, 232
Twelfth Night, 39, 47, 48
Two April Mornings, 152
Two Cheers for Democracy, 253
Two Drovers, 155
Two in the Campagna, 200–201
Two Voices, 194
Tyger, 143
Tyndale, William, 87
Typhoon, 245

Ulysses (Joyce), 257–259, 260, 325
Ulysses (Tennyson), 193
Unconditional Surrender, 275
Under Ben Bulben, 247
Under Milk Wood, 288–289
Under The Greenwood Tree, 232
Under the Net, 293
Under Western Eyes, 243
Undertones of War, 267

Unnameable, The, 281
Upon Julia's Clothes, 73
Upon Julia's Voice, 74
Utley, Alison, 252

Valediction Forbidding Mourning, 66
Valediction of Weeping, 67
Vanbrugh, John, 94
Vanity Fair, 198–199
Vanity of Human Wishes, 117
Vaughan, Henry, 65, 84–85
Vicar of Wakefield, 128
Victor, 283
Victory, 245
View of a Pig, 307
Vile Bodies, 275
Village, 134–135
Village Minstrel, 177
Villette, 212, 213
Virgil, 26, 59, 79
Virtue, 76
Vision of Judgment, 172
Volpone, 60

Waiting for Godot, 281–282, 322
Walpole, Horace, 125
Walsingham, 28
Walton, Izaak, 65, 67
Wanderings of Oisin, 248
War of the Worlds, 249
Warden, 210
Warner, Rex, 283
Wasp in a Wig, 230
Waste Land, 29, 267, 269
Watercolour of Grantchester Meadows, 303
Watt, 281
Waugh, Evelyn, 275–276
Waverley, 155
Waves, The, 260
Way Through The Woods, 246
Way We Live Now, 210
Weathers, 233
Webster, John, 34, 65, 71–73

Wells, H.G., 249–250, 260
Welsh Landscape, 286
Wesker, Arnold, 298
Wessex Poems (Hardy), 233
Wessex Tales, 232
Wheels Within Wheels, 308
When I am dead, my dearest…, 229
When I consider how my life is spent…, 81
When the Lamp is Shattered, 176
When We Were Very Young, 252
Where Angels Fear to Tread, 253
White Devil, 71
Whiting, John, 297
Whitsun Weddings, 294–295
Wife a-Lost, 188
Wild Oats, 294
Wild Swans at Coole, 249
Wilde, Oscar, 106, 201, 236–237, 306
Williams, William Carlos, 317
Wind, 301
Wind at the Door, 188
Windhover, 235
Wind in the Willows, 251
Winnie-the-Pooh, 252
Winslow Boy, 296
Wintering Out, 308
Winter's Tale, 39, 53, 54
Withered Arm, 232
Wives and Daughters, 197
Woak Hill, 187–188, 192

Wodehouse, P.G., 276
Wodwo, 302
Woman in White, 227
Woman of no Importance, 237
Women in Love, 262–263
Woodlanders, 232
Woolf, Virginia, 93, 221, 250, 254, 259–261, 268, 274
Wordsworth, William, 29, 35, 79, 130, 134, 139, 144, 148–152, 157, 159, 160, 161, 167, 192, 200, 221, 222, 223, 234, 282, 310
World, 85
Wreck of the Deutschland, 235
Wuthering Heights, 214–216
Wyatt, Thomas, 25–26, 55
Wycherley, William, 93
Wycliffe, John, 87

Ye Banks and Braes o'Bonnie Doon, 145
Yeats, William Butler, 29, 75, 239, 247–249, 268, 315
You're, 303
Youth, 245

Zola, Emile, 250